The Management of Savagery

The Management of Savagery

How America's National Security State Fueled the Rise of Al Qaeda, ISIS, and Donald Trump

Max Blumenthal

London • New York

First published in paperback by Verso 2020
First published by Verso 2019

1 3 5 7 9 10 8 6 4 2

Verso
UK: 6 Meard Street, London W1F 0EG
US: 20 Jay Street, Suite 1010, Brooklyn, NY 11201
versobooks.com

Verso is the imprint of New Left Books

ISBN-13: 978-1-78873-230-7
ISBN-13: 978-1-78873-228-4 (US EBK)
ISBN-13: 978-1-78873-227-7 (UK EBK)

British Library Cataloguing in Publication Data
A catalogue record for this book is available from the British Library

The Library of Congress Has Cataloged the Hardback Edition as Follows:

Names: Blumenthal, Max, 1977– author.
Title: The management of savagery : how America's national security state fueled the rise of Al Qaeda, ISIS, and Donald Trump / Max Blumenthal.
Description: London ; Brooklyn, NY : Verso, 2019. | Includes bibliographical references and index.
Identifiers: LCCN 2019001125| ISBN 9781788732291 (hardback : alk. paper) | ISBN 9781788732284 (US ebook) | ISBN 9781788732277 (UK ebook)
Subjects: LCSH: United States—Foreign relations—Middle East. | Middle East—Foreign relations—United States. | Middle East—Politics and government—1979– | Qaida (Organization) | IS (Organization) | Imperialism. | United States—Politics and government—1989– | National security—United States. | Trump, Donald, 1946–
Classification: LCC DS63.2.U5 B58 2019 | DDC 327.73056—dc23
LC record available at https://lccn.loc.gov/2019001125

Typeset in Sabon by MJ & N Gavan, Truro, Cornwall
Printed and bound by CPI Group (UK) Ltd, Coydon, CR0 4YY

Let's remember here, the people we are fighting today, we funded twenty years ago, and we did it because we were locked in this struggle with the Soviet Union ... There's a very strong argument, which is—it wasn't a bad investment to end the Soviet Union, but let's be careful what we sow because we will harvest.

—Secretary of State Hillary Clinton to the House Appropriations Committee, April 23, 2009

AQ [Al Qaeda] is on our side in Syria.

—Jake Sullivan in February 12, 2012, email to Secretary of State Hillary Clinton

We underscore that states that sponsor terrorism risk falling victim to the evil they promote.

—President Donald Trump, June 6, 2017

Contents

Introduction

The Unstable State

It was the week after Labor Day and Washington was filling up again with its chattering class, just back from summer sojourns up and down the coast. President Donald Trump was in town as well, paying the White House a visit after a series of golf trips and rowdy rallies before his Rust Belt loyalists. The White House, however, had been in a state of siege throughout the summer, as former FBI director Robert Mueller had led an investigation into Trump's 2016 campaign and an allegation that the Russian government had subverted the presidential election in his favor. Though the Russiagate inquiry had produced nothing so far to demonstrate collusion, with the political season kicking back into high gear, the stage was set for two dramatic events carefully timed to turn up the heat on the president.

The first event was the funeral of John McCain, a former prisoner of war turned Republican senator. Branded as a "maverick" by the Beltway press corps, which he half-jokingly referred to as his political base, McCain had operated throughout his career in complete lockstep with the military-intelligence apparatus. Over the years, he had junketed from one theater of conflict to the next, marketing jihadist insurgents and far-right militiamen to the American public as "freedom fighters," clamoring for military intervention and enriching his donors in the arms industry. A budget-busting $717 billion defense bill authorized days before his death on August 13 was appropriately dedicated in his name.

Days later, the authors of some of the most destructive wars in recent history, from Dick Cheney and George W. Bush to Henry Kissinger and Barack Obama, filed into the National Cathedral to pay homage to the late senator. Trump was pointedly uninvited, a snub that prompted the *New Yorker* to dub the event "the biggest Resistance meeting yet." The president was persona non grata among the guest list, which represented a bipartisan establishment that he had ridiculed, denigrated and menaced to the delight of millions of ordinary Americans. From the dais, McCain's daytime talk show host daughter, Meghan, delighted her audience with twenty minutes of nationalistic cant peppered with subtle digs at Trump—"America was *always* great." A line in her eulogy that repackaged the Vietnam War as a fight for the "life and liberty of other peoples in other lands" passed by without controversy. The spectacle had gone off just as McCain had planned: as a celebration of American empire and a rebuke to the rogue president who was viewed by its architects as a clear and present danger to its survival.

The following week, a second attack on the president was launched—this time from within his administration. An anonymous figure, self-described as a "senior administration official" and posing as "the Resistance inside the administration," published an editorial excoriating Trump's "amoral" leadership. The author homed in on Trump's supposedly sympathetic posture to Russia and his fulsome and utterly unexpected support for a peaceful resolution to the six-decade-long conflict between North and South Korea. The president had crossed red lines in both areas, the official argued, breaking from the Washington consensus of regime change in North Korea and resisting the aggressive containment of Russia. Summoning the spirit of McCain and branding him "a lodestar for restoring honor to public life and our national dialogue," the official revealed that top figures had begun wresting control of important foreign policy decisions from Trump. If the anonymous author was to be believed, then the national security state had effectively conducted a soft coup inside the White House, just as had been done against so many foreign governments.

"This isn't the work of the so-called deep state," the official claimed, referring to the unelected and opaque chambers of government that spanned the Pentagon to the intelligence services to America's diplomatic corps. "It's the work of the steady state," the writer insisted.

The irony behind this claim could hardly be overstated, though it was probably lost on most readers of the op-ed and certainly on its author. The national security state that the anonymous official claimed to represent had certainly maintained a steady continuity between successive administrations, regardless of whether the president was Republican or Democrat. However, the ideology that animated its agenda has spread unsteadiness around the globe, especially in the Middle East, where American-led regime change wars had unleashed refugee crises of unprecedented proportions and fomented the rise of transnational jihadism. The toxic effects of the West's semi-covert intervention in Syria—where the United States and its allies contributed billions of dollars to the arming and training of Islamist militias that ultimately fought under the black banners of Al Qaeda and the Islamic State of Iraq and Syria (ISIS)—continue to reverberate to this day.

The backlash from America's proxy wars and direct interventions has begun to destabilize the West as well. In Europe, a new breed of ultra-nationalist political parties are extracting a record number of votes out of a growing resentment of Muslim migrants, and swinging elections from Italy to Sweden while driving the Brexit agenda in the UK. Trump, too, owes much of his success at the polls to the anti-Muslim hysteria whipped up by a well-funded Islamophobia industry that grew dramatically after the 9/11 attacks, but whose existence predated the traumatic daylight assault.

For several days after the attacks, while George W. Bush and top Bush officials shrunk from public view, Trump absorbed the belligerent sensibility of New York's tabloid media. He preserved his image as a B-list celebrity through regular appearances with nationally famous shock jock Howard Stern. And he likely listened as Stern translated the outrage of ordinary New Yorkers into a genocidal tirade that was delivered live as the Twin Towers came crashing down. Trump also watched carefully as a shell-shocked Dan Rather, the trusted voice of network news, appeared on David Letterman's late-night talk show days after the attacks to spread rumors of Arab Americans celebrating on rooftops across the Hudson River.

Trump learned the crude lessons delivered to the American public through trusted mainstream voices after 9/11 and distilled them into the 2016 campaign with his trademark flair. On the campaign trail, he gave the ideologues of the Islamophobia industry a charismatic voice they had never enjoyed before, pledging a total ban on Muslim travelers from seven nations before a captive audience of millions of CNN viewers. On the debate stage, meanwhile, he channeled the rage of Middle American families who had suffered the moral injury of Iraq and Afghanistan by humiliating the national security state's great white hope, Jeb Bush, over his brother's failed wars. Insincere as he might have been, Trump was willing to tap into the deep wellsprings of anti-interventionism across the country while his opponent, Hillary Clinton, was clamoring for a no-fly zone in Syria.

This book makes the case that Trump's election would not have been possible without 9/11 and the subsequent military interventions conceived by the national security state. Further, I argue that if the CIA had not spent over a billion dollars arming Islamist militants in Afghanistan against the Soviet Union during the height of the Cold War, empowering jihadist godfathers like Ayman al-Zawahiri and Osama bin Laden in the process, the 9/11 attacks would have almost certainly not taken place. And if the Twin Towers were still standing today, it is not hard to imagine an alternate political universe in which a demagogue like Trump was still relegated to real estate and reality TV.

Tragically, after laying the groundwork for the worst terrorist attack on American soil, the US national security state chose to repeat its folly in Iraq, collapsing a stable country run along relatively secular lines and producing a fertile seedbed for the rise of ISIS. Libya was next, where a US-led intervention created another failed state overrun by jihadist militias. The regime change machine then moved on to Syria, enacting a billion-dollar arm-and-equip operation that propelled the spread of ISIS and gave rise to the largest franchise of Al Qaeda since 9/11. In each case, prophetic warnings about the consequences of regime change were buried in a blizzard of humanitarian propaganda stressing the urgency of dispatching the US military to rescue trapped civilians from bloodthirsty dictators.

It should be considered a national outrage that so many of those who have positioned themselves as figureheads of the anti-Trump "Resistance" were key architects of the disastrous interventions that helped set the stage for Trump and figures like him to gain power. But in the era of Russiagate, when so many liberals cling to institutions like the FBI and NATO as guardians of their survival, the dastardly record of America's national security mandarins has been wiped clean. This book will excavate their crimes and expose the cynicism behind their appeals to democratic values.

A 2004 paper by a pseudonymous jihadist ideologue in Iraq, Abu Bakr Naji, provided the inspiration for this book's title. Entitled "The Management of Savagery," Naji's paper outlined a strategy for building an Islamic State by exploiting the chaos spawned by America's regime-change wars. He urged jihadist forces to fill the security vacuum opened up by Western intervention by establishing "administrations of savagery" at the state's outer reaches, while waging ruthless "vexation operations" against the central institutions of the state. Naji's paper dovetailed neatly with the regime-change blueprints conceived by national security hard-liners in Washington, and it hints at the symbiotic relationship that these two extremist elements have enjoyed. In Libya and Syria, where the CIA provided arms and equipment to jihadist insurgents, this ideological symbiosis was consolidated through direct collaboration. But as I will demonstrate in the coming pages, savagery by its very definition cannot be managed. In fact, it has already found its way back home.

—Max Blumenthal
Washington, DC
September 11, 2018

1

The Afghan Trap

On February 11, 1979, the West lost its frontline client government in the Middle East when Iranians ousted the corrupt, repressive monarchy of Mohammad Reza Shah Pahlavi. The shah was and ultimately replaced with a glowering theocrat, Ayatollah Ruhollah Khomeini. As Khomeini declared full support for the Palestinian national struggle and swore to repel the West's imperial designs across the region, American media overflowed with Orientalist commentaries on "the Persian psyche." "American television treated the Iran crisis either as a freak show, featuring self-flagellants and fist-wavers, or as a soap opera," *Wall Street Journal* columnist Morton Kondracke observed in January 1980.

The anxiety over Iran's revolution was also palpable in Israel, where the right-wing Likud Party had wrested power for the first time from the Zionist movement's Labor wing. In Jerusalem, just months after Khomeini swept to power, a young Likud Party upstart named Benjamin Netanyahu organized a conference under the auspices of the Jonathan Institute, a think tank he named after his brother, who had been killed while leading the legendary 1976 Israeli raid at the Entebbe airport in Uganda.

In attendance was George H.W. Bush, neoconservative standard bearers like Senator Henry "Scoop" Jackson, staff from newfangled conservative think tanks like the American

Enterprise Institute and the Center for Strategic and International Studies, and sympathetic policymakers and journalists from across the West. Netanyahu's goal was to internationalize the Israeli understanding of terrorism. In short, he sought to deny rational motives to the Arabs, who had been militarily occupied for decades or had seen their nations ravaged by Western colonialism, casting their violence instead as the product of the most primitive impulses—"part of a much larger struggle, one between the forces of civilization and the forces of barbarism," as he wrote in his 1986 tract on terrorism and "how the West can win."

Netanyahu had cleverly reimagined right-wing scholar Richard Pipes' vision of a global struggle between communist and "anti-communist" nations as a battle over "values" waged between the civilized "Judeo-Christian" West and the barbaric Eastern hordes. When Washington embarked on a "war on terror" two decades later, the clash of civilizations narrative Netanyahu helped construct provided the George W. Bush administration with the language it needed to market its unilateral military doctrine to a discombobulated American public. The crude mantra of the post-9/11 era in America, "They hate us because we're free," seemed to have flowed directly from Netanyahu's worldview and into George W. Bush's teleprompter. History had been erased and the West was cast as a blameless victim of stateless totalitarians driven by nothing more than a pathological urge to dismantle democracy. Anyone who attempted to place Al Qaeda in context, particularly by explaining how its early antecedents emerged thanks to semi-covert US warfare, was likely to be accused of "blaming America first." Either you were "with us, or you're with the terrorists," Bush and his supporters often said, putting a distinctly Texan spin on Netanyahu's Manichean discourse.

But only a few months after the first Jonathan Institute conference, in December 1979, Netanyahu's understanding of "terror" had begun to resonate throughout the West. By this point, much of the American public was transfixed by the US embassy crisis in Iran that had erupted a month before, tuning in to nightly news coverage that focused in on the ayatollah as the new icon of international terror. Meanwhile, another event was unfolding largely below the radar of the Western media that would impact the future of the Middle East at least as much as Iran's revolution. Islamist fanatics had laid siege to the Grand Mosque at Mecca, trapping some 100,000 pilgrims inside. The insurgents were guided by a millenarian preacher named Juhayman al Utaybi, who had been trained in the Saudi Arabian National Guard and inspired by the resurgent Wahhabi religious movement.

During breaks from the guard, Utaybi soaked in the jeremiads of Saudi Arabia's Abdul Aziz bin Baz, the blind and unsightly cleric who was far and away the leading opponent of Saudi Arabia's process of modernization. Bin Baz issued decrees against the display of wall art by the royals, urging his followers to destroy it wherever possible. He opposed the public clapping of hands and railed against the appearance of women on national news broadcasts, warning that the mere sight of them could cause ten-year-old boys to become sexually aroused. The sybaritic, American-oriented royal family was destroying Islam from within, he declared, and he fumed at its flagrant disregard for his orders. Under the influence of bin Baz, Utaybi fantasized about a popular uprising that would drive out the royals and replace them with a pious order that adhered to the true origins of Islam—at least, as he and other Wahhabi cadres saw it.

Drawn from the philosophy of eighteenth-century cleric Abd al-Wahhab and the Salaf, the original followers of the Prophet Muhammad, Wahhabism represented much more than an exceedingly fundamentalist vision of Islam; it was also a socio-political movement that saw non-Sunni Muslims as rejectors and encouraged conflict with non-believers. It therefore provided the basis for the toxic doctrine that labeled Muslims who opposed its sectarian designs as *takfir*, or self-hating apostates. This concept of belief served as the ideological justification for groups like Al Qaeda to massacre fellow Muslims, whether they were Shia or conscripted Sunni soldiers of secular governments.

Because the strictures of Islam forbade violence within the Grand Mosque, the royals were forced to turn to their sworn foe, bin Baz, for a fatwa authorizing the use of force to retake the mosque from Utaybi's militia. In exchange for his edict, the royals entered into a Faustian bargain with the country's rigidly conservative clerical class, agreeing to spend billions in petro-cash to project Wahhabism across the Muslim world.

The deal also expanded the clergy's domestic influence, granting it more authority than ever to impose its hyper-conservative vision on Saudi society. Rather than repressing the extremism gestating within its borders, the House of Saud decided to co-opt it as a tool of internal political suppression and external soft power.

In the months and years after the traumatic battle to extricate Utaybi's band of fanatics from the holy heart of Mecca, bin Baz rolled out more characteristically fanatical pronouncements. He issued a fatwa denouncing photography, condemned driving by women, forbade them from shaking hands with men (although he endorsed the use of Viagra), and urged Muslims to make exodus from non-Muslim countries, or at least, "less evil countries." Under the watch of Crown Prince Fahd bin Abdulaziz Al Saud, Saudi morality police known informally as the *mutawain*, or the Committee for the Promotion of Virtue and Prevention of Vice, were given free rein to crack down on gender mixing, seize "anti-Islamic" films and outlaw movie theaters. Even as the kingdom's modernization process continued, Sharia law prevailed.

On December 25, just three weeks after the siege of the Grand Mosque was broken, the Soviet Union invaded Afghanistan to prop up a loyalist communist government facing a swelling armed rebellion. A deeply conservative rural population led the insurgency, ferociously rejecting the secular modernization projects organized out of Kabul. The invasion was triggered by a scheme enacted five months prior by President Jimmy Carter's national security advisor, Zbigniew Brzezinski, who sought to bleed the Soviet Union from its soft underbelly by funneling billions in arms and aid to the mujahedin.

A hard-line anticommunist born to Polish nobility and seared by his family's experience in World War II, Brzezinski was the driving force behind the Carter administration's strategy in Afghanistan. He eventually conceded that his intention had been "to induce a Soviet military intervention," explaining to the French journal *Nouvel Observateur* in 1998, "That secret operation was an excellent idea. It had the effect of drawing the Russians into the Afghan trap and you want me to regret it? The day that the Soviets officially crossed the border, I wrote to President Carter, essentially: 'We now have the opportunity of giving to the USSR its Vietnam war.'"

To fulfill Brzezinski's policy, Carter was forced to roll back hopes for comprehensive reforms to restore public trust in the intelligence agencies following revelations of the Phoenix assassination program that the CIA conducted during the Vietnam War. A 1977 interagency memo distributed by none other than Brzezinski concluded, "Public trust and confidence in the Intelligence Community have been seriously undermined by disclosures of activities in the past that were illegal, injudicious or otherwise improper by today's standards." Two years later, however, the Carter administration was setting the stage for perhaps the most consequential covert intelligence operation in US history. Worse, Carter allowed Pakistan's Islamist-oriented military dictator Muhammad Zia-ul-Haq and his Inter-Services Intelligence agency (ISI) to control the distribution of American military assistance to the mujahedin, giving him and his military junta a free hand, while dooming any chance to impose more transparency on the CIA.

Washington was furthermore forced to look away as Pakistan's nuclear weapons program advanced. As Jack Blum, the staff attorney with the Senate Antitrust Subcommittee and the Senate Foreign Relations Committee who led several investigations into the CIA's illicit activities, later explained to me, "Pakistan was a wonderful staging area for war, it was so convenient. We needed it as a refuge for the mujahedin, so we completely ignored the fact that they were building a nuclear bomb. We knew about this way before this became public."

It was also thanks to the CIA's Afghan proxy war that President Zia was able to consolidate his regressive national vision. "Pakistan is like Israel, an ideological state," Zia explained in 1981. " Take out the Judaism from Israel and it will fall like a house of cards. Take Islam out of Pakistan and make it a secular state; it would collapse."

In doling out cash and US arms, Zia's ISI gave preference to Afghanistan's radical Islamist factions and thereby propelled them from the fringe to the mainstream. As the Ugandan scholar of international affairs Mahmood Mamdani wrote of the elements armed by the CIA and ISI, "the right-wingers had no program outside of isolated acts of urban terror. Until the Afghan jihad, right-wing Islamists out of power had neither the aspiration of drawing strength from popular organization nor the possibility of marshaling strength from any alternative source. The Reagan administration rescued right-wing Islamism from this historical cul-de-sac."

For Brzezinski, who worried that the Soviet Union might fill an "arc of crisis" that ran across the global South, the mujahedin and backers like Zia's Pakistan and the Saudi royals represented a reactionary "arc of Islamism" that could be encouraged to provide a powerful counterweight to communist influence. He urged Carter to "concert with Islamic countries both a propaganda campaign and a covert action campaign to help the rebels."

The anti-Soviet jihad in Afghanistan therefore offered the Saudis an opportunity to project its state religion into Central Asia, but also provided a convenient ventilation mechanism for the extremism gestating within its borders. Saudi Arabia arranged a special fund that matched every dollar the CIA gave to the cause of the mujahedin. Bolstered by the contributions of ideologically inclined princes, the Saudi backing was crucial in purchasing hundreds of Stinger antiaircraft missile systems without congressional knowledge. By backing the covert US war effort, the Saudi royal family was able to provide the most fanatical members of their society with a one-way ticket to Pakistan, where they could be shepherded over the border to vent their pent-up aggression against the atheistic Soviet invaders. At the urging of his government, bin Baz—now the Saudi Grand Mufti—issued a new fatwa compelling worldwide Muslim participation in the anti-Soviet jihad.

Thanks to Saudi support, the indigenous mujahedin in Afghanistan were supplemented by tens of thousands of foreign fighters locally referred to as the "Afghan Arabs." Many of the foreign fighters flocking to the battlefield were drawn by the preaching of a Palestinian theologian named Abdullah Azzam. Before arriving in Pakistan, Azzam had spent several years teaching at Saudi Arabia's King Abdulaziz University, educating students on the texts of proto-Wahhabi clerics like Ibn Taymiyyah, the medieval scholar who laid the basis for *takfiri* doctrine. In Jeddah, Azzam instructed a young Osama bin Laden, helping him hone the religiously zealous sensibility that set him apart from his more secular siblings.

The seventeenth son of billionaire construction baron Mohammed bin Laden, Osama had been shaken by the scenes of Saudi tanks barreling into the Grand Mosque to break the siege in December 1979. His family had been renovating the mosque at the time, and its construction blueprints were used by the military to devise the assault. Bin Laden's revulsion at the ensuing bloodbath left him captivated by Utaybi's vision. But his growing resentment of the royal family momentarily dissolved in the anti-Soviet jihad it was backing in Afghanistan. His family was contributing heavily to the war effort at the time, and it eventually dispatched young bin Laden to join his mentor, Azzam, in Peshawar. There, he joined several of Utaybi's former cohorts, including Muhammad Amir Sulayman Saqr, who became one of Al Qaeda's most skilled document forgers.

In 1984, Azzam and bin Laden founded the international Islamist organization known as Maktab al-Khidamat (MAK), or the Services Bureau. With bin Laden's wealth and Azzam's ardor, this network functioned like a jihadist Abraham Lincoln Brigade, providing free lodging, training and ideological indoctrination to many of the tens of thousands of Islamist fundamentalists from forty-three countries who flocked to the Afghan battlefield. The effort was bolstered by the involvement of Benevolence International, a charity funded by prominent Saudi businessman Adel Batterjee, whom Azzam had praised for being "at the forefront" of jihad.

The following year, President Ronald Reagan formalized US support for the Afghan insurgents when he issued National Security Directive 166. Among the directive's goals was to "improve the military effectiveness of the Afghan resistance in order to keep the trends in the war unfavorable to the Soviet Union."

From this classified authorization, the largest covert operation in CIA history was born. Known as Operation Cyclone, it committed over a billion dollars to the mujahedin, affording them state-of-the-art weapons and advanced hunter-killer training. While the American national security state cheered the gradual collapse of the Soviet military campaign, its efforts transformed Afghanistan into a petri dish for international jihadism.

Adopt a Muj

Vincent Cannistraro, a CIA counterterrorism officer who served as director of intelligence for Reagan's National Security Council at the height of Operation Cyclone, monitored intelligence operations from Nicaragua to Afghanistan. He likened briefing Reagan to talking at a brick wall: "Reagan was a very amiable, likable person," Cannistraro told me, "but you weren't going to get any burst of mental energy from him on the questions of the day."

The president's rapidly advancing Alzheimer's rendered him incapable of absorbing the details of foreign policy, leaving a cast of hard-liners and rogues with substantial control over covert operations. For some Cold War cowboys, the war in Afghanistan offered a chance to get revenge on the Soviets for the humiliation they experienced as enlisted soldiers in Vietnam. For others, it was an opportunity to realize the lucre and glory of war without risking American lives. For Representative Charlie Wilson, it was a bit of both.

On Capitol Hill, Wilson was known as an alcoholic vulgarian who did little for his largely African American constituency back in east Texas but provided the timber industry with a loyal servant. He had also cultivated a reputation as the most ardent supporter of the mujahedin in Congress, leveraging his position on two congressional committees to double funding for the covert war in Afghanistan. He did this with a single phone call to the staffer in charge of the House Appropriations Committee's black operations budget. "I was expecting to have to debate it and justify it and all that," Wilson said, "but when it was read out in the closed session of the appropriations committee, nobody said a word."

Covert proxy wars were easy this way. The public never had to know how or where their money was being spent. And by subverting the democratic process, policymakers insulated themselves from antiwar agitation and scrutiny from the fourth estate. Opaque operations like these were also perfect vehicles for war profiteering.

Wilson made sure to insert special language into the appropriations bill requiring the Pentagon to buy $40 million in .22-millimeter cannons produced by a Swiss weapons company called Oerlikon. The guns were deemed utterly worthless against Soviet airpower and required the rebels to cart them onto the battlefield by mule and cart. But Wilson was attached to the weapon, successfully lobbying for its approval with an almost messianic zeal. According to Cannistraro, the CIA had reason to suspect a financial relationship between Wilson and Oerlikon. Wilson also owned some $250,000 worth of stocks in an oil company that became a Pakistani subsidiary right before he developed his sudden interest in Afghanistan. The mutually beneficial relationship with Pakistan paved the path for Wilson to serve as a registered lobbyist for the country upon his retirement from public life.

In the meantime, Cannistraro joined Wilson on a fateful congressional delegation to Pakistan at the height of the anti-Soviet jihad. In Islamabad, during a dinner with President Zia, the Pakistani junta leader rose spontaneously before his guests and demanded they ship shoulder-mounted Stinger antiaircraft missiles to the mujahedin. "Everyone was taken by surprise," Cannistraro recalled, "but then they said, okay, we agree. And that's what broke the opposition." The Stingers turned the tide of the battle, enabling the mujahedin to take down the Soviet Mil Mi-24 Hind combat helicopters and MiG jets that had been pulverizing the supply convoys flowing over the border from Pakistan.

The rapid improvement in weapons to the rebels complemented a CIA-built complex of tunnels and mujahedin training camps near the border city of Khost in Afghanistan's mountainous Paktiya province. To complete the job on time, the agency tapped an experienced contractor named Osama bin Laden, who dutifully carted in his family's earthmoving equipment. "My job was to raise the alarm and if there was an opportunity to do it and I failed to do it, it would be my failure," Cannistraro said. "And none of us knew who bin Laden was at the time."

Weapons were not all that flowed into Afghanistan courtesy of the US government. A $51 million grant from the United States Agency for International Development (USAID) to the University of Nebraska's Center for Afghanistan Studies and a former Peace Corps volunteer who directed the center, Thomas Gouttierre, produced some 4 million third-grade textbooks that helped transform Afghan schools into jihadist indoctrination centers. Introduced in 1986, the books encouraged Afghan children to gouge the eyes and amputate the legs of Soviet soldiers.

"One group of mujahedin attacks 50 Russian soldiers. In that attack 20 Russians are killed. How many Russians fled?" read one arithmetic question in the textbook. An aid worker counted forty-three violent images in just 100 pages of one of the books. The Taliban later adopted the books as their own, blotting out the faces of soldiers to comport with religious restrictions on depicting the human form while maintaining the language that described the mujahedin as holy warriors fighting in the service of God. (In a 1989 briefing report to his funders at USAID,

Gouttierre argued that educating women would anger the men whom the US depended upon as anti-Soviet proxies. "This type of reform must be left to the Afghans to be solved at their own pace," the University of Nebraska academic wrote.)

Perhaps the greatest recipient of CIA funding through Operation Cyclone was Gulbuddin Hekmatyar, a ruthless Afghan warlord described in a 1985 congressional study as "a relatively young leader often compared to the Ayatollah Khomeini in his intense ideological fundamentalism."

Hekmatyar had been a CIA asset for years before the anti-Soviet jihad, joining a secretive Islamist academic group called "the professors" in 1972. This collection of Islamist ideologues was established with the help of the Asia Foundation, a CIA front group, to counter the rise of leftist popular organizing at Kabul University. The professors there were led by Burhanuddin Rabbani, who taught Islamic law and led the campaign to drive women off campus, inciting followers like the young Hekmatyar to throw acid in the faces of female students and to murder left-wing activists. Over a decade later, Hekmatyar remained in the CIA's favor because, as Cannistraro bluntly put it, "He was the one who was the most effective fighter."

Cannistraro worked directly with Hekmatyar during the 1980s, escorting him to Washington to meet Reagan alongside a group of mujahedin commanders. Hekmatyar ultimately refused the face-to-face with Reagan, a flamboyant and calculated maneuver that put his contempt for the United States on international display. The warlord was furious, Cannistraro recalled, by what he considered insufficient American support for the anti-Soviet cause. That eventually changed with the infusion of some $600 million in aid and weapons directly to Hekmatyar's Hezb-i-Islami militia, including Stinger antiaircraft missiles. (During our interview, Cannistraro referred to Hekmatyar as "Gulbud," hinting at the guerrilla commander's cozy relationship with Washington's intelligence community.)

While the CIA and Pakistani ISI armed Hekmatyar to the teeth, diplomats in the region worried that his Hezb-i-Islami was playing a long game, allowing other mujahedin factions to do the bulk of the fighting against the Soviets and focusing his militia's energy on dominating the opposition. Loathed by fellow mujahedin commanders, Hekmatyar was strongly suspected to be involved in the murder of a British cameraman and the killings of two American escorts. He rejected all negotiation, declaring his goal as "a pure Islamic state in Afghanistan."

In 1981, before the mujahedin were junketed to Washington, British prime minister Margaret Thatcher traveled to a refugee camp on the Pakistani-Afghan border alongside President Zia. She appeared in a tent before a male-only crowd of some 1,500 mujahedin fighters. Promising an extra $4 million in aid, she encouraged them: "I want to say that the hearts of the free world are with you." Then, moments later, Britain's first female prime minister moved to a private tent with a few female refugees. No cameras—or men—were allowed inside. "We will never rest until Afghanistan is free again," Thatcher declared. Shortly after that, she hustled away on a helicopter, remarking to Zia, "We had better leave while they're friendly."

The visit highlights a burgeoning love affair between the salt-of-the-earth mujahedin and Western elites. Hollywood paid tribute to the anticommunist guerrillas in the highly successful *Rambo III*, which defined Reagan-era Hollywood. The film was an unrestrained tribute to CIA field operatives and the Islamist rebels they trained, even featuring a dedication in its closing credits "to the brave mujahideen fighters of Afghanistan." (The tribute was later edited to refer to "the gallant people of Afghanistan.") US mainstream media sided almost reflexively with the rebels, with CBS anchor Dan Rather leading the charge. Branded "Gunga Dan" by media critic Tom Shales for the sensationalist coverage he produced for *60 Minutes* while embedded with a band of mujahedin, Rather accused Soviet forces of "genocide" and of borrowing their methods from "early Hitler."

Radek Sikorski, a young Polish exile and journalist for the UK's *Spectator*, took his affection for the mujahedin a step further, donning Pashtun guerrilla garb, toting a rifle and even participating in a raid on a Soviet barracks, during which he fired three cartridge clips of ammo. According to the UK's *Telegraph*, the reporter-cum-guerrilla "succeeded only in hitting the outer wall of a Soviet barracks." After the Cold War, Sikorski went on to serve as Poland's foreign minister and marry the vehemently anti-Russian *Washington Post* columnist, Anne Applebaum.

American media coverage of the Afghan conflict was substantially influenced by advocacy NGOs like the Afghanistan Relief Committee (ARC). The ARC received the bulk of its funding from the National Endowment for Democracy, a US government-backed organization that advanced American soft power by supporting political parties, media and civil society groups in countries where Washington sought regime change.

ARC's operations were overseen by John Train, the founding manager of the *Paris Review*, a CIA-backed literary journal that served as a cover for agency writers. In 1982, Train volunteered his NGO as a funding vehicle for a propaganda film hyping the suffering and courage of the Afghan mujahedin. The film's goal, according to Train, was "to impose on the Soviet Union in Afghanistan the sort of television coverage that proved fatal to the American presence in Vietnam."

He imagined his film being aired on public television, shown on college campuses and broadcast on right-wing televangelist Pat Robertson's Christian Broadcasting Network. And he proposed Hekmatyar, the CIA-backed Islamist warlord, as the local fixer. In a memo to Freedom House, the US government-supported NGO, Train spelled out the kind of footage he was hoping to capture: "Russians: Coverage live of air assault and destruction of a rural village and mosque. Reprisal killings, use of CBW [chemical or biological weapons]."

In Train's spy-ops fantasy, ordinary Afghans were little more than imperial stage props. As journalist Joel Whitney wrote in his investigative book *Finks*, which exposed the CIA's role in Cold War cultural propaganda, "This seemed to take propaganda to a whole new level that completely dehumanized the victims of the violence in the service of some apocalyptic bet between angels and demons."

~

In 1985, as US support for the mujahedin reached its height, journalist Helena Cobban discovered how deeply the fetishization of the Afghan rebels had penetrated American culture. Cobban had been invited to an event advertised as an academic conference at a resort hotel in Tucscon, Arizona. When she entered the hotel, Cobban found herself inside a Cold War political rally. "I remember mingling with all of these wealthy Republican women and being asked, 'Have you adopted a muj?" Cobban recalled to me. "Each one had pledged money to sponsor a member of the Afghan mujahedin in the name of beating the communists. Some were even seated at the event next to their personal 'muj.'"

The keynote speaker of the evening, according to Cobban, was a hard-charging freshman member of Congress named John McCain. During the Vietnam War, the North Vietnamese Army had captured McCain after he was shot down by a Soviet officer on his way to bomb a civilian light bulb factory. He spent two years in captivity at the so-called Hanoi Hilton, during which he provided the Vietnamese with valuable intelligence on US war planning. McCain returned from the war with a deep, abiding loathing of his former captors, remarking in 2000, "I hate the gooks. I will hate them as long as I live." His visceral anticommunist resentment informed his vocal support for the mujahedin as well as the right-wing Contra death squads in Central America.

So committed was McCain to the anticommunist cause that he momentarily served on the advisory board of the United States Council for World Freedom, the American affiliate of the World Anti-Communist League (WACL). Geoffrey Stewart-Smith, a former leader of WACL's British chapter, described the organization as "a collection of Nazis, Fascists, anti-Semites, sellers of forgeries, vicious racialists, and corrupt self-seekers. It has evolved into an anti-Semitic international."

Joining McCain in the organization were notables such as Yaroslav Stetsko, the Ukrainian Nazi collaborator who helped oversee the massacre of thousands of Jews during the 1941 Lviv pogrom; the brutal Argentinian former dictator Jorge Rafael Videla; and Guatemalan death squad leader Mario Sandoval Alarcón. Ignoring the rogue's gallery that comprised WACL's leadership, Reagan honored the group for playing "a leadership role in drawing attention to the gallant struggle now being waged by the true freedom fighters of our day."

Before journalists Scott and Jon Lee Anderson published their damning investigative book on the WACL, *Inside the League*, in 1986, the unsavory connections fostered by the Reagan White House and its Republican congressional allies received little attention from the mainstream press. The same was generally true for Washington's anticommunist proxies, from Central America to Afghanistan.

When mujahedin rebels committed atrocities, like the massacre by bin Laden's fighters of seventy Afghan government officers who had surrendered at Torkham in 1988, newspaper editors generally turned their attention elsewhere. The rebels' rampage on Kunduz in 1988, which saw rape and pillaging on a mass scale, also drew little attention. And when Hekmatyar's forces butchered thirty fellow rebels—all top CIA trainees—State Department spokesman Richard Boucher casually dismissed a lone reporter's critical questions: "I think what you're doing is taking one incident and blowing it out of proportion," Boucher protested.

A year later, with encouragement from the CIA to "put pressure" on Kabul, Hekmatyar's Hezb-i-Islami opened up a campaign of terrorist bombings around the city. When Ed McWilliams, a foreign service officer at the US embassy in Kabul, attempted to report back to Washington about a car bombing by one of Hekmatyar's men that had torn through a neighborhood of minority Hazaras and left a pile of dead civilians, he was rebuked. McWilliams explained to journalist Andrew Cockburn that the CIA had demanded that he "report a little less specifically about the humanitarian consequences of those vehicle bombs."

The American covert war in Afghanistan helped inflame the worst refugee crisis in history, turning Afghans into the largest refugee group in the world at the time and what Rüdiger Schöch, a researcher for the United Nations High Commission on Refugees (UNHCR), described as "victims of political instrumentalization" by the powers driving the conflict. According to Schöch, the Afghans were not received in Pakistan as refugees fleeing persecution in their own country, but rather as "partisan holy warriors in a struggle against atheist tyranny" who were "accepted practically under the condition of their outspoken opposition against the regime in Kabul."

His report concluded that "even though UNHCR confines its humanitarian programme to persons of its concern, there is ample evidence that the [Pakistani] government as the operational partner is permitting, by acts of commission or omission, humanitarian assistance to flow into the hands of freedom fighters participating in the 'Holy Jehad.'"

As the refugees from Afghanistan and other destabilized nations began to reach Europe during the 1980s, right-wing forces that had lain dormant since the end of World War II began to mobilize for a new Kulturkampf. In 1985, Norway saw its first right-wing terror attack with the firebombing of the Nor Mosque in Oslo, a congregation of the demonstratively "moderate" Ahmadiyya sect. The attack was preceded by public remonstrations by the right-wing National Popular Party against liberal politicians for allowing the entry of "thousands of Muslims who now demand the right to practice their religion."

As the number of refugees rose in the late 1980s, far-right elements that had organized around their loathing of European Jews now transferred their resentment onto Muslims, declaring followers of Islam the main threat to the survival of Western civilization. As Norwegian social anthropologist Sindre Bangstad noted, the far-right Popular Movement Against Immigration drew its activist core from former volunteers for the Waffen SS Nordic division. Among them was Arne Myrdal, who publicly heralded the birth of a "resistance movement" that was "fighting against the Muslim invasion of our country and against the national traitors who assist them."

Back in Washington, where the Reagan administration made the call to arm the most ferocious Islamist commanders of the Afghan mujahedin, the administration was becoming suspicious of America's well-educated, rapidly assimilating Arab population. In 1987, Reagan's Immigration and Naturalization Service drew up a formal blueprint to hold Arab Americans at a concentration camp in Oakdale, Louisiana, in the event of a future war with Middle Eastern countries. Slowly but surely, the government was establishing the groundwork for holding American Arabs and Muslims collectively responsible for the actions of the band of fanatics the government had secretly armed and trained.

Ali the American

In the United States, an archipelago of front organizations shepherded men and money to the Afghan battlefield right under the nose of the FBI. The top recruitment center in the United States was an inauspicious storefront on Atlantic Avenue in Brooklyn called the Al-Kifah Afghan Refugee Center. Acting as staffers of a relief organization, the center's leadership dispatched impressionable young Muslim men to Afghanistan while raising money from private sources across the country. Al-Kifah was, in fact, the American branch of the Peshawar-based Services Bureau funded by bin Laden and overseen by his mentor, Azzam. Historian Alfred McCoy later described Al-Kifah as "a place of pivotal importance to [the CIA's] Operation Cyclone, the clandestine American training effort to support the mujahadeen."

An Egyptian immigrant, Mustafa Shalabi, directed the Al-Kifah operation and answered directly to Azzam. Throughout the 1980s, Azzam barnstormed America, rustling up money and manpower for the anti-Soviet jihad. Barnett Rubin, a scholarly expert on Afghanistan and Pakistan, told journalist Robert Friedman that Azzam "was 'enlisted' by the CIA to unite fractious rebel groups operating in Peshawar." His anticommunist agenda dovetailed neatly with the CIA's; indeed, few figures played as pivotal a role as Azzam did in exporting Islamism into secular Arab societies and undercutting socialist movements in the Middle East. Azzam coordinated his efforts abroad with

Omar Abdel-Rahman, the so-called "Blind Sheikh" who was adored in jihadist circles for his masterfully accessible application of tracts by Ibn Taymiyyah and other proto-Wahhabist scholars to the contemporary crises facing the Islamic world. Credited with the fatwa that provided justification for the 1981 assassination of Egyptian president Anwar al-Sadat, Abdel-Rahman wound up being expelled from Egypt instead of jailed. Like Azzam, the CIA paid Abdel-Rahman's way to Peshawar, where he joined Hekmatyar, the CIA's favorite warlord, and functioned as his charismatic sidekick.

Ayman al-Zawahiri, a wealthy surgeon who led Al-Jihad, rounded out the Services Bureau leadership by bringing Egypt's most potent jihadist organization to the table. Unlike Abdel-Rahman, Zawahiri had done hard jail time for the Sadat assassination plot and suffered grisly abuses in the dungeons of Egyptian state security. After his release, Zawahiri testified to being whipped with electric cables and attacked by wild dogs that, according to journalist Lawrence Wright, had been trained to rape prisoners. Over time, Zawahiri became obsessed with revenge. "In striking the enemy, he would create a new reality," Wright wrote. "His strategy was to force the Egyptian regime to become even more repressive, to make the people hate it."

One of Zawahiri's most potent weapons came in the form of an Egyptian special-forces soldier drummed out of the army for his untethered extremism. Muscular and six foot two, a martial arts expert who boasted a degree in psychology and proficiency in four languages, the army veteran had somehow managed to find work as a security advisor for Egypt Air, the national airline. Sensing an enticing opportunity, Zawahiri assigned the recruit with his first mission: scout out Cairo's airport and prepare a detailed plan for an aerial hijacking. Thus began the saga of Ali Abdel Saoud Mohamed, a brazen and brilliant covert operator known in Al Qaeda's inner circle as "Ali the American."

With startling ease, Mohamed infiltrated the CIA, FBI and US Army, tapping his high-level government connections to evade investigation while he provided invaluable intelligence to the Al Qaeda handlers to whom he owed his loyalty. Though

Mohamed's case might seem extraordinary, it fit within the CIA's Cold War–era modus operandi, which flagrantly disregarded national security imperatives to achieve imperial goals—in this case, anticommunism—that seemed much more urgent at the time.

Again and again, Mohamed furnished his superior officers with specific information about Al Qaeda's existence and its determination to strike American assets. His intelligence was even used to warn President George W. Bush about the 9/11 plot. But each time, the red flags were ignored, allowing the plots to move ahead while international jihadism metastasized. And as journalist Peter Lance argued in his book *Triple Cross*, the CIA was so determined to protect its relationship with the Blind Sheikh, it "may have run interference for Ali [Mohamed] as he sought entry to the United States and a position of influence at Fort Bragg, the heart of the US military's black operations."

Mohamed's career as a US intelligence agent began in 1985 when he showed up uninvited at the US embassy in Cairo to offer his services. Despite warnings from Egyptian intelligence, the CIA assigned him to Hamburg, Germany, where he was to spy on a mosque supposedly tied to Hezbollah, the Lebanese Shia-based political movement that preoccupied the agency while Sunni jihadism flourished under its watch. Mohamed immediately blew his cover, informing senior figures at the mosque that he was a CIA operative.

Having betrayed the agency, the State Department put him on a terrorist watch list. This should have been the end of his career in intelligence, but somehow Mohamed was still able to enter the United States on a State Department visa. On the flight over, he successfully courted a young American woman and married her weeks later at a drive-through wedding chapel in Reno, Nevada. At her home in California's Silicon Valley, he proceeded to set up a jihadist sleeper cell while apparently maintaining his relationship with the CIA. "Everyone in the community knew he was working as a liaison between the CIA and the Afghan cause," Ali Zaki, a local obstetrician, told journalist Peter Lance.

In 1986, Mohamed enlisted in the US Army at Fort Bragg's

John F. Kennedy Special Warfare Center and School. His commanding officer, Lt. Col. Robert Anderson, was convinced that the invisible hand of the intelligence community engineered Mohammed's assignment to a special-forces unit. "If you proposed this to any army non-commissioned officer [or] commissioned officer, they'[d] tell you, it didn't happen without support form an outside agency," Anderson said. "Now, what outside agency? I would say that it would have to have been the CIA getting him into the United States. And then once in the United States, the Federal Bureau of Investigation."

With his physical prowess and battlefield experience, Mohamed quickly rose to the rank of supply sergeant, gaining access to special-forces equipment and training manuals. During a joint exercise between American and Egyptian forces, however, Mohamed was sent home after Egyptian intelligence informed his army superiors that he was a potentially dangerous radical with ties to Al-Jihad. The army responded by simply reassigning him to another unit at Fort Bragg, where he served under the command of Colonel Norville "Tex" De Atkine.

As the director of the JFK School's Middle East studies department, De Atkine fancied himself an expert on the history and culture of Arab societies. Among his most notable contributions was the foreword to *The Arab Mind*. Written by Raphael Patai, an Israeli American cultural anthropologist, the book presented a collection of lurid colonial stereotypes about Arabs. Patai devoted a full twenty-five pages to the supposed sexual dysfunctions of contemporary Arabs, musing about "the Arab view that masturbation is far more shameful than visiting prostitutes." Thanks to De Atkine, the Orientalist tract became required reading for officers serving in the Middle East.

"It is essential reading," De Atkine wrote in the book's foreword. "At the institution where I teach military officers, *The Arab Mind* forms the basis of my cultural instruction."

The colonel arranged for Mohamed to lead a series of cultural training seminars for officers on their way to the Middle East. He presented the religiously devout Egyptian as the embodiment of the Arab mind. In one such forum, Mohamed offered a vision of Islam so extreme that it could have been lifted from the pages of Patai's book. "We have to establish an Islamic state because Islam without political domination cannot survive," Mohamed declared before an array of stone-faced army officers. "Actually," he continued, "if you look at the religion, we do not have moderates. You have one line. You accept the one line or not."

De Atkine later defended his relationship with Mohamed, stating, "I don't think he was anti-American. He was what I would call a Muslim fundamentalist, which isn't a bomb thrower."

At the time, Mohamed was situated in one of the most important hubs of the Afghan proxy war. Indeed, Fort Bragg was known to CIA operatives as "the Farm." When investigative journalist John Cooley visited the onsite JFK Special Warfare Center, he found that "Green Beret officers, many of them seasoned veterans of Vietnam, took draconian secrecy oaths and then began the secret training assignments for the Afghanistan war." From this "farm" and others across the American south, including a CIA black site in rural Virginia, according to Cooley, special-forces soldiers trained Pakistani officers and visiting Afghan mujahedin in use and detection of explosives; surveillance and counter-surveillance; how to write reports according to CIA "Company" standards; how to shoot various weapons, and the running of counter-terrorism, counter-narcotics and paramilitary operations.

In 1988, Mohamed informed his army superiors that he would take his leave in Afghanistan, where he planned to kill as many Russians as he could. Despite the diplomatic peril of allowing an active-duty US soldier to participate directly in a war that was supposed to be covert, he was given a green light. Before long, he was on his way to the Services Bureau in Peshawar, and then across the Afghan border to rendezvous with his handler, Zawahiri. On the Afghan frontier, Mohamed presided over the training of newly arrived jihadists, including a gloomy Egyptian American named El-Sayyid Nosair.

Mohamed returned to his unit at Fort Bragg proudly bearing the belt of a Russian soldier and maps of the training camps he toured. De Atkine rewarded him by assigning him to lead an officer-level seminar on the tactics of the Soviet Spetnaz. Other officers, meanwhile, were stunned that Mohamed was not harshly punished for his freelance participation in a foreign war. "I believe that there was an [FBI] agent that controlled Ali and knew Ali Mohamed's actions," Anderson remarked to Lance.

According to Mohamed's army evaluation report, his duties included "translat[ing] military briefings from English to Arabic." This gave him access to training manuals demonstrating how to load and fire shoulder-mounted M72A2 antitank rockets and M16 rifles, as well as dispatches from the Joint Chiefs of Staff to US embassies in cities across the Middle East marked "top secret for training." Mohamed highlighted the embassies in Kenya, Tanzania and Yemen, translated the documents into Arabic and smuggled them to jihadist cadres of the Services Bureau.

The Disposal Problem

In Kabul, as the tide of battle turned against the Soviets, women who had been empowered by the communist government fretted about a future under mujahedin control. "Without the revolution, what would I be?" a college-educated Afghan Red Crescent worker named Mina Fahim declared in 1988. "I would be staying at home, and maybe only going out with the veil—like my mother did. And for marriage, I could be bought like so much property. This is why so many Afghan women are with this revolution, and why we will fight so hard to defend it."

A reporter from the Knight Ridder news service noted at the time:

> The differences in how the two sides view women are enormous. When asked why they had left Afghanistan for the refugee camps, many Afghans in Pakistan don't talk about the bombing or land reform, or even the suppression of Islam. What they did not like, those Afghans said recently, was that the Communists in Kabul wanted to send their daughters to school.

The anti-Soviet jihad had altered Afghanistan for good. The cultural tensions that flared throughout 1970s Kabul, with Islamists battling student leftists in the streets, had been settled through conventional warfare, with the former camp winning out. The modernizing reforms of the communists, advanced against the will of the rural clan-based population, were about to be washed away in a green tide that not only restored traditional patriarchal values, but introduced new strains of Islamism cultivated in the ideological hothouses of Saudi Arabia and Pakistan. The United States was hardly an innocent bystander to this development; if anything, its role was decisive.

On February 15, 1989, the last of the Red Army's beleaguered forces retreated from Afghanistan. On the eve of Soviet withdrawal, that country's premier, Mikhail Gorbachev, proposed to President Bush a ceasefire, with an end to weapons shipments and the establishment of a coalition government that welcomed the mujahedin into power. So determined was Gorbachev to prevent the Afghan state from collapsing, he proposed free elections supervised by the UN. "If we score any points, we can do it only together. If we try to score points alone, nothing good will happen," the Soviet premier had told Bush and then president Reagan weeks earlier at the UN, beseeching them for American cooperation. His entreaties were ultimately met with a cold shoulder from Washington, which had adopted the mujahedin position as its own: full regime change or perpetual insurgency. With the Soviet-backed government of Mohammad Najibullah still in power, the arms continued to flow to the rebels.

The Afghan trap laid more than a decade before by Brzezinski had successfully ensnared the Soviet Union. The Reagan doctrine seemed to have been ratified and America's nemesis was teetering on the brink of collapse. The war had worked out nicely for the arms industry as well, enabling the battlefield testing of new weapons systems and record sales to oil-rich allies. Reagan's secretary of defense, Caspar Weinberger, was a former president of Bechtel, and the construction and pipeline company did billions of dollars in business in Saudi Arabia. As a reward for the kingdom's support for the anti-Soviet jihad, Weinberger helped arrange a whopping $8.5 billion arms deal that granted the Saudis advanced AWACS surveillance aircraft. It was the beginning of a very special relationship.

Peter Tomsen, an Afghanistan specialist working in the State Department under the first Bush administration, was a voice in the wilderness when he warned of the consequences of Najibullah's government falling. "An extremist seizure of Kabul would plunge Afghanistan into a fresh round of warfare, which could affect areas adjoining Afghanistan," Tomsen wrote in a secret 1991 cable to Washington. He added that if Hekmatyar reached the city, "extremists in the Arab world would support them in stoking Islamic radicalism in the region, including the Soviet Central Asian republics, but also in Saudi Arabia and elsewhere in the Arab world."

Tomsen called for a political settlement, but few in Washington were listening. In the final years before the CIA and Soviet Union agreed to cut off arms to Afghanistan, the CIA pumped unprecedented amounts of cash and weapons to Hekmatyar. Tomsen, for his part, saw to it that an almost equal amount went to Ahmad Shah Massoud, his guerrilla rival, who was seen as more moderate and was favored by the State Department. As soon as Kabul fell, a collection of warlords took control, each with an array of foreign backers, often in competition with one another, and none with any interest in maintaining a semblance of functional government. The country remained a magnet for foreign jihadists while droves of women empowered by communist rule were forced to flee for their lives, their worst fears realized thanks in no small part to the freedom-loving United States.

With one superpower vanquished, an emboldened cadre of zealots introduced to the Afghan battlefield through the Services Bureau set out to wage jihad across the world. The tactics the CIA brought to Afghanistan were on display virtually anywhere jihadist militancy took root. "Time and again," Cooley noted, "these same techniques reappear among the Islamist insurgents in Upper Egypt and Algeria, since the 'Afghani' [*sic*] Arab veterans began returning there in the late 1980s and early 1990s."

Abdurajik Abubakar Janjalani, a Filipino jihadist who'd fought alongside bin Laden in Afghanistan, returned home to wage an insurgency for an independent Islamic State under the banner of the Abu Sayyaf terrorist group. According to Cooley, Abu Sayyaf was "the most violent and radical Islamist group in the Far East, using its CIA and ISI training to harass, attack, and murder Christian priests, wealthy non-Muslim plantation owners, and merchants and local government in the southern Philippine island of Mindanao." Filipino senator Aquilino Pimentel was gripped with outrage after reading Cooley's reporting. Pimentel branded Abu Sayyaf a "CIA monster," demanding a government inquiry into the agency's role in establishing the jihadist organization.

In Bosnia, where some 3,000 foreign Islamic fundamentalists flocked to fight the Russian-aligned Serbs, Senator Jesse Helms, far-right former WACL member and powerful Senate Foreign Relations Committee member, said it was time to "begin treating the Bosnians as we did the Contras and mujahedin—as freedom fighters engaged in a war of liberation."

At that point, the Bosnian forces had purchased as much as $200 million in illegal weapons through a shadowy group called Third World Relief Agency, with funding provided by countries like Saudi Arabia and, according to the *Washington Post*, "the wealthy Saudi Arabian emigre [sic] Osama Binladen." (The 1995 report represents one of the first mentions of bin Laden in the American media.) A Western diplomat complained at the time, "We were told [by Washington] to watch [the Third World Relief Agency] but not interfere. Bosnia was trying to get weapons from anybody, and we weren't helping much. The least we could do is back off. So we backed off."

Another charity that was instrumental in shepherding jihadist fighters from Afghanistan to new flashpoints like Bosnia was Benevolence International. Overseen by Saudi businessman Adel Batterjee, Benevolence International had established a camp to train fighters in Afghanistan in 1991, then followed bin Laden into Sudan, where he set up training grounds the following year. The charity also established an office that year in suburban Chicago, Illinois. Though a 1996 CIA report found that Benevolence International was among a chain of charities that "employ members or otherwise facilitate the activities of terrorist groups operating in Bosnia," the FBI took no action against it.

As the *Chicago Tribune* later explained, "the United States did not push the matter because of a long political understanding: America would defend the kingdom [of Saudi Arabia] militarily and not meddle in its internal affairs if the Saudis remained a loyal oil supplier and Middle East ally." Another undeniable reason for Washington's passive attitude was that the Islamist guerrillas in Bosnia were becoming valuable proxies in the NATO-orchestrated destruction of Yugoslavia.

Thus Central Europe became the next petri dish for international jihadism, as thousands of foreign fighters flocked there to battle the Serbs, or jaunted over to Chechnya to confront Russia once again.

Former Senate Foreign Relations Committee investigative counsel Jack Blum was among a tiny handful in Washington who raised the alarm about the anti-Soviet jihad's unintended consequences. When Blum testified before the Senate Select Committee on Intelligence in October 1996 about allegations of the CIA trafficking drugs to fund the Nicaraguan Contras during the 1980s, he warned that the agency was facing a new and especially troublesome "disposal problem."

The problem first arose, according to Blum, when Cuban mercenaries trained by the CIA returned to Miami after the botched amphibious Bay of Pigs landing. "And when you teach people how to change their identity, how to hide from the law, how to build bombs, how to assassinate people," Blum testified, "they don't forget how to do it, and you wind up, after the covert action is over, with a disposal problem. We've never been very good at handling disposal."

After 1961, CIA-trained Cuban exiles had wreaked havoc around the world, from the assassination of Chilean socialist diplomat Orlando Letelier to the downing of Cubana Flight 455 by right-wing Cuban CIA asset Orlando Bosch. But the danger presented by the veterans of the anti-Soviet jihad was exponentially greater, Blum warned: "We have all kinds of people who have been trained in bomb-making, and by God, they've been with us everywhere from the World Trade Center to Paris and all over the world, wherever there's somebody who doesn't suit their ideological tenor."

Two decades after his testimony, Blum's frustration has only grown. "By creating a motley assortment of volunteers and bringing them to Afghanistan," he remarked to me, "we created the monster of all monsters. And nobody seemed to care. It was not only a disposal problem, they were totally abandoned. It went well beyond disposal. They all went home and went to work doing what we trained them to do. And nobody, I mean nobody, has been held accountable for this."

The Ghosts of Operation Cyclone

Upon his triumphant return home from the Afghan battlefield, Osama bin Laden held court with one of his most generous wartime patrons. Prince Bandar bin Sultan, former Saudi ambassador to the United States, had once helped the CIA manage mass transfers of arms to Afghan rebels and Nicaraguan Contras. He had even coordinated with the CIA to arrange the assassination of Iranian assets. Seated before the well connected prince, bin Laden gushed about the American aid he received. "Thank you!" he exclaimed to Bandar. "Thank you for bringing the Americans to help us get rid of the secularist, atheist Soviets."

Bin Laden's friendly attitude to Washington was fleeting, however. Almost as soon as the last Soviet tanks left Afghanistan, he was mapping out plans for an organization that could expand the battlefield across the globe, and ultimately to American shores. Alongside Zawahiri, the founder of Al-Jihad, bin Laden named the new network Al Qaeda—"the base"—after their old military camp in Afghanistan. Zawahiri maintained control over his old organization, which aimed to topple Egypt's government and implement Islamist rule, while serving as one of

Al Qaeda's top tacticians. However, Zawahiri faced a powerful internal rival in Azzam, founder of the CIA- and ISI-backed Services Bureau.

A Palestinian refugee who had endured the bitterness of forced displacement, Azzam was determined to return to his homeland as a leader of a newfangled Islamist resistance against the Israeli occupiers. During 1970's Black September, when the Jordanian monarchy brutally ejected Palestinian forces from its realm, Azzam refused to retaliate. His neutrality stemmed not only from his belief that the secular, left-oriented Palestine Liberation Organization (PLO) was a rival to his Islamist camp, he warned that in battling fellow Muslims, "forbidden blood would be spilled." Twenty years later, Azzam insisted again that killing Muslims was not only counterproductive, but sinful; he demanded that Israel, not a "near enemy" like Egypt, be the next target. He thus placed himself in direct conflict with Zawahiri over Al Qaeda's fundamental strategy.

On November 24, 1989, a massive bomb planted on a Peshawar roadside tore Azzam to pieces. Lawrence Wright, who chronicled the rise of Al Qaeda in his book *The Looming Tower*, speculated that Zawahiri might have been behind the assassination, noting that he had been overheard spreading rumors that Azzam was an American agent that same day. But the killers could have come from any number of outfits—from the Israeli Mossad, which sought to liquidate another implacable foe, or from the CIA, which might have decided that Azzam had outlived his usefulness. At the time, Peshawar was a haven for operatives from virtually every intelligence agency meddling in Afghanistan. Whoever the culprits were, Azzam's killing left Zawahiri in the driver's seat, with bin Laden by his side.

Months after Azzam's killing, Abdel-Rahman (the Blind Sheikh) entered the United States on a visa he had obtained at the US consulate in Sudan, despite having been on a US terrorist watch list for three years. The CIA had reviewed seven applications made by Abdel-Rahman between 1986 and 1990, during the height of the anti-Soviet jihad, when he had been a key recruiter for Azzam's Services Bureau. CIA officers turned him down only once due to his links to international terrorism. At the same time, the FBI had been closely monitoring Azzam's recruitment of young Muslims in the United States to fight in Afghanistan. Its investigators ultimately found a curious rationalization for closing its inquiry into the matter: "This will not be considered as mercenary recruiting, since they did not sign any documents nor did it appear that they were recruited to Afghanistan to fight."

Five years later, a 1995 report in the *Boston Globe* featured a rare public acknowledgement of Abdel-Rahman's relationship with the CIA. The article essentially revealed that the Blind Sheikh had entered the United States on the clandestine CIA Department of Operations visa waiver program, which provided privileged access to valuable assets. "In May 1993, the Egyptian government newspaper *Al Gomhuria* quoted Egyptian president Hosni Mubarak as saying that Rahman had worked with the CIA," the report noted. It also quoted Mubarak complaining that the United States could have prevented the first World Trade Center bombing if it had heeded his warnings about Abdel-Rahman. Under pressure from the US State Department, the newspaper's editor retracted the story a few days later. But in July 1993, US press reports asserted that CIA officers working under consular cover in Egypt and Sudan had reviewed seven US visa applications made by Rahman between 1986 and 1990. The CIA officers approved six of the requests."

For all his supposed erudition, Abdel-Rahman displayed almost baffling naivete when he arrived in the United States. In his mind, he was the Salafi version of Iran's Shi'ite theocrat Ayatollah Ruhollah Khomeini. Modeling his move to the New York area after Khomeini's exile in Paris, Abdel-Rahman fantasized about returning to Egypt as the spiritual guide of a new, Islamist government after the old, corruption-addled dictatorship fell, just as Khomeini had done in Iran. The United States had supported Abdel-Rahman's cause abroad for years, so why would it have a problem with him preaching jihad within its borders? He arrived to US shores with supreme confidence, but he was walking into a trap.

Abdel-Rahman's first order of business was to take control of Brooklyn's Al-Kifah center. The center represented a remnant of Azzam's old CIA and Saudi-backed Services Bureau, which had directed foreign fighters into Afghanistan to bleed the Soviets. According to Osama el-Baz, former security advisor to Egypt's Hosni Mubarak, the CIA and Saudi Arabia had kept the Services Bureau afloat for future operations against Iran, relying on Al-Kifah to launder funding. "It's all the fault of those stupid bastards at the CIA," el-Baz complained to journalist Andrew Cockburn. "They trained these people, kept them in after the Russians left, and now we get this."

At Al-Kifah, millions of dollars were left over from fundraising campaigns during the height of the anti-Soviet jihad, and $100,000 was still pouring in each month. Abdel-Rahman insisted that half of the donations be committed to toppling Mubarak's government—the ultimate goal of Zawahiri's Al-Jihad. But Shalabi wanted to spend the funds backing the establishment of an Islamist government in Kabul.

On March 1, 1991, following a sustained campaign of incitement by the Blind Sheikh, Shalabi was found soaked in his own blood on the floor of his Brooklyn apartment, bludgeoned with a baseball bat and hacked with knife wounds. As in any gangland style murder, the killer's methods were designed to make an example of the victim.

Despite ample evidence pointing to Abdel-Rahman's network, and the disappearance of $100,000 in Al-Kifah donations from the apartment, the murder investigation was hastily closed with no arrests. Ali Mohamed, who had been a confidant of Shalabi and his family, was not even questioned. This allowed the Blind Sheikh to complete his takeover of Al-Kifah, which meant that bin Laden had taken over the Services Bureau network once and for all—providing his Al Qaeda network with easy access to the United States.

The ghosts of Operation Cyclone hovered over early-1990s New York City. One of them, Nosair, had been an understudy of Abdel-Rahman and trained on the Afghan battlefield by Ali

Mohamed. A highly educated immigrant to the United States, Nosair had turned to fundamentalist Islam in reaction to the repression of Egypt's dictatorship. Once he arrived in the United States, he grew depressed, popping Prozac and reeling in disgust at the socially permissive, hyper-consumerist atmosphere in which he was suddenly immersed. Trained as an engineer back in Egypt, he toiled as an air conditioner repairman, developing an inferiority complex and suffering a painful industrial accident that left him with lingering injuries. He became a constant presence at Al-Kifah, joining fellow veterans of the Afghan War for excursions to a shooting range in Long Island, where Mohamed schooled them in the use of high-powered assault rifles. Undercover FBI agents tailed them to one session and photographed them wearing Services Bureau T-shirts emblazoned with a map of Afghanistan. No action was taken, however.

Before long, though, Nosair applied his firearms and infiltration skills to target the Jewish fanatical rabbi, Meir Kahane. Kahane had made his name clamoring for the overthrow of Israel's civil law-based government and replacing it with a fascist theocracy cleansed of all Palestinians—the State of Judea. He was the Jewish analog to Zawahiri, who aimed to do the same thing in Egypt by toppling a putatively secular government and installing a fundamentalist Islamic State that purged religious minorities.

And like Zawahiri, Kahane was a hard-line anticommunist who had been used by the US government to advance an ulterior political agenda that did lasting damage to America's social fabric. Indeed, Kahane had enjoyed a long relationship with the FBI, dating back to his infiltration of the right-wing John Birch Society in the 1950s. During the early 1970s, Kahane and his Jewish Defense League served as tools in the FBI's campaign of subterfuge against the Black Panthers. Agents agitated Kahane with fabricated anti-Semitic messages authored in the name of black radicals, inflaming long-standing racial tensions, sparking street fights and advancing the FBI's plan to shatter efforts at leftist black-Jewish political coalition building. The FBI-fomented paranoia ultimately enabled the militant rabbi to paint himself as the only thing standing between Jews and a second Holocaust at hands of blacks, Arabs and their liberal Jewish donors.

On November 5, 1990, Kahane appeared at the Marriott East Side hotel in Manhattan for the founding conference of a group he called ZEERO, or the Zionist Emergency Evacuation Rescue Organization. In characteristic fashion, the rabbi conjured up a scenario of imminent doom for the Jews, urging his hundred or so supporters to abandon life in America before the flames of anti-Semitism consumed them. Their only sanctuary, he declared, was within the militarized frontiers of the self-proclaimed Jewish state.

Suddenly, a man dressed as an ultra-Orthodox Jew approached Kahane. With a crazed look in his eyes, he unloaded a .357 Magnum revolver into the rabbi's torso. It was Nosair, demonstrating the tactics he had learned from years of training in Afghanistan and under the watch of Ali Mohamed. The fascist rabbi died that night. His funeral, held days later in Jerusalem, where he had served as a lawmaker in Israel's Knesset, was the largest to date in that country's history and was even addressed by Israel's chief rabbi.

Martyred by a fellow religious fanatic, Kahane's views moved steadily into the Israeli mainstream in the years after his death, particularly his proposals for the ethnic cleansing of Palestinian citizens from Israel. The fallout from his killing demonstrated the success of the logic both Al Qaeda and his own followers embraced: terror begets extremism and collapses the fragile space where multi-confessional societies survive.

In Nosair's home, FBI and NYPD investigators found the trove of documents stolen by Ali Mohamed from Fort Bragg, including classified dispatches from the Joint Chiefs to US embassies across the Middle East and Green Beret training manuals that Mohamed had translated into Arabic. They found Nosair's notebooks containing detailed plans, in his words, for an attack "to be done by means of destroying—exploding—the structures of [America's] civilized pillars such as the tourist infrastructure which they are proud of and their high world buildings which they are proud of and their statues which they endear and the buildings in which gather their leaders." The investigators also discovered maps of the World Trade Center and audiotapes of the Blind Sheikh calling for holy war.

Besides training him in firearms, Mohamed had instructed Nosair in the use of dead mail drops, prompting him to register a post office box at a check-cashing store in Jersey City called Sphinx Trading. It was the same mailbox center that the 9/11 ringleaders relied on to exchange messages as the plot developed. Despite uncovering a massive cache of evidence that connected Nosair to an international terror network and suggested active plots underway in New York City, Nosair was tried as a lone gunman. His lawyer, the leftist firebrand William Kunstler, easily outmaneuvered a clumsy government prosecution team. In the end, Nosair got off with an illegal gun rap—a stinging defeat for the government.

The FBI had failed to stop Al Qaeda before it could metastasize into a major global force. Meanwhile, bin Laden was turning against his former patrons and preparing ambitious plans to wage war on a global scale.

2

At the Dawn of the Forever War

When Iraqi president Saddam Hussein invaded Kuwait in 1991, a new chance for glory arrived on bin Laden's doorstep—or so he thought. The wealthy scion had warned for years that Saddam would eventually threaten Saudi Arabia, and now, here he was, with his million-man army just miles from the kingdom.

Desperate for action after a year of dithering, bin Laden appeared in the office of the Saudi defense minister, Sultan bin Abdulaziz al-Saud. Bin Laden had brought battle plans and an entourage of Afghan war vets spoiling for a new fight. He beseeched Sultan to send his own private militia and a supplement of unemployed Saudi conscripts against the battle hardened Iraqi Republican Guard. Later, he made the same pitch to Prince Turki al-Faisal, one of the few principals who shared bin Laden's resentment of Saddam. Turki left the meeting astounded by bin Laden's arrogance and the harebrained quality of his plan, and sent him away almost as soon as the royal family welcomed the American military in as the protectors of its kingdom.

For bin Laden, the rejection revealed to him that his country's army was little more than a neo-imperial shell and confirmed in his mind how its leadership acted as tools of the godless West—just as Utaybi, the millenarian coup leader, had described them back in 1979.

This offered bin Laden further fuel for his wrath against the United States. A few years earlier, he had celebrated them for supporting the anti-Soviet jihad, but now he echoed Reagan's language about the Soviet Union, inverting it to slam the United States as an Evil Empire that had to be bled at its weakest points.

For Americans, thousands of miles away, the Gulf War unfolded for the first time on 24-7 cable network broadcasts, with commercial breaks. In a series of essays provocatively entitled *The Gulf War Did Not Take Place*, French philosopher Jean Baudrillard captured the way that round-the-clock cable news spoon-fed Americans a simulacrum of the actual event, an electronic war game of camera-tipped, laser-guided missiles, stealth bombers and embedded journalists. For Baudrillard, the war was "a virtual and meticulous operation which leaves the same impression of a non-event where the military confrontation fell short and where no political power proved itself."

Widely misunderstood as a denial of the carnage and human toll of the war, Baudrillard had produced one of the most enduring critiques of the way post–Cold War conflicts were marketed to the Western public as clinical exercises in freedom-spreading. For most Americans, the digital abstraction of the war and the dual layer patina of patriotic hoopla and humanitarian goodwill overwhelmed their critical faculties and ensured their consent. The stage was set for the era of drone warfare that saw the United States carrying out robotic assassinations from Yemen to the Philippines with little political backlash at home.

Of the few Kuwaitis the American public got to know during the Gulf War, and the most aggressively promoted one, turned out to be a fraud. She was the product of a massive cash infusion from that country's emir into at least twenty public relations firms through a front group called Citizens for a Free Kuwait. One of those firms, Hill & Knowlton, arranged for an anonymous young woman known as "Nayirah" to testify that she had seen Iraqi soldiers unplug the incubators of Kuwaiti babies.

Another firm raking in $100,000-a-month from the Kuwaitis, the Rendon Group, relayed to the US media the girl's testimony. The human rights group Amnesty International gave the story a veneer of legitimacy when it falsely claimed in a poorly sourced eighty-four-page report that "300 premature babies were reported to have died after Iraqi soldiers removed them from incubators, which were then looted."

Nayirah arrived in Washington alongside Representative Tom Lantos, a neoconservative Democrat who brought her to testify before his Congressional Human Rights Caucus. At the time, his caucus was renting discounted office space from Hill & Knowlton and had taken a $50,000 payment from Citizens for a Free Kuwait. Before Nayirah appeared in Congress, she was coached by Hill & Knowlton's vice president, who directed her to deliver false testimony. Reporters repeated the heart-wrenching story of Nayirah in a virtual feedback loop until President George H.W. Bush spun the tall tale during a national address. The star witness of interventionist forces was later revealed to be the Kuwaiti ambassador's daughter—a fact that Lantos knew but knowingly concealed. In fact, the entire story she promoted was a fabrication. But by the time it was exposed, US boots were already on the ground in Kuwait.

"Of all the accusations made against [Saddam Hussein]," wrote John R. MacArthur, author of the seminal book on Gulf War propaganda, *The Second Front*, "none had more impact on American public opinion than the one about Iraqi soldiers removing 312 babies from their incubators and leaving them to die on the cold hospital floors of Kuwait City."

For Americans consuming the war through the warped lens of cable news, the enemy appeared either in the form of an imposing Arab dictator or as faceless, pixelated dots in the crosshairs of a "smart bomb." Mainstream media coverage was driven by public relations firms like Hill & Knowlton, which had market tested the most effective anti-Saddam talking points, and were supplying taped releases to news outlets that published them without acknowledging their source. Nearly unanimous public approval flowed from the coverage, turning generals like Colin

Powell and Norman Schwarzkopf into national heroes and dreary studio personalities like Wolf Blitzer into overnight celebrities. Back home, pop stars gathered in studios and football stadiums for elaborately produced tributes to the troops. The tidal wave of nationalistic propaganda ensured that close to 80 percent of the American public supported the war effort, a thirty-point surge from the days before the United States attacked. A study that year by Martin Lee and Norman Solomon found that the more Gulf War-related news Americans watched, the less they knew about the war, and the more likely they were to support Bush's intervention.

Behind the star-studded hoopla, the FBI embarked on an unprecedented campaign to gather information on Arab American business and community leaders under the guise of "interviewing" them voluntarily. In hundreds of interviews, FBI agents asked Arab Americans about their views on the war, what they thought about Israel, and if they were personally familiar with any terrorists. For the first time, the Department of Justice began fingerprinting and photographing anyone entering the country from Iraq or Kuwait.

The American Civil Liberties Union's then director, Kate Martin, described the panicked mood consuming communities of Arab Americans: "One of the questions that we don't know the answers to is, where did they get the list of people they are interviewing? Did they already have a list of people to be talked to in the event of war with Iraq? That's the first thing you need to repeat the World War II experience. That also began with interviews, and then it accelerated."

For those targeted by the government as ethnically disloyal subversives, the war was hardly the simulacrum that Baudrillard described. But for the rest of the public, the victory over a far-off army of evildoers represented a ratification of the post–Cold War "new world order" that George H.W. Bush touted. The country's reaction to the spectacle of the Gulf War sent the signal that its Vietnam syndrome—the brief national affliction of skepticism toward foreign interventions—had been salved.

Francis Fukuyama, the neoconservative scholar, excitedly

proclaimed in a 1989 essay later adapted into a book called *The End of History and the Last Man* that the world was witnessing "not just the end of the Cold War" but "the end point of mankind's ideological evolution and the universalization of Western liberal democracy as the final form of human government." According to Fukuyama, "The triumph of the West, of the Western idea, is evident first of all in the total exhaustion of viable systematic alternatives to Western liberalism." His essay perfectly channeled the sense of triumphalism that pervaded the Beltway foreign policy establishment and that led Washington to claim "victory" in the Cold War. The growing cult of American exceptionalism not only assumed an international consensus around market-style democracy, it received the Soviet collapse as carte blanche to spread the system around the world, by force if politically possible.

Following the Gulf War, Wesley Clark, a young general possessed with the realist outlook that characterized many in the military brass, entered the Pentagon and headed to the office of Paul Wolfowitz. Clark had come to congratulate him on the victory against Iraq, but instead found himself engaged in a disquieting exchange with one of the neoconservative movement's leading spokesmen. "With the end of the Cold War, we can now use our military with impunity," Wolfowitz remarked to a stunned Clark. "The Soviets won't come in to block us. And we've got five, maybe ten, years to clean up these old Soviet surrogate regimes like Iraq and Syria before the next superpower emerges to challenge us ... We could have a little more time, but no one really knows."

Al Qaeda's Trial Runs

While the neoconservatives plotted a global upheaval, the graduates of the anti-Soviet jihad had metastasized into a revolutionary force. They had benefited as much as any transnational corporation from the process of free market globalization that whittled down nation-states, hollowed out public institutions, evaporated borders, dislocated vulnerable populations and spurred economic disruption. Like the West's emerging class of disaster capitalists and neoconservatives who preached permanent war, the jihadists made instability their lifeblood, translating crises across the globe into unprecedented opportunity.

The first Gulf War progressed, on the rural outskirts of Sudan's capital, Khartoum, an alternative desert storm was gathering. Effectively excommunicated by his own government in 1991, bin Laden had migrated to Sudan, where an Islamist-inspired junta had taken power. There, he joined Zawahiri and members of Al-Jihad to train and share lessons from the battlefield. At one dusty plot outside Khartoum, bin Laden hosted veterans from the Afghan theater while showcasing to visiting journalists the ambitious infrastructure projects he had staked out around the country. Robert Fisk, the veteran Middle East correspondent, returned from the camp in 1993 with bin Laden's first interview by a Western reporter. His dispatch for the UK's *Independent*, detailing bin Laden's myriad businesses and building plans around the country, was headlined, "Anti-Soviet Warrior Puts His Army on the Road to Peace."

However, this portrayal was difficult to square with the knowledge that bin Laden had already taken credit for inspiring a December 1992 attack on US military installations in Aden, Yemen, a key link to America's archipelago of bases in the Persian Gulf. Then, a few months later, he admitted responsibility for a rocket attack on the US embassy in Yemen's capital Sana'a. Scott Stewart, then a special agent for the State Department's Diplomatic Security Service, came away from the scene of the bombings with a startling conclusion: "The CIA had trained whoever had conducted them," he wrote. "Several specific elements of those attacks matched techniques I had learned when I attended the CIA's improvised explosive device training course."

At the time, Stewart did not realize he had stumbled onto evidence of a new terror network with global reach. "It would be almost a year before I heard the term 'al Qaeda,'" he recalled, "and several months after that before I realized the term was the name of a group of former mujahideen who fought in

Afghanistan and had turned their sights against the United States."

Just months before the bombing, a crafty explosives engineer and master of disguises named Ramzi Yousef entered New York City on a tourist visa. Yousef, who had pioneered the use of improvised remote trigger devices, was the nephew of Khalid Sheikh Mohammad, the Pakistani jihadist who honed his craft at the Services Bureau under Azzam's watch. Yousef refined his skills in the Philippines, arriving as a personal envoy of bin Laden and operating through a constellation of Saudi-backed charities to help establish Abu Sayyaf, the Al Qaeda affiliate founded by fellow Afghan war veteran Janjalani.

Once in the United States, Yousef was determined to detonate a series of bombs at the base of the World Trade Center that would kill as many as 250,000 in a "Hiroshima-like event." His plan recalled Nosair's hand-scrawled fantasy of destroying "the structures of [America's] civilized pillars," and presaged the September 11 attacks.

On February 26, 1993, Yousef and two assistants personally trained by Ali Mohamed drove a 1,500-pound bomb into the basement lot below the World Trade Center's North Tower and detonated it with a remote trigger. They killed five and injured around 1,000, wreaking havoc but failing in their mission to topple one tower against the other. "We promise you that next time will be very precise and the Trade Center will be one of our targets," Yousef warned in a manifesto typed out from the first-class lounge of the Pakistan airline at New York's JFK International Airport.

In the months after the attack, Pakistani intelligence agencies homed in on the Saudi-founded charity Mercy International and an affiliated charity, the Muwafaq Foundation. Pakistani newspapers had reported that the foundation's local director, Zahid Shaikh, was Yousef's uncle, prompting the investigation. Pakistani authorities also looked into "the possibility that Yousef worked for Pakistani and U.S. security agencies during the Afghan war but later turned against them after developing links with the Islamic militants," according to the newswire, UPI. French journalist Richard Labévière alleged that Mercy International was "able to establish its headquarters in the United States, in the state of Michigan, with the assistance of ... the CIA. The [Central Intelligence] Agency provided significant logistical and financial support to this 'humanitarian' organization, enabling it to act clandestinely in the various Balkan conflicts as well as within the Muslim communities of several Russian republics."

Just months before the first World Trade Center attack, another Al Qaeda operative hovering in the immediate orbit of US intelligence agencies, Ali Mohamed, was summoned by bin Laden to train his cadres at the Khost camp—the same mujahedin training base built along the Afghan-Pakistani border during the 1980s with CIA support. During that time, Mohamed also managed a trip to stake out US embassies in Kenya and Tanzania and to train a special Kenyan cell for a future bombing plot.

On his way back from one of his trips to the Middle East, Mohamed landed at Vancouver International Airport and nearly blew his cover. He was accompanied by Essam Hafez Marzouk, an Al-Jihad member who handled military logistics for Zawahiri and was traveling on a passport that was clearly forged. Both men were immediately detained by the Royal Canadian Mounted Police (RCMP) and subjected to an extended interrogation session. This could have been the end of Mohamed's career in spying, and perhaps another chance to unravel Al Qaeda's expanding international network. But the FBI had other plans.

When it became clear that the Canadians suspected their two detainees were top-level terrorist operatives, Mohamed demanded his interrogators place a call to the FBI's San Francisco field office. There, according to journalist Peter Lance, they reached Mohamed's contact, Special Agent John Zent, who instructed the RCMP to let his asset go. And so they did. Once again, with the help of the US government, Ali the American maintained his cover.

By this time, Mohamed had revealed the existence of Al

Qaeda and his own membership in the organization to the FBI. In a remarkably candid discussion with Zent after the World Trade Center bombing, Mohamed had previously freely detailed his training of Al Qaeda recruits and outlined the organization's network of camps from Afghanistan to Sudan. According to a 1998 affidavit, he even named bin Laden to the FBI as Al Qaeda's leader. Mohamed then offered more information in a subsequent chat with Pentagon counterintelligence agents. Without explanation, the FBI and Pentagon disappeared the notes of Mohamed's interview sessions.

A month later, with the full confidence of the FBI, Mohamed led his mentor, Zawahiri, on a speaking tour of California. Posing as a field doctor from the Kuwaiti Red Crescent and traveling with a US tourist visa under an assumed name, Zawahiri surreptitiously raised hefty sums of cash for Al Qaeda, stirring crowds with heartrending stories of Afghan civilians suffering at the hands of Soviet marauders. He found his rapt audiences within mosques and Muslim charities, whose rank-and-file were almost certainly unaware Zawahiri was connected to an international terror network.

Back in Brooklyn, the Al-Kifah center was sending foreign fighters to Bosnia, where they waged jihad in support of immediate American interests and against the Russian-aligned Yugoslav army. Among those dispatched from the center to the Bosnian battlefield was Clement Rodney Hampton El, an African American convert to Islam who had been trained in firearms by Mohamed at the Calverton, Long Island, gun range. Back in 1989, the FBI had photographed Hampton-El at the range alongside Nosair and others, clad in their Services Bureau T-shirts.

As the CIA's "disposal problem" festered in the heart of the Big Apple, the FBI decided it was finally time to move against the Afghan war veterans who gathered around Al-Kifah. But first, it needed a plot it could indict them for. The result was a dubious dragnet that triggered a courtroom cover-up of the government's ongoing covert operations.

The CIA on Trial

In the weeks before the 1993 bombing, the FBI dismissed a former Egyptian army officer it had been employing as an informant. Emad Salem had become close to the Blind Sheikh, but he secured a promise to never have to wear a wire, and he would not take a polygraph test to back up some of his more questionable reports. Salem had once lied under oath in a criminal court, claiming he'd been wounded while trying to protect Egyptian president Anwar Sadat from assassination in 1981. And he lied to his FBI handlers when he told them he'd been an Egyptian intelligence officer; he was, in fact, a desk officer who never fired a shot in combat. A serial fabulist with a shady background seeking income and intrigue, Salem fit the classic profile of an FBI informant.

Following the 1993 attack on the World Trade Center, Salem leaked audio to the press of conversations with his government handlers to create the impression that the FBI was aware of the bombing plot and had sat on its hands. Chastened by Salem's leaks and embarrassed by its failures in the field, the FBI brought him back on to take down Al-Kifah's inner circle. To guarantee Salem's enthusiasm for the ambitious new undercover assignment, the bureau paid him a whopping $1 million.

Salem effortlessly wormed his way back into the Blind Sheikh's inner circle, recording tapes of himself encouraging followers of the Egyptian cleric to hit targets around the city, from the Lincoln Tunnel to the UN building to the FBI headquarters. The World Trade Center was not among those targets. Some of the zealots Salem approached seemed willing to bomb anything and everything, but they never possessed the actual materials to do so. In fact, many appeared on tape as a gang of comically bumbling idiots. Among Salem's dupes was Victor Alvarez, a twenty-nine-year-old idler who was judged by a psychiatrist as a mentally unstable cocaine addict and "borderline retarded"—an especially easy mark for an experienced hustler like Salem.

Following months of surveillance, the government arrested the Blind Sheikh and eight of his followers. They were indicted on an obscure, Civil War-era charge of conspiracy to commit sedition against the United States. The prosecution branded the legal extravaganza as the "Day of Terror" trial, suggesting that the defendants had been captured before they could cripple New York City's vital infrastructure and slaughter hundreds of thousands. It placed a carefully selected jury in isolation and under strict guard, impressing upon them the sense that they could be next if the Blind Sheikh's gang was not locked away for good.

Abdeen Jabara, a lawyer and founder of the American-Arab Anti-Discrimination Committee, was a member of the legal team that defended the Blind Sheikh. He described the prosecution's case to me as contrived and ethically dubious. "Emad Salem was as unsavory a character as you can imagine, a real slimeball," Jabara remarked to me, referring to the informant who became the FBI's star witness. "What he really did was help a group of Keystone Kops put together something that was indictable."

Jabara learned that the government had initially been reluctant to indict Abdel-Rahman. He suspected the hesitation stemmed from its fear of exposing the Sheikh's long-standing relationship with the CIA, which dated back to Afghanistan. "There was a whole issue about [Abdel-Rahman] being given a visa to come into this country and what the circumstances were around that," Jabara said. "The issue related to how much the government was involved with the jihadist enterprise when it suited their purposes in Afghanistan and whether or not they were afraid there would be exposure of that. Because there's no question that the jihadists were using the Americans and the Americans were using the jihadists. There's a symbiotic relationship."

Joining Abdel-Rahman in the dock was Nosair, whose lawyers had humiliated the government four years before. With the government back for another round, Nosair procured the services of Roger Stavis, a veteran defense attorney who had conceived a novel and potentially explosive strategy. With his client on trial for sedition, Stavis decided to focus his defense on Nosair's role as a soldier in America's most crucial proxy war.

During the trial, Stavis took every possible opportunity to highlight the services the defendants had provided to the CIA, referring to them constantly as "Team America." In effect, he was putting the CIA and its covert operations on trial. "I spent days in the courtroom saying, 'It's all about Afghanistan. Afghanistan! Afghanistan!'" Stavis recalled to me.

Stavis compiled a remarkable body of evidence, beginning with the JFK Special Warfare Center training manuals discovered in Nosair's apartment by police investigators after his arrest in 1990. The manuals led Stavis to the office of Colonel De Atkine. During his conversations with De Atkine, he learned about Ali Mohamed, the army cadet who had drilled with Fort Bragg's Green Berets, led seminars on "the Arab mind" before De Atkine's students and smuggled the special operations manuals to jihadist cadres like Nosair. Stavis soon discovered that Mohamed had participated in the Afghan war through the Services Bureau and that he had frequently visited the Blind Sheikh's crew in Jersey City. "I had him at Fort Bragg, I had him in New Jersey with the guys from the mosque, and I had him in Afghanistan," Stavis said. "I called it completing the triangle."

Stavis now saw Mohamed as the key to his client's defense. When he moved to subpoena him as a defense witness, he had no idea that Mohamed was busy training a terror cell in Nairobi, Kenya. Nor did he know that the FBI had hired Mohamed as an informant. But it had become abundantly clear to him that the government had a lot to hide.

The prosecution team was led by Patrick Fitzgerald, an assistant US attorney appointed by Reagan who was considered one of the government's strongest prosecutors. He was joined by Andrew McCarthy, an unabashed right-wing ideologue who exhibited what Jabara described somewhat charitably as "a linear and un-nuanced understanding of Islam." The federal judge presiding over the case, Michael Mukasey, shared McCarthy's hard-line views and formed a working relationship with him after the trial. (McCarthy, for instance, used his column at the right-wing *National Review* to tout Mukasey's antiterror cred—"Bravo, Attorney General McCarthy," read one blog—after the latter was appointed US attorney general under George W. Bush.)

In late 1994, the FBI located Mohamed in Nairobi and summoned him back to California for an urgent discussion. Determined to maintain his standing with the bureau, Mohamed obliged, tapping Al Qaeda financiers to cover his flight. McCarthy, as assistant US attorney, rushed over from New York to meet Mohamed in Santa Clara. According to a letter submitted by Nosair's cousin, Ibrahim El-Gabrowny, a defendant in the "Day of Terror" verdict, "McCarthy advised Ali Mohamed to ignore the subpoena's order and not to go to testify on Nosair's behalf and that Mr. McCarthy will cover up for him regarding that."

The government knew that Mohamed had been involved with the Blind Sheikh while he'd had access to sensitive material at Fort Bragg. And it also apparently knew—a year before the first mention of his name in American media and three years before his first major attack—the identity of Al Qaeda's top figure. Stavis recalled how Fitzgerald asked one of his defense witnesses seemingly out of the blue if he had ever met Osama bin Laden at the Services Bureau office in Pakistan. The witness answered that he had. As Stavis later recalled, "I said to myself, I don't know who this bin Laden guy is, but he's really in Fitzgerald's crosshairs."

Oddly, the government took no action against Mohamed after meeting him in California. Whether El-Gabrowny's startling account of McCarthy's scheming was accurate or not, Mohamed never testified. Instead, he was listed by the prosecution as an "unindicted co-conspirator," a legally empty designation. When Stavis attempted to bring Mohamed's commanding officer, De Atkine, to the stand in his place, the government blocked him too, this time on the suspect grounds that the military academician was not a competent witness.

Finally, when Stavis attempted to introduce Mohamed's army records as evidence, McCarthy vehemently objected, arguing they were irrelevant to the case. At every turn, the prosecution fought to cover up the US government's past collaboration with the defendants and its ongoing relationship with Mohamed.

Despite the stonewalling, Stavis managed to extract a

stipulation from the government. It read: "From shortly after the start of the Soviet invasion of Afghanistan in 1979 through September 1991, the United States, through one of its intelligence agencies, provided economic and military support to the Afghan Mujahideen through a third country intermediary." The document represented the first official acknowledgement by the government of one of its worst-kept secrets.

Stavis's relentless focus on Ali Mohamed also generated the first mention of the shadowy operative's name in American media. It came in the form of a February 3, 1995, article in the *Boston Globe* that detailed Mohamed's relationship with the CIA, his presence at the Al-Kifah Center in Brooklyn, and the fact that he had trained most, if not all, of the defendants in weapons use.

"His presence in the country is the result of an action initiated by Langley," a senior CIA official told the *Boston Globe*, referring to Mohamed and to the CIA headquarters in Langley, Virginia.

The "Day of Terror" trial was the largest and most complex terror conspiracy prosecution of its day. Despite its contrived foundations, or perhaps because of this, it served as a blueprint for future terror prosecutions. The trial ended with a verdict that surprised no one: a local jury found all the defendants guilty of conspiracy to commit sedition. They delivered their verdict almost immediately, with minimal deliberation. Mukasey proceeded to sentence Abdel-Rahman and Nosair to life and slapped the others with lengthy sentences that amounted to life in jail. Despite the fact that the plot was conceived by an FBI informant in a controlled environment, Mukasey claimed it "would have resulted in the murder of hundreds if not thousands of people."

Among those found guilty was Mohammed Saleh, a Palestinian refugee and gas station owner who was accused of selling the diesel fuel the would-be bombers planned to use. Despite his insistence that he had no idea whom he was selling gas to or what they intended to do with it, Saleh was sent away for thirty-five years. "I think my client was set up by the FBI," Saleh's lawyer, John Jacobs, declared after his conviction. "They bought their conviction with a million dollars they gave the informant. They bought it with the misconduct of the agents."

Mukasey concluded the trial by launching into a tirade that put his right-wing political outlook on full display: "This country has experienced militant fascism that failed and militant communism that failed," he railed at the defendants, suggesting that the militant Islam they embraced would be the next ideological movement in America's crosshairs.

Earlier that day, the Blind Sheikh had belted out a 100-minute jeremiad before Mukasey and the packed courtroom that gained legendary status among his followers. He ticked off a litany of transgressions the United States had committed against Muslims (at least, in his view), from its support for the secular Turkish revolution of Kamal Atatürk in 1923 to its full-scale backing of Israel to the Gulf War. At the crescendo of his address, Abdel-Rahman predicted that the United States would substitute the hammer and sickle with the Islamic crescent as its new national enemy. With America's Cold War against communism over, he foresaw a hot war in and against the Islamic world. Unlike Mukasey, who appeared to wish for the same scenario, the Sheikh warned that the coming clash of civilizations would end in catastrophe for America. "God will make (America) disappear from the surface of the Earth, as it has made the Soviet Union disappear," he said, invoking the triumph of the mujahedin over the Red Army. The sheikh appeared to see no irony in the fact that the United States was the guarantor of that victory, or in his own role as a CIA asset.

There were no warnings of any terror plots after the trial and no sign of danger as a result of the verdict. Yet the Clinton administration decided to place airports and government buildings under a sweeping security clampdown, amplifying and extending the atmosphere of fear the trial had inspired. "We're preparing for the worst," declared FBI deputy director Weldon Kennedy. Attempts to provide a confused public with a historical framework for understanding the new threat, meanwhile, were harshly punished. When Robert Fox, the FBI's New York City director, mentioned in a nationally televised 1993 broadcast that the CIA had trained many of the perpetrators of the World Trade Center attack, he was swiftly transferred to a faraway post. The subject was considered taboo thereafter.

While inconvenient truths about CIA collusion with international jihadists were swept away, a coterie of militarists hyped the Al Qaeda threat to weave crank conspiracy theories that advanced an ulterior, interventionist agenda, attracting interest and promotion from influential quarters. Laurie Mylroie, a disgruntled, obscure former foreign policy advisor to President Bill Clinton, had published a dubious 1997 article claiming that Yousef had actually been an Iraqi intelligence agent. Former CIA director James Woolsey and an ex-Reagan administration official named Frank Gaffney seized on Mylroie's crackpot theory as proof that Saddam Hussein posed an existential threat to the United States. Her research, which linked minuscule islands of truth with bridges of bunkum, became the linchpin for Woolsey and a close-knit band of neoconservative zealots to initiate a multiyear project to build the case for a full-scale military confrontation with Iraq.

Throw Reason to the Dogs

Meanwhile, in Afghanistan, a war of warlords had erupted after the removal of the country's socialist government. As the former proxies of the United States battled one another for control of the capital, destabilizing the country and driving it into further ruin, they gradually set the stage for another American intervention.

The legacy of the CIA's program in Afghanistan was not only the unraveling of the Soviet Union, but also the systematic destruction of a country. By 1994, half of Kabul lay in ruins thanks to the vicious power struggle that erupted between some of the CIA's main proxies after they successfully dislodged Najibullah's Soviet-backed government.

Much of the destruction was the handiwork of Hekmatyar, the ruthless warlord and now heroin kingpin who had received some $600 million in CIA support over the years. Flush with rocket-propelled grenades, munitions supplied by Washington through Pakistan, Hekmatyar's Hezb-i-Islami released thousands of violent convicts to rampage through enemy-controlled areas and rocketed entire neighborhoods. Kabul was left without electricity, water or functioning telephones—a total reversal from the fleeting period of development during communist rule.

After the ousting of Najibullah, Burhanuddin Rabbani, one of the mujahedin's founding fathers and a Reagan administration favorite, took over the government. He explicitly opposed democracy and sought to install an Islamic State that governed under strict Sharia law.

With Hekmatyar's militia at the outskirts of Kabul, Rabbani relied on his defense minister, Ahmad Shah Massoud—the guerrilla tactician regarded by the CIA during the anti-Soviet jihad as a kind of pro-Western Che Guevara—to repel the assault. For years, Massoud and Hekmatyar waged a battle of all against all that reduced half of the city to rubble. Hekmatyar's brutality knew no limits; when journalist Leslie Cockburn arrived in 1993 to interview him, he had just beheaded five political opponents—and would later kill Cockburn's translator. The post-communist regime had been reduced to the squabbling of despotic warlords with no political vision or bureaucratic competence. Its agenda was focused entirely on battling for power.

Abdullah Mirzoy served as a diplomat in Afghanistan's Foreign Ministry in Kabul under successive governments from 1979 to 1994. He described himself as an Afghan nationalist who supported any government that was committed to his country's development, irrespective of its ideology. When the former mujahedin commanders entered power, Mirzoy watched in agony as his country was systematically plunged into despotism. Today, like many of Afghanistan's brightest minds, he resides far from his homeland, in the city of Lafayette, Indiana.

"I was in Kabul and I saw with my eyes the fighting there, how they destroyed the city," Mirzoy recalled to me. "The city was not destroyed before, it was a nice city, and [Massoud and Hekmatyar] completely ruined it."

Mirzoy recalled the day a delegation of European diplomats arrived in Kabul to discuss ending the civil war with Massoud. "He didn't even have a logical explanation why he fought," he said. "I had some discussion with Massoud and his people and they didn't have any vision for the country. All they wanted was power. They had no economic plan, nothing. They even destroyed a very strong army and took all of the tanks to Pakistan, sent all the weapons away. In the end, we had nothing."

Mirzoy said he pleaded with the government to salvage what was left of the country. "If you would have seen the children in the city you would have cried. But they didn't care," he said of the warlords. "They were all fighting for somebody else, they were slaves for outside powers without thinking about their own country and what is human dignity. Sure, you have to have money but not at the expense of the other people."

In the areas that Hekmatyar's Hezb-i-Islami controlled, Mirzoy said the warlord attempted to impose a de facto Islamic state on the local population. During a bus trip from Peshawar to Kabul, the vehicle was stopped at a Hezb-i-Islami checkpoint in the Surobi district east of the Afghan capital. He said militiamen demanded as a matter of policy that each passenger leave the bus to recite the *shahada*, the Muslim profession of faith.

"I told the commander, 'I'm already Muslim, why are you trying to convert me?'" Mirzoy said. "'How is it logical to force people to say the *shahada* and convert to Islam?' I asked him. 'Why should I say if I'm Muslim or not, it's my problem, not yours.'" Thanks to Mirzoy's protests, he and his fellow travelers were allowed to go without reconverting to Islam.

"It was a really bad situation there," Mirzoy remembered. "Out of all my friends in the [Foreign] ministry, I was the only one who didn't have fear. One of them passed me in the office and asked why I even bothered showing up to work in a suit."

Hekmatyar's rampage ultimately led to the collapse of his popular base. His support of Saddam's invasion of Kuwait also lost him the patronage of Saudi Arabia and bin Laden. As his influence faded, Pakistan shifted its support to a little known group of religious zealots known as the Taliban. Educated in Saudi-funded religious schools in Pakistan's northwest frontier region, the Taliban's founders modeled themselves after the Saudi morality police. With powerful allies in the West, they were poised to suffocate Afghanistan's tradition of diverse Islamic scholarship and practice beneath a uniformly fundamentalist, ruthlessly enforced theocracy.

For many average Afghans driven into ruin under the rule of former mujahedin commanders, the Taliban were a welcome change. "Nobody had ever imagined that the situation could get this bad," reflected Mullah Mohammad Omar, a famed Afghan war veteran who helped found the Taliban. "Nobody thought it could be improved, either."

By September 1995, with Kabul under siege by the Taliban, Washington backed a secret Pakistani-Saudi plan to replace the Rabbani government with a coalition that included the Taliban. The Pakistani government of Benazir Bhutto wanted to go further and made installing the Taliban in sole power a top priority. Pakistan then helped to set up a wireless network for Taliban commanders, repairing its airports and fleet of captured Soviet jets, providing it with a communications network to advance its radio propaganda, while the Saudis directly armed the movement with Datsun pickup technicals that provided its forces with superior mobile warfare capacity.

In contrast, the Clinton administration's considerations were guided largely by a plan from petroleum company Unocal to build a pipeline through Afghanistan that would break Russia's control over oil from the Caspian Sea and marginalize Iran. As Ahmed Rashid, a leading journalistic chronicler of the Taliban's rise to power, wrote, "There was not a word of US criticism after the Taliban captured [the Afghan city of] Herat in 1995 and threw out thousands of girls from schools. In fact the USA, along with Pakistan's ISI, considered Herat's fall as a help to Unocal and tightening the noose around Iran."

That same year, a Unocal executive named Chris Taggart publicly volunteered his opinion that the Taliban would ensure the most secure environment for the pipeline. His employer had even bribed warlords like Hekmatyar with "bonuses" in exchange for guarding of the pipeline.

With the backing of Saudi Arabia and Pakistan, the Taliban bristled with firepower that left its foes stunned. Human Rights Watch documented a white-painted C-130 Hercules transport aircraft identified by journalists as Saudi Arabian on the tarmac at Kandahar airport in 1996 unloading artillery and small-arms ammunition to Taliban soldiers. With its superior firepower and political discipline, the Taliban drove the Rabbani government from Kabul in 1996 and announced the birth of the Islamic Emirate of Afghanistan that same year.

To secure the Taliban's theocratic stronghold, Saudi Arabia kicked in millions for its own morality police: the Committee for the Promotion of Virtue and Prevention of Vice. The sister organization of the Saudi service that bore the same name and meted out similarly harsh punishments to those who violated Wahhabi interpretation of Sharia law, this ministry was the most generously funded and powerful of all the Taliban's government agencies.

Draconian rule descended on Afghanistan, with women forbidden from attending school and required to wear full facial and head-to-toe covering. Music was banned and public executions in stadiums became the order of the day, with walls bulldozed atop accused homosexuals. Forced out of jobs in the civil service and education system, many women turned to begging in the street. An entire generation of Afghan children was subjected to the Taliban's indoctrination, with recycled USAID-designed textbooks as their guide.

In fact, the CIA-backed author of those textbooks, University of Nebraska's Gouttierre, was paid by Unocal to train the staff that would maintain its expected pipeline in Afghanistan. In July 1999, when Taliban commanders and a few Al Qaeda operatives were junketed to the United States by the American government and Unocal, Gouttierre was assigned as their personal guide. For several weeks, the professor escorted his guerrilla guests to local malls for all-expenses paid shopping sprees, and to Mount Rushmore, where they gazed blankly at a rendering of the vehemently anticlericist Thomas Jefferson. When he brought the illiterate Taliban men to his university department, a horrified female Afghan assistant took shelter in the basement. Back in Afghanistan, the Taliban's Saudi-trained religious police adopted the slogan "Throw reason to the dogs."

For at least the initial period of its rule, the dystopian regime the Taliban imposed on a once vibrant society was at best a secondary concern to Washington. As State Department spokesman Glyn Davies said at the time, the United States found "nothing objectionable" in the new Afghan government's intention to impose Sharia law. A top State Department diplomat justified the Faustian bargain with the Taliban to Rashid in February 1997: "The Taliban will probably develop like Saudi Arabia. There will be [the Saudi-owned oil company] Aramco, pipelines, an emir, no parliament and lots of Sharia law. We can live with that."

In a remarkable interview five years after 9/11, Iranian American filmmaker Samira Goetschel asked Brzezinski, the original author of the strategy that aimed to induce a Soviet invasion of Afghanistan by covertly supplying the mujahedin, if he had any regrets about the role the United States had played in Afghanistan. He was entirely unrepentant.

"Can you imagine what the world would be like today if there was still a Soviet Union?" Zbigniew Brzezinski asked indignantly. "So yes, compared to the Soviet Union, and to its collapse, the Taliban were unimportant."

A Very Hard War

Years of US-backed war had not only deluged Afghanistan with weapons and left its infrastructure in ruins; the country was also being flooded all over again with foreign fighters magnetized by the rise of a Saudi-backed Islamic Emirate. Among them was bin Laden, who had been driven from his haven in Sudan by American pressure and was desperate for new sanctuary. Though the Taliban viewed him with deep suspicion, it was in desperate need of his patronage. A marriage of convenience was born that breathed new life into bin Laden's movement just as Al Qaeda had reached its nadir. "I call on Muslims to support this nation, because God willing, this nation will raise the banner of Islam," bin Laden said of Taliban-controlled Afghanistan, linking his own fate to that of the government.

In 1996, soon after bin Laden's arrival to Afghanistan, British reporter Gwynne Roberts, working at the time on a documentary about Saudi opposition movements, secured an interview with the Al Qaeda leader. Before meeting bin Laden in Jalalabad, Roberts stopped in on one of his associates, a Saudi professor teaching in the crumbled, hollowed out classrooms of Kabul University, which was now off-limits to female students. He was one of many Saudi dissidents who had found sanctuary within the realm of the Taliban and who was determined to ultimately seize power in the country of his birth. What would happen if the United States insisted on maintaining its military presence inside Saudi Arabia? Roberts asked the professor.

"An international war that will affect everyone," he replied matter-of-factly. "A very hard war between Muslims and Westerners in ten years."

Back in Egypt, Zawahiri's Al-Jihad was on a rampage. Activists connected to the group, many of them Afghan war veterans, had killed over a thousand people throughout the early and mid-1990s. But the worst was yet to come. The Egyptian government had struck a deal in July 1997 that saw thousands of Islamist activists formally renounce violence in exchange for freedom from prison. Abdel-Rahman, the Blind Sheikh, signed off on the initiative from his own cell. Having just joined bin Laden in Afghanistan, Zawahiri raged against the deal, blasting it as a catastrophic sellout. He immediately put into motion a plot to shatter Egypt's tourism sector, the beating heart of the country's economy.

On November 17, 1997, six jihadist cadres methodically butchered fifty-eight tourists and six Egyptian locals at Luxor. Just a month prior, the same resort on the banks of the Nile had been the site of a performance of Verdi's *Aida* attended by

President Mubarak and Sean Connery. The killers' methods—aiming at victims' legs before executing them at close range, and disemboweling their bodies with knives—had been seen before on the Afghan battlefield, and as Cooley put it, "had been so rare as to be unknown until then in Egypt." The sheer savagery of the attack turned the Egyptian public wholly against the jihadists, giving the government all the space it needed to clamp down.

Zawahiri's dream of an Islamic State in Egypt had been extinguished, and with it, the war against the "near enemy" seemed over. From Kandahar, he and bin Laden festered in a squalid encampment with little food or provisions for their bedraggled underlings. Brought to their lowest point by their own hubris, they hashed out an ambitious plan to strike America and its assets abroad. Their former frenemy was now the "far enemy."

In Washington, the threat from Al Qaeda was little understood. "We probably should have been more concerned about it at the time than we were, but in the first term we did not see Osama bin Laden and Al Qaeda as a major factor, or one that we were concerned with," then defense secretary William Cohen reflected years later.

In March 1998, Muammar Gaddafi's Libya became the first country to issue an international Interpol arrest warrant for bin Laden. The warrant was studiously ignored by American and British intelligence, which had apparently judged toppling Gaddafi a greater priority than disrupting Al Qaeda's growing global network, according to French journalist Guillaume Dasquié and Jean-Charles Brisard, an advisor to French president Jacques Chirac. At the time, the British MI6 was grooming a group of veterans of the anti-Soviet jihad in Afghanistan who had formed into the Libyan Islamic Fighting Group (LIFG), an Al Qaeda ally dedicated to assassinating Gaddafi and replacing his rule with an Islamist theocracy.

Five months after Gaddafi's Interpol warrant was ignored, on August 7, 1998, Al Qaeda struck the US embassies in Kenya and Tanzania, killing 224 people. The attack was carried out under bin Laden's personal orders as retaliation for the American military intervention in Somalia.

The most deadly Al Qaeda attack to date had been a pet project of Ali Mohamed. It was Mohamed who scouted the US embassy in Nairobi in 1993—right after being released from Canadian police custody on the word of his FBI handler. ("I took pictures, drew diagrams and wrote a report," he later admitted, describing how he passed off his files to bin Laden in Sudan.) And it was Mohamed who personally trained the local cell, which was led by a former Al-Kifah staffer named Wadih el-Hage. Mohamed's involvement with the Al Qaeda unit in Kenya should not have been a secret to the national security officials working on a budget of around $40 billion a year. By the spring of 1996, they knew of the existence of the East African cell and had received Foreign Intelligence Surveillance Act warrants to monitor Mohamed and el-Hage's calls, even as they paid Mohamed's salary as an informant. But the presence of an admitted terror operative in eastern Africa failed to trigger any action by the FBI.

Ten months before the bombings, US attorney Patrick Fitzgerald had a rare chance to meet with Mohamed in person. Having gained acclaim prosecuting the "Day of Terror" trial, during which his ultra-conservative assistant counsel, Andrew McCarthy, apparently prevented Mohamed from taking the witness stand, Fitzgerald was appointed to direct I-49, the government's newly formed "bin Laden Unit." And now, inside a restaurant in Sacramento one block from the California statehouse, he sat face-to-face with Al Qaeda's top spy in America.

Fitzgerald listened to the seasoned operative freely declare that he did not require any fatwa to attack the United States, that he "loved" bin Laden, and that he had personally trained bin Laden's bodyguards. "This is the most dangerous man I have ever met. We cannot let this man out on the street," Fitzgerald concluded. And yet, Mohamed was allowed to do just that—he walked out of the restaurant a free man.

Why was Mohamed allowed to walk away? Did Fitzgerald believe he did not have enough to indict him? Was the FBI concerned with losing its eyes and ears on Al Qaeda? Or did the fear of public exposure and embarrassment over the FBI and CIA's long-standing relationship with Mohamed—as well as many of the founding fathers of Al Qaeda—trump any concern about Mohamed's danger to the public? For raising these questions in his book-length investigation into the case of Ali Mohamed, *Triple Cross* journalist Peter Lance was faced with a libel lawsuit by Fitzgerald. (Fitzgerald was ultimately forced to drop his claim.)

It would not be until September 10, 1998, that the government began to take measures against Mohamed—and it was only because of Mohamed's own arrogance that the United States took the opportunity to scrutinize him. Following the arrest of el-Hage and the subsequent indictment of the key figures behind the East African embassy bombings, Mohamed scrapped his plans to join bin Laden in Afghanistan and accepted a subpoena to testify before a secret grand jury in New York.

Having outsmarted the feds for years, Mohamed probably thought he could remain one step ahead if he faced them down one more time. But Fitzgerald had had enough. Concluding that Mohamed had lied to the grand jury, he ordered his arrest. When FBI agents arrived at Mohamed's hotel room to cuff him, they allowed him a visit to the bathroom. There, he tore pages from his notebook containing Zawahiri's address and satellite phone number, and then flushed them down the toilet.

In federal custody, Mohamed's name was registered as "John Doe." A date was set for sentencing, but the hearing never took place. He gave up his right to appeal and the defense raised no objections. Mohamed was sent to a secret location that was most likely the witness protection wing of a federal prison. His file remained sealed and Fitzgerald kept him off the witness stand in the embassy bombing trial, once again averting embarrassment to the CIA, the Department of Defense and the FBI.

It is unclear if Mohamed was ever sentenced, or if he struck a secret deal with the government. The thick shroud of secrecy draped over his very existence meant that Fitzgerald denied the American public a chance to learn about their government's colossal failures in judgment—and its sordid history of collusion with jihadist elements. As former FBI special agent Joseph F. O'Brien told Lance, if Mohamed had been allowed to testify in open court, he "would have been opened up by defense lawyers and told the whole sad tale of how he'd used the Bureau and the CIA and the DIA for years. The Bureau couldn't risk that kind of embarrassment."

On November 4, 1999, Mary Jo White, the US attorney who oversaw Ali Mohamed's peculiar prosecution, was asked about his case at a press conference about his activities. All she could do was reply, "I've read what you read and I can't comment." The cover-up to protect the reputation of Ali the American's employers in the US government had turned into a disappearing act.

A Catastrophic and Catalyzing Event

Two weeks after the embassy bombings, Clinton authorized Operation Infinite Reach. It was the most aggressive US response to a terrorist attack since the country tried and failed to assassinate Libyan president Muammar Gaddafi in 1986 for his supposed role in downing Pan Am flight 103. As with that botched missile strike, which wound up burnishing Gaddafi's image as an anti-imperialist lion, Infinite Reach revived the beleaguered bin Laden's global status.

From both a military and political standpoint, the American operation was a disaster. Cruise missiles fired from a navy warship in the Persian Gulf had aimed to destroy an Al Qaeda nerve gas factory in Sudan that, according to Clinton, was co-owned by bin Laden. Instead the strikes, launched on the basis of bunk intelligence, decimated a pharmaceutical plant that supplied 50 percent of the medicine to one of the poorest countries in the world. The bombing wiped out Sudan's supply of TB vaccinations and eliminated its supply of crucial veterinary drugs that prevented the transfer of parasites from animals to small children.

Furthermore, several cruise missiles failed to explode; Al Qaeda seized them and sold them on the black market for $10 million each, allegedly to China. A separate series of cruise missile strikes hit an Al Qaeda camp in Khost—the old network of bases and tunnels that bin Laden had built for the CIA—but he and Zawahiri were hundreds of miles away thanks to a likely tip-off from the Pakistani ISI. "It was like a script [bin Laden] has written for the Americans and the Americans just went along," Khaled Batarfi, a childhood friend of bin Laden's, remarked to an interviewer. "He wanted to provoke the Americans into such actions against Muslim countries."

"Bin Laden's interest was not in killing a few Americans in the embassies. He intended to have a response from Clinton—this cowboy response," said Sa'ad Al-Fagih, a Saudi dissident who had known bin Laden since the days of the anti-Soviet jihad. Citing his contacts in Saudi intelligence, Al-Fagih alleged that no less than 11,000 people enlisted to participate in Al Qaeda–related organizations between 1998 and 2001. He explained, "It's all because of the successful PR service from the Americans."

The response authorized by Clinton might have been badly off the mark, but it did not produce the kind of cataclysmic effect that Al Qaeda could exploit to the fullest extent. As Al-Fagih explained, "What bin Laden wants is a full chaos in the region. And with the chaos in the region, those local regimes will collapse very easily and the culture of jihad will supersede. It's not just a matter of a military coup or one or two operations, it's going to be a new culture of jihad, a new thinking in the mind of the people is going to be default."

It would not be long before bin Laden was presented with the situation he sought. Frustrated by Clinton's insufficient belligerence, a coterie of endowed university chairs and neoconservative zealots nested in think tanks was hatching plans for military interventions that would topple governments across the Middle East. In the global war bin Laden envisioned, these foreign policy fanatics would make the perfect partners.

Benjamin Netanyahu's 1996 election victory as Israel's prime minister electrified a group of foreign policy zealots stationed in think tanks on America's coasts. A graduate of MIT from suburban Philadelphia who later worked at Boston Consulting alongside Mitt Romney, Netanyahu was at least as American as he was Israeli. During the Gulf War, Netanyahu became a familiar face on American cable news, single-handedly turning CNN into what one PLO official called "a propagandist for the Israelis." For his extended tirades branding the PLO as a front organization for Saddam Hussein, the *Washington Times* recommended Netanyahu for an Emmy Award, the honor bestowed on American daytime TV actors. The new prime minister was intimately connected to ideological movement that extended from Jerusalem to a network of neoconservative think tanks and policy journals in Washington, all dedicated to advancing the imperatives of Israel's right-wing Likud Party.

At the heart of this network was Richard Perle, a neocon hard-liner who emerged during the 1970s out of the office of Democratic Senator Henry "Scoop" Jackson, a cold warrior who favored massive defense buildups. While on Jackson's staff, Perle was overheard on an FBI wiretap furnishing classified information that he had received from a National Security Council staffer to an Israeli embassy official. When Perle entered the Reagan administration's Department of Defense, he hired the son of a major pro-Israel donor and Likud Party activist named Douglas Feith. In 1983, Feith was fired from a job at the National Security Council and stripped of his security clearance when he became the target of an FBI investigation for forking over classified material to the Israeli embassy. Perle continued to promote his understudy, however, shielding him from scrutiny for allegations of double-dealing.

Following Netanyahu's ascension to the prime minister's office in 1996—a victory made possible by the assassination of Prime Minister Yitzhak Rabin, whose widow openly blamed Netanyahu for inciting his murder—the prime minister tapped Feith and his allies to help him devise a strategic doctrine for engaging and disrupting the region. Gathered under the auspices of the Institute for Advanced Strategy and Political Studies, an Israel-based think tank with offices in Washington, Feith joined Perle and a collection of neocon and Likudnik ideologues, from

David and Meyrav Wurmser to former Mossad commander Yigal Carmon, to draft a sweeping blueprint for remaking the Middle East in Netanyahu's vision.

They called their vision for the incoming Israeli administration, "A Clean Break: A New Strategy for Securing the Realm." The document recycled many of the revisionist Zionist ideas introduced in Ze'ev Jabotinsky's high colonial-era "Iron Wall" manifesto, which urged the application of pure force against the native Palestinian population to secure the Jewish state's deterrent capacity, and reapplied them to the post–Cold War Middle Eastern geopolitical chessboard. Essentially, the neocons' paper amounted to a call to violently replace the leadership of any regional state that challenged Israel's expansionist agenda—a feat that could only be accomplished with direct American military intervention.

The "Clean Break" authors envisioned the first target as Saddam Hussein's Iraq, which had supported the PLO and fired Scud missiles at Israel during the first Gulf War. As Feith and his co-authors wrote, "removing Saddam Hussein from power in Iraq [was] an important Israeli strategic objective in its own right." But Iraq would only be a stepping-stone to a greater war that would extend to Syria, a country under the control of Hafez al-Assad that based its strategy of deterrence on close alliances with Iran, Russia and Hezbollah, the Lebanese Shia militia that was well on its way toward dislodging the occupying Israeli military from southern Lebanon.

Through a joint effort by US-allied countries like Jordan, Turkey and a new, US-friendly Iraqi regime, the neoconservatives hoped to "squeeze and detach Syria from the Saudi Peninsula. For Syria … this could be the prelude to a redrawing of the map of the Middle East which would threaten Syria's territorial integrity." They proposed weaponizing the heavily religious, rural Sunni population as a proxy force in Syria's eastern hinterlands: "Israel has an interest supporting diplomatically, militarily and operationally Turkey's and Jordan's actions against Syria, such as securing tribal alliances with Arab tribes that cross into Syrian territory and are hostile to the Syrian ruling elite," the neocons argued, alluding to the Salafi-centric rural population that would later rally behind Al Qaeda in Mesopotamia and the Islamic state.

"A Clean Break" presented a microcosm of the vision outlined on a global scale in an essay published the same year, 1996, by two of the neoconservative movement's principal ideologues, Robert Kagan and William Kristol. Published in the journal of the Council on Foreign Relations, the essay's title, "Toward a Neo-Reaganite Foreign Policy," was clearly intended to soften the nakedly militaristic thrust of its contents. Kagan and Kristol called for exploiting the void left by the Soviet Union's collapse to intervene wherever and whenever the United States felt it could exert "preponderant influence and authority over all others in its domain." The goal, they wrote, was "benevolent global hegemony."

In the post–Cold War status quo, where under Pax Americana the United States had no viable competitors to fear, Kagan and Kristol pointed to a pacific domestic atmosphere and latent antiwar sentiment as the key obstacle to a renewed drive for imperial expansion. "In a world in which peace and American security depend on American power and the will to use it," they wrote, "the main threat the United States faces now and in the future is its own weakness."

A year after the publication of "A Clean Break," Kagan and Kristol organized a virtual who's who of neoconservatives into an informal working group to push for the "benevolent global hegemony" they sought. Centered in the offices of the American Enterprise Institute, the nest of Washington's neoconservative second generation, this group called itself the Project for the New American Century, or PNAC.

Signatories of PNAC's first letter included civilian national security figures like Feith, Perle, Paul Wolfowitz, Donald Rumsfeld and Christian right moralists like Gary Bauer, William Bennett and the blue-blooded Republican political upstart Jeb Bush. The neocons found a few liberal allies as well, like *New Republic* editor Leon Wieseltier, an ardent Zionist and reflexive military interventionist who tended to favor progressive social policies at home. PNAC was determined to maintain a patina of bipartisanship, but its true base lay in the Republican Party. In the Clinton era, this meant that its membership would be relegated to firing off open letters, delivering congressional testimony and publishing op-eds.

While the neocons cooled their heels in Beltway think tanks, they conjured up dreams of a national emergency that would electrify their imperial agenda. One PNAC manifesto read, "Further, the process of transformation, even if it brings revolutionary change, is likely to be a long one, absent some catastrophic and catalyzing event—like a new Pearl Harbor."

In Iraq, to the great dismay of the regime change advocates in neoconservative circles, the Clinton administration was then invested in a strategy its foreign policy hands described as "dual containment," adapting the prevailing American approach to the Soviet Union from the days of the Cold War. The concept was formally introduced in 1993 by Martin Indyk, a former staffer for the pro-Israel lobbying group, American Israel Public Affairs Committee (AIPAC), who was appointed to Clinton's National Security Council. Rather than removing Iraq's government in one fell swoop, dual containment aimed to erode the country's stability through slowly imposing unilateral "no fly zones" that enabled the United States to bomb Iraq once a week at a cost of over a billion dollars. It was complemented by crushing sanctions that targeted Iraq's infrastructure and civilian population. While the sanctions' death toll remains hotly disputed, one 1995 study by the medical journal *Lancet* and sponsored by the United Nations Food and Agricultural Organization found that 576,000 children under the age of five had died. Grilled by Leslie Stahl of *60 Minutes*, then secretary of state Madeleine Albright infamously declared that the containment policy was "worth it"—even if it triggered half a million infant deaths.

Though Clinton resisted neoconservative calls for a full-scale invasion, he gave PNAC a boost in 1998 when he signed the Iraq Liberation Act, a congressional resolution that budgeted $97 million to assist anti-Saddam proxy groups and that called for complete regime change. The money went straight to Ahmad Chalabi, a shady Iraqi exile who had been sentenced to twenty-two years in jail for a banking scandal in Jordan before resurfacing in London as the leader of the Iraqi National Congress. At the time, the four-star general who oversaw US military operations in the Persian Gulf, Anthony Zinni, privately dismissed the scheme as "harebrained."

The congressional sponsors of the Iraq Liberation Act drew explicit inspiration from the Reagan-era strategy of undermining sovereign states from within by arming and training opposition groups as proxy militias. "At the height of the Cold War, we supported freedom fighters in Asia, Africa and Latin America willing to fight and die for a democratic future. We can and should do the same now in Iraq," said Republican senator Trent Lott in his argument for the bill's passage. Senator Jesse Helms, the old anticommunist stalwart, declared that the Iraq Liberation Act "harkens back to the successes of the Reagan doctrine, enlisting the very people who are suffering most under Saddam's yoke to fight the battle against him." Thus, the Cold War's covert anti-Soviet operations were adapted by the world's lone superpower to violently destabilize the states that remained opposed to Western influence. In the case of Ba'athist-run Iraq, then Democratic senator Bob Kerrey insisted America should accept nothing less than the messianic goal of "replacing it with a transition to democracy."

Though the rising aggression against Iraq was a bipartisan effort in Washington, it met with stiff resistance from a burgeoning grassroots antiwar movement. In February 1998, when Clinton's secretary of state, Madeleine Albright, National Security's Sandy Berger and Defense Secretary William Cohen convened a special CNN town hall to defend their plan to launch a punishing military strike on Iraq, they faced withering criticism from among the audience of 6,000.

Challenged by a caller over the hypocrisy of American support for ruthless dictators in allied countries while Washington sanctioned Iraq, Albright responded, "No one has done what Saddam Hussein has done, or is thinking of doing. He is producing weapons of mass destruction, and he is qualitatively and quantitatively different from other dictators." When an audience member grilled Berger about the casualties US bombing had already exacted on Iraqi civilians, the national security advisor claimed without evidence, "you're dealing with someone who uses people as human shields."

The botched attempt at pro-war public relations helped expose the flabby justifications for bombing a country whose danger to the United States was questionable at best. What's more, it boldly displayed the American public's healthy skepticism of military interventionism. A caller from Oklahoma wondered if the United States was entering a state of permanent war. He pleaded, "How many times are we going to send our children and our children's children to fight Saddam Hussein?"

The exponents of empire were unable to answer inconvenient questions like these. They could only draw up plans and wait for some "catastrophic and catalyzing event."

3

Waves Flanked by Arrogance

Two hours' drive from Kandahar, in the southern Afghan desert city where the Taliban were born and where bin Laden maintained his operational base, a February 2001 wedding ceremony became the stage for bin Laden's first public appearance in several years. Seated in the shade of palm trees was the Al Qaeda leader's seventeen-year-old son, Mohammed, his father's personal protector and likely successor. To his left was Mohammed Atef, an Egyptian comrade of Zawahiri who acted as the chief military strategist of Al Qaeda—the brains behind its operations. To Mohammed's right sat his father, who smiled proudly as his son prepared to marry Atef's fourteen-year-old daughter.

Ahmad Zaidan, a correspondent for the Qatari outlet Al Jazeera, was ferried to the wedding with a camera crew in an effort to provide bin Laden with the publicity he had been denied by the Taliban. Zaidan witnessed bin Laden rise before the guests to deliver verses of jihadist poetry: "She sails into the waves flanked by arrogance, haughtiness and false power. To her doom she moves slowly," the wealthy sheikh exclaimed. "Your brothers in the East readied themselves. And the war camels prepared to move."

In his verse, bin Laden appeared to be alluding to the October 2000 attack by two Al Qaeda assets on the USS Cole, a naval destroyer stationed in Yemen's Aden harbor—another daring strike at the strategic point of access for the US military to its bases across the Gulf states. The bombs, detonated from a fiberglass boat piloted by two suicide attackers, had torn a forty-foot hole in the hull of the Cole and caused it to nearly capsize. Seventeen sailors were killed and thirty-eight more wounded, most of them blown apart while taking lunch. "The destroyer represented the West," bin Laden said. "The small boat represented Muhammad."

Later, Atef took Zaidan aside to detail Al Qaeda's plan to drag the West into an endless war. "He was explaining to me what will happen in the coming five years," Zaidan recalled, "and he said, 'Look, there are two or three places in the world which are the most suitable places to fight America: Afghanistan, Iraq and Somalia. We are expecting the United States to invade Afghanistan and we are preparing for that. We want the United States to invade Afghanistan."

The strategy to trigger a series of American interventions and bleed an overstretched empire represented an especially ironic adaptation of Brzezinski's "Afghan trap." Bin Laden and his lieutenants reasoned that it would only require a single violent cataclysm to draw the Americans in. His goal was to enact the very thing that the neocon authors of the PNAC's first letter envisioned: "some catastrophic and catalyzing event."

Early in 2000, an operation was set into motion to fulfill the American trap. An Al Qaeda operative named Khalid al-Mihdhar was deployed into the faceless suburbs of Southern California alongside his friend, Nawaf al-Hazmi. Both men were sons of Saudi Arabia, products of its Wahhabi-influenced school system, and had followed the jihadi trail through Bosnia and Chechnya during the 1990s. Mihdhar later trained in Afghanistan, likely under the watch of Ali Mohamed. The two landed at Los Angeles

International Airport on January 15, 2000, on a flight from Kuala Lumpur, Malaysia. Together, they represented part of the team that would execute what Al Qaeda informally referred to as "the planes operation."

While the two were in Malaysia, CIA operatives broke into Mihdhar's hotel room there and photographed his passport. Mihdhar was known to Saudi intelligence as a jihadist and was photographed by Malaysian secret police at a planning meeting for the "planes operation." Also in attendance at the meeting was Khalid Sheikh Mohammed, widely considered the "mastermind" behind the plot. The photos were immediately shared with the CIA. Two months later, the agency learned that Mihdhar, now a known Al Qaeda member, had traveled to Los Angeles on a multiple-entry visa, and that he was seated next to Hazmi on the flight. Curiously, the CIA refused to supply the information to the FBI.

Why did the agency sit on its hands? Lawrence Wright, one of the leading chroniclers of Al Qaeda's rise, speculated that, "Mihdhar and Hazmi could have seemed like attractive recruitment possibilities—the CIA was desperate for a source inside Al Qaeda, having failed to penetrate the inner circle or even to place someone in the training camps, even though they were largely open to anyone who showed up."

Neither Mihdhar nor Hazmi spoke English or were familiar with American culture. When they arrived in Los Angeles, they were met at the airport by Omar Bayoumi, a Saudi civil aviation authority official who did no known work for the bureau—he was a ghost employee. Bayoumi had held a mysterious closed-door meeting at the Saudi consulate just moments before meeting the two men. Though he had never met Mihdhar or Hazmi before, he was clearly acting as their advance man. Upon arrival, the two worshipped at the King Fahad Mosque in Los Angeles, a Saudi-funded institution. There, they met Fahad Al-Thumairy, an accredited Saudi consular official who served as the mosque's imam. According to an FBI investigation carried out years later, they were "immediately assigned an individual to take care of al-Hazmi and al-Mihdhar during their time in the Los Angeles area." That individual was almost certainly Bayoumi.

In February, Bayoumi took Mihdhar and Hazmi to San Diego, where they co-signed an apartment lease under his name. Neither man had any credit. Bayoumi was able to muster up large amounts of cash to cover his guests' expenses, far more than any ordinary government worker should have had access to. As soon as he took Mihdhar and Hazmi in his charge, his salary shot up from $500 a month to $3,500. "One of the FBI's best sources in San Diego informed the bureau that he thought that al-Bayoumi must be an intelligence officer for Saudi Arabia or another foreign power," a heavily redacted congressional investigative committee report later concluded. Bayoumi and Thumairy's phones registered twenty-one calls between them spanning from Mihdhar and Hazmi's arrival to May 2000. Bayoumi logged nearly 100 calls to Saudi officials in that period and traveled frequently to Saudi consular offices in Los Angeles and Washington during that time.

At a welcoming party Bayoumi organized for Mihdhar and Hazmi, he introduced them to Anwar al-Awlaki, one of the more notable Muslim religious figures in San Diego. On the day that Bayoumi helped Mihdhar and Hazmi find a local apartment, he logged four calls to al-Awlaki. Al-Awlaki was a charismatic imam from Yemen whose flawless English and engaging style made him a star among many younger Muslims raised in the West. The cleric betrayed little sign of extremism, though he would later turn up in Yemen as top propagandist of Al Qaeda in the Arabian Peninsula. At the time, Mihdhar and Hazmi each considered him a kind of spiritual advisor, worshipping at his Al-Ribat Al-Islami mosque in La Mesa and meeting in private with him.

It may never be known if al-Awlaki was aware that the two represented the advance team for a handful of operatives preparing a deadly operation. But neighbors of Mihdhar and Hazmi suspected some sort of criminal plot was underway: "There was always a series of cars driving up to the house late at night," said one neighbor. "Sometimes they were nice cars. Sometimes they had darkened windows. They'd stay about 10 minutes."

On March 5, 2000, a cable arrived to the CIA headquarters in Langley, Virginia, alerting the agency to Hazmi's presence in the United States. It read, "Action Required: None."

The FBI had eyes and ears on Mihdhar and Hazmi almost as soon as they arrived in California. Indeed, a bureau informant had extensive contacts with the two men, reporting back to his handler about them, but the bureau did nothing. The FBI's inaction might have been understandable considering the CIA had inexplicably withheld evidence of Mihdhar and Hazmi's presence at what the agency knew to be a gathering of top Al Qaeda operatives in Kuala Lumpur. It was not until August 2001 that Mihdhar was placed on a terror watch list. By then, the "day of the planes" plot was in its final stages.

The Summer of the Shark

George W. Bush entered the White House after months of friendly coverage from the Washington press corps. With only a few exceptions, the pundits portrayed Bush as the consummate centrist, a uniter who could calm a badly divided nation. ABC's Dean Reynolds called him a "different kind of Republican [who could] show middle of the road voters—both white and black that he is more moderate than they would have suspected." The *New York Times*' Jim Yardley praised Bush's "bipartisan, above-the fray image," while CNN trumpeted Bush's supposed steps toward "healing a divided nation."

On Bush's selection as vice president, Representative Bill Paxon assured a CNN audience that "Dick Cheney is the ultimate man of moderation." As for Condoleezza Rice, Bush's national security advisor, CNN's Tony Clark insisted she "doesn't not believe the US military should be what is described as a 911 global police force."

The neoconservatives that honeycombed the Bush administration had flown almost entirely under the media's radar. A close look at the civilian wing of the Pentagon or the State Department's Middle East handlers revealed a virtual government jobs program for the signers of PNAC. They included Elliott Abrams, the State Department's undersecretary of Middle East affairs; Paul Wolfowitz, the deputy secretary of defense; Douglas Feith, a "Clean Break" author hired as undersecretary of defense for policy; his mentor, Richard Perle, now chairman of the Pentagon's Defense Policy Board; and David Wurmser, an advisor to Cheney on Middle East policy. Having burrowed deep within the administration's bureaucracy without any real scrutiny, these figures maintained their laser-like focus on Iraq, bringing in Laurie Mylroie, the crank conspiracist who blamed Saddam for the Oklahoma City Federal Building bombing, as a terror consultant in the Pentagon.

On June 6, 2001, Wolfowitz appeared before an auditorium full of cadets to deliver the commencement address at the West Point Academy in New York state. His remarks centered on the sixtieth anniversary of Pearl Harbor and its relevance at the time. Years later, his words are chilling. "Interestingly," Wolfowitz said, "that surprise attack was preceded by an astonishing number of unheeded warnings and missed signals ... Surprise happens so often that it's surprising that we're surprised by it. Very few of these surprises are the product of simple blindness or simple stupidity. Almost always, there have been warnings and signals that have been missed, sometimes because there were just too many warnings to pick the right one out."

The following month, a senior executive intelligence brief was delivered to the White House entitled "Bin Laden Threats Are Real." Wolfowitz dismissed the report out of hand, insisting to the deputy national security advisor, Stephen Hadley, that bin Laden was simply trying to study Washington's reactions by leveling empty threats.

The US media spent the summer of 2001 swarming around the office of Representative Gary Condit, a previously unknown Democratic backbencher who was wrongly suspected of murdering Chandra Levy, his former intern and mistress who had disappeared while jogging in Washington, DC's Rock Creek Park. In between fever-pitched dispatches about Condit's whereabouts, the networks declared the weeks after July 4, 2001, "the summer of the shark," blitzing viewers with reports of an unprecedented wave of Jaws-level carnage.

The number of shark attacks was actually down from the year before, but without any other source of sensational storylines, American media ginned up a Sharknado epidemic that was leaving half-chewed appendages bobbing in bloody seas. George Burgess, director of shark research at the Florida Museum of Natural History, said he fielded thirty to fifty calls from reporters every day that summer. At the time, according to CIA director George Tenet, "the system was blinking red" with warnings about an imminent, massive terror attack on American soil.

Bush spent the summer of 2001 on the longest recorded vacation in presidential history. Tenet and National Security Council chief Condoleezza Rice were not present at his luxury ranch in Crawford, Texas, when he reviewed presidential daily briefings (PDBs) on August 6. That afternoon, Bush was handed one PDB with a headline that should have sent him rushing back to Washington. It read, "Bin Laden Determined to Strike Inside the US." The document was a page and a half—an exceptional length that highlighted its importance. Its source was described as an "Egyptian Islamic Jihad [EIJ] operative ... a senior EIJ member [who] lived in California in the mid-1990s." According to the brief, he warned that "a Bin Laden cell in New York was recruiting Muslim American youth for attacks."

There was no doubt that that source was Ali Mohamed, who had by then been disappeared into federal custody. The "bin Laden cell" was a clear reference to the remnants of the Al-Kifah Center, which had served as one of the CIA's major pipelines for sending jihadist fighters to Afghanistan in the 1980s, and then Bosnia and Chechnya throughout the '90s. Deep within the federal prison system, where Mohamed had been registered as "John Doe," the former triple spy appeared to be dishing everything he knew about Al Qaeda's infrastructure and agenda.

While Bush reviewed the briefing document, several Al Qaeda operatives who had recently entered the country for the "Day of the Planes" plot maintained mailboxes at the Jersey City–based Sphinx Trading Company. This was the same mailbox center where Mohamed's trainees and the Blind Sheikh exchanged dead drop messages. The owner of Sphinx, Waleed al-Noor, was well known to the FBI; he had been named as an unindicted co-conspirator in the trial of the Blind Sheikh in 1995. But the bureau's New York office was not paying attention to Sphinx or to al-Noor's longtime business partner, Mohamed el-Atriss, who was selling fake IDs to several of the plotters, including Mihdhar. (During el-Atriss's 2003 trial, where he was sentenced to six months' probation, Passaic County detectives accused then US Attorney Chris Christie, later the Republican governor of New Jersey and failed Republican presidential candidate, of bullying them into ending an investigation into el-Atriss's links to the 9/11 hijackers.)

Bush did not appear to take the PDB seriously. He exuded an "expansive mood," according to two *Washington Post* reporters, as he took a round of golf the day after reviewing the document. One week later, at the Pentagon's annual convention on counterterrorism, CIA counterterrorism chief Cofer Black concluded his briefing by exclaiming, "we are going to be struck soon, many Americans are going to die, and it could be in the US."

Despite the doomsday predictions, Bush did not meet with his cabinet heads to discuss terrorism until September 4, his first meeting after returning from vacation. The "Day of Planes" plot would be executed a week later.

Pam Anderson's Jet

The catastrophic and catalyzing events of September 11, 2001, unfolded live on one of New York City's top morning talk shows. At 9:01, Howard Stern delivered a brief update about the first plane hitting the World Trade Center, gashing open the face of the tower and sending plumes of smoke into the sky. "I don't even know how you begin to fight that fire," he commented. Then, without missing a beat, the legendary shock jock returned to an inane yarn about his date with former Baywatch star Pamela Anderson at a seedy Midtown bar called Scores.

"I felt her butt," Stern bragged to his randy co-hosts. A highly involved discussion ensued about his failure to "bang Pam Anderson." "I wasn't gonna sit there and work it all night," Stern explained moments before the second plane hit. Then, as soon as Tower 2 caught fire, he quipped, "I'm telling you, it was Pam Anderson's jet."

Minutes later, Stern's producers began piping in audio from the local CBS affiliate, setting a traumatizing aural atmosphere that recalled Orson Welles' "War of the Worlds." Stern apparently realized the flames were the product of a terror attack, probably by Muslim extremists. Confronted with a national calamity, he and his shrieking sidekick Robin Quivers immediately shifted gears.

"We've gotta go bomb everything over there," Quivers insisted.

"We've gotta bomb the hell out of them!" Stern added. "You know who it is. I can't say but I know who it is. This is more upsetting than me not getting Pam Anderson!"

As the smoke engulfed lower Manhattan, Stern descended into a series of genocidal tirades. "We've gotta drop an atomic bomb," he proclaimed.

"There has got to be a war," Quivers demanded.

"But a devastating war, where people die. Burn their eyes out!"

Thirty minutes later, as the news of mass civilian casualties poured in, Stern had transformed into a cartoon villain: "Now is the time to not even ask questions. To drop a few atomic bombs. Do a few chemical warfare hits! Let their people suffer until they understand!"

"Because we haven't been bothering anybody," Quivers interjected. "They started screaming about colonialism. *We stopped.*"

Moments later, Stern repeated his call for nuclear annihilation. "Blow them all to sky high!" he said. "Atom bombs! Just do it so they're flattened out and turned into a paved road and we'll take the oil for ourselves."

This was not right-wing radio, but one of the consistently most highly rated morning shows in the country. Stern's exterminationist diatribes demonstrated how deeply the neoconservative mind-set had been inculcated into mainstream American culture, how it had been simmering just below the surface of the bawdy blather that normally dominated the drive-time airwaves and was waiting to explode upon what PNAC described as "some catastrophic and catalyzing event." The sleaze-laden shock jock who compared himself to Dan Rather as the attacks unfolded had given voice to large sectors of a shell-shocked public, earning him praise for channeling the outrage that average New Yorkers felt on that clear blue day.

Exactly a week later, before an audience of millions on the *Late Show with David Letterman*, the real Dan Rather appeared in the guest chair to render Stern's tirades into smooth, vaguely Texas-accented sound-bites. "This will be long, the casualties will be greater," Rather informed Letterman. "We've suffered casualties but there will be more. When we send our sons and daughters into this kind of war, into this twilight zone that they're going, there will be great casualties."

Visibly exhausted after nights of long, emotionally taxing broadcasts, Rather broke down several times. Following one teary display, he gathered his composure just enough to issue a vow of loyalty to the nation's leader. "George Bush is the president," said Rather. "He makes the decisions. As just one American, wherever he wants me to line up, just tell me where."

When Letterman attempted a mild intervention—"What are the events that pissed [bin Laden] off?"—Rather insisted on the most comforting explanation possible, one that formed the basis of Bush's talking points: "They hate America. They hate us. This is one of those things that makes this war different. They don't want territory. They don't want what we've got. They want to kill us and destroy us ... Some evil, it can't be explained."

Letterman explored another line of critical questioning, this one slightly more daring than the last, but softened it with a humorous tinge: "I think about the CIA, they can't even find the drinking fountain. Have we made some mistake, or done something we shouldn't have?"

Rather quickly pivoted away from the uncomfortable question to one of the Bush administration's pet obsessions. "Saddam Hussein—if he isn't connected to this," Rather stated, "he's connected to many other things. He's part of this 'hate America' thing ... His hate is deep for us ... It's a new place and we're headed for a new place."

And where was that new place? According to Rather, delivering an eerily faithful recitation of neoconservative plans for the Middle East, "the focus is on, and we should understand, not just Afghanistan—Afghanistan, Sudan, Iran, Iraq, Syria and Libya."

Like Stern, Rather could hardly be associated with the exclusive, almost incestuous family of the neoconservatives. But the outlook they had insinuated into the country's political culture and impressed upon the Bush administration had clearly shaped his understanding of the Middle East, terrorism and warfare. Through familiar, trustworthy faces like Rather, the American public was seeded with the mentality of interventionism and military unilateralism.

Down at the Pentagon, whose western wing had been smoldering only days before, Wesley Clark, the former head of the military's European Command, strode into the office of a member of the military's Joint Chiefs of Staff. "We're going to attack Iraq," the general grumbled to him, a look of anguish on his face. "The decision has basically been made."

Clark returned to the same general six weeks later to revisit the issue of invading Iraq, a source of rising exasperation among the Pentagon brass. "Oh, it's worse than that," the general told Clark. He waved around a classified memo he had just received. "Here's the paper from the Office of the Secretary of Defense [Donald Rumsfeld] outlining the strategy. We're going to take out seven countries in five years."

He then rattled off the Bush administration's targets for regime change: first Iraq, then Syria and finally Iran, with Lebanon, Libya, Somalia and Sudan somewhere in between.

The memo was a virtual mimeograph of the neoconservative "A Clean Break" produced in 1996 for Netanyahu. The momentum toward an invasion of Iraq was almost unstoppable.

Truthers and Experts

On September 17, 2001, President George W. Bush appeared at the Islamic Center in Washington, DC, a mosque dedicated in 1957 by then president Eisenhower. Before a crowd of dignitaries and diplomats, Bush delivered an impassioned address stressing the "invaluable contribution" Muslims had made to American life. "In our anger and emotion, our fellow Americans must treat each other with respect," he continued. "Women who cover their heads in this country must feel comfortable going outside their homes. Moms who wear cover must be not intimidated in America. That's not the America I know. That's not the America I value."

With his nobly worded address, Bush sought to calm the wave of anti-Muslim attacks that had erupted since 9/11. In the suburban Chicago town of Bridgeview, where thirty percent of residents were Arab, a "pro-American" vigil days after the attacks transformed into a racist mob as 300 marched toward a local mosque, chanting "USA! USA! USA!" and bellowing "Kill the Arabs!" They were halted only by a last-minute mobilization of police. Elsewhere, across the country, Sikhs were targeted with verbal abuse and physically attacked by patriots who mistook them for followers of bin Laden, now the omnipresent, bearded face of evil.

While Bush's rhetoric may have helped reduce the anti-Muslim tide spreading across the country, he nonetheless signed off on the Patriot Act, granting the executive branch unprecedented wartime powers to investigate and prosecute Americans. The bill comprised a scattershot of sweeping surveillance proposals that represented a wish list of the FBI, giving the bureau unprecedented latitude to spy on, among others, Muslim American communities. Christopher Smith, the Republican congressman from New Jersey, credited a 1994 documentary, *Terrorists Among Us: Jihad in America*, with playing a "real role" in the bill's passage. In the days after 9/11, with an eye on passing a bill like the Patriot Act, the documentary was distributed to every member of the House of Representatives.

The film was produced by Steven Emerson, a self-styled terror expert who had wrongly blamed Arabs for bombing the Oklahoma City Federal Building and held expansive civil liberties protections responsible for transforming the United States into "occupied fundamentalist territory." Funded by right-wing billionaires including Richard Mellon Scaife and criticized by investigative journalist Robert Friedman for "creating mass hysteria against American Arabs," Emerson's "Jihad in America" consisted of grainy footage of the extremists that inhabited the Al-Kifah center in Brooklyn during the time they were serving American foreign policy goals in Afghanistan. Having been assets in the CIA's program during the Cold War, evildoers like Rahman and Azzam were exploited all over again, this time as props in America's new "war on terror."

Passed by a vote of ninety-nine to one in the Senate, the Patriot Act undoubtedly benefited from the folk myth of terrorist sleeper cells and Arab Americans celebrating Al Qaeda's terror. Dan Rather had popularized the rumor during his post-9/11 Letterman show appearance when he cited "a report" that "there was one of these cells across the Hudson river ... they got on the roof of the building, they knew it was going to happen, they were waiting for it to happen, and when it happened, they celebrated." Howard Stern also spread the canard on the country's most popular radio show in the days after 9/11.

In fact, the FBI had registered only one incident of people appearing to celebrate the attacks. The bizarre event consisted of three men suspiciously filming the flaming World Trade Center from atop a white van. "They were, like, happy, you know," a witness observed. According to investigations by ABC News and *Jewish Daily Forward*, those men were not part of any Islamist terror cell. They were, in fact, Israeli intelligence agents. "We are Israeli. We are not your problem," one of them told the FBI agents who rushed to the scene. "Your problems are our problems. The Palestinians are the problem."

The events of 9/11 real were all too real, so much so that most Americans could only experience the horror as what philosopher Jean Baudrillard described as a televised simulacrum. For too many, the images of planes suddenly slamming into Manhattan's iconic downtown skyline and sending workers tumbling from the burning towers to their agonizing death—the sheer magnitude of the terror and the tragedy—defied the bounds of comprehension. And the stories that emerged when the clouds of ash cleared raised more questions than they answered.

It was only natural that in the days after a traumatizing event like 9/11, millions of Americans gravitated toward conspiratorial thinking to make sense of the cataclysm. In July, just two months before the attacks, a radio personality in Austin, Texas, had prophesied what many came to believe was the hidden truth: "Please! Call Congress. Tell 'em we know the government is planning terrorism," the gravelly voiced host intoned, warning that the target would be the World Trade Center. Next, he identified the name of the government's patsy: "bin Laden is the boogeyman they need in this Orwellian, phony system."

At the time, Alex Jones was on the cutting edge of alternative talk radio. Branded by *Talkers* magazine as "an early trailblazer" of the "digital, independent model of the 21st century," he was broadcast on 100 stations across the country. Jones had made a memorable cameo in his friend Richard Linklater's 2001 animated docufiction film, *Waking Life*, barreling down the barren streets of downtown Austin in an old car and barking through a public address system, "The twenty-first century is gonna be a new century, not the century of slavery, not the century of lies and issues with no significance, and classism and statism and all the rest of the modes of human control," Jones ranted, unwittingly echoing rhetorical PNAC themes. "It's gonna be the age of humankind standing up for something pure and something right!"

Following the shock of 9/11, Jones stood almost alone among his peers. On that morning, when he sat behind the microphone, he pointed his finger directly at the government, accusing it of orchestrating "controlled demolitions" inside both towers of the World Trade Center. It was an inside job, he insisted, the handiwork of a nefarious network of sociopathic globalists. Within days, Jones was unceremoniously dropped by radio affiliates until he virtually disappeared from the commercial airwaves. But he spoke to the masses of confused and suddenly inquisitive Americans who sensed that they were being lied to; who sensed that their media was manipulating them into war and that their simpleton president was little more than a front man for a sinister elite willing to sacrifice countless lives to deepen its control over the masses.

As the Bush administration spun out a case for invading Iraq almost immediately after 9/11, the mainstream media fell in line with the march to war. Pundits on both sides of the partisan divide acted out the sentiments that Dan Rather expressed days after the attacks: "wherever [Bush] wants me to line up, just tell me where." Antiwar outliers like MSNBC's Phil Donahue were summarily driven from their jobs while neoconservative conspiracy theorists like Laurie Mylroie found a mostly uncritical national media platform to make the dubious link between Saddam Hussein and Al Qaeda. The case for invading Iraq on the basis of nonexistent weapons of mass destruction only compounded popular skepticism of the official narrative. By the summer of 2002, public trust in the federal government had plummeted twenty-four points from October 2001, when trust levels were at their highest point in forty years.

Amid the deluge of disinformation, Alex Jones emerged as a cult hero. With each rant about the government plot to engineer the most devastating terror attack on American soil in history, the barrel-chested, ruddy-faced agitator attracted thousands of new listeners, many of them deeply disillusioned young men with negligible economic prospects. His Infowars network ballooned into a multimillion-dollar empire with more online listeners than America's top conservative radio jock, Rush Limbaugh, enabling Jones to roll out a highly profitable, nutritionally questionable line of dietary supplements, from Caveman True Paleo Formula to Silver Bullet colloidal silver, all marketed as antidotes to the government's "chemical war." (Ironically, the Center for Environmental Health found that Jones' True Paleo Formula and another of his supplements contained toxic levels of lead, enough to increase risk of heart attacks and sperm damage. In a custody battle with his ex-wife, Jones' own attorney described him as "a performance artist," not an ideologically committed journalist.)

But even if he was just playing an online carnival barker, Jones put his money where his mouth was. Among the shock jock's myriad pet projects was the 2005 *Loose Change 9/11* documentary series, produced by Dylan Avery, a twentysomething waiter at Red Lobster at the time he edited it. The film is an eighty-minute scattershot of compelling theories and probing questions about the 9/11 attacks, clinically scripted and set with an impressively high production value. Avery's narrative seemed to expose serious flaws in the government's case, demonstrating that it at least had foreknowledge of the attacks and did nothing to stop them.

The insinuation that runs through the documentary is that, even more than an official cover-up, there was ample evidence of active government involvement in planning and implementing the attacks by planting bombs inside the World Trade Center. Inspired by the 9/11 Truth movement, Jones quickly recognized the film's potency and invested heavily in its distribution, making himself its executive producer. Over the course of several editions, *Loose Change* garnered more than 10 million views, becoming the central recruiting vehicle of the Truth movement. Avery became a celebrity in his own right, finding interest from filmmaking legend David Lynch, actor Charlie Sheen and the oligarch Mark Cuban. *Loose Change* drove public opinion in an undeniable direction: by the time the film had reached several million views, in 2006, 42 percent of Americans told pollsters from Zogby—in a poll sponsored by the Truther organization 911Truth.org—that they believed the 9/11 Commission had

either ignored or "concealed" evidence that contradicted the "official explanation."

There was no doubt the 9/11 Commission had endeavored to cover up inconvenient truths surrounding the attacks. Twenty-eight pages of the commission's final report had been redacted. These sections dealt with the Saudi connection to 9/11, delving into the relationship between Saudi officials like Fahad al-Thumairy and Omar Bayoumi, and the hijackers Khalid al-Mihdhar and Nawaf al-Hazmi. The pages also included information showing contacts between one of the hijackers and a corporation managing the Aspen, Colorado, home of Prince Bandar bin Sultan, who was then the Saudi ambassador to Washington. The Saudi government had forked over millions to powerhouse DC firms like Qorvis to lobby against the public release of those twenty-eight pages. And despite sustained pressure campaigns from the families of 9/11 victims, both the Bush and Obama administrations stood staunchly against any action that would embarrass a top ally like Saudi Arabia.

Then there was the issue of Operation Cyclone. Al Qaeda had been a natural outgrowth of the covert war the CIA oversaw during the 1980s in Afghanistan, where the agency armed and trained Islamist mujahedin like the warlord Hekmatyar. The 9/11 Commission Report glossed over this crucial piece of context in a short page and a half, referring to the mujahedin as "an Afghan national resistance movement" and noting only in passing that the United States covertly backed some of its most extreme elements. On this central point, the report was a historical whitewash.

If the government had advance warning of the 9/11 attacks; if it turned a blind eye to the devious schemes of the hijackers; and if it callously sacrificed the security of its own citizens, the reason was imperial ambition. Indeed, the American national security state had been so hell-bent on defeating the Soviet Union that the long-term consequences of weaponizing Islamist proxies were irrelevant—"compared to the Soviet Union, and to its collapse, the Taliban were unimportant," as Brzezinski had reflected in 2006. It was also undeniable that America's special relationship with Saudi Arabia had necessitated a passive attitude toward the country's funding and propagation of extremism across the Middle East, and may have caused the intelligence services to look the other way even when Saudi activities on American soil in the months leading up to 9/11 had their own systems "blinking red." For many of the disillusioned youth that gravitated into 9/11 Truth circles, however, these critical pieces of historical and political context seemed overly complex and utterly unsatisfying.

Loose Change avoided any exploration of the blowback from American empire. By homing in instead on the granular details of the explosions that brought down the Twin Towers (and getting many of them wrong in the process), and by omitting any historical discussion of the American government's relationship with the forces directly implicated in the attacks, turning to crude insinuations about an inside job, the Truthers inadvertently ran interference for the imperialist power elite they claimed to disdain.

There was probably one direction a national movement bound together by conspiratorial thinking could go, and that was hard right. The hyper-ambitious Jones proved eager to channel antiestablishment energy into right-wing mobilization. Having put 9/11 Truth on the national radar, Jones opened up a new front against undocumented immigrants, joining forces with the white nationalist border vigilantes known as the Minutemen to paint illegal immigration as a globalist plan to destroy American culture. He focused intensely on the threat of "chemtrails," alleging that government jets were engaged in a secret plot to spray chemicals that promoted mind control and "could possibly cause flooding akin to Noah's ark." And he continued to push the claim—not far afield from self-styled terror expert Steven Emerson's baseless speculation—that the Clinton administration had engineered the 1995 Oklahoma City Federal Building bombing to advance gun control and other liberal policies.

Thanks to Jones, principled skeptics of the official narrative surrounding 9/11 could be dismissed as cranks, while millions

of youthful, disillusioned citizens were plunged into a morass of paranoid bunk that could only lead them away from mass antiwar organizing. Jones' followers were building the basis not for an alternative politics based on "humankind standing up for something pure and something right," as he once claimed he sought, but for an authoritarian right-wing subculture with alternative aesthetic trappings. If Jones had not existed, the establishment might have had to create him. Or perhaps, if one wants to get conspiratorial, it did.

For Americans struggling to make sense of 9/11, there was an explanation that was far more accessible than the "inside job" conspiracy, and which did not threaten to undercut their sense of national exceptionalism. This theory held the Islamic faith of the attackers responsible for inspiring 9/11 and cast suspicion on Muslims living across the United States. It had been trafficked in various forms by mainstream figures like Dan Rather, who stated without evidence before a national audience on the *Late Show with David Letterman* that Arab "sleeper cells" lay in wait for the next attack and that Arab Americans had been seen celebrating the World Trade Center's collapse from across the Hudson River in New Jersey.

The rumors of terrorist sleeper cells across America had some basis in reality, but this was thanks entirely to the CIA's post-Afghanistan "disposal problem," which reared its head most prominently, and dangerously, at the Al-Kifah Center in Brooklyn. After 9/11, bin Laden's network in the States had run its course, with most of its members in jail or abroad. And yet the Bush administration had reinforced the unfounded fears by promising to take down the global network that connected Al Qaeda to a network of sleeper cells.

Thus the Bush administration found itself in a political quandary. How could it generate the dramatic counterterror busts it had promised an outraged and traumatized public? And how could it do so without offending imperial partners like Saudi Arabia? It responded by casting its net as widely as possible, ensnaring people who had no intention to attack America, but who could be branded as a threat to the country and the freedoms it supposedly stood for. These were the Palestinian academics and activists whom Emerson, a dedicated ultra-Zionist, had hounded for years.

The first major terror bust of the Bush administration was the 2003 indictment of Sami al-Arian, a Palestinian computer science professor at Tampa's University of South Florida and prominent Muslim civil rights activist who had forged relationships with both Presidents Bill Clinton and George W. Bush. In fact, al-Arian had known both men, having spent years leading up to 9/11 personally lobbying both to end the use of secret evidence against criminal suspects. The practice of secret evidence had been authorized under Clinton and was directed almost exclusively against Arabs and Muslims, denying them the right to see the material the government was using to prosecute them.

Starting in 1998, al-Arian worked across the aisle in Congress, winning strong advocates in the liberal Democratic representative David Bonior and the Republican libertarian representative Bob Barr. He organized a packed meeting inside the US Capitol on the perils of secret evidence, and fundraised for members of Congress from both parties who showed concern on the issue. The powerful judiciary chairman, Representative Henry Hyde, was among them. By September 2000, with the presidential campaign entering its final stage, a bill to end secret evidence passed with strong bipartisan support in the House Judiciary Committee. According to al-Arian, the measure was the first congressional lobbying effort by Muslims and Arabs in America, and it appeared to be proceeding successfully. All the bill needed was a signature by the president.

The campaign of Democrat Al Gore had given al-Arian and the organized Muslim community the cold shoulder, stonewalling their demands to meet. But the Bush campaign was eager to cooperate. On October 6, 2000, al-Arian received a call from a Republican lobbyist who made clear that he was speaking on behalf of Bush campaign guru Karl Rove. The lobbyist and the activist worked out a deal: Bush would agree to denounce secret evidence in a presidential debate and support the Senate

legislation to end the practice. When Bush made good on the first part of the pledge, the lobbyist phoned al-Arian again. "I delivered," he said. "Now it's your turn."

The Bush campaign expected al-Arian and his allies to shepherd their Muslim constituents to the polls on Election Day. And when the time came, they delivered on their end of the bargain as well, phoning the leader of every Muslim organization in the country to emphasize that a vote for Bush was a vote for civil liberties. "We campaigned around Florida and we said, 'This isn't about Iraq or Palestine; it's about civil rights," al-Arian recalled. "Our analysis was that after polling, we delivered 14,000 votes more to Bush than Gore. So we reversed the trend, and [Bush] won Florida by 537 votes."

Indeed, al-Arian's backroom deal with Bush was a crucial factor in one of the closest and most contested elections in American history. Days later, he stood inside the White House at a private reception with a collection of senior Republicans, including Republican House majority leader Newt Gingrich. "They said without you, Bush wouldn't have been president," he recalled. "I said immediately, this is about secret evidence and we expect a change of policy."

Bush appeared to take his pledge seriously. Months after his inauguration, he scheduled a press conference to announce his support for ending secret evidence. The presser was set for 3:00 p.m. on September 11. It never took place.

In the days and weeks after the attacks of 9/11, al-Arian fell under a constantly rising wave of attacks from right-wing radio jocks and media allies of Steve Emerson. Claiming without evidence that "one of the world's most lethal terrorist factions was based out of Tampa," Emerson had contended for years that al-Arian was the top American financier of Palestinian Islamic Jihad (PIJ), a Palestinian nationalist faction that had struggled violently against Israel but had never targeted the United States or American assets. Emerson offered no evidence to show that al-Arian had broken any law or that he was operationally active with any terror group, and neither did the federal prosecutors who oversaw his trial. All they had were recordings of strident anti-Israel statements by al-Arian and hints that he had once sympathized with PIJ's aims.

The Bush administration that owed its victory at least in part to al-Arian now set out to destroy him. In a nationally televised press conference, Attorney General John Ashcroft touted the case of *United States v. al-Arian* as the first major test of the Patriot Act—and the opening phase of the war on terror's legal strategy. But the trial ended in a hung jury, with al-Arian pleading guilty to a minor charge. He wound up spending the next ten years in federal custody, often in solitary confinement, and then under house arrest. Gordon Kromberg, an outspoken supporter of Israel who had once traveled to the country on a paid pro-Israel junket, oversaw his prosecution, hounding al-Arian for refusing to testify in a separate, peripherally related case. For Kromberg, pursuing the Palestinian professor appeared to be a crusade driven by ideological zeal.

During his first trial, al-Arian's defense team inadvertently exposed the birth of a counterterror industry that leveraged dubious, seemingly endless dragnets into inflated paychecks. By their account, two full-time court translators had been paid $94,000 a year to transcribe the 21,000 hours of phone calls the FBI had recorded from phone taps on al-Arian's home line. Prosecutors then had to spend $550,000 to convert the FBI's outdated magnetic tapes to compact discs. Matthew Levitt, a self-proclaimed expert on Palestinian militant groups who worked at the neoconservative Washington Institute for Near East Policy (the former think tank of the Beltway's main pro-Israel lobbying arm, AIPAC), admitted in court to raking in a whopping $250,000 for his supposedly expert testimony, according to a member of al-Arian's defense team.

Government prosecutors and FBI agents revealed to the court as many as twenty taxpayer-funded junkets to Israel, where their intelligence counterparts fed them information that turned out to be useless innuendo. Meanwhile, the government flew Israelis to the scene of the trial for the dramatic press conference. They were survivors of Palestinian suicide bombings and none of them had ever encountered al-Arian before. An investigation and prosecution that protected no one and led nowhere cost taxpayers upwards of $50 million. It also marked a deep, seemingly irreparable rift between the US government and an aspirational community of American Muslims whose leadership had once been eager to collaborate with it—and even with Republican Party leadership—to achieve mutually beneficial political objectives.

In the end, al-Arian was exonerated. Having been denied citizenship by the United States and deprived of citizenship in historic Palestine due to Israel's half-century-long military occupation, he found a home in Turkey thanks to the personal intervention of President Recep Tayyip Erdoğan, the leader of the Islamist-oriented AKP (Justice and Development) party. Speaking to me from Istanbul, al-Arian lamented his experience in post-9/11 America: "Why would they want to solve the terror threat? They just exacerbate it to make more money."

The pressing post-9/11 need for private experts to explain the government's "war on terror" resuscitated Emerson's flagging career, earning him a paid gig as an NBC commentator and hefty fees on the lecture circuit. Through his Investigative Project on Terrorism (IPT), he amassed donations from major right-wing and pro-Israel foundations, then transferred millions to a private for-profit company he owned called SAE Productions. Emerson's acolytes also emerged during this period as sought-after celebrity "experts," hyping threats before captivated and often credulous audiences in courtrooms and cable news studios.

Among Emerson's top disciples was Evan Kohlmann, now a counterterror correspondent for MSNBC with no serious scholarly or journalistic credentials. In the years after 9/11, Kohlmann emerged as a top expert witness in government prosecutions, providing "big picture" analysis before credulous juries in exchange for lucrative paychecks. Before testifying against two men accused of providing "material support" to Southeast Asian extremist groups, Jaish-e-Mohammed and Jamaat-e-Islami (one of the defendants initially thought the groups were the names of Bangladeshi music acts), Kohlmann admitted he previously knew little about either faction. The research he planned to present had been cobbled together through a weekend's worth of Google searches, he conceded. As journalist Petra Bartosiewicz noted, Kohlmann "admitted he had never interviewed any members of the group. He was unable to name the paramilitary elements of the group or even recent major political parties in Bangladesh." Ultimately, however, his testimony helped generate a swift conviction for the government.

Another leading terror "expert" to emerge from under Emerson's watch was Rita Katz, the daughter of an Iraqi Jew executed by the Iraqi government for spying for Israel. Like Kohlmann, Katz had no scholarly credentials; her field work largely consisted of entering Muslim gatherings in hijab and trolling for signs of extremism. She told a reporter that she modeled her lifestyle after the second generation of educated, middle-class jihadis who sacrificed everything for the sake of the mission. Katz even wrote an anonymous autobiography portraying herself as an "extraordinary woman who went undercover to infiltrate the radical Islamic groups operating in America." She appeared on *60 Minutes* to promote the book disguised as "Sarah," and wearing a fake nose and wig. Her identity was ultimately uncovered by two Saudi-backed, US-based charities she targeted, who sued her for defamation. Katz went on to form her own company, Search for International Terrorist Entities, or the SITE Institute. The outfit earned her a lucrative income selling subscriptions to media and law enforcement agencies seeking access to her constantly updated, sometimes questionably translated catalog of jihadist videos and manifestos.

In many cases, the militant fanboys who populated the dark corners of digital chat rooms were happy to see Katz provide their favorite militant gangs with a mainstream platform. "They translate the statements into English on our behalf, and they do not analyze them. Why do we not grab the opportunity?" one jihadist commenter insisted.

Katz and her fellow jihadologists rose to prominence just as Al Qaeda was beginning to harness the power of online media.

The impact of the organization's propaganda was exponentially magnified thanks to a single American recruit named Adam Gadahn. A Generation Xer magnetized by the brave new world of online propaganda, Gadahn could have just as easily wound up as a member of the Truther army galvanized by Alex Jones' Infowars network, but in Salafi-oriented Islam he discovered a sense of spiritual community that was absent from online conspiracy culture.

Gadahn's father, Philip Pearlman, had been the guitarist for an obscure psychedelic band, Relatively Clean Rivers, that attained cult status decades after it faded from the scene. During the post-counterculture come-down of the 1970s, Pearlman retreated from the social mainstream, earning a living as a goat farmer in rural southern California and converting to evangelical Christianity. Adam Gadahn was homeschooled and lived a cloistered existence. During his early adolescence, he emulated his father's affinity for music, writing about his obsession with death metal for a magazine called *Xenocide*. But at age 16, when he took a job at a computer store, he was able to access the Internet for the first time.

Drawn into the cyber-world of Islamic chat rooms, Gadahn realized his true spiritual calling. He converted a year later, in 1995, instinctively embracing the most rigid interpretation of Islam, an inverted expression of his father's Christian fundamentalism accented with an Orientalized version of the black-and-white iconography that drew him to death metal. Gadahn slipped into the *takfiri* mind-set, leading him to denounce the imam of his local mosque as a Jew. He soon found his way to the preachings of the Blind Sheikh, Omar Abdel-Rahman, and then fell into the hands of Khalid Sheikh Mohammed, who recruited him as Al Qaeda's top English language spokesman in 1998. He was the poster child for a new generation of jihadists drawn from the neoliberal West, the vanguard of an emerging cast of suggestible, hyper-alienated losers and outcast, racially abused *enragees* with little left to lose.

Gadahn's "State of the Ummah" series, produced through the As-Sahab media company he founded, represented the jihadist reboot of the World War II–era propaganda film *Why We Fight*. Blending footage of American and Israeli atrocities with extended diatribes by bin Laden, Zawahiri and their inner circle, Gadahn aimed to convince viewers that America's war was not against terrorists, or "evil," as Bush called it, but against Islam itself. The video was the first Al Qaeda propaganda vehicle aimed specifically at the hearts and minds of Muslims in the West. Like *Loose Change*, it became a key recruiting vehicle for disillusioned youth seeking immersion into a totalistic atmosphere that grounded their disrupted existences.

Al Qaeda recruits seeking to make their escape from freedom had found a base in Afghanistan under the nervous watch of the Taliban. In Washington, plans were underway that would not just target the base of Al Qaeda's operations, but the entire state apparatus.

Into the Quagmire

On the eve of America's invasion of Afghanistan, George W. Bush was determined to revive the *mission civilisatrice* that Washington and its proxies in the mujahedin had already crushed when they ousted the pro-Soviet government from Kabul. "Civilized people throughout the world are speaking out in horror—not only because our hearts break for the women and children in Afghanistan, but also because in Afghanistan, we see the world the terrorists would like to impose on the rest of us," his wife, Laura Bush, declared in a November 18, 2001, radio address.

After the United States routed its former allies in the Taliban, driving them too from Kabul, Anna Wintour, the editor-in-chief of *Vogue*, arrived on thc scene with an ambitious initiative to establish a 1,200-square-foot fashion salon in the new Afghan Ministry of Women's Affairs compound. "There will be 300-page [haircare] manuals and instructional videos," the *New York Times* reported in September 2002. "There will be ample supplies of Matrix hair-care products and MAC cosmetics and

Revlon nail polish. There may even be an Aveda herb garden to bring aromatherapy to a land that has smelled too much of death and destruction and too little of lavender and lemon grass."

Those who were supposed to benefit from Wintour's project were the same class of Afghans the United States had doomed a generation before when it backed a grotesque gallery of fundamentalist warlords who had earned their stripes crusading to drive women out of Kabul University. As the American occupation took hold, Hekmatyar returned to his former power base, funding and directing the insurgency while the Afghan women that provided the occupation with its moral justification suffered once more.

For the Bush administration's Middle American base, any interest in the welfare of foreign civilians, especially Muslim ones, was faint at best. To them, the war was an opportunity to exact righteous revenge for the humiliation of 9/11. Country music star Toby Keith channeled the Red States' mood into his song, "Courtesy of the Red, White and Blue," which debuted at the top of the Billboard 200 on July 2002:

> Soon as we could see clearly
> Through our big black eye
> Man, we lit up your world
> Like the Fourth of July.

In the days before Keith's song was released—July 1, to be precise—the United States "lit up" a wedding celebration in the Kandahar region of Afghanistan, killing at least twenty civilians. They were among the first casualties of a war that harvested the lives of as many as 10,000 Afghan civilians a year.

An unmitigated disaster for American military grunts and the civilians in their way, the occupation was a boon for US-backed opportunists like the man installed as Afghanistan's interim president, Hamid Karzai, in December 2001. During the 1980s, Karzai was one of the so-called "Gucci Guerrillas" who helped the CIA organize shipments to the mujahedin from Quetta,

Pakistan. By 1996, he was advising Unocal on its pipeline through Afghanistan, working closely with his fellow Pashtun tribesman, Zalmay Khalilzad, a charter member of PNAC who lent his name to the neoconservative grouping's letter urging regime change in Iraq. Before the Clinton administration backed the Taliban as the pipeline's most reliable guardian, Karzai helped organize the movement into a potent force around his hometown of Kandahar.

Soon after the Taliban took power, Karzai was recruited by Mullah Omar to serve as its UN ambassador, but the movement's rule was never formally recognized. Karzai attained his country's presidency thanks largely to the patronage of Khalilzad, who led Bush's Pentagon transition team. From Kabul, he had the opportunity to enrich himself, his restauranteur brother, and his brother Ahmed Wali Karzai, an accused heroin trafficker, at the expense of American taxpayers, looting government coffers while slowly edging back into the orbit of the Taliban. Despite widespread allegations of drug trafficking Ahmed Wali Karzai was put on the CIA payroll and used to organize a paramilitary force outside Kandahar. The CIA-backed militia operated out of the former compound of Taliban founder Mullah Omar.

The doomed American occupation of Afghanistan followed one of the most consequential military failures in the country's history, as the forty-four-year-old bin Laden and about 1,000 loyalists escaped the American siege of the Tora Bora cave complex with only fifty-seven captured. The precipitous incline from the road to the caves made a direct infantry approach nearly impossible, while the caves themselves rendered even enormous 15,000-pound American daisy cutter bombs ineffective.

Bin Laden knew these fortified caves well; they had been constructed with the help of the CIA during the anti-Soviet jihad in which he fought during the 1980s. In those halcyon years, he flew in earthmoving equipment from his father's Saudi Binladin Group and impressed his underlings by trundling around in a bulldozer across the rocky heights as they dug out a network of tunnels and depots. "He knew every ridge and mountain pass, every CIA trail," wrote journalist Mary Anne Weaver. "For this was the area where bin Laden had spent more than a decade of his life."

By the time the main American assault began at Tora Bora in December 2001, about seventy US special forces soldiers had been relegated to a supporting role for a collection of local warlords that George Friedman, the founder of the private intelligence firm Stratfor, described as "a shifting kaleidoscope of brigands, fanatics, and opportunists, all with agendas and grievances going back generations." Rented with wads of cash flown in by the CIA, the warlords began cutting deals with Al Qaeda, capitulating one after another rather than sending their men to die in a futile uphill battle on behalf of a foreign invader.

Bin Laden slipped across the Pakistani border, traveling by horseback over the same paths the CIA had carved out for him and the mujahedin during the anti-Soviet jihad. His loyalists dispersed with plans to regroup, just as the Taliban had done after being driven from Kabul by the Americans. The Bush administration, for its part, did not publicly admit to its failure at Tora Bora or to bin Laden's escape until April 2002, four months after the assault.

Following its failure to achieve the central goal of the Afghan invasion, the American military proceeded to expand its footprint across the country, establishing a semipermanent presence and embarking on a $65 billion program to train a new Afghan army. Reconstruction was earmarked for $117 billion, more than was spent on the Marshall Plan for Europe, with hundreds of millions in kickbacks to contractors and billions for failed opium eradication programs. The more costly the mission was, the more dedicated its generals became.

The war had been blessed by Congress, which had given the president constitutional authority to "take action to deter and prevent acts of international terrorism against the United States." The vague language contained in the congressional Authorization for Use of Military Force resolution meant that the war Bush had pledged would not only be global in scope, but a perpetual battle against an array of enemies, including many who were sworn enemies of Al Qaeda. Congress thus voluntarily abdicated its constitutional authority and gave its blessing to America's forever war.

4

In for the Rudest of Awakenings

While Al Qaeda regrouped, the neoconservatives who had burrowed within the Pentagon's bureaucracy were finally able to pursue the fantasy spelled out in "A Clean Break"—"seven countries in five years." The neoconservative vehicle was the Office of Special Plans (OSP), a pet project that the Senate Foreign Relations Committee later called "an unofficial 'Iraqi intelligence cell' ... to circumvent the CIA and secretly brief the White House on links between Saddam Hussein and Al Qaeda." Set up through the patronage of Defense Secretary Donald Rumsfeld and given the green light from Vice President Dick Cheney, the OSP was a playpen for the neoconservatives to stovepipe cooked intelligence past the CIA and directly to the Oval Office.

To establish the nonexistent link between Saddam and bin Laden, Feith and the OSP cobbled together testimony from shady Iraqi defectors and the neoconservatives' favorite exile, longtime CIA proxy Ahmad Chalabi. Recruited to lead the anti-Saddam opposition after the 1991 Gulf War, Chalabi remained on the US payroll thanks to Clinton's 1998 Iraq Liberation Act, which committed the United States to regime change and doled out $97 million to Chalabi's Iraqi National Congress (INC) to help the effort along.

In 2002, Bush's State Department attempted to appropriate $8 million for Chalabi while absorbing his INC into the so-called Iraqi National Movement, a collection of Sunni exiles with a $315,000 budget and a wing in Damascus (an antecedent to the Western-backed opposition to Syrian president Bashar al-Assad). Chalabi assured his neoconservative patrons that American troops would be welcomed into Baghdad as liberators, a pledge that Feith found "quite moving." But before the US 82nd Airborne could be pelted with candy by the grateful Iraqi masses, the American public had to be moved to back a ground invasion.

The INC—and, by extension, Feith's OSP—scored the public relations coup it had been seeking when Chalabi delivered Adnan al-Hadeiri, a defector from Iraq's civil engineering corps, to the *New York Times*' Judith Miller and the Australian Broadcasting Corporation (ABC). Both Miller and the ABC dutifully reported al-Hadeiri's claims that Saddam Hussein oversaw chemical, nuclear and biological weapons facilities and that he was on his way toward developing a nuclear weapon he could deploy against the United States. Miller cited anonymous "government officials" who called al-Hadeiri's information "reliable and significant." One of those officials was later revealed to be Lewis "Scooter" Libby, a neoconservative fellow traveler who served as a liaison between Cheney's office and the OSP. Chalabi allegedly received $1 million for generating the testimony about weapons of mass destruction.

Though al-Hadeiri had failed a polygraph test administered by the CIA, his lies were packaged for mass consumption with the help of a $16 million contract the Pentagon paid to public relations firms with the explicit aim of promoting regime change in Iraq. Among those that cashed in on the contract was the Rendon Group—the PR company that previously helped spin out the fake news of babies torn from their incubators by Iraqi troops prior to the first Gulf War. The INC spokesman who had coached al-Hadeiri on spinning his story, Zaab Sethna, was, in fact, a former Rendon Group staffer. So was the INC's chief lobbyist in Washington, Francis Brooke. "It was the first in a long line of hyped and fraudulent stories that would eventually propel the US into a war with Iraq—the first war based almost entirely on a covert propaganda campaign targeting the media," wrote journalist James Bamford.

The Bush administration made its public case for invading and occupying Iraq largely on the basis of the link between Saddam Hussein and Al Qaeda—a connection that the 9/11 Commission rejected, and which the Pentagon inspector general and senator, Jay Rockefeller, later called "inappropriate." Feith's former boss, then Israeli opposition leader Benjamin Netanyahu, had done his best to reinforce the perception of such a link, telling Congress in a 2002 testimony, "There is no question whatsoever that Saddam is seeking, is working, is advancing towards the development of nuclear weapons. Once Saddam has nuclear weapons, the terror network will have nuclear weapons." While the Israeli interest in encouraging a US war of regime change in Iraq was clear, the American interest had to be contrived by Netanyahu's neoconservative cutouts in Washington.

Thanks to their efforts, the bogus Al Qaeda–Saddam connection formed the basis of one of the most memorable—and deceptive—talking points of the Bush presidency: "America must not ignore the threat gathering against us," Bush declared on October 8, 2002. "Facing clear evidence of peril, we cannot wait for the final proof—the smoking gun—that could come in the form of a mushroom cloud." The line was the brainchild of two speechwriters, Michael Gerson and David Frum, who had previously conceived Bush's infamous phrase, the "axis of evil," to spur public support for military interventions after 9/11.

But support for an invasion of Iraq was hardly limited to Republican foreign policy hawks. "It seemed to me that almost anybody in Washington who dealt with security issues supported that war," recalled Max Abrahms, an assistant professor of political science at Northeastern University who was a fellow at the neoconservative Washington Institute for Near East Policy during the invasion of Iraq. "What's been really frustrating to me [is that] there wasn't a large empirical record of US-led regime change in the Muslim world. It was much more reasonable in 2003 to think that this could work."

Indeed, when the *New York Times*' Thomas Friedman—the paper's former Middle East bureau chief, its chief liberal interventionist and most brazen promoter of corporate globalization—argued, "We needed to go over there [to Iraq], basically, and take out a very big stick right in the heart of that world and burst that [terror] bubble," he was merely restating the so-called "Ledeen doctrine" of arch-neoconservative Michael Ledeen: "Every ten years or so, the United States needs to pick up some small crappy little country and throw it against the wall, just to show we mean business."

In the Senate, most Democrats fell in line with the conventional wisdom spun out by editorial pages and Beltway think tanks. In October 2002, then senator Hillary Clinton echoed Bush, arguing for invading Iraq and basing her argument on the misinformation churned out by Feith's OSP and Chalabi's Potemkin village-style exile operation. From the Senate floor, Clinton declared that "intelligence reports show that Saddam Hussein has worked to rebuild his chemical and biological weapons stock, his missile delivery capability, and his nuclear program. He has also given aid, comfort, and sanctuary to terrorists, including Al Qaeda members."

One of the lone dissenters in the Senate was Democratic senator Robert Byrd, a Rust Belt populist at the end of his decades-long career. Before an almost empty chamber, Byrd bellowed out his protestations of the war with righteous fury. He opened with an incendiary indictment of his colleagues' drone-like consensus: "Yet this chamber is, for the most part, silent—ominously, dreadfully silent," Byrd roared. "There is no debate, no discussion, no attempt to lay out for the nation the pros and cons of this particular war. There is nothing." Warning of the destabilization and radicalization the war would inspire, Byrd ended by praying that America was not "in for a rudest of awakenings."

I was among the hundreds of thousands who protested the war across the country. The movement's size and reach was surprising considering the tsunami of pro-war media: it was later calculated that there were six positive stories about the case for war for every critical one. Among cable news management, efforts to silence dissent were scarcely disguised. MSNBC's top-rated host, Phil Donahue, was summarily yanked from the airwaves for his refusal to conform to NBC management's pro-war narrative. Clear Channel, the corporation that owned a disproportionate number of radio stations across the country, had circulated an internal memorandum listing 158 songs that could not be played in the wake of the 9/11 attacks. The banned songs ranged from anything and everything by the antiauthority hardcore quartet Rage Against the Machine to "Leaving on a Jet Plane" by Peter, Paul and Mary. As I stood outside the Federal Building in Los Angeles, California, on March 20, 2003, alongside a few hundred antiwar demonstrators, I endured hours of abuse hurled from passing cars and pickup trucks. "Go back to Baghdad!" was among the most common refrains. Drunk on the delusions spun out by the White House and corporate media, American nationalists were due for a rude awakening indeed.

That night, some 200,000 American troops stormed into Iraq alongside nearly 50,000 British soldiers, commencing an invasion that would turn into a grisly eight-year-long occupation and leave as many as a million dead. The removal of Saddam's government fueled chaos almost immediately, with irreplaceable antiquities looted from the National Museum of Iraq while Defense Secretary Rumsfeld directed troops to protect the Iraqi Ministry of Oil. "Freedom's untidy," Rumsfeld grumbled in response to critics. Amid the turmoil, some 250,000 tons of ammo and explosives disappeared from depots across the country.

Saddam Hussein had been befuddled by the Americans' hostility. After all, he had provided Washington with a reliable ally during the 1980s, turning the heavy weaponry and chemical weapons it provided him against his Kurdish and Iranian foes while using an iron fist against his own country's communist and Islamist forces. When John Nixon, the CIA leadership analyst and Iraq specialist, briefed Saddam after his capture by US troops, he found that the deposed dictator viewed himself as a force for stability, one who had kept the lid on incipient Sunni extremist groups like Al Qaeda.

"Wahhabism is going to spread in the Arab nation and probably faster than anyone expects. And the reason why is that people view Wahhabism as an idea and a struggle," Saddam told Nixon in one interrogation session. "Iraq will be a battlefield for anyone who wants to carry arms against America," he continued. "And now there is an actual battlefield for face-to-face confrontation."

Just as Saddam warned, the chaos brought by the invasion was electrifying religious extremists on both sides of the conflict, enabling Christian and Islamic fanatics to advance their messianic aims from whatever territory they could control. Thousands of pamphlets published by an Atlanta-based evangelical ministry, In Touch, were found among American troops. The tracts branded the war in Iraq as "A Christian's Duty"—a holy war—and they urged the troops to "pray for the President and his advisors regardless of critics."

When Franklin Graham, the Christian right-wing scion and vitriolic Islamophobe, announced his intention to proselytize Iraqi Muslims from the backs of American M1A1 tanks, he inspired a ferocious response from Islamic fanatics. In response, Khilafah.com, an English-language propaganda website run by Hizb ut-Tahrir, a fundamentalist Islamist group that actively promoted the establishment of an Islamic state, denounced Graham by name. Next, it published a downloadable pamphlet urging Muslims from the West to flock to the Iraqi battlefield. It was entitled "Destroy the Fourth Crusader War."

A war that had been sold to a shell-shocked American public as a campaign against the top state sponsor of Al Qaeda was soon fertile ground for bin Laden and his supporters. The plague of international jihadism that the United States helped unleash through its covert intervention in Cold War–era Afghanistan was to expand and metastasize due to its full-scale occupation of Iraq.

The Green Zone and the Green Man

The nerve center of the American occupation of Iraq lay within a hyper-fortified conglomeration of pop-up offices, air-conditioned residential structures and familiar fast food joints known as the Green Zone. Described as "Baghdad's little America" by journalist Rajiv Chandrasekaran, who chronicled the Green Zone in his book *Imperial Life in the Emerald City*, the Coalition Provisional Authority's (CPA) home was a study in neocolonial arrogance, nepotism and libertarianism run amok. The CPA's hiring prioritized ideological alignment over experience, with applicants questioned on political loyalty and their commitment to conservative ideals. Staffers at the Heritage Foundation, the unofficial think tank of the Republican Party's right wing, were given special priority. Peter McPherson, a Cheney official and Reagan administration veteran, was parachuted in to deregulate the Iraqi economy. He defended the rampant looting as "privatization that sort of occurs naturally."

L. Paul Bremer, a veteran of Kissinger Associates appointed to oversee the CPA's Republican libertarian playpen, turned Iraq into a disaster capitalist laboratory. He imposed a flat tax and imposed the notorious Order 39 on foreign investment. This order, enacted without any local input, privatized some 200 Iraqi state companies, allowing foreign corporations to usurp their assets and move all of their profits out of Iraq. The move was implemented by BearingPoint, a company that reaped a $250 million government contract to "establish the basic legal framework for a functioning market economy."

Like an imperial lord, Bremer issued dozens more orders that enabled foreign investors to take over Iraqi banks; he also eliminated tariffs and provided international contractors, including private security firms like Blackwater, with full immunity in Iraqi courts. As expected, local suppliers were wiped out and highly skilled former government employees—mostly Sunni beneficiaries of the Ba'ath Party—were sent into the streets among the swelling ranks of the suddenly unemployed.

"De-Ba'athification," a romantic concept drawn from the

de-Nazification project of post–World War II Germany, was one of the neoconservatives' pet fetishes. The plan, which called for purging thousands of employees of the Ba'ath Party, had been cooked up in the OSP by Feith with encouragement from Chalabi.

Feith first presented his proposal for a "De-Ba'athification of Iraqi Society" to Bush at a March 10, 2003, National Security Council meeting. Two months later, he forwarded it to Bremer, who promptly implemented a wholesale purge of Iraq's public sector. Not only did Bremer oust the top level of Ba'athist hard-liners, his order forced as many as 100,000 people out of work, including some 40,000 schoolteachers who, according to then CIA director George Tenet, "had joined the Ba'ath Party simply to keep their jobs."

The toxic blend of libertarian and neoconservative ideology imposed on a postcolonial Arab state by a collection of Beltway hacks created the perfect atmosphere for armed insurgency. Two generations of skilled government workers had been put out in the street while Iraq's army and intelligence services were fully disbanded. In practice, this meant that the highly adept overseers of Saddam's police state and the battle hardened commanders of the elite Iraqi Republican Guard were incandescent with rage and open to employment from any outfit that might help them strike out at the Americans.

"What happened to everyone there? Did they join the new army?" the reporter Chandrasekaran asked an American soldier at the time, referring to the disbanded army.

The soldier replied, "They're all insurgents now."

The CIA had warned of the possibility of a post-invasion insurgency led by Sunni extremists in a January 2003 National Intelligence Council paper. But it did so in cursory fashion, devoting a mere two lines to the scenario, while focusing more extensively on the prospect of intertribal fighting.

"The ability of Al Qaeda or other terrorist groups to maintain a presence in northern Iraq (or more clandestinely elsewhere) would depend largely on whether a new regime were able to exert effective security and control over the entire country," the intelligence briefing noted. "In addition, rogue ex-regime elements could forge an alliance with existing terrorist organizations or act independently to wage guerrilla warfare against a new government or coalition forces." The Republican-led Senate Intelligence Committee refused to initiate a follow-up report after the insurgency began.

Iraq's armed revolt against American occupation immediately assumed an extreme Islamist flavor and a sectarian bent. This was largely thanks to advance planning conducted by a Jordanian militant named Abu Musab al-Zarqawi. Born Ahmad Fadhil al-Nazal al-Khalaylah, Zarqawi took the namesake of his hometown of Zarqa, an impoverished city considered the capital of radical Islam in Jordan. There, locals referred to him as the "green man," a nickname owing to his sleeves' worth of tattoos. He was a common thug, a hard drinking, street-fighting thief and alleged rapist who only found self-discipline by submitting himself to the rigid Salafist theology gaining popularity among his neighbors.

Like so many others, Zarqawi found his path to jihad through Azzam's Services Bureau. By the time he reached the Afghan battlefield, however, the Soviet Red Army had already been vanquished, so he wound up honing his skills during the "war of the warlords" in the early 1990s under Hekmatyar's command.

Zarqawi returned to Jordan with sophisticated military techniques in hand and plans to organize a coup against his country's authoritarian, US-aligned monarchy, alongside fellow veterans of the Afghanistan theater. He did not get far before he was thrown in prison, where he was hardened even further, organizing a dedicated cadre of veteran jihadists while having most of his toenails extracted under harsh torture. In 1999, when he was released under a general prisoner amnesty, he was hounded by Jordanian intelligence, forcing him to strike out abroad.

Zarqawi had correctly read Washington's intentions to invade Iraq after it entered Afghanistan in 2001. That year, he organized the advance guard of an insurgent network in the autonomous Kurdish region of Iraq, out of reach of Saddam's security forces.

He was an utterly insignificant figure at the time, leading a small deployment of foreign fighters. Contrary to Secretary of State Colin Powell's February 5, 2003, testimony to the UN Security Council, where Powell falsely described Zarqawi as the link between Saddam and Al Qaeda, Zarqawi had to station himself outside the reach of a deeply hostile Iraqi government. As soon as the Americans removed Saddam, Zarqawi and his newfangled organization, Monotheism and Jihad [Jama'at al-Tawhid wal-Jihad], were able to enter the chaotic terrain of the country's Sunni Triangle and transform it into their personal playground. For Zarqawi, Al Qaeda had been insufficiently violent, too concerned with cultivating support from the local Sunni population. He sought an open war with the Shia majority of Iraq that was poised to enter power through elections.

Zarqawi had denigrated the Shia as snakes, idolaters and literal agents of Satan. He proceeded to target them at their holiest sites, slaughtering ninety-five pilgrims, for example, at Najaf's Imam Ali Mosque on August 29, 2003. His strategy hinged on polarizing Iraq along sectarian lines, provoking the Shia into a brutal religious war that then forced the Sunni population to seek protection under a banner of an Islamic state. "If we are able to strike them with one painful blow after another until they enter the battle, we will be able to reshuffle the cards," Zarqawi said, referring to the Shia. "This is what we want, and whether they like it or not, many Sunni areas will stand with the mujahedin."

Borrowing a tactic from his former mentor, Hekmatyar, Zarqawi established checkpoints along roads where Shia civilians traveled, forcing passengers from buses for religious tests. Unlike Hekmatyar's Hezb-i-Islami, however, Zarqawi's men simply slaughtered the Shia. In 2008, during the height of sectarian violence, Al Qaeda members stopped a bus in Anbar, on its way into Syria. A businessman in his mid-sixties, Taleb Al-Haddad, on his way out of Iraq's killing fields to Syria, was forced out and asked for his papers. When the Al Qaeda insurgents noticed on his ID card that he was born in the majority Shia city of Najaf, they shot him on the spot and threw his corpse in a mass grave. This was a typical experience for Shia civilians across the country.

"There's this common saying we have now—that our lives don't matter," said Ruba Ali Al-Hassani, the niece of Taleb Al-Haddad. Now a refugee activist living in Toronto, Canada, Al-Hassani told me, "The sectarian hatred has become a regional problem, and Shia are quite literally fighting for their right to exist. America's 2003 war in Iraq definitely allowed for the festering of terrorism, but there was also the fact that the Shia were the majority in Iraq so anyone who had profound hate for Shia from around the region would come there so they could bomb them."

Bin Laden and Zawahiri expressed severe reservations about Zarqawi's grisly methods. They had hoped to mobilize a united Iraqi struggle first against the American and British occupiers before settling internal sectarian issues between Muslims. Zawahiri, a highly educated denizen of the Arab elite who had engaged with Muslims around the world, including on his 1992 speaking tour in California, saw Zarqawi as a destructive ruffian. He warned the young hothead that his penchant for videotaped beheadings only won over "zealous young men" while losing "the hearts and minds of our community." But Zarqawi was changing the facts on the ground through the application of terror, and gradually, he was forcing the Shia majority to respond. In 2004, Al Qaeda accepted his pledge of loyalty, establishing its first franchise in Iraq: Al Qaeda In Mesopotamia.

A year later, Chatham House, the NATO-funded British security consulting outfit, issued a paper concluding that the American invasion and occupation of Iraq had provided "a boost to the al Qaeda network's propaganda, recruitment and fundraising, caused a majority split in the coalition, and provided an ideal targeting and training area for al Qaeda linked terrorists." Abdel Bari Atwan, editor-in-chief of the Arabic daily *Al Quds Al Arabi* and a leading chronicler of Al Qaeda's rise, understood how the destabilization process that accompanied the American presence in the region had become a boon to jihadist elements. He warned at the time that "al Qaeda would also very much welcome a US military intervention in Syria."

In the meantime, the allied forces continued their attritional progress. By October 2006, the number of Iraqi civilian casualties stood at 665,000, according to the *Lancet*. The country had become a meat grinder, with the death count surging rapidly toward the million mark, thanks in no small part to the Western presence and the insurgency it spawned. By this point, Zarqawi was among the dead, killed in a US air strike on June 7. But he had already won the argument with Zawahiri.

On October 15, 2006, Al Qaeda's franchise in Iraq declared a caliphate and ordered all Sunni Muslims in the country to pledge allegiance to its new emir, a previously unknown character named Abu Umar al-Baghdadi. Slowly and haltingly, and with exceptional brutality, an Islamic state was coming to life in the heart of the Levant.

Israelification

The brutality behind the American attempts to suppress Iraq's mounting insurgency was on full display at the Abu Ghraib prison, where leaked photographs showed guards, some of them former employees of America's Supermax prisons, gleefully torturing nude prisoners with attack dogs and Marquis de Sade-style acts of sexual humiliation.

These scenes, first exposed by Seymour Hersh in the *New Yorker* in May 2004, were part of a range of allegations of grisly torture, brutality and even rape that were emerging. Hersh noted the influence of Patai's *The Arab Mind*—the "neocon Bible on Arab behavior," which portrayed Arabs as sexually dysfunctional primitives who only understood force—on the torture techniques implemented at Abu Ghraib. Intended to help guide a successful allied counterinsurgency program, the book and the torture it inspired wound up inflaming resistance to the occupation of Iraq.

As the insurgency intensified, the US military turned to Israel for lessons on military occupation, allowing Israeli officers to train American troops in urban warfare techniques based on their experience in razing the occupied West Bank's Jenin refugee camp in April 2002. American officers not only emulated these tactics at Fallujah, they adopted Israeli-style hunter-killer death squad tactics to take out insurgents, Sunni clerics and even politicians, deepening local hatred of the American presence. "It is bonkers, insane," a senior intelligence official complained. "We're already being compared to [Israeli prime minister and accused war criminal Ariel] Sharon in the Arab world, and we've just confirmed it by bringing in the Israelis and setting up assassination teams."

That program was informally known as the "Salvador Option," after the CIA-sponsored right-wing Contras that operated in the 1980s in Central America, often with Israeli training and arms. The man who led the assassination program was James Steele, a special-forces veteran who oversaw the training and daily operations of right-wing Salvadoran death squads during the CIA's Cold War–era covert operation in El Salvador. Steele dipped into an $8.3 billion slush fund overseen by General David Petraeus, his de facto boss and collaborator, to establish a special police commandos brigade comprised largely of Shia militia members.

Eager to exact revenge on the Sunni insurgents who had slaughtered members of their sect, the Shia fighters poured into Baghdad for training. When, after minimal training, Steele and Petraeus turned them loose in Iraq's Sunni Triangle, simmering sectarian tensions exploded. Thousands of dead bodies piled up on Iraqi streets each week, inadvertently ratifying Zarqawi's polarization strategy and swelling the ranks of the nascent Islamic state in response.

Steele's death squads were complemented by a network of secret torture centers—as many as fourteen in Baghdad—where Sunni insurgents were pumped for information in an almost literal sense. "If somebody gets arrested and we hand them over to [Iraq's Ministry of Interior] they're going to get their balls hooked, electrocuted or they're going to get beaten or raped up the ass with a coke bottle or something like that," an American soldier who arrested insurgents told the *Guardian*. Munthader

Samari, a former Iraqi general who worked with the United States to rebuild the country's police force after the neoconservatives' de-Ba'athification project, said he personally witnessed Steele near the torturing of prisoners. "He [the victim] was hanging upside down and Steele got up and just closed the door, he didn't say anything—it was just normal for him," Samari told the *Guardian*.

Under Petraeus' watch, the American military furthered sectarian rivalry by adopting the draconian Israeli tactic of encircling occupied enclaves with vast walls. In Iraq, the United States imposed these walls between Sunni and Shi'ite neighborhoods. Iraqis were keenly aware that the plan described by self-styled counterinsurgency master David Kilcullen as the "gated communities" strategy had made them Palestinian refugees in their own backyards.

"Iraq is a prison, and now I live in my own little prison," a resident of the Baghdad neighborhood of Adhamiya complained. "Adhamiya will be isolated from all the other areas. We'll be like the Palestinians, and we do not accept that."

The US military's fascination with Israeli occupation techniques inevitably blew back into American life as local police departments initiated training programs with their Israeli counterparts. This was largely thanks to a project overseen by the Jewish Institute for National Security of America (JINSA), the Jerusalem- and DC-based neoconservative think tank that had been advised by neocon Iraq War authors Douglas Feith and Richard Perle. Through its Law Enforcement Exchange Program (LEEP), JINSA claimed to have arranged Israeli-led training sessions for over 9,000 American law enforcement officials at the federal, state and municipal levels.

"The Israelis changed the way we do business regarding homeland security in New Jersey," Richard Fuentes, an ex-New Jersey state police superintendent, said after attending a 2004 JINSA-sponsored trip to Israel and a subsequent JINSA conference alongside 435 other law enforcement officers. Cathy Lanier, the former chief of the Washington, DC, metropolitan police, remarked, “No experience in my life has had more of an impact on doing my job than going to Israel.”

Among the most prominent Israeli government figure to have influenced the practices of American law enforcement officials is Avi Dichter, a right wing politician and former head of Israel’s Shin Bet. In 2002, Dichter guided a notorious assassination bombing in the Gaza Strip that resulted in the death of fifteen innocent people, including eight children, and 150 injuries. “After each success, the only thought is, ‘Okay, who’s next?’” Dichter said of the “targeted” assassinations he had ordered. Seated beside FBI director Robert Mueller and then attorney general Alberto Gonzalez at the 2006 convention of the International Association of Chiefs of Police, Dichter told the 10,000 police officers in the crowd that there is an “intimate connection between fighting criminals and fighting terrorists.” Dichter declared that American cops were actually “fighting crimiterrorists.” The *Jerusalem Post* reported that Dichter was “greeted by a hail of applause, as he was hugged by Mueller, who described Dichter as his mentor in antiterror tactics.”

The surge in arms manufacturing driven by the invasions of Afghanistan and Iraq left the Pentagon with more weapons systems than it could handle. In 2006, the Pentagon ushered in its 1033 Program, establishing a Law Enforcement Support Office that doled out almost 84,258 assault rifles and $699 million in military vehicles to local police departments across the country, including in small towns where violent crime was almost nonexistent. As a result, the Ohio State University campus police armored up with an eight-ton mine-resistant ambush protected vehicle (MRAP). Meanwhile, cops in the sleepy town of West Springfield, Massachusetts, obtained two M79 grenade launchers. The Department of Justice supplemented the flood of military-grade weaponry with the $111 million COPS Hiring Program that ensured a steady flow of Afghanistan and Iraq veterans into the ranks of local police departments.

An occupiers’ mentality toward policing blew back into American life from the post-9/11 militarization process, as a new breed of warrior cops treated American cities as havens of "crimiterrorists." Such fear seemed to play up a potential threat hiding among largely black and brown urban poor and immigrant communities. "They move unnoticed through our cities, neighborhoods, and public spaces. They wear no uniforms. Their camouflage is not forest green, but rather it is the color of common street clothing," Attorney General Ashcroft warned as he announced the National Security Entry-Exit Registration System (NSEERS). The program, initiated in 2002, was a de facto Muslim registry that authorized the surveillance of adult male visitors to the United States from twenty-five Muslim-majority countries and forced them to persistently check in with immigration officials.

The NYPD added another layer to the new surveillance regime by establishing a secret "Demographics Unit" designated to spy on and monitor Muslim communities around the city. The Israeli imprimatur on the unit was unmistakable. As a former police official told the Associated Press, the Demographics Unit attempted to "map the city's human terrain" through a program "modeled in part on how Israeli authorities operate in the West Bank."

The unit was developed with the input and intensive involvement of the CIA, which placed the former agency director of operations, David Cohen, inside the NYPD's intelligence division to oversee its implementation. Run at a cost of $60 million a year and with 600 employees, including Muslim cadets press-ganged into service as informants, the unit targeted Muslims on the basis of their religion and national origin. Cohen, according to reporters Adam Goldman and Matt Apuzzo, aimed to send "mosque crawlers" into every mosque and "rakers" into every hookah bar or business within a 250-mile radius, often to gauge community anger over US military activity in the Middle East. The NYPD's semisecret unit went as far as spying on the Muslim Students' Association at Yale University, located hundreds of miles from New York City.

The entire program was administered under the watch of NYPD commissioner Ray Kelly, a frequent visitor to conferences of Israeli securitocrats in Tel Aviv. In the end, it wound up disrupting the lives of an untold number of Muslim residents of the New York metropolitan area and a grand total of zero terror plots.

Born from the perception of Muslim communities in the West as a willing host body for terrorist plots, the new surveillance apparatus represented the domestic echo of the war on terror. Meanwhile, members of a new generation of veterans returning from Afghanistan and Iraq became symbols of the latest phase of the right wing's culture war.

No Worst Enemy

By the end of the Bush era, the pro-war consensus that prevailed after the trauma of 9/11 had been turned on its head. After five years of occupation, the American public's reflexive support for the invasion of Iraq had fallen by thirty-four percentage points. A Pew Research poll found that by mid-2007, a majority of Americans favored a comprehensive withdrawal of troops from the country. However, the polls could not measure the depth of resentment Americans felt toward the authors of the war, particularly the president and his advisors, as their sons and daughters came back with limbs missing from roadside explosives or, worse, in bodybags. By the end of 2008, 4,222 Americans had been killed in Iraq.

Corporal Cloy Richards helped lead the Marines' artillery barrage that preceded the American assault on Fallujah, then held by Al Qaeda and its allies. It was what was known as a "shake and bake" operation, in which a salvo of depleted uranium shells was followed by white phosphorous, an internationally banned substance that heats human flesh to 5,000 degrees Fahrenheit. Richards' mother, Tina, described to me how her son entered Fallujah after the artillery strike to discover "burned body parts of little kids, old women." His commanding officer dropped an AK-47 among the charred corpses and exclaimed, "Justified kill. They're all listed as insurgents."

"That was, I think, the moment that my son was completely

destroyed, and why, when he got back, he tried to commit suicide so many times," Tina Richards explained. "He had a shotgun in his mouth where I stopped him from pulling it. He can't seem to live with himself."

Richards managed to find a sense of redemption in antiwar activism, helping to lead the protest group Iraq Veterans Against the War and counseling other veterans struggling with post-traumatic stress. But countless others succumbed to the psychological wounds inflicted on the battlefield. In 2016, a Department of Veterans Affairs study concluded that as many as twenty veterans killed themselves each day—a staggering number that accounted for a full one fifth of all suicides in the country.

Then there were the veterans who projected their violent wrath outwards at the Muslims and Arabs they encountered after returning from the failed "war on terror." Ilario Pantano, a well-to-do New York University graduate and investment banker who enrolled in the marines after the shock of 9/11, distinguished himself in Iraq by firing sixty rounds into two Iraqi civilians, both detained in a car and unarmed, and even stopped to reload his M16A4 automatic rifle. When Pantano was done, he scrawled a phrase on a piece of cardboard and left it on the windshield of the car where his two victims' corpses lay. "NO BETTER FRIEND, NO WORST ENEMY," it read. It was the motto of General James "Mad Dog" Mattis, the marine commander in Iraq who testified as a witness in Pantano's subsequent trial for murder. The legal proceedings became a high-profile passion play that earned Pantano victim-hero status among the right-wing grassroots and translated into a run for Congress on an explicitly anti-Muslim platform.

Like Pantano, Republican Representative Allen West had returned from Iraq determined to make a career out of his resentment of Muslims and Islam. While serving in Iraq, West was discharged from the military and fined $5,000 after he brutally beat an Iraqi policeman, then fired his pistol behind the immobilized man's head. As in Pantano's case, reports of the disturbing incident only helped propel West to victory. After a campaign that saw members of a far-right biker gang, the Outlaws, serving as his private security team, West secured a seat in a solidly Republican district in south Florida. He made hectoring Muslims the centerpiece of his career, claiming Islam was "not a religion" but a "theo-political belief system and construct" that had to be crushed.

As the post-9/11 wars wound down in ignominious defeat, the American right found its hero in the battle-scarred terminator known simply as the "American Sniper." He was Chris Kyle, the Navy SEAL and serial fabricator who falsely claimed to have chalked up 160 "confirmed kills" in Fallujah, inflated the number of service medals he was awarded, and churned out tall tales about picking off black looters while perched atop the New Orleans Superdome during Hurricane Katrina. Kyle also told an unverified story about gunning down two carjackers at a gas station in Midlothian, Texas, claiming he sent police investigators away with a quick call to the Pentagon. He even claimed to have punched Jesse Ventura in a bar fight, a story that cost him $1.8 million when the former pro wrestler and Minnesota governor sued Kyle successfully for libel. When Kyle was killed at a shooting range by a fellow Iraq veteran suffering from post-traumatic stress disorder in February 2013, his celebrity only grew, making him the subject of a Clint Eastward-directed Hollywood blockbuster and martyr of the burgeoning populist right wing.

Marcus Luttrell, a fellow Navy SEAL and close friend of Kyle's, cultivated his right-wing cult status with the publication of his autobiography, *Lone Survivor*. The book was a memoir of Afghanistan, detailing his legendary battle with Taliban recruits on the Pakistani border that left him with a broken back and badly wounded leg. Luttrell chronicled how he was saved by Mohammad Gulab, a local timber worker who selflessly sheltered him from the Taliban and nursed him back to health before he was rescued by a team of army rangers. The publicity Gulab received in a bestselling paperback cast him as the noble Tonto to the gallant Lone Ranger, resulting in his name being added to a Taliban kill list and forcing him to seek sanctuary in Texas.

When Luttrell's book went into production as a major Hollywood feature starring Mark Wahlberg, Gulab could not resist contradicting key elements of the SEAL's story of courage under fire, even claiming his unit's target was not an international terrorist, but a marginal band of local bandits. Luttrell, who had become a multimillionaire with his own clothing and ammunition lines, cut Gulab loose. "He totally changed," Gulab told journalist R.M. Schneiderman. "If it wasn't for the movie, Marcus would never have asked me to come here."

Unable to obtain the green card Luttrell had promised him, Gulab returned to Afghanistan, where he was ruthlessly pursued by the Taliban and forced to take shelter for a time at the US embassy in Kabul. Meanwhile, Luttrell raked in millions in royalties and speaking fees, titillating his growing right-wing fan base by starring in a viral ad for the National Rifle Association in which he rumbled defiantly against "Islamic extremist[s] who would kill me for my beliefs."

"My freedom is more powerful than anything you can possibly do," Luttrell intoned at imaginary Muslim evildoers, "and I will never, *never* surrender my rights to your terror. I will say what I think, worship according to my beliefs and raise my children how I see fit. And I defend it all with the Second Amendment to the Constitution of the United States."

Islamophobia had become the language of a wounded empire, the guttural roar of its malevolent violence turned back from the sands of Iraq and the mountain passes of Afghanistan, and leveled against the mosque down the turnpike, the hijabi in the checkout line, the Sikh behind the cash register—the neighbors who looked like The Enemy. The "very hard war between Muslims and Westerners" that a member of bin Laden's inner circle had foreshadowed in 1996 was coming home.

5

The Counter-Jihad

Decades of American military interventions across the Muslim world, from proxy wars to invasions with "boots on the ground," had sent waves of immigrants and refugees fleeing rubble-strewn conflict zones for the safety of the West. Those recent arrivals and their children arrived to confront a new threat, as an incipient political movement held them under suspicion of plotting to undermine liberal democracy from within. The belief in "creeping Sharia," a conspiracy between Muslim civil society organizations and naive liberals to transform the West into Islamic-occupied territory—an adaptation of well-worn anti-Semitic tropes about Jewish influence—was gaining currency among a new coalition of right-wing populist forces that fancied themselves to be "counter-jihadists."

Like the jihadists they claimed to abhor, the so-called counter-jihadists organized across national boundaries, embraced a *takfiri* mind-set that branded co-religionists as sellouts for refusing to embrace its rigid worldview and expressed themselves in an often genocidal language. Movement adherents fed off of the extremist energy emanating from organizations like Al Qaeda, exploiting its violent imprecations to implicate the masses of Muslims as potential threats. The relationship between the counter-jihadists and jihadists was a comfortable, mutually reinforcing symbiosis that relied on a constantly escalating sense of antagonism.

A former Goldman Sachs vice president and longtime Hollywood hack named Steven Bannon was quick to recognize the power of the new anti-Muslim crusade. Bannon was a former Democrat who had begun dabbling in political film and online media, hoping to find the right vehicle to mobilize a right-wing populist insurgency against the ossified political establishment. In 2007, Bannon arranged a power lunch at an Italian restaurant in Washington with Steven Emerson to hash out a documentary film project called "Destroying the Great Satan: The Rise of Islamic Facism [sic] in America." The proposal that resulted from the meeting offered a neat distillation of the Islamophobia industry's emerging narrative.

Bannon's treatment envisioned the inauguration of an "Islamic States of America" thanks to a "fifth column" of "Islamic front groups" that "preach reconciliation and dialogue in the open but, behind the scenes, advocate hatred and contempt for the West." In Bannon's dystopian fantasy, Muslim "cultural jihadists" find allies among "the American Jewish community" and mainstream media as they push their stealthy plot to impose Sharia law. Bannon promised to introduce viewers to "an unbroken chain of 'thinkers' who epitomize the culture of hate" along with the avatars of the new counter-jihadist movement.

The cast of narrators that Bannon proposed represented a who's who of the growing Islamophobia industry. It included Walid Phares, a former commander of the Lebanese Forces militia that aimed to establish an exclusively Christian enclave modeled after Israel, its main military sponsor. During Lebanon's civil war, Phares worked in the Lebanese Fifth Bureau as a psychological warfare specialist. After moving to the United States, he marketed himself as a counterterror expert, earning a fellowship at the Foundation for Defense of Democracies, a neoconservative think tank with close ties to the Israeli military-intelligence apparatus.

Bannon's documentary treatment also called for on-screen "expert" commentary from Robert Spencer, a monomaniacal promoter of creeping Sharia theories at his blog, Jihad Watch, and author of tracts like *The Truth About Muhammad: Founder of the World's Most Intolerant Religion*. Spencer, a bookish, bespectacled pseudo-scholar, had forged a close partnership with Pamela Geller, a trash-talking former Long Island, New York, used car dealer given to video fulminations against "left-tards" and "Nazi Hezbollah." Together, they became the unusually prolific odd couple of the Islamophobia industry.

Like so many other counter-jihadists, Geller developed a fixation on the perceived threat that Muslims posed to the Western way of life after 9/11. She harnessed the new platform of blogging, founding a personal online journal, *Atlas Shrugged*, which emerged as one of the major hubs of anti-Muslim organizing. With $4 million she won in a 2007 divorce settlement with her ex-husband, Michael Oshry, Geller had unlimited amounts of free time to spin out elaborate tirades. Her ex, Oshry, wound up dying in 2008, a year after being indicted for an alleged $1.3 million criminal enterprise he was accused of running out of a Long Island used car dealership he co-owned with Geller. The scam had enabled mafia straw buyers to procure cars under false identities. After one of Oshry and Geller's cars was used in the murder of two New York police officers, an employee uncovered what appeared to be an illegal scheme. Soon after, the employee was found dead, the victim of an execution-style killing.

With $5 million in hand from her husband's life insurance policy, Geller invested it into a new outfit, Stop the Islamicization of America (SIOA), which she cofounded with Spencer. The group provided a new breed of grassroots anti-Muslim activists with step-by-step legal guides for preventing mosque construction. They were prepared with significant input from SIOA's in-house lawyer, David Yerushalmi, a Jewish white supremacist who lamented how "democracy has seeped through the cracks" and destroyed a political order previously controlled by "essentially Christian white men." Yerushalmi was also the author of a swath of bills introduced in

Republican-controlled statehouses across the country that banned the implementation of Sharia law, an extreme and purely symbolic initiative that nonetheless attracted a surge of support from the new generation of right-wing lawmakers organizing under the banner of the Tea Party Patriots.

Geller and Spencer's SIOA provided an online community for the most vitriolic Islamophobes to clamor for Muslim genocide. One meme posted on SIOA's site depicted American and British troops dropping a nuclear bomb in the midst of thousands of Muslim pilgrims in Mecca. "Who ya gonna call? Shitbusters," the meme read. A second image portraying a nuclear mushroom cloud declared: "DEALING WITH MUSLIMS—RULES OF ENGAGEMENT; Rule #1: Kill the Enemy. Rule #2: There is no rule #2." Another posted on SOIA's Facebook page displayed the bullet-riddled, blood-soaked bodies of Muslim civilians splayed by a roadside—it could have been a rendering of any of Pantano or Chris Kyle's Iraqi victims. "ARMY MATH," the caption read, "4 Tangos + (3 round burst × 4 M 4's) = 288 virgins."

Geller and Spencer's efforts benefited from a network of multimillionaire patrons cultivated by the veteran right-wing activist David Horowitz. A former communist agitator who turned to the hard right during the Reagan era, reaping millions of dollars in the process, Horowitz was an early promoter of the Islamophobia industry. His David Horowitz Freedom Center provided a tax-exempt nonprofit mechanism for transferring millions from ultra-Zionists like tech mogul Robert Shillman and the security industry baron Aubrey Chernick to anti-Muslim groups like SIOA and Spencer's Jihad Watch. Another top supporter of the Islamophobia industry, Sears Roebuck heiress Nina Rosenwald, also emerged from right-wing pro-Israel circles, funding Israel lobbying groups like AIPAC and JINSA while driving the rise of anti-Muslim politics across the West.

Horowitz organized "Islamofascism Awareness Week" on college campuses around America, delivering tirades before college Republican chapters, flanked by a cavalcade of grim private security guards. The national campaign provided a new generation of right-wing activists with a flood of outside resources and the sense that they were waging a transcendent civilizing mission. At Duke University in 2007, a student named Stephen Miller collaborated with Horowitz to establish a "Terrorism Awareness Project" that aimed to correct what he saw as academia's insufficient interest in "Islamofascism."

"American kids attend school in an educational system corrupted by the hard left. In this upside-down world, America is the villain and Jihadists the victims of our foreign policy," Miller wrote at the time. "Instead of opening eyes, we are fastening blindfolds." On campus, Miller worked closely with Richard Spencer, a classmate and fellow conservative activist who later emerged as the face and voice of the white nationalist movement in America. As advisors to the Duke Conservative Union, the duo organized screenings of anti-Muslim propaganda films and brought the white nationalist pundit Peter Brimelow to campus for a "debate" on immigration.

While at Duke, Miller also made common cause with Rabbi Ben Packer, an open supporter of the Meir Kahane and self-proclaimed "rabbi on campus." Packer invited Miller, who was Jewish, on a free tour of Israel through the so-called Birthright Israel program, then guided him around the ultra-right Jewish settlement communities in the occupied West Bank city of Hebron. "Stephen [Miller] thanked me for my efforts to show them around and remarked that 'putting on the Tefilin [Jewish holy phylacteries] at Machpelah was one of the most spiritual experiences of my life,'" Packer recalled.

Packer tapped his contacts in Jerusalem to link Miller with a figure at the center of the Islamophobia industry, a filmmaker who was building on the close bond between the pro-Israel lobby and the new generation of right-wing activists in the West. He was Raphael Shore, a Canadian-Israeli activist who worked at Aish HaTorah. Housed in a giant complex in Jerusalem's occupied Old City, Aish was a cipher for millions in donations from wealthy supporters of Israel. The center coordinated directly with Israel's Foreign Ministry to amplify Israel's public relations across the West. At Aish, Shore oversaw the creation of a film company, the Clarion Project, which became the central propaganda arm of the Islamophobia industry. He had accomplished what Steven Bannon failed to do in Hollywood.

During the 2008 American presidential election campaign, the Clarion Fund distributed 28 million DVDs of a film called *Obsession*, slipping it into newspapers as inserts that reached residents of swing states around the country. *Obsession* hewed closely with the narrative of Bannon's "Islamic States of America," introducing viewers to the self-styled experts of the Islamophobia industry, from Steven Emerson to Robert Spencer, and to the narrative of creeping Sharia. The mass mailing also capitalized on an ongoing right-wing disinformation effort to portray the Democratic Party's nominee, Senator Barack Obama, as a secret Muslim, born outside the United States.

Though the Clarion Fund's disinformation campaign failed to keep Obama out of the White House, the president became a convenient screen onto which to project the Islamophobia industry's phantasmagoria. With the rise of a "birther" movement that challenged Obama's American citizenship, thus calling his very legitimacy into question, Pam Geller published a lengthy series of posts claiming Obama was, in fact, the lovechild of Malcolm X.

Meanwhile, Frank Gaffney, the obsessively anti-Soviet former Reagan administration defense official, emerged as one of the Republican Party's key Islamophobia channels. Gaffney tendered donations from a combination of wealthy pro-Israel sources as well as arms industry giants like Raytheon, building his Center for Security Policy into the Islamophobia industry's central hub in Washington. His self-published book, *The Muslim Brotherhood in the Obama Administration*, gave birth to one of the most pernicious of the far right's conspiracy theories. The book's cover featured Hillary Clinton conferring with her aide, Huma Abedin, whom Gaffney accused of operating a secret Muslim Brotherhood cell inside Obama's State Department.

Despite its conspiratorial content and bigoted slant, the literature of the Islamophobia industry found an increasingly receptive audience within federal law enforcement circles.

Starting in 2009, the FBI's new recruits were exposed to curricula that included Patai's *The Arab Mind* and Spencer's *The Truth About Muhammad*. Meanwhile, agencies from the FBI down to local police departments called on the industry's network of hucksters for counterterror training. Among them was Walid Shoebat, a far-right confidence man who falsely marketed himself as a former Palestinian terrorist and who raked in speaking fees from the International Counter-Terrorism Officers Association as he ranted, "A secular dogma like Nazism is less dangerous than is Islamofascism today."

Sebastian Gorka, a Hungarian American ultra-nationalist with no military background and no academic expertise in Islam, was able to made a career as a counterterror instructor at Marine Corps University in Quantico, Virginia, and teach classes at the FBI's Counterterrorism Center. Gorka was a proud member of the Vitezi Rend, a Hungarian nationalist order whose founders collaborated with Nazi Germany's occupying authorities to organize the deportation of tens of thousands of Jews, and then battled with communists as Hungary fell under the control of the Soviet Union. He received his PhD from Corvinus University, a diploma mill in Budapest, under suspicious circumstances. His thesis on "the rise of the transcendentalist terror" was approved by his former co-author and a far-right Hungarian legislator who proposed placing pig's heads on spikes at the country's borders to deter Muslim migrants. Like many other self-styled counterterror experts, Gorka had spent no time in the Middle East and did not speak Arabic.

Despite Gorka's apparent lack of credentials, he was hired as the lead instructor for the Special Operations Combating Terrorism course at Fort Bragg's JFK School of Special Warfare. (The same special operations center that had employed Ali Mohamed while he spied for Al Qaeda.) "Dr. Gorka has a long history as an Associate Fellow and instructor at the Joint Special Operations University," US Special Operations Command public affairs officer Kenneth McGraw told me. According to McGraw, Gorka provided "strategic analysis and education about counterterrorism and irregular warfare."

Just as the military and law enforcement drew from the ranks of the Islamophobia industry, anti-Muslim forces placed irate veterans of the failed wars in the Middle East alongside retired federal officials at the front of protest rallies that increasingly focused on mosque construction around the country. Besides Pantano and West, the industry found eager recruits in Gary Berntsen, a CIA team leader in the failed raid at Tora Bora, and Andrew McCarthy, the former federal attorney who oversaw the prosecution of the "Blind Sheikh," Abdel-Rahman, while allegedly coaching the triple agent Ali Mohamed to avoid testifying and blowing his cover. While Berntsen ran a long-shot Tea Party campaign against Democratic Senator Charles Schumer, touting his support for the summary execution of all prisoners at Guantanamo Bay and the use of torture, McCarthy pushed Islamophobic conspiracy theories in a series of books that included *How Obama Embraces Islam's Sharia Agenda*.

Berntsen and McCarthy were star speakers at the highest profile anti-Muslim rally in American history. It took place on July 7, 2010, as hundreds of right-wing zealots gathered in downtown Manhattan to protest the planned construction of an Islamic community center by Feisal Abdul Rauf, a demonstratively moderate Sufi Muslim imam who regularly traveled abroad representing the United States at the behest of the State Department. Geller had organized the protest and demanded "a center to the victims of hundreds of millions of years of jihadi wars, land enslavements, cultural annihilations and mass slaughter" in place of what she called Rauf's "Ground Zero mosque." Her rally treated the ruins of the World Trade Center as a holy shrine, the Kaaba of the counter-jihadists, and the presence of Muslims in its proximity as a contaminant. Former House speaker and Republican presidential wannabe Newt Gingrich reinforced the righteous narrative when he compared the planned community center to a Nazi sign next to the Holocaust Memorial Museum.

Though Geller claimed credit for the antimosque movement, the campaign would not have become a national outrage were it not for the beneficence of the reclusive billionaire hedge funder

Robert Mercer, who paid for a $1 million ad blitz against the center's construction. The ads were part of a much wider agenda that relied on Mercer's millions. By this point, the billionaire had teamed up with Steven Bannon and the hot-tempered Internet entrepreneur Andrew Breitbart to establish an online media empire that would serve as a hub for a far-right insurgency against the Obama administration.

The idea to launch the Breitbart News Network arrived in 2007 when Breitbart and a group of right-wing bloggers were junketed to Israel for one of the government's routine propaganda tours. After a meeting with Benjamin Netanyahu at the Likud Party's Jerusalem offices, Breitbart convinced Larry Solov, a wealthy lawyer from Los Angeles, to invest in his media empire. "I decided right there and then to 'throw away' (my Mom's phrase) a perfectly good, successful and safe career in order to start a 'new media' company with Andrew Breitbart out of his basement and my home office," Solov recalled.

Under Breitbart's direction and with Mercer's millions, the online media network emerged as a force in national politics with a series of sting-style operations against liberal activist groups. Breitbart thrived off his image as the Internet's most influential troll and mobilized an army of beta male underlings against Obama and the Democratic Party. Hovering on the periphery of Breitbart's political network was Bannon, a figure he praised as "the Leni Riefenstahl of the Tea Party movement." Unlike Breitbart, Bannon had a coherent political vision for the future of the West under far-right rule.

Though Breitbart cultivated a moderate image, promoting black and gay conservatives wherever he could find them, he and Bannon were united by an obsessive resentment of an ideology they described as "cultural Marxism." The two had been heavily influenced by a short documentary produced by the right-wing Free Congress Foundation and called *The Roots of Political Correctness*. The film was produced by William Lind, an iconoclastic right-wing intellectual and military theorist. A subscriber to the "retroculture" movement, which emphasized rejecting modern tech culture and postmodern thought, Lind struck a strong contrast with Breitbart, the perpetually wired, social media-savvy online impresario. Lind lived in Cleveland, Ohio, in the home where his parents raised him, and worked without email, a cell phone or even a computer. There, he produced all of his writing on an IBM Selectric typewriter that he regularly repaired with tweezers and a hammer.

Lind told me his lifestyle was "a response to the catastrophe brought on by cultural Marxism of the generation of elites in the 1960s. We have to go back to the way we used to live, and we know it works."

Lind's documentary on political correctness charted the origins of cultural Marxism back to a collection of mostly Jewish socialist intellectuals who fled Nazi Germany following Hitler's rise to power. Calling themselves the Frankfurt School, these academics brought to American shores "the vehicle that translated Marxism from economic to cultural terms, giving us what we now know as political correctness ... a cultural revolution against Western society," Lind said.

The Frankfurt Group's landmark studies of authoritarianism in America encouraged the standard bearers of political correctness to label their opponents as fascists and to subject them to psychological therapy in the form of "sensitivity training," Lind's documentary alleged. Amid the 1960s counterculture, they provided the inspiration for the birth of critical theory, the postmodern academic trend that took the form of courses in gender studies, black studies and gay studies. Lind and his collection of talking heads, including the radical leftist-turned-far-right provocateur David Horowitz, posited this development as nothing short of an anti-American plot.

Having given up on the American working class as a revolutionary vanguard, according to Lind, the Frankfurt Group turned instead to victimized minority groups—gays, blacks, women and immigrants—as its vanguard. Political correctness was their enforcement method, enabling them to impose "radical multiculturalism" on white men and shatter the foundations of traditionally Judeo-Christian Western societies. The narrative rang true to a new generation of campus conservatives gripped with the sense that they were under siege by intolerant leftists.

Together, Bannon and Breitbart aimed to give birth to an alternative right united by the resentment of political correctness, concepts like "safe spaces" and hypersensitive liberal "snowflakes." They ingested identity politics and spit it out in reactionary form, helping to spawn a movement that upheld the straight white male as the persecuted target of the elitist establishment. "With cultural Marxism, the left created a white political consciousness and very few whites are going to vote for the left now," Lind reflected to me. "The identity politics has screwed them."

Following Breitbart's collapse on a sidewalk outside his home and sudden death at age forty-three, Bannon took control of the Breitbart News Network. He set about galvanizing a new coalition of hyper-nationalist forces capable of stirring up middle American resentment against the Republican establishment and ultimately supplanting it, transforming his online empire into what he pithily described as "a platform for the alt-right." On the side, he pressed ahead with his interest in political documentaries, producing *Generation Zero*, a film that blamed the financial collapse on cultural Marxism and the social and racial permissiveness of the 1960s—not on Wall Street greed.

Among Bannon's significant hires at Breitbart was Julia Hahn, a hyper-ambitious online writer in her early twenties who hailed from the same affluent Southern California environment as Stephen Miller. Hahn's top contributions to the newly weaponized Breitbart included a 4,000-word essay on an obscure French novel that Bannon described as one of his favorite political tracts. Titled *The Camp of the Saints*, the book was authored by Jean Raspail, a leading voice of the French New Right that transmuted traditional anti-Semitism into resentment of the country's Arab immigrants. Raspail weaved a lurid narrative depicting black- and brown-skinned migrants holding orgies on rickety boats overflowing with "rivers of sperm, streaming over bodies, oozing between breasts, and buttocks, and thighs, and lips, and fingers." Pointing to the Middle Eastern refugee crises deluging Europe with waves of migrants, Hahn concluded that "all around the world, events seem to be lining up with the predictions of the book."

Bannon clearly sought to transplant the clash of civilizations narrative into domestic politics, with Muslim immigrants and their "cultural Marxist" defenders as the target of a reborn "alt-right." In a 2011 radio appearance, he spun out an apocalyptic scenario that bore echoes of bin Laden's grand narrative but also recalled neoconservative visions of a Fourth World War: "Against radical Islam, we're in a 100-year war."

That year, events aligned in favor of Bannon and his ideological fellow travelers, fanning the flames of Islamophobia to unprecedented heights.

A Focusing Event

The mainstreaming of anti-Muslim politics in America was thanks in no small part to the proliferation of Islamophobic propaganda by a well-funded network of online media outlets and the growing presence of the far right on social media. But a less understood factor in the onslaught of Islamophobia was the persistence of Al Qaeda and its offshoots after a decade-long "war on terror" that had cost American taxpayers untold billions.

After two campaigns of regime change deceptively sold under the banner of a "war on terror," US troops were still in Afghanistan in 2011, where they were battling two of the CIA's former favorites, Islamist warlords Hekmatyar and Jalaluddin Haqqani. In 2007, a "surge" of American troops to Iraq's Sunni-dominated Anbar province had been sold as a silver bullet against Al Qaeda, the product of the sophisticated COIN (counterinsurgency) doctrine honed by Petraeus and his understudy, H.R. McMaster. But as soon as American payments to the Sunni tribes involved in the so-called Anbar Awakening ended, their loyalty did as well.

The so-called "war on terror" expanded with each passing

day, with drone strikes across seven countries and special forces seeing action around the globe, yet the one figure that triggered the war, Osama bin Laden, was still at large. For a decade, bin Laden had remained the singular face of terror in the American mind—perhaps the only international terrorist with national name recognition. For most of those who experienced the shock of 9/11, killing him was paramount and the rest was commentary.

On the evening of May 1, 2011, Obama strode out of the West Wing and appeared before the media for an impromptu press conference.

After lengthy remarks about the horror of 9/11, the president emphasized that he made "the killing or capture of bin Laden the top priority of our war against Al Qaeda." Finally, he revealed that after receiving a "possible lead" about bin Laden's whereabouts at a "compound deep inside Pakistan," he had authorized an operation. Obama claimed that following a "firefight," an American special-forces team had killed the Al Qaeda leader. He then thanked Pakistan's ISI for its cooperation in hunting down bin Laden.

"The American people did not choose this fight. It came to our shores and started with the senseless slaughter of our citizens," Obama concluded, casting the United States as an island of innocence targeted by irrational maniacs and whitewashing the American role in fueling Al Qaeda's creation.

Obama's remarks raised serious questions about the raid that killed bin Laden and opened the door for skepticism. Indeed, there was reason to believe that well before members of the CIA-led SEAL Team Six had rappelled from a Blackhawk helicopter, barged into bin Laden's house in Abbottabad, Pakistan—not a "compound," as Obama called it—the terror financier's coordinates were no secret.

Seymour Hersh, the veteran journalist, reported in 2015 that bin Laden had been in the custody of Pakistan intelligence since 2006, and that the Saudi royal family was paying Pakistan to keep bin Laden under a form of house arrest, just down the road from a major intelligence station, in the resort city of Abbotabad. For the Pakistani ISI, keeping bin Laden under its watch provided it with a line to jihadist cells in the disputed region of Kashmir, where it deployed them against India.

Hersh's revelations paralleled those previously reported by the *New York Times*' Carlotta Gall, who had also noted that the Pakistani military knew of bin Laden's whereabouts. There was also the journalism of R.J. Hillhouse, an academic and intelligence expert who relied on apparently separate sources to publish a strikingly similar account of bin Laden's death in 2011. The reports of Pakistani collaboration with Saudi Arabia to maintain control over jihadist proxies had the ring of truth as well; the dynamic harkened back to the role the two nations had played against the Soviets in Afghanistan.

Like Hersh, Hillhouse reported that the United States had planned to wait until a week or two after the raid before announcing (falsely) that bin Laden had been killed on the Afghan-Pakistani border in a drone strike. But with a tough re-election battle coming up and right-wing elements painting him as everything from a terrorist mollycoddler to a foreign-born crypto-Muslim, Obama's dramatic press conference could hardly wait.

Within minutes of Obama's late-night announcement, thousands of revelers spontaneously appeared outside the White House and in downtown Manhattan, waving flags and hand-scrawled signs featuring messages like, "America Fuck Yeah." College students scaled street lamps to spray champagne on the crowds below, and rambunctious frat boys alternated between drunken renditions of the national anthem and the Miley Cyrus hit, "Party in the USA." In the middle of a World Wrestling Entertainment Extreme Rules match, pro wrestling hero John Cena strode shirtless and drenched in sweat into the middle of the ring to announce that "Oh-sama bin Laden" had been "compromised to a permanent end." Pandemonium broke out, followed by chants of "USA! USA! USA!" A similar scene took place at Philadelphia's Veterans Stadium, where fans interrupted an otherwise dull pitcher's duel between the Phillies and Mets with innings worth of nationalistic chanting.

By the time of his death, bin Laden was a bedraggled, home-bound shadow of his former self, a semiretired basement dweller who was much more a symbol of international terrorism than an operational shot caller. Much of his influence had been transferred to Zawahiri, his longtime éminence grise, and was increasingly outsourced to the commanders of Al Qaeda's local franchises. By dangling bin Laden's figurative corpse before the American public, however, Obama imbued the gray-bearded jihadist with ferocious power and restored his mystique.

Instead of fostering a sense of closure among Americans, the killing of bin Laden drove vengeful anti-Muslim attitudes to an all-time high. A poll by Erik Nisbet, a researcher at Ohio State University, revealed that the percentage of Americans who believed that Muslims living in the United States "increased the likelihood of a terrorist attack" surged to 34 percent—a whopping 27 percent surge from prior to the killing. While conservatives' almost invariably hostile views of Muslims remained largely static after bin Laden's death, liberal suspicion of followers of Islam spiked dramatically, with 24 percent of them agreeing with the statement that Muslims "make America a more dangerous place to live." Before the wall-to-wall coverage of bin Laden's death, only 8 percent of self-declared liberals had voiced such an opinion.

"The death of bin Laden was a focusing event. There was a lot of news coverage and a lot of discussion about Islam and Muslims and Muslim Americans," Nisbet explained. "The frenzy of media coverage reminded people of terrorism and the September 11 attacks and it primed them to think about Islam in terms of terrorism."

Though thousands of Americans had partied in the streets as though the "war on terror" had finally been won, Nisbet found that the event had only inflamed their fears. The fears of those Americans would soon be realized, though not necessarily as retaliation for bin Laden's killing. The beer-soaked revelers cheering the raid could have never imagined that the Obama administration was set to embark on a series of foreign policy follies that would deliver Al Qaeda and its offshoots with US arms and unprecedented power in the heart of the Middle

East—a posthumous victory for bin Laden amid the tumult of the so-called Arab Spring. These ill-conceived imperial disasters would spawn a new refugee crisis, accelerate the rise of the far right in Europe and bring its influence to previously unimaginable heights in Washington.

Into the Abyss

The next American-led regime change catastrophe was set in Libya, a country that had largely shed its deterrent capacity in a desperate bid to normalize relations with the West.

Libyan strongman Muammar Gaddafi had held his country together for forty years with a combination of political repression, a cult of personality and social welfare programs that guaranteed citizens full access to education and health care. Under his rule, "gays, beer drinkers and pot smokers all say they could get away with a lot, as long as they never hinted at opposing the regime," noted the *Washington Post*'s Marc Fisher.

After years of diplomatic isolation stemming from his support of anticolonial armed movements like the PLO and African National Congress, as well as harsh sanctioning for his perceived role in the terrorist bombing of Pan Am flight 103, Gaddafi had taken considerable steps to normalize with the West. He had formally abandoned his nuclear program, which was barely at an embryonic phase. He also handed over Libya's stockpile of chemical weapons, the centerpiece of its strategy of deterrence against outside invasion. Gaddafi's government even took out a contract with a lobbying firm in Boston, the Monitor Group, to "introduce to Libya important international figures that will influence other nations' policies towards the country." Academics and elite policymakers like Anne-Marie Slaughter were junketed to the country and came away with mostly positive impressions.

But for all his concessions, and they were many, Gaddafi held fast to his ambitions to lead in an independent direction. The political anthropologist Maximilian Forte demonstrated in his book-length survey of the Libyan catastrophe, *Slouching*

Towards Sirte, that Gaddafi could never be compliant enough to satisfy Washington. Gaddafi infuriated the George W. Bush administration, for instance, when he denied a contract to Bechtel, the oil service firm that had enriched scores of US government officials, most notably Vice President Cheney. Gaddafi also delivered a browbeating to the CEO of ConocoPhillips, demanding that he pressure Washington into halting its exploitative actions against Libya. Most crucially, Gaddafi embraced a Pan-Africanist foreign policy that placed him in direct conflict with AFRICOM, the pro-Western coalition that represented the main vehicle for American financial and military interests on the African continent.

In February 2011, as the protest wave branded the "Arab Spring" gathered steam, an armed insurgency erupted in Libya. The governments of France and Britain clamored for military action to propel the rebellion. Though the Obama administration could not come to a consensus on whether there was any concrete American interest in intervening, the president had "signed a secret finding authorizing the CIA to provide arms and other support to Libyan rebels," according to the *New York Times*. CIA operatives were already on the ground across the country, the paper noted. Sensing that an Iraq-style invasion was on the horizon, Gaddafi reached out to Tony Blair, the former British prime minister who had cut the "deal in the desert" that brought Gaddafi out of the wilderness in 2004.

In a series of panicked phone calls that day, Gaddafi warned Blair that his removal would open the floodgates for a jihadist takeover. "I want to tell you the truth," he said to Blair. "It is not a difficult situation at all. The story is simply this: an organization has laid down sleeper cells in North Africa called the Al Qaeda organization in North Africa. They don't use Arabic words, they use Islamic [ones]. The sleeper cells in Libya are similar to the ones in America before 9/11."

Gaddafi then mentioned the name of a former Guantanamo detainee who had joined Al Qaeda and trained at a camp run by bin Laden in Afghanistan. He was referring to Abu Sufian Ibrahim Ahmed Hamuda bin Qumu, a member of the LIFG who had been captured by the United States in Pakistan thanks to a tip from Gaddafi's own intelligence services. Gaddafi complained that Qumu was now leading the forces seeking his ousting, a claim confirmed by the *Wall Street Journal* two months later when it described the rebel leader as "a US ally of sorts." He predicted that if they succeeded, they would set up an Islamic State in the country, or what he called an "Al Qaeda Emirate."

Blair brushed Gaddafi's ominous warnings aside and calmly urged him to relinquish power through a "peaceful transition." A week later, Obama declared, "Muammar Gaddafi has lost legitimacy to lead and he must leave." That same month, as the insurgency intensified with the help of a flood of weapons from the United States and Qatar, Gaddafi issued another warning about the consequence of his removal, this one a direct appeal to Europe's right-wing antimigrant forces. "There are millions of blacks who could come to the Mediterranean to cross to France and Italy, and Libya plays a role in security in the Mediterranean," he told France 24.

Gaddafi's son, Saif, sounded a similar note, declaring at the time, "Libya may become the Somalia of North Africa, of the Mediterranean. You will see the pirates in Sicily, in Crete, in Lampedusa [the Italian island home of migrant detention facilities]. You will see millions of illegal immigrants. The terror will be next door."

A secret 2008 US embassy cable had corroborated Gaddafi's presentation of his regime as a bulwark of stability. "Libya has been a strong partner in the war against terrorism and cooperation in liaison channels is excellent," the cable read.

> Muammar al-Qadhafi's criticism of Saudi Arabia for perceived support of Wahabi [sic] extremism, a source of continuing Libya-Saudi tension, reflects broader Libyan concern about the threat of extremism. Worried that fighters returning from Afghanistan and Iraq could destabilize the regime, the [government of Libya] has aggressive[ly] pursued operations to disrupt foreign fighter flows, including more stringent monitoring of air/land ports of entry, and blunt the ideological appeal of radical Islam.

The author of that cable was a longtime foreign service officer named J. Christopher Stevens.

Stupid, Stupid Facts

The American decision to lead NATO's military intervention in Libya was the brainchild of a group of foreign policy ideologues nested in the Obama administration and united by their faith in military humanism. Unlike the neoconservatives, who made the case for unilateral armed interventions on the messianic grounds of eradicating "evil," these liberals argued for military action out of the urgent need for "civilian protection," or to prevent a genocide that appeared imminent. Whenever trouble arose, they reflexively advocated for "no-fly zones" and "safe zones" where only American attack jets could operate, and asserted the authority to do so without UN Security Council or US congressional approval, always in the name of saving some group supposedly threatened with imminent destruction.

The military humanists marketed their doctrine of preemptive military action as "Responsibility To Protect," or R2P. By weaponizing the discourse of human rights to justify the use of force against governments that resisted the Washington consensus, this group of well-connected liberals was able to stir support where the neocons could not. Their brand of interventionism appealed directly to the sensibility of the Democratic Party's metropolitan base, large swaths of academia, the foundation funded human rights NGO complex, and the *New York Times* editorial board. The exhibition of atrocities allegedly committed by adversarial governments, either by Western-funded civil society groups, major human rights organizations or the mainstream press, was the military humanists' stock in trade, enabling them to mask imperial designs behind a patina of "genocide prevention." With this neat tactic, they effectively neutralized progressive antiwar elements and tarred those who dared to protest their wars as dictator apologists.

Samantha Power was the celebrity icon of military humanism.

Standing close to six feet tall, with a long strawberry blonde mane and given to effusive gestures, Power gained renown among the pack of Western journalists who descended on the killing fields of Yugoslavia in the 1990s. As the country was split into pieces, she wrote George Orwell-style dispatches highlighting Serb brutality and the urgent need for intervention. "In 1995, the same year Power enrolled at Harvard Law School, NATO bombed Serb forces, and she rejoiced. She told me, 'These guys who had been terrorizing these people were going to be stopped!'" the *New Yorker*'s Evan Osnos wrote in a profile of Power.

In her Pulitzer Prize–winning book, *A Problem From Hell*, Power lashed out at "bystanders to genocide" and exposed the failures of "people in offices" in Washington who had missed countless opportunities to halt the mass killing in Rwanda. Her polemic became the bible of military humanism. Soon enough, she presided over her own "human rights center" at Harvard's Kennedy School of Government, was hailed as the "femme fatale of the humanitarian-assistance world" by journalist Tara McKelvey, and earned the title "the Smartest Woman in America" from the fashion magazine *Marie Claire*.

When Obama entered the Oval Office, he appointed Power as senior director for multilateral affairs and human rights on the National Security Council. The important-sounding job seemed custom tailored for America's smartest woman. Power found a kindred spirit in the US ambassador to the United Nations, Susan Rice (no relation to Condoleezza), a fellow product of elite academic institutions who had a similar thirst for promotion. While serving in the Clinton administration, Rice had been one of the officials that Power accused of being "bystanders to genocide" in Rwanda. But when the Libyan civil war broke out, Rice was handed the perfect opportunity to atone for her past sins, and she leapt at it with full force. For her part, Power finally had the opportunity to put her principles to the test. Power "really put on the agenda the use of military power to respond to what was happening [in Libya], at a time when the President wasn't sure," recalled Dennis Ross, then one of Obama's top Middle East advisors.

Power and Rice found an eager patron in Secretary of State Hillary Clinton, a reliable champion of military action from the former Yugoslavia to Iraq. Clinton's director of policy planning, Anne Marie Slaughter, was the intellectual author of the R2P doctrine. She urged Clinton to ignore those voices warning that removing Gaddafi would spawn chaos: "People will say that we will then get enmeshed in a civil war, that we cannot go into another Muslim country, that Gaddafi is well armed, there will be a million reasons NOT to act," Slaughter emailed Clinton. "But all our talk about global responsibility and leadership, not to mention respect for universal values, is completely empty if we stand by and watch this happen with no response but sanctions."

At a March 14, 2011, meeting in Paris arranged by the French celebrity philosopher Bernard Henri-Lévy, a dedicated interventionist who claimed credit for the West's intervention in Libya, Clinton made up her mind to push for war. There, Clinton was lobbied by Mahmoud Jibril, a former University of Pittsburgh international relations professor and ex-Gaddafi official now leading the National Transitional Council (NTC) that intended to replace Gaddafi. With Clinton apparently eager to place a successful intervention on her resume—what is known in Washington as a "democratic transition"—Jibril became her personal Ahmad Chalabi.

"I talked extensively about the dreams of a democratic state ... and how the international community should protect civilians from a possible genocide like the one [that] took place in Rwanda," Jibril told the *Washington Times*. "I felt by the end of the meeting I passed the test. [Opposition stronghold] Benghazi was saved."

"They gave us what we wanted to hear. And you do want to believe," Clinton's assistant secretary, Philip Gordon, later admitted.

Obama, who had devoted his 2009 Nobel Peace Prize lecture to challenging Europe's "deep ambivalence about military action" and "reflexive suspicion of America," wilted under intense lobbying from the triad of Clinton, Power and Rice. According to then secretary of defense Robert Gates, a staunch opponent of the Libyan intervention, the youthful idealists he derided as "backbenchers" convinced Obama that amid the revolutionary ferment of the Arab Spring, the president had to be "on the right side of history."

On March 17, the UN Security Council authorized a no-fly zone over Libya. That same day, Gaddafi's son, Saif, offered a ceasefire and transition of power to the United States. A Pentagon official described the fig leaf as "a peaceful solution ... that keeps Saif on our side without any bloodshed in Benghazi." But Clinton immediately shut the initiative down, opting for a war for regime change that threatened the lives of tens of thousands.

Clinton was so wedded to war and averse to what an American intermediary described as "stupid, stupid facts," that some Democratic members of Congress and the Pentagon opened a separate channel of communication with Gaddafi. In one conversation between Saif Gaddafi and American officials, Gaddafi warned that the Libyan insurgents were "not freedom fighters" but a collection of "gangsters and terrorists."

"And now you have NATO supporting them with ships, with airplanes, helicopters, arms, training, communication," he lamented in vain. "We ask the American government [to] send a fact-finding mission to Libya. I want you to see everything with your own eyes."

By the time NATO entered the conflict, Gaddafi's forces had recaptured most of Libya's cities at a cost of about 1,000 dead, including hundreds of government soldiers. In his meticulous study of the intervention, Alan Kuperman of Harvard's Belfer Center for Science and International Affairs concluded, "Qaddafi did not perpetrate a 'bloodbath' in any of the cities that his forces recaptured from rebels prior to NATO intervention ... so there was virtually no risk of such an outcome if he had been permitted to recapture the last rebel stronghold of Benghazi."

Yet Clinton justified the intervention on the basis of preventing an imminent slaughter in Benghazi, or what the liberal legal scholar David Cole forecasted in classic military humanist language as "another Srebrenica." Soliman Bouchuiguir of the

Libyan League for Human Rights, a Geneva-based exile group tied to the NTC, conjured up the perfect appeal to the liberal sensibility, predicting "a real bloodbath, a massacre like we saw in Rwanda." Obama echoed the apocalyptic rhetoric, proclaiming, "Gaddafi threatens a bloodbath that could destabilize an entire region," and boasted that he "refused to wait for the images of slaughter and mass graves before taking action."

Rice took the humanitarian hysteria to new heights, claiming without a shred of evidence that Gaddafi was handing out supplies of Viagra to his troops to encourage mass rape. The risible allegation, first broadcast by the Qatari-run outlet Al Jazeera, was soon picked up by the BBC and Associated Press. Luis Moreno-Ocampo, the chief prosecutor of the International Criminal Court, declared excitedly, "There's some information with Viagra. So, it's like a machete. It's new. Viagra is a tool of massive rape."

A Libya inquiry by the British House of Commons' bipartisan Foreign Affairs Committee later exposed the hysterical rhetoric emanating from Washington as untrustworthy. "Despite his rhetoric," the British report found, "the proposition that Muammar Gaddafi would have ordered the massacre of civilians in Benghazi was not supported by the available evidence ... In short, the scale of the threat to civilians was presented with unjustified certainty."

The report also concluded that a network of Libyan expats waged a propaganda campaign designed to accelerate military action by NATO in the name of saving lives. "Émigrés opposed to Muammar Gaddafi exploited unrest in Libya by overstating the threat to civilians and encouraging Western powers to intervene," the inquiry concluded, summarizing findings by George Joffé, a Middle East and North Africa expert from King's College, London University. But the Obama administration and its allies were not about to let these "stupid, stupid facts" get in the way.

The NATO assault on Libya ended in Sirte, where Gaddafi had announced his Pan-Africanist "Al-Fateh Revolution" back in 1969. The city had become the site of some of the war's worst atrocities, committed not by Gaddafi's soldiers but by NATO during a seven-month-long bombing campaign that blanketed the country with more than 7,700 missiles. A *New York Times* investigation found "scores of civilian casualties the [US-led] alliance has long refused to acknowledge or investigate" in Sirte, while reporters who entered the city after the bombing campaign discovered some sixty corpses splayed out on the lawn of the Mahari Hotel, all Gaddafi loyalists killed execution style by the Islamist rebels. When the International Red Cross was finally able to access the city, it discovered "at least" 200 more corpses. In towns like Tawergha, thousands of mostly black residents were killed or ethnically cleansed by Western-backed Islamist rebels, who accused them of loyalty to Gaddafi and cast them as foreign mercenaries. The avatars of military humanism had apparently felt no responsibility to protect these civilians.

The most famous casualty of the rebels' march on Sirte was Gaddafi himself. As the insurgents charged into the city on flatbed technical trucks and in tanks, bristling with advanced weaponry supplied by the United States and its Gulf allies, Gaddafi's convoy assembled and attempted to escape. It did not get far before it was struck by a Hellfire missile from an American drone controlled by a joystick jockey from thousands of miles away inside an air base near Las Vegas. The convoy then came under attack by French warplanes. With at least fifty mutilated bodies lying about, the rebels riddled the convoy with bullets, sending Gaddafi and his bodyguards staggering out of their vehicles to seek cover in a drainage pipe. The rebels captured Gaddafi after executing his black African bodyguards, then proceeded to sodomize him with a bayonet. Finally, they shot him in the head and chest and paraded his ravaged corpse atop a car.

By late October, Sirte was in ruins and on its way toward becoming a base of the "Islamic emirate" Gaddafi had warned that his opponents aimed to establish. Meanwhile, Gaddafi's body was laid out to rot on a cheap mattress on the floor of a meat store in Misrata, a gruesome rebel trophy for cell phone victory selfies. When Clinton learned of the strongman's killing during a series of interviews in Tripoli, she lit up with glee. "We came, we saw, he died!" she exclaimed with a self-satisfied cackle.

Liberal cheerleaders of the Obama administration's gruesome intervention celebrated the NATO intervention as "a reminder that sometimes it is possible to use military tools to advance humanitarian causes," as the *New York Times*' in-house liberal interventionist Nicholas Kristof put it. But they were hardly prepared for its aftermath.

Libyan Patriots

The British Foreign Affairs Committee report issued in the House of Commons was perhaps the most authoritative autopsy on the NATO war of regime change that targeted Libya. In one of its most damning passages, the report concluded that the UK, France and its American allies had little idea about the ideological composition of their Libyan armed proxies, and even less interest in vetting them. "Intelligence on the extent to which extremist militant Islamist elements were involved in the anti-Gaddafi rebellion was inadequate," the report found.

"The possibility that militant extremist groups would attempt to benefit from the rebellion should not have been the preserve of hindsight," the committee concluded. "Libyan connections with transnational militant extremist groups were known before 2011, because many Libyans had participated in the Iraq insurgency and in Afghanistan with Al Qaeda."

In the rush for American influence in North Africa and control of Libya's mineral resources, the Obama administration had abandoned any reasonable caution. The blowback from arming Islamist proxy groups during the Cold War had been enormous, culminating in the 9/11 attacks, and the invasion of Iraq that followed had handed Al Qaeda its first opportunity to hold territory and declare an Islamic state. But when America's allies in Qatar and the United Arab Emirates began dumping weapons into Libya, funneling them into the hands of the most hard-line Islamist elements, the Obama administration decided that the most prudent move would be to send weapons of its own to rebels it had judged to be "moderate."

(At the time, some self-styled left-wing academics slammed "anti-imperialist polemics" for undermining "the imperative for solidarity with the Libyan rebels," whom they marketed as "reformist revolutionaries.")

Clinton framed arming the rebels as a means to get some American "skin in the game," according to her Middle East advisor, Dennis Ross. In practice, this nakedly imperial gambit entailed arming the supposedly "moderate" rebels overseen by the NTC. Ignoring warnings from NATO's supreme allied commander, Admiral James Stavridis, about the presence of Al Qaeda in the opposition, Obama approved shipments of TOW missiles, armored Humvees and advanced radar systems to the insurgents.

When she learned of the newly armed rebels' rapid advances, Clinton reportedly exclaimed, "Good! This is the only language that Gaddafi is understanding."

The French president, Nicolas Sarkozy, urged his Western allies to "ask our Arab friends" to distribute weapons to the NTC. When a French shipment of missiles and machine guns arrived through the port of Benghazi, the NTC's acting defense minister handed them over to Abdelhakim Belhaj, the leader of the LIFG. It was a fateful move that would set the stage for the Islamist domination of Libya's opposition.

Comprising "Afghan Arab" veterans of the anti-Soviet jihad in Afghanistan, the LIFG functioned as an ally of Al Qaeda in Libya, dedicated to Gaddafi's overthrow and his replacement with an Islamic State. In 1991, when bin Laden moved his operations from Afghanistan to Sudan, Belhaj had followed. Five years later, according to an MI6 document leaked online and covered by the *Guardian*, British intelligence tapped its contacts in the LIFG to attempt to assassinate Gaddafi.

According to the leaked document, British intelligence was aware of a plot in 1995 to kill Gaddafi that included "Libya veterans who served in Afghanistan"—Belhaj and his men. It took the attacks of 9/11 and the inauguration of the so-called "war on terror" to make Belhaj a target of the West. The CIA captured him in 2001 in Pakistan, where he had fled after fighting alongside the Afghan Taliban, and was rendered to Libya two months later. In 2004, the United States listed the LIFG as a terrorist organization.

By 2010, Belhaj was free again, released from prison thanks to a de-radicalization program overseen by Saif Gaddafi and facilitated through negotiations with the Qatari government. Pronounced "no longer a danger to society" by the younger Gaddafi, Belhaj swiftly returned to militancy as soon as the opportunity arose, becoming the NTC's Tripoli Military Council commander.

As the insurgency against Gaddafi gathered steam, Belhaj found an eager promoter in John McCain, chairman of the Senate Foreign Relations Committee. After a friendly meeting with Belhaj and his militiamen in Benghazi on April 22, 2011, McCain called on "responsible nations" to provide the Libyan rebels with "battlefield intelligence, training, and weapons." McCain emerged from the meeting stirred with inspiration. "I met these courageous fighters, and they are not al-Qaeda," the senator stated. "On the contrary: they are Libyan patriots who want to liberate their nation. We need to help them do that."

Throughout the insurgency, Belhaj partnered closely with Ali Sallabi, a Muslim Brotherhood leader who had led the Islamist opposition to Gaddafi from exile in Qatar. Sallabi became Qatar's main conduit for $2 billion in arms to the rebels, emerging after Gaddafi's overthrow as "the architect of the new Libya," according to the *Washington Post*. For his part, Belhaj moved into mainstream politics as a leader of Libya's Islamist Al Watan Party and founder of an Al Jazeera–style private media network with backing from Qatar. Under the influence of Sallabi and other ultra-conservatives, the Libyan General National Congress scrapped Gaddafi's secular apparatus and formally declared: "Islamic law is the source of legislation in Libya. All state institutions need to comply with this."

The new government's first appearance at the United Nations in February 2012 featured an angry protest against a panel on antigay violence, with Libya's representative ranting that homosexuality "affect[s] religion and the continuation and reproduction of the human race." That same year, the Nawasi Brigade militia, operating under the Libyan Interior Ministry, threatened to mutilate a dozen men it had kidnapped from a private party in Tripoli, accusing them of belonging to "the third sex."

The Obama administration's war for "universal values" had established a failed state where the vulnerable populations that its military humanists like Samantha Power had sworn a responsibility to protect were hunted by revanchist warlords. And there was no clear path out of the abyss.

The Revenge of Sam Bacile

Back in the fever swamps of America's online bigotsphere, anti-Muslim activists Frank Gaffney and Robert Spencer seized on news of Middle Eastern chaos as proof of the regressive agenda of Muslims as a whole. The "counter-jihadists" had fallen into a symbiotic, mutually reinforcing relationship with the jihadists, with each side feeding off the other's propaganda and deepening the dynamic of mutual radicalization among their respective followers. That the release of an obscure propaganda flick could ignite a regional conflagration was a testament to the malevolent power of their death dance.

A bizarre Islamophobic film called *The Innocence of Muslims* became the trigger point for inflaming extremist sentiment across a region already torn by revolutionary ferment. The film was the brainchild of a group of far-right Egyptian Coptic scam artists determined to sabotage an uprising in their home country that had led to the election of the Muslim Brotherhood. Produced by Nakoula Basseley Nakoula, a militant Coptic separatist and felon convicted of check fraud posing as an Israeli Jew named "Sam Bacile," the film was an almost laughably amateurish portrayal of the Prophet Muhammad as a mass-murdering rapist.

The 2011 film featured an all-volunteer cast of aspiring actors in Los Angeles who had been duped into believing they were acting in a benign biblical epic about "how things were 2,000 years ago." Entitled "Desert Warrior," its contents made no mention of Muhammad—his name was dubbed into the film during post-production. On the set, a gray-haired Egyptian man who identified himself only as "Sam" (Nakoula) was seen chatting aimlessly in Arabic with a group of friends off set while posing as the director. A casting notice for "Desert Warrior" listed the film's real director as "Alan Roberts," a veteran softcore porn director responsible for such masterpieces as *The Happy Hooker Goes Hollywood* and *The Sexpert*.

Behind the scenes, Nakoula had hired a self-styled "counter-jihadist" activist named Steve Klein as a consultant, relying on him to sharpen the film's Islamophobic framing. A regular commenter on Pamela Geller's anti-Muslim *Atlas Shrugged* blog, Klein had posted memes urging armed attacks on American mosques on his own website. After consulting on the script of *The Innocence of Muslims*, Klein recruited a pair of Coptic extremists, Joseph Nasrallah, the owner of a private Arabic satellite station who appeared seemingly out of nowhere to speak at Geller's 2010 Ground Zero rally; and Morris Sadek, a far-right zealot who was filmed parading around Washington, DC, on September 11, 2010, with a crucifix in one hand and a Bible embossed with the American flag in the other. "Islam is evil!" Sadek roared. "Islam is a cult religion!"

In early September 2011, Nakoulah promoted the video in the United States through a fanatically anti-Muslim preacher, Terry Jones, who had gained notoriety by staging a public burning of the Quran. Sadek translated a YouTube clip of the film's trailer into Arabic and phoned Gamal Girgis, a correspondent for the Egyptian daily *Youm Al Sabaa*. In a brief write-up of the film published in atmosphere wracked with religious tension, Girgis dismissed it as "just a passing crisis that doesn't affect the bond between Muslims and Copts." But when Khalid Abdullah, the most prominent voice of the Salafi-Wahhabi satellite station Al Nas, aired a clip on his show, demands appeared across Islamist social media networks for protests on September 11—the tenth anniversary of Al Qaeda's "day of the planes" attacks on Manhattan.

The US embassy in Cairo was caught on the back foot by the gathering storm; by the time it attempted to quell the wave of demonstrations, it was too late. Egypt's al-Nour Party, a Salafist faction that was actively colluding with the Supreme Council of the Armed Forces—the bulwark of Egypt's "deep state"—in a coup plot against the elected Muslim Brotherhood government, had already sent its members into the street. On September 11, the American embassy in Cairo was stormed by hundreds of protesters, who managed to scale its heavily reinforced gates, tear down an American flag and replace it with the black flag of the Islamic State.

Echoing anti-Muslim commentators across the West, Sadek blamed Islam itself for the chaos he had deliberately provoked, declaring that "the violence that [the film] caused in Egypt is further evidence of how violent the religion and people [are]."

The coming days saw an escalation of protests and lethal clashes from Sudan to Afghanistan. *Newsweek* seized on the demonstrations to publish a cover story that represented a high-brow distillation of the Islamophobic film's essence, repackaged for mass consumption by Americans in airports and supermarket checkout lines. Authored by Ayaan Hirsi Ali, a former right-wing Dutch legislator who had advocated a "war with Islam," the *Newsweek* cover depicted a mob of rabid-looking Islamist protesters beneath the boldface headline: MUSLIM RAGE.

Amid the wave of attacks on American diplomatic interests, the US consulate in Benghazi became the site of the deadliest assault and the greatest source of intrigue. On September 12, the consulate was stormed by looters and overrun by gunmen from Ansar al-Sharia, a local band of armed extremists that had become a fearsome fighting force thanks to the weapons that flowed into the country under the watch of the Obama administration. In the gun battle that followed, four American staffers of the diplomatic mission were killed—two security guards, one information officer, and J. Christopher Stevens, the ambassador who been the Obama administration's direct line to Belhaj and his allies.

At the time of the attack, the *New York Times*' Cairo-based correspondent David Kirkpatrick noted that "Egyptian satellite television networks popular in Benghazi were already spewing outrage against [*The Innocence of Muslims*]." After interviewing several witnesses to the attack and its participants, Kirkpatrick concluded, "There is no doubt that anger over the video motivated many attackers. A Libyan journalist working for the *New York Times* was blocked from entering by the sentries outside, and he learned of the film from the fighters who stopped him. Other Libyan witnesses, too, said they received lectures from the attackers about the evil of the film and the virtue of defending the prophet."

Though the film had been established as a factor in the attack, its role as a primary motivator of Ansar al-Sharia was hotly disputed in Washington as the Republican congressional majority convened the Select Committee on Benghazi. The special congressional investigation into the attack on the consulate and killing of Stevens was a transparently partisan weapon aimed at undermining Hillary Clinton's presidential ambitions. Members of the panel homed in on administration claims that *The Innocence of Muslims* had played a part in the attacks, accusing officials like Rice and Clinton of lying about the film's influence to cover up their failure to protect American personnel. Clinton's approval rating sank under withering attacks emanating from the Benghazi committee, which centered almost entirely on the deadly night at the consulate and omitted its wider context.

With Washington consumed in partisan political games, the real scandal of Libya was conveniently ignored. As David Mizner wrote, "For loyal Democrats and liberal ironists, including many who supported the US war on Libya, 'Benghazi' is a joke about GOP obsession. For Libyans, Benghazi is a ravaged city in a ravaged country."

Inside the Beltway information bubble, partisan political warriors were content to ignore the fact that the United States and its allies had destroyed a functional state, plunged its economy into ruin, handed it over to warlords and zealots, and doomed an entire region in northern and central Africa to chaos. Virtually everything Gaddafi prophesied at the dawn of Western intervention was coming true, from his prediction that Al Qaeda and its affiliates would fill the security void to his warning about Libya becoming the primary disembarkation point for a new wave of refugees fleeing militia-run human trafficking camps that UNICEF called "living hellholes."

Since the campaign, over 180,000 asylum seekers—including at least 25,000 unaccompanied children—have poured into Italy from Libya each year, with thousands perishing along the way in the depths of the Mediterranean. Meanwhile, weapons from Libyan military depots flowed into the hands of Al Qaeda affiliates in other theaters of conflict like Boko Haram in northern Nigeria, whose brutality deepened the refugee crisis, displacing over 1 million people in the regions it had declared an "Islamic caliphate."

A 2013 report by the UN Security Council concluded, "In the past 12 months, the proliferation of weapons from Libya has continued at a worrying rate and has spread into new territory: West Africa, the Levant and, potentially, even the Horn of Africa," where the Al Qaeda affiliate al-Shabaab operated. The report added, "Illicit flows from the country are fueling existing conflicts in Africa and the Levant and enriching the arsenals of a range of non-state actors, including terrorist groups."

Heavy weapons had also flowed to the battlefields of Syria, thanks in no small part to Belhaj, who had met with Syrian rebel leaders on the Turkish border to coordinate arms shipments. "Having ousted one dictator, triumphant young men, still filled with revolutionary fervour, are keen to topple the next," the *Telegraph* concluded in a report on Belhaj's trip. In September 2012, the *Times* of London reported that "a Libyan ship carrying the largest consignment of weapons for Syria since the uprising began has docked in Turkey and most of its cargo is making its way to rebels on the front lines." The shipment, which included SAM-7 surface-to-air missiles and rocket-propelled grenades, was likely a part of a wider CIA operation to arm Syria's rebels.

Obama openly lamented the Libyan intervention as his "greatest mistake." But he remained a prisoner of the military humanist forces he had empowered within his administration. Like the hyper-confident Vietnam-era White House advisors panned in the book *The Best and the Brightest*, Obama's foreign policy brain trust had, as David Halberstam wrote, "for all their brilliance and hubris and sense of themselves, been unwilling to look and learn from the past." In the face of the rapidly mushrooming human catastrophe they caused, they patted themselves on the back and groped across the ravages of the Middle East for another opportunity.

With Libya and Iraq in the throes of chaos, two countries had fallen from the neoconservatives' blueprint for regime change in seven countries in five years. Now, with Syria in the midst of a blood-soaked civil war and jihadist insurgents entering the fray, the military humanists embedded in the Obama administration moved in to check a third government off the list. Reaching for a sports metaphor, one top Clinton aide called the coming arm-and-equip operation the "bank shot."

6

The Next Dirty War

The revolt that erupted across areas of Syria in March 2011 presented a wide and often contradictory theatre of demands. At protests led by the idealistic, plugged-in youth that typified the Arab Spring, grievances centered on the repression and cronyism of President Bashar al-Assad's inner circle. This included neoliberal policies such as placing Syrian public holdings in the hands of Rami Makhlouf, Assad's billionaire first cousin and the gatekeeper of the state's private sector. "The youth's civil resistance is unfettered by ideology—what they want is simply that democracy be consolidated and that the resources of the country be used for the good of its people—without exception, exclusion, marginalization or discrimination," wrote Haytham Manna, a secular progressive voice of the Syrian opposition, days after the revolt broke out.

In the countryside, where religiously conservative Sunni populations had been worn down by drought and the gradual collapse of the Ba'athist agrarian reform policies, protests took on a different flavor. On March 18, 2011, in the town of Baniyas, an area with a mixed population of Sunnis and Alawites near the loyalist city of Tartous, within wider protests, a Sunni crowd gathered to make their demands clear. From a balcony atop a mosque, Anas al-Ayrout, a hard-line Salafist cleric, belted out the list of dictates: "We demand, first, banning [gender] mixed schools!" Ayrout bellowed into a megaphone, sending gales of applause through the all-male crowd. After calling for improving local electricity, the preacher demanded that the government "re-allow women wearing niqab [full face covering] to teach in schools." The ultra-conservative religious demands were followed by calls that were familiar to reformist demonstrations: release political prisoners and cease arresting protesters.

In Houla, another rural, mostly Sunni town, protest leaders expressed similar grievances to journalist Nir Rosen: "They were upset about the ban of the niqab, or full veil, on women in public schools—while the medical student complained that the books of the medieval Islamic scholar and Salafi source, Ibn [Taymiyya], were banned," Rosen wrote in October 2011.

In March 2012, a large crowd of protesters was filmed in Homs chanting, "We are all jihadists! We will exterminate Alawites!" Around this time, the supposedly peaceful pro-democracy uprising was disturbed when government forces came under fire from snipers inside the city.

In response, hundreds of thousands marched in Syria's largest cities, Damascus and Aleppo, in support of Assad and the government. In numbers, these demonstrations far outstripped those of the opposition. More strikingly, a Yougov poll funded by the Qatar Foundation—an official arm of the Qatari government clamoring for regime change in Syria—revealed that 55 percent of Syrians living inside the country wanted Assad to stay. But Western media largely dismissed these numbers and cast the revolt as a popular mass uprising against a universally reviled dictator. The politicized framing of the divided nation dovetailed closely with the opposition's narrative, fueling the sense in Western capitals that Assad's rule would collapse any day.

This blinkered view was further consolidated as Western media chose to report on the government's violent repression of its own opposition's protests far more extensively than similar brutal crackdowns by allies, like Bahrain, that took place at the same time. Bahrain was a critical Persian Gulf outpost where the US Navy docked its Fifth Fleet and could not be allowed to fall under the control of a restive Shia population and into the Iranian sphere of influence. The humanitarian crisis that soon gripped Yemen as a result of the Saudi and American military campaign to oust its Houthi government was met with a similarly revealing dearth of official Western consternation.

Meanwhile, in Homs and elsewhere, the opposition's activities were depicted in mainstream Western media as almost universally peaceful; this was hardly the case, though. In Baniyas, for example, sectarian Sunnis spurred on by Salafi preachers like Ayrout slashed to death of a local fruit vendor, Nidal Janoud, a member of the Alawite sect. Two days later, on April 12—only weeks after the revolt broke out—the opposition staged a sophisticated guerrilla raid on a military convoy on a bridge in Baniyas, killing nine soldiers. As news of the killings emerged, the Syrian opposition falsely claimed the soldiers were killed by their own commanders for refusing to open fire on protests. Outlets like the *Guardian* and AFP fell for the spin and conveyed it uncritically to the Western public. Meanwhile, the violence continued. "Every day, members of the Syrian army, security agencies and the vague paramilitary and militia phenomenon known as shabiha ["thugs"] are also killed by antiregime fighters," Nir Rosen told Al Jazeera in February 2012.

By the summer, the revolt was careening toward a full-scale armed insurgency. On June 6, 2011, in Jisr al-Shughour, a city in the northern Idlib municipality that lay on a strategic road to Aleppo, rebel groups massacred over 100 Syrian government soldiers, destroyed tanks and even downed army helicopters. Once again, the opposition claimed the soldiers had been killed by their own commanders for refusing orders. In August, opposition members burned government employees alive at the post office in al-Bab and threw government soldiers to their deaths from a bridge in Hama.

Weapons eventually began pouring in through Turkey, where shipments had been arriving from Libya thanks to the CIA's ratline and were delivered to galvanizing insurgent forces. This was what a Clinton advisor meant by the reference to "the bank shot" from Libya. Foreign powers were already asserting their influence over the uprising, with the governments of Turkey and Qatar successfully pushing for the disproportionate representation of the Muslim Brotherhood on the opposition's de facto political body, the Syrian National Council. As in Libya and Afghanistan during the 1980s, the West and its Gulf allies found the most effective, deeply motivated fighters among the Islamists.

But even as the arms began pouring into Syria under the CIA's watch, American media denied the very presence of armed groups inside the country. A remarkable exchange between CNN's Anderson Cooper and Bashar Ja'afari, the Syrian ambassador to the United Nations, perfectly illustrated Western media's tendency to paint the Syrian conflict as a one-sided war between a maniacal dictator and his defenseless subjects.

"The government is running against the terrorist armed groups," Ja'afari insisted after Cooper recited the narrative of peaceful protesters being mowed down by security forces.

"What terrorist armed groups? Who are they? Name them," a befuddled Cooper exclaimed.

"Those who have killed so far 500 officers and soldiers of our army and police officers," Ja'afari responded.

"Okay, you haven't named who these unnamed, mysterious armed terrorists are."

"They are the outcomes of the American and British invasion of Iraq, Anderson," explained Ja'afari. "They are the Salafists, they are the *takfiri* groups, they are the Muslim Brotherhood military wing, they are all these kinds of extremist groups in the area. All of them spread all across the area after the American and British invasion of Iraq."

Cooper shot back that given the decades of rule of the Assad family, "it seems incomprehensible that all of a sudden you have thousands of Salafists that are calling for the overthrow of the government. It just doesn't make logical sense."

~

Like most Americans, Cooper was unaware of how the history of clashes, dating back to the 1970s, between the Syrian government and armed Sunni Islamist groups had set the stage for the unfolding civil war. At that time, Hafez al-Assad, father of Bashar and president following a coup in 1971, sparked massive Muslim Brotherhood demonstrations by issuing a stringently secular constitution. By 1979, the Brotherhood's protests had turned into a campaign of violent subterfuge, as an underground Combat Vanguard of Fighters slaughtered eighty-three cadets at a Syrian military academy in Aleppo. The next two years saw an assassination attempt on Assad, a car bombing that massacred some 200 civilians in Damascus, the killings of hundreds of Alawite members of the ruling Ba'ath Party, and the murder of Assad's personal doctor.

Tensions came to a head in 1982 in the city of Hama, a hotbed of conservative Sunni sentiment. Bogus reports that Assad had been overthrown sent the Brotherhood into a violent frenzy. According to Talcott Seelye, then the US ambassador to Syria, "The Islamists killed all of the Ba'athist officials in the city." Before long, over 10,000 troops led by Assad's brother, Rifaat, were bearing down on Hama. They rampaged across the city in tanks and blanketed it with artillery shells, leaving thousands dead. Islamist sources claimed that more than 20,000 had been killed, while other estimates in Western media ranged from one to five thousand. The iron-fisted crackdown effectively crushed Syria's Brotherhood affiliate.

The surviving members of the Muslim Brotherhood fled abroad, some to join up with the Islamist guerrillas gaining experience in Afghanistan, and others to the West, where they helped lay the groundwork for an exiled political network.

By summer 2012 whatever was left of a supposedly peaceful uprising had already folded into a brutal civil war fueled by cynical outside powers and carried out along sectarian lines. It was clear at this stage that the armed opposition was edging decisively toward the hard-line Salafi-jihadi ideology that Al Qaeda's leadership had espoused. The messaging beamed out of Saudi Arabia's private satellite channels by figures like Adnan al-Arour, an exiled Muslim Brotherhood televangelist, played a critical role in the sectarian bent of the insurgency. Infamous for his theatrical animadversions, elegant garb and the Sunni supremacist overtones of his sermons, Arour had impelled Syrian protesters to violence in the early days of the revolt, urging them to "grind the flesh" of Alawite government loyalists and "feed it to the dogs." As the rebellion descended into a bloodbath, Arour remained in the safety of his Saudi TV studio, ensconced in luxury as his wealth and influence grew daily amid bloodshed back home.

The pseudonymous Edward Dark was a student in Aleppo who joined the early campus protests in his city. In spring of 2012, Islamist rebels stormed from the countryside into the poorer neighborhoods in the city's east, waging a campaign of bombings and destroying Aleppo's Old City in a bid to establish the base of their insurgency. They proceeded to loot local factories and sell their wares off to Turkey, driving much of the local population into the government-controlled west. "A particular incident I can clearly remember was seeing black Qaeda flags at a checkpoint in my city, and having a foreign fighter ask Syrian people for their IDs," Dark recounted to journalist Rania Khalek. "That's when I knew everything had gone horribly wrong, and it was all over for our side of the 'revolution.'"

Dark recalled how fellow youth activists rejected the armed insurgency and its explicitly Islamist flavor. "Those who switched to the armed camp did so mostly out of sectarian, or personal reasons—revenge over a death, for example," he explained. "The rest who remained either turned their back on the armed uprising, or actually turned against it as they saw it was now being used [as] a vessel to destroy the country and no longer championed any ideals of freedom and democracy, and instead encompassed a violent Islamic extremism that was contrary to what they were struggling for."

Like Saddam Hussein's Iraq and Gaddafi's Libya, Assad's Syria posed little present threat to American national security. Within

America's bipartisan national security state, however, imperial imperatives often trumped national security concerns. Syria was the only state in the Arab League aligned with Russia, a relationship dating back decades. Hafez al-Assad had secured his independent foreign policy through the alliance government loyalists referred to as the "resistance axis": Russia, Iran and the Iranian-sponsored Shia militia Hezbollah, which had dealt Israel a bloody nose during the failed 2006 invasion of southern Lebanon. This was why Syria was listed atop the neoconservatives' post-9/11 targets for regime change. And it was why a convergence of forces applied pressure on Obama to check the country off the list once and for all.

The Syrian regime change lobby comprised an array of elements, from the military humanists gathered around Hillary Clinton's State Department to regional experts housed at Gulf-funded Beltway think tanks, to the leaders of organizations like Human Rights Watch, to the quietly influential Syrian American political apparatus, which provided cover for many Muslim Brotherhood-affiliated exiles to lobby Washington for military intervention against their mortal nemesis. Then there were the neoconservatives who had made clear in their 1996 "Clean Break" blueprint that the menace that the Syrian government presented to Israel—and its alliance with Iran—made collapsing Damascus a top priority.

True to his passive sensibility, Obama initially acceded to the interventionist pressure, setting the stage for an intensified proxy war in the country. "It will be the policy of the United States to promote reform across the region, and to support transitions to democracy," the president proclaimed in a May 2011 speech to the State Department. By August 2011, Obama announced, just as he had with Gaddafi, that "the time has come for President Assad to step aside."

Most foreign policy pundits and Western governments seemed convinced that Assad would be forced from power within a matter of months. As an administration official told the *Washington Post* in August 2011, the White House was "certain Assad is on his way out." However, Washington had badly misread the signs from Damascus, appearing to rely more on the Western media's information bubble than any human intelligence assets it might have cultivated.

As the uprising dragged on and mutated into a grinding civil war, the United States watched as Qatar began funneling weapons and logistical support to the same Sunni Islamist elements it had unleashed in Libya. The Arabic arm of Al Jazeera became a key element in the information war, spurring chauvinistic attitudes across the region. Opening an episode of *Opposite Direction*, a popular Al Jazeera debate program, Faisal al-Qasim introduced a viewer poll: "Do you think Alawites brought genocide upon themselves?" Then he read out the results, with only 3.8 percent of viewers answering "no."

"Allah must never forgive anyone who shows mercy towards the Alawites, screams the opposition activists of Syria," Qasim then ranted. "The question should rather be, should we wipe out Alawites in their entirety, including their children?"

"I am warning the Alawites to get out of the country or they will be slaughtered," responded Qasim's guest, Maher Sherafedinne, whom Qasim introduced as a "Syrian intellectual."

"Basically, it is the right of the [Sunni] people to demand the slaughter of the Alawites!" Qasim interjected.

"Of course! Of course!" answered Sherafedinne.

Having plunged into a full-scale proxy war, Syria began to look more and more like Afghanistan in the 1980s. President Erdoğan allowed Turkey to assume the role of being the transfer point for foreign fighters, weapons, and a way station for the flood of refugees the proxy war inevitably created. Billions in foreign aid and private NGO donations flooded into Turkey, fostering a parallel economy in its southern border regions that was intimately tied to the civil war and its prolongation. As with Pakistan in the 1980s, the millions of Syrian refugees Turkey warehoused in its camps were cynically weaponized against the Syrian government and its allies.

Saudi Arabia also reverted to the role it played in the anti-Soviet jihad, supplementing the West's arms shipments to the rebels through the same figure, Prince Bandar bin Sultan, who had directed weapons to the mujahedin. While the Saudi monarchy pumped aid into rebel-controlled areas, private interests in Jeddah and Riyadh spread Wahhabi-inspired messaging through its private media channels. Together, Qatar, Saudi Arabia and Turkey formed an axis with the West that stirred Syria's civil war, alongside a quiet but crucial assist from Israel, which surreptitiously supported the rebel forces operating around the Golan area on its northern frontier. Republican senator John McCain, the old cold warrior, celebrated the role the Gulf states were playing in weaponizing Syria's Sunni-led insurgency. McCain exclaimed, "Thank God for the Saudis and Prince Bandar, and for our Qatari friends."

Washington's desire to replace Syria's government with a pliant, pro-Western Sunni government, like the kind that ruled Jordan, dated back to the Cold War. A recently declassified 1986 CIA memo entitled "Syria: Scenarios of Dramatic Political Change," unearthed by writer and researcher Brad Hoff, offered a window into the cynical, sectarian thinking that informed the national security state. "In most instances the regime would have the resources to crush a Sunni opposition movement," the memo read, "but we believe widespread violence among the populace could stimulate large numbers of Sunni officers and conscripts to desert or mutiny, setting the stage for civil war."

Noting that the majority of conscripts in the Syrian Arab Army (SAA) were Sunni while the army's officer corps was dominated by members of the Alawite minority, the CIA asserted that "a renewal of communal violence between Alawis and Sunnis could inspire Sunnis in the military to turn against the regime." The authors of the agency's assessment pointed to a more militant Muslim Brotherhood as a vehicle for driving a revolt against Assad, with government retaliations "prompt[ing] large numbers of Sunni officers and conscripts to desert or stage mutinies in support of dissidents, and Iraq might supply them with sufficient weapons to launch a civil war."

Though the document was framed as objective intelligence analysis of the fault lines within Syrian society, the authors in the memo stated in no uncertain terms that the United States aimed to produce a pliant Sunni-led government completely delinked from Russia and Iran: "In our view, US interests would be best served by a Sunni regime controlled by business-oriented moderates. Business moderates would see a strong need for Western aid and investment to build Syria's private economy, thus opening the way for stronger ties to Western governments."

In an afterthought, the authors added that though "Syria's secular traditions would make it extremely difficult for religious zealots to establish an Islamic Republic," there was the chance that the overthrow of Assad could "provide support and sanctuary to terrorists groups."

Exactly twenty-five years later, the worst-case scenario was taking shape. Thanks to the campaign of regime change that the United States and its allies were waging in Syria, and had already completed in Iraq, the Sunni "business-oriented moderates" feared for their lives while an Islamic state was taking territory across the country's eastern hinterlands with shocking success.

Administrations of Savagery

In a lengthy paper published in January 2010, a group of Iraqi jihadists issued a "Strategic Plan" that would allow Al Qaeda to get back on its feet. The authors urged a "popular jihad" modeled along the lines of Mao Zedong's famous dictum: first, control the peasants, then the countryside and finally the country. (Abu Ubaid al-Qurayshi, another leading jihadist ideologue, frequently quoted Mao in his weekly magazine column, along with conservative ideologue William Lind's theories on "Fourth Generation Warfare.") They counseled a ruthless guerrilla war against the state and the establishment of efficient local councils modeled after those sponsored by the US military's Anbar Awakening.

Though the jihadist blueprint was intended for the Iraqi theater, the revolutionary ferment in Syria presented a perfect laboratory for its application. In late 2011, Zawahiri, now the main figure in charge of Al Qaeda's global operations, dispatched a veteran jihadist named Mohammed Jolani to "form a group and send it to" Syria.

A top commander in the grueling Al Qaeda–led insurgency in northern Iraq, Jolani had wound up in Camp Bucca, the American military prison named after a New York fire marshal killed on 9/11, Ronald Bucca. Within the prison's barbed wire confines, jihadists like him found fertile soil for training, study and political networking with seasoned former members of Saddam's intelligence services and army. Many of these veterans had no religious conviction whatsoever, but all had been left disgruntled by the Bush administration's de-Ba'athification program and were desperate for new work. From the former Ba'athists, the jihadists learned to implement an authoritarian bureaucracy, and from the jihadists, the Ba'athists gained a sense of transcendent purpose. Together, the inmates planned the next stage of the insurgency right under the noses of their American jailers. "Bucca was a factory. It made us all. It built our ideology," a former inmate told the *Guardian*.

When Jolani returned to his native Syria, it was not known at the time by outside observers or even by Syrians that he was operating under the command of an obscure Iraqi cleric named Abu Bakr al-Baghdadi. Born Ibrahim al-Awwad, Baghdadi gained a PhD at the Islamic University of Baghdad, enabling him to claim a greater wealth of Islamic education than either bin Laden or even Zawahiri. He had turned toward jihadism under the tutelage of Muhammad Hardan, a Syrian Muslim Brotherhood cadre and veteran of the anti-Soviet jihad in Afghanistan in the 1980s. The two wound up sharing a cell with Jolani inside Bucca, where Baghdadi was also held.

When the jihadists emerged from Bucca, the leadership of Al Qaeda's Iraqi outfit had been badly depleted by sustained warfare with the Americans and the Sunni Awakening tribes around Anbar. The death of Abu Umar al-Baghdadi, the previous caliph of the failed Islamic state in Iraq, left Abu Bakr al-Baghdadi at the top of the totem pole.

Baghdadi promptly set in motion a ruthless purge of the officials he held responsible for the failure of the Islamic state's previous iteration, replacing them with former members of Saddam Hussein's intelligence services and army. With stunning ease, they applied their experience managing Iraq's old police state to erect a totalitarian security apparatus under the black banner of jihad. At the time, Baghdadi was an unknown quantity outside of the Islamic state's inner circle.

Baghdadi's agenda hinged on the immediate establishment of an Islamic state fully eradicated of "impure" elements—inadequately pious Sunnis and religious minorities—that would serve as a base for international terrorism. His strategy, which led to his organization's formal rupture with Al Qaeda, was outlined in an exceptionally influential document published in 2004 by an Al Qaeda ideologue known as Abu Bakr Naji. The document's title offered a concise distillation of its content: *The Management of Savagery*.

Naji advised jihadist groups to exploit the chaos that resulted from the destabilization of previously stable states. He pointed to the collapse of the Soviet Union as the initial pivot point that allowed jihadist organizations to move from the stage of "vexation and exhaustion," or guerrilla-style militancy, to the establishment of "administrations of savagery." Naji cited Chechnya and Afghanistan as the first examples of "administrations of savagery" transitioning to the highest stage: governments run along the lines of Islamic law. But these projects turned out to be fleeting, with military interventions by Russia and the United States shattering both.

With the formerly stable state of Iraq thrown into chaos by an American invasion, however, new opportunities lay on the horizon. And then there was Syria, separated from Iraq by colonially imposed Sykes–Picot borders with a Sunni population on both sides. In producing a blueprint for destabilizing the Middle East and fragmenting it along sectarian lines, Naji's manifesto echoed the agenda outlined in the neoconservatives' "A Clean Break," albeit from an alternately opposed ideological angle.

"If we succeed in the management of this savagery, that stage will be a bridge to the Islamic state which has been awaited since the fall of the caliphate," Naji wrote. "If we fail it does not mean an end of the matter; rather, this failure will lead to an increase in savagery."

On December 23, 2011, a series of bombings rocked security installations in Damascus, leaving forty-four dead. The Syrian government declared that the attacks "had the fingerprints of Al Qaeda all over them." Next, on January 5, bombs struck a crowded Damascus neighborhood, killing twenty-six. The "vexation operations" had begun.

The CIA, meanwhile, was poised to implement a multibillion-dollar covert program to arm and equip Syria's supposedly moderate rebels. With critical assistance from Washington and its Sunni allies, jihadist elements would soon find new ground to establish "administrations of savagery."

The Hard Men with Guns

Obama and the National Security Council had all the intelligence they needed to accurately assess the situation in Syria, if only they were willing to acknowledge it. In August 2012, the Pentagon's Defense Intelligence Agency (DIA), then under the direction of Lieutenant General Michael Flynn, produced a memo that was widely distributed across administration channels warning that jihadist forces emanating from Iraq aimed to exploit the security vacuum to establish a "Salafist principality in eastern Syria." The DIA accused Saudi Arabia, Qatar and Turkey of encouraging such an outcome: "This is exactly what the supporting powers to the opposition want, in order to isolate the Syrian regime, which is considered the strategic depth of the Shia expansion (Iraq and Iran)."

The Syrian civil war, according to the DIA report's authors, "creates the ideal atmosphere for AQI [Al Qaeda in Iraq] to return to its old pockets in Mosul and Ramadi, and will provide renewed momentum under the presumption of unifying the Jihad among Sunni Iraq and Syria, and the rest of the Sunnis in the Arab world against what it considers one enemy, the dissenters. ISI could also declare an Islamic State through its union with other terrorist organizations in Iraq and Syria, which will create grave danger in regards to unifying Iraq and the protection of its territory."

Referring to Al Qaeda's Syrian affiliate by its name, Jabhat al-Nusra, before Western media ever had, the DIA emphasized the intimate ties the group had fostered with Syria's opposition forces: "AQI supported the Syrian opposition from the beginning, both ideologically and through the media. AQI declared its opposition to Assad's regime from the beginning because it considered it a sectarian regime targeting Sunnis."

When the secret memo was declassified three years later, the US State Department dismissed questions about its accuracy as "sweeping generalizations." In the meantime, the Obama administration ignored the intelligence and aligned itself with the Syrian opposition's Gulf backers.

Asked if the Obama administration had ignored the intelligence his agency was producing, Flynn said, "I don't know if they turned a blind eye. I think it was a decision, I think it was a willful decision."

In April 2012, months before the DIA's warning was issued, Secretary of State Clinton joined the nations backing the Syrian rebels at a conference in Istanbul. These countries, which were united by a desire for the removal of the Syrian government, called themselves the "Friends of Syria." At the gathering, Clinton forcefully rejected a mediation effort by the UN secretary general, Kofi Annan, that had been personally approved by President Assad.

For the first time, Clinton announced America's intention to directly fund the Syrian rebels and provide the opposition with "communications equipment" to advance the goal of regime change. Clinton stated her belief that "the hard men with the guns are going to be the more likely actors in any political transition than those on the outside just talking."

To smooth the way for regime change, Obama and his British counterpart, Prime Minister David Cameron, reportedly attempted to arrange for Assad to receive legal immunity if he stepped down. Clinton, meanwhile, continued to pressure Annan and the UN against negotiating a settlement to the conflict. Instead, she urged him to host a conference on regime change "using the transition on Yemen as the model," according to the *Guardian*.

By June 2012, CIA operatives had set up shop on the southern Turkish border with Syria, in the city of Adana, home to the American air base Incirlik. From there, the *New York Times* reported, "automatic rifles, rocket-propelled grenades, ammunition and some antitank weapons, [were] being funneled mostly across the Turkish border by way of a shadowy network of intermediaries including Syria's Muslim Brotherhood and paid for by Turkey, Saudi Arabia and Qatar."

To justify the arms shipments, Washington conjured up the label "moderate rebels," stamping it on an umbrella organization of Syrian army defectors and former Muslim Brotherhood cadres that called itself the Free Syrian Army (FSA). The Obama administration and a collection of pundits, many housed in Gulf-funded think tanks in Washington, zealously promoted the FSA as the best hope for combating ISIS. Douglas Laux—acknowledged by the CIA as the lead member of its Syrian Task Force and a key figure behind the plan for then agency director David Petraeus to topple the Syrian government with insurgent proxy forces—later acknowledged what few of the FSA's promoters in the West ever would: "There were no moderates."

Laux's appointment as the CIA's Syria regime change point man highlighted the agency's harebrained approach to the conflict. A veteran of Afghanistan with little command of Arabic, a bad alcohol habit and no experience inside Syria, Laux described how he thrust himself into the mission of recruiting insurgents to take down Assad: "I stopped drinking, bought myself a cool cane with a cowboy boot on the top, rode a bike at the gym daily, and read up on Syria. I learned that the situation on the ground was extremely complex and reflected the ethnic and religious diversity of Syria itself."

While the CIA's Syria handler was boning up on the situation from the seat of an indoor recumbent bike, the *New York Times* was issuing reports that should have sent up red flags within Western intelligence services. "Most of the arms shipped at the behest of Saudi Arabia and Qatar to supply Syrian rebel groups fighting the government of Bashar al-Assad are going to hard-line Islamic jihadists," it reported in October 2012. Chief among the extremist forces referred to by the *Times* was Mohammed Jolani's Al Qaeda affiliate, Jabhat al-Nusra.

In November 2012, FSA representatives delivered a revealing report to the State Department that further highlighted the CIA-run insurgent army as a de facto arms depot for jihadists: "From the reports we get from the doctors," it read, "most of the injured and dead FSA are Jabhat al-Nusra [Al Qaeda], due to their courage and [the fact they are] always at the front line."

Thanks to the surge of weapons from the United States and its Gulf allies, the jihadists were rapidly subsuming the FSA. As the FSA cable noted, the Syrian battlefield was witnessing "more [mergers] of extreme groups within Jabhat al-Nusra as it becomes more and more franchised. Their risk is paying off. They are on a high [rate] of growth."

There was no shortage of public sources to put the lie to the CIA-spun idea of "moderate rebels." "The so-called moderate rebels have often been very immoderate and ineffective," Representative Adam Schiff, the ranking Democrat on the House Intelligence Committee and generally a reflexive supporter of military interventions, complained.

"You are not going to find this neat, clean, secular rebel group that respects human rights and that is waiting and ready because they don't exist," explained Aron Lund, a Syria expert at the

Carnegie Institute for International Peace. "Even the groups that the US has trained tend to show up in the same trenches as the Nusra Front eventually."

But the weapons continued to flow into Syria, and al-Nusra expanded its footprint as a direct result.

The success that the local Al Qaeda affiliate Jabhat al-Nusra enjoyed nestling within the overall armed opposition presented its leader, Mohammed Jolani, with a fateful dilemma. His Iraqi spiritual guide, Abu Bakr al-Baghdadi, had dispatched him to carry out a series of grisly tasks, each of which conflicted with the strategy of "popular jihad." First, Baghdadi demanded that Jolani exploit his relationship with his former cellmate at Camp Bucca, Muhammad Hardan, to assassinate him, rubbing out a rival who likely held damaging information about Baghdadi's past. Next, Baghdadi ordered Jolani to stage an attack on the Syrian opposition's Istanbul-based umbrella group, the National Coalition of Syrian Revolution and Opposition Forces, in order to eliminate the Western-backed exiles vying for control of the opposition.

Zawahiri, as the international leader of Al Qaeda, intervened against Baghdadi, vetoing his demand for attacks inside Turkey. He argued that the Islamist oriented government of President Erdoğan was playing a critical role in supplying the insurgency with training and arms and that exacerbating the relationship risked stifling the lifeblood of the Syrian jihad. Jolani concurred, sending Baghdadi into a fit of anger. On April 9, 2013, Baghdadi announced the foundation of the Islamic State in the Levant and al-Sham (ISIS), appointed himself its caliph, and demanded total fealty from Jolani. He and Zawahiri bristled at the ultimatum, and by January 2014, Al Qaeda had formally divorced itself from ISIS.

Though Al Qaeda and ISIS waged a sporadic turf battle, the news of a jihadist civil war inside Syria was greatly overstated. Throughout the conflict, both groups displayed a willingness to partner with one another when convenient and often forged alliances with the CIA-vetted "moderate" rebels of the FSA, including prominent rebel leaders who had gained the personal blessing of American and British diplomats. With covert American support, this coalition not only enabled the rebels to seize new territory and threaten Damascus, it paved the way for ISIS to establish the de facto capital of its caliphate.

The Moderates at Menagh

In August 2013, the Free Syrian Army launched its most ambitious offensive to date, Operation Liberation of the Coast. The goal of the operation was to strike at the heart of the Syrian government's popular base, the Alawite communities along the Mediterranean coast, which had so far been untouched by the civil war, even while supplying the bulk of the army's officer corps.

The FSA entered the battle with training and arms supplied directly by the CIA and with an assortment of jihadist fighters by their side. Their allies in the operation ranged from ISIS to al-Nusra to Ahrar al-Sham, a Turkish-backed Salafi militia also dedicated to the establishment of an Islamic State. Some 300 foreign fighters from Tunisia, Saudi Arabia, Jordan and Libya bolstered the ranks of the Syrians. (Among those who would be killed in the fighting was one of the emirs of Libya's newly minted Islamic State, which was based in the NATO-"liberated" city of Sirte.)

Driven by sectarian resentment, the rebels placed their genocidal agenda on bold display. Anas Ayrout, the Islamic cleric who led some of the uprising's first demonstrations in the town of Baniyas in 2011, called for the rebels bearing down on the Alawite communities to "create a balance of terror." He added, "We have to drive them [the Alawites] out of their homes like they drove us out. They have to feel pain like we feel pain." Besides being the would-be emir of Baniyas, Ayrout was a leading member of the Syrian National Coalition, the opposition's Istanbul-based government-in-exile that was formally backed by the United States.

Most male residents of the Alawite majority were away on army duty at the time of the assault, a fact the rebels were undoubtedly aware of. Human Rights Watch researchers visited the towns after the rampage and documented the summary execution of sixty-seven civilians "even though they were unarmed and trying to flee." The NGO's on-the-ground examination found that the rebel onslaught was "planned as part of an attack on a civilian population" and featured "the systematic killing of entire families."

"When we got into the village of Balouta I saw a baby's head hanging from a tree. There was a woman's body, which had been sliced in half from head to toe and each half was hanging from [a] separate apple tree. It made me feel I wanted to do something wild," a Syrian army officer recounted to the *Guardian* after retaking one village from the rebels.

"We found two mass graves with 140 bodies. They were not shot. They had their throats slit. About 105 people of different ages were kidnapped," an army conscript commented. "The whole area is unusable. Salafists from abroad were behind the attack."

The events around the Syrian military's Menagh air base provided another opportunity to see the US-backed Free Syrian Army operate alongside jihadist groups like ISIS. For ten months, starting in August 2012, the FSA had tried and failed to overtake the isolated base. Its leader was Abdul Jabbar al-Okaidi, an FSA colonel described by the British *Daily Telegraph* as "a main recipient of the limited western aid" to the Syrian armed opposition.

Benjamin Hall, a Western journalist embedded in the FSA camps outside Menagh, also reported on how the base "only fell when the FSA were joined by the ISIS leader Abu Omar al-Shishani and his brutal gang of Chechens." Born Tarkhan Batirashvili in the former Soviet republic of Georgia, Shishani emerged as a leader of the country's US-trained special forces during its 2008 war with Russia over the breakaway republic of Ossetia. "We trained him well, and we had lots of help from America," a former Georgian defense official told reporter

Mitch Prothero. "In fact, the only reason he didn't go to Iraq to fight alongside America was that we needed his skills here in Georgia."

Once the army base was taken, Okaidi, the "moderate" Western proxy, and Shishani, the US-trained ISIS leader, gathered together for a triumphant and undeniably chummy press conference. The *New York Times* characterized the media event as "a mix of jihadist and Free Syrian Army leaders, who stood together, each praising his men, like members of a victorious basketball team." Before an Al Jazeera camera crew, Okaidi hailed Shishani's ISIS fighters as "heroes," before the latter commander pledged to clear Syria of the nonbeliever *kuffar*. (The Syrian army officers were eventually executed en masse.)

"I swear to Allah, oh Alawites, we came to slaughter you!" an ISIS fighter exclaimed to a cameraman from inside Menagh. "Await what you deserve!"

Later on, Okaidi commented to a reporter, "My relationship with the brothers in ISIS is good. I communicate with brothers in ISIS to settle these disputes and issues ... There are some who have the wrong ideology but when we sit down with them ... they don't have this ideology. And the relationship is good, even brotherly."

In a separate interview with official FSA media, Okaidi praised Al Qaeda's Syrian affiliate: "We truly did not see from them anything except good morals and brave and heroic fighting against this regime."

Just months before taking the air base at Menagh, Okaidi received one of his main patrons, then US ambassador to Syria Robert Ford. Ford had played a central role in the Syrian conflict, promoting the fantasy of "moderate rebels" in Washington and pushing Obama relentlessly to authorize military intervention. According to Michael Scheuer, a former CIA field operative, Ford was "running around the country trying to encourage groups to overthrow the Syrian government." On the Turkish border, Ford personally delivered seven trucks worth of food and supplies to General Salim Idris, the FSA's supreme commander and someone "considered to be moderate," according to National Public Radio.

The press conference at Menagh, the open admission of admiration for ISIS from Okaidi and any objective analysis of the facts on the ground should have exposed the FSA as a cover for the very elements the United States claimed to be fighting in its "war on terror." As early as February 2013, a United Nations independent inquiry report concluded that "The FSA has remained a brand name only." The UN further issued a damning assessment of the role of the United States, UK and their Gulf allies in fueling extremism across Syria. "The intervention of external sponsors has contributed to the radicalization of the insurgency as it has favoured Salafi armed groups such as the al-Nusra Front, and even encouraged mainstream insurgents to join them owing to their superior logistical and operational capabilities," the report stated.

Yet the continuous flow of arms to the FSA eventually enabled ISIS to establish its de facto capital in the city of Raqqa. In March 2013, when a coalition of Syrian rebel forces representing the US-backed FSA, Ahrar al-Sham and the jihadist al-Nusra overwhelmed the Syrian army in the isolated city, the Islamic State was as yet an unknown entity in Syria. Opposition activists declared the city the "icon of the revolution" and celebrated in the town center, waving the tricolor flags of the FSA alongside the black banners of al-Nusra, which set up its headquarters in the city's town hall. Disorder quickly spread throughout the city as its residents attempted to order their affairs through local councils.

A month after Raqqa was taken, ISIS commander Baghdadi revealed that al-Nusra had been a Trojan horse for his organization, referring to its commander, Jolani, as "our son." Jolani, in turn, admitted that he had entered Syria from Iraq as a soldier of the Islamic State, declaring, "We accompanied the jihad in Iraq as military escorts from its beginning until our return [to Syria] after the Syrian revolution."

It was only a matter of weeks before the process of Talibanization took hold in Raqqa, with jihadist forces subjecting activists to arbitrary detention and imposing a draconian regime of Sharia law that punished violators with public floggings. By August, Baghdadi completed his bloodless coup, announcing total ISIS control over the city. True to form, the US-backed FSA avoided all confrontation with ISIS; many of its fighters quickly jumped ship to either the Islamic State or al-Nusra.

"The [FSA] battalions are scared to become the weakest link, that they will be swallowed by ISIS," a media activist named Ahmed al-Asmeh told journalist Alison Meuse on NPR. "A number joined ISIS, and those who were with the people joined Jabhat al-Nusra." Another activist told Meuse that the ISIS takeover led to a swelling of the ranks of Al Qaeda's local affiliate, al-Nusra, by fighters from the CIA-backed FSA. "Not all, but the majority of FSA have joined Nusra because of ISIS," he said. "Al-Nusra are Syrian and ISIS is not. Al-Nusra, at the end of the day, is essentially FSA, in that they are fighting to bring down the regime."

By the end of 2013, ISIS had consolidated its control over Raqqa and was well on its way toward establishing the caliphate. Jolani, as al-Nusra commander, had once again broken with Baghdadi and separated his organization formally from the Islamic State. Meanwhile, ISIS set about to the totalitarian tasks that defined it, burning Christian churches in Raqqa, jailing activists and instilling fear in the hearts of anyone who might consider protesting its rigid rule. "Imagine your favorite city in Syria, and pray that it is not liberated," a local activist told Meuse, "because liberation means occupation."

As ISIS expanded its realm of control and al-Nusra rapidly subsumed the armed opposition, the Syrian lobby in Washington was pushing the Obama administration to authorize another war of regime change. A strange series of events outside Damascus had spread outrage in capitals across the world, and Obama found himself on the verge of intervening.

Astonished at the unfolding folly, Representative Dennis

Kucinich, the most outspoken among a dwindling band of anti-war members of Congress, wondered aloud, "So what, we're about to become Al Qaeda's air force now?"

7

Until We Meet in Damascus

The policy adopted by the Obama administration on Syria focused on an imaginary "red line." Under heavy pressure from the Syrian opposition's government in exile, the Syrian National Council, Israel's intelligence services, which were determined to create a pretext for war on Syria, and from the military humanist elements in his own administration, Obama inaugurated the policy on August 20, 2012: "the red line for us is we start seeing a whole bunch of chemical weapons moving around or being utilized [by Assad]. That would change my calculus. That would change my equation."

A former US ambassador to the Middle East later complained to journalist Charles Glass, "The 'red line' was an open invitation to a false flag operation."

With the implementation of the strategically dubious policy, the opposition had incentivized its own forces to allege the use of chemical attacks against rebel-held areas. Over the coming months and years, the opposition's international public relations apparatus would complain of hundreds of chlorine attacks, but would supply little more than online photos of children breathing into oxygen masks, or coughing men in hospitals. But the proliferation of sophisticated social media accounts, US- and UK-supplied communications gear in rebel-held territories, and the inability of Western journalists to access these areas meant that the rebels had a monopoly on the flow of information. Even before evidence arrived of chemical weapons use or proof of the Syrian government's culpability was established, the dissemination of online images of children foaming at the mouth could trigger instant calls from Washington to London for a US-led bombing campaign. Thanks to the red line, the simulacra that provided Westerners with a digital window into Middle Eastern conflict zones had become the ultimate weapon in the hands of Syria's jihadi-oriented rebels.

In private, Obama bridled at the prospect of another war of regime change that would exacerbate the unfolding chaos in the Middle East. He grumbled that the Libyan intervention was a "shit show" and sought insulation from advisors who sought another war. In public, however, Obama did nothing of substance to counter the intensifying drumbeat for regime change. "The pressure [on the president] was multivalent," Steven Simon, Obama's former national security director for the Middle East and North Africa, explained to me. "It was coming from the Saudis, the Emiratis, the liberal interventionists in the administration and outside of it. Then there was the president's own desire to try something, despite his skepticism."

As during the fateful days before NATO's intervention in Libya, the most forceful voice for intervention was Obama's ambassador to the UN, Samantha Power. According to the *Atlantic*'s Jeffrey Goldberg, Power and her fellow interventionists had convinced themselves that the Syrian rebels were a ragtag band of "farmers and doctors and carpenters, comparing these revolutionaries to the men who won America's war for independence." Obama, on the other hand, had become so irritated with Power's persistent lobbying for intervention that he snapped at her, "Samantha, enough, I've already read your book."

On August 20, 2013—exactly one year after Obama announced

the red line on chemical weapons—the Syrian opposition produced videos of children writhing on the ground in extreme pain, the alleged victims of a chemical weapons attack in East Ghouta, an area outside Damascus held by Saudi-backed Liwa al-Islam. With an estimated 1,200 dead in the attack, haunting footage was disseminated through opposition media channels depicting piles of lifeless, glassy-eyed children.

As the images were broadcast across the world, diplomats scrambled to respond. In a hastily prepared intelligence report, the US government blamed the Syrian government for the attack, claiming that Syrian government "chemical weapons personnel were on the ground, in the area, making preparations." Secretary of State John Kerry declared his "high confidence" in the Syrian government's culpability, but at that point, no evidence from international investigative bodies was available. The White House refused to provide documentation to support its claims, however, and declined to name its sources on security grounds. James Clapper, then the director of national intelligence, warned Obama at the time that the case against Damascus was no "slam dunk."

The timing of the attack was unusual. Five months before it occurred, in March, the director general of the Organisation for the Prevention of Chemical Weapons (OPCW), Ahmet Üzümcü, had issued a statement of deep concern regarding an unverified allegation of another chemical attack by rebels against the Syrian army in the town of Khan al-Asal. The OPCW team was given approval to travel to Syria on August 1. On the way to Damascus, one investigator sounded a pessimistic note to the *Guardian*: "Some people say that it's already too late, and I can definitely understand that."

Three weeks later, the chemical attack in East Ghouta took place, leaving hundreds dead. Would the Syrian government have authorized such an assault right under the noses of the OPCW inspectors it had formally invited into the country, and one that would have likely triggered the Americans' "red line" policy? Was it stupid to the point of being suicidal? The answer was elusive.

Though Western governments pointed the finger at Damascus, there was a plentitude of evidence that the rebels had acquired chemical weapons of their own. Carla Del Ponte, the head of the United Nations independent commission of inquiry on Syria, oversaw an investigation in May 2013 that collected testimony from doctors and victims of the civil war. Del Ponte found that "there are strong, concrete suspicions but not yet incontrovertible proof of the use of sarin gas, from the way the victims were treated. This was use on the part of the opposition, the rebels, not by the government authorities."

Investigative journalist Seymour Hersh presented the most thorough case against the White House's "red line." In a series of articles, Hersh cited testimony from former US military officials who insisted that al-Nusra had acquired sarin gas through the weapons stockpile shipped to Syria from Libya, and that it may have been behind the attack in East Ghouta. According to Hersh, the Defense Intelligence Agency issued a classified briefing on June 19, 2013, that warned of "one of the most advanced sarin lots since al-Qaeda's pre-9/11 effort." The report asserted that "Turkey and Saudi-based chemical facilitators were attempting to obtain sarin precursors in bulk, tens of kilograms, likely for the anticipated large scale production effort in Syria."

When Hersh's story later appeared in the *London Review of Books*, he was blitzed with attacks by rivals who branded him a conspiratorial loon. But skepticism about the attacks and the necessity of a military response was widespread. In the UK, where David Cameron's government seemed dead set on intervention, parliamentarians from his own Conservative Party staged an unlikely revolt, joining up with antiwar stalwarts like Labour's Jeremy Corbyn to torpedo the bill authorizing the use of force in Syria.

In Arizona, Senator John McCain, one of the most ardent proponents of wars of regime change, fell under a tirade of criticism from his constituents. A town hall in Phoenix on September 5, 2013, became a theater for protest as a woman identifying herself as a Syrian Christian rose from the crowd and excoriated the senator, accusing him of supporting Al Qaeda–linked rebels determined to exterminate her fellow religious minorities. "We can not afford another Iraq!" the woman intoned. "We can not afford to turn Syria into Iraq or Afghanistan." Her comments were met with gales of applause from a crowd that was decidedly hostile to the idea of another intervention.

Ten days after the alleged chemical attack, Obama announced his own plan to request congressional approval for a campaign of air strikes and cruise missile attacks on Syrian military infrastructure. Well aware that the votes were not there, Obama had cleverly arranged a political escape hatch. The Syrian opposition was furious at the president's refusal to intervene unilaterally and set its Beltway lobbying apparatus into motion.

At the heart of the opposition's lobbying push was a Washington-based group called the Syrian Emergency Task Force (SETF). Funded by the US State Department and a collection of anonymous donors, the group acted as a direct line between the FSA and Congress. SETF's Syrian American point man, a hip, youthful DC-based activist named Mouaz Moustafa, had been a consultant to the Libyan National Transitional Council during the run-up to the NATO invasion.

In 2014, an obscure documentary called *Red Lines* was produced as a public relations vehicle for Moustafa and the SETF, but the film wound up exposing the Syrian opposition's lobbying apparatus as an almost comically bumbling vehicle for advancing the converging agendas of arms dealers, fanatical insurgents and neoconservative operatives.

The documentary recorded Moustafa shuttling from Washington to the Syrian-Turkish border, and then jaunting into the heart of the country to smuggle a fighter into the rebel-held city of Homs. It also portrayed his cellphone discussion of a shipment of heavy weapons and tanks to the rebels from an unnamed American company that was buying up weapons from the Ukrainian military after its war with pro-Russian separatists. "They made millions!" Moustafa exclaimed.

Moustafa's costar in *Red Lines* was the SETF's Razan Shalab al-Sham, a Syrian opposition activist from an elite family. She is filmed on a visit to an old friend who was leading a unit of Liwaa al-Umma, which was at the time a unit of the Free Syrian Army. Al-Sham was visibly queasy when she discovered that Liwaa al-Umma fighters were holding captives in a school basement. She was then forced to listen with disgust as they made plans to loot a local cement factory. (Over the course of the civil war, business owners from Aleppo complained that the rebels stripped their factories to the bone and sold their wares off to Turkey.)

In a subsequent scene, Moustafa is seen meeting with officials from Ahrar al-Shama. "We're not democratic, frankly," Abu Abdulrahman al-Suri, an Ahrar al-Sham founder and administrator of its Sharia courts system, explained to him. "Ballot boxes are not a precondition to know the people's opinion. We live with the people. We know their demands ... They all want Islamic law to be their law because that's their instinct."

Having arrived at the meeting with plans to establish transitional governing councils that could be marketed to Washington as the basis for a democratic post-Assad Syria, Moustafa was instead mugged by the reality of the Syrian opposition.

But nothing could deter the ambitious young lobbyist from his goal of regime change. In May 2013, Moustafa approached Senator John McCain, the most zealous cheerleader for war in Congress, and convinced him to take an illegal trip across the Syrian border and meet some freedom fighters. An Israeli millionaire named Moti Kahana, who coordinated efforts between the Syrian opposition and the Israeli military through his NGO, Amaliah, claimed to have "financed the opposition group which took senator John McCain to visit war-torn Syria."

"This could be like his Benghazi moment," Moustafa hoped excitedly. "[McCain] went to Benghazi, he came back, we bombed."

During his brief excursion into Syria, McCain met with a small group of rebel fighters and blessed their struggle for regime change. "The thoughts and prayers of millions of Americans are with you," McCain told the insurgents. "I will never rest until we meet in Damascus." McCain's office promptly released a photo of the meeting showing the senator posing beside a beaming Moustafa and two grim-looking gunmen.

Days later, the men were named by the Lebanese *Daily Star* as Mohammad Nour and Abu Ibrahim. Both had been implicated in the kidnapping a year prior of eleven Shia pilgrims, and were identified by one of the survivors. McCain and Moustafa returned to Washington the targets of mockery from *Daily Show* host Jon Stewart and the subject of harshly critical reports from across the media spectrum. But they remained undaunted in their quixotic mission for regime change.

In June, after arranging a meeting in Syria between FSA fighters and Evan McMullin, a former CIA field officer with presidential ambitions, Moustafa angrily protested the State Department's designation of Al Qaeda's Syrian franchise as a terrorist group. "It was a mistake," he told *Foreign Policy*. "The feeling among Syrian fighters was, 'Why are you telling us what we can or can not do when you should be doing so much more to help us?'"

Two months later, the chemical attack in eastern Ghouta took place and intervention was suddenly at the forefront of Washington's agenda.

The debate to intervene in Syria culminated at a September 3, 2013, meeting of the Senate Foreign Relations Committee. There, both Secretary of State Kerry and Senator McCain cited a *Wall Street Journal* editorial by a previously unknown researcher named Elizabeth O'Bagy to support their assessment of the Syrian rebels as predominantly "moderate" and potentially Western-friendly.

"She works with the Institute of War," Kerry said of O'Bagy. "She's fluent in Arabic and spent an enormous amount of time studying the opposition and studying Syria. She just published this the other day. Very interesting [*Wall Street Journal*] article, which I recommend to you." Kerry concluded, "I just don't agree that a majority [of the rebels] are al-Qaida and the bad guys."

The Institute for the Study of War (ISW) that employed

O'Bagy was a Washington-based think tank founded by Kimberly Kagan, the daughter-in-law of neoconservative ideologue Donald Kagan and wife of his son Fred Kagan—a perfect family portrait of the revolving door culture that festered inside Washington's national security state. The group was funded by the arms industry and private surveillance firms that reaped windfall profits from the military interventions the ISW has lobbied for and advised. (Kimberley Kagan and her husband, Frederick, had served on General Stanley McChrystal's strategic review team in 2009, advocating for a dramatic expansion of the US presence in Afghanistan. She also advised General Petraeus during his surge in Iraq, before feting him at a $10,000-a-plate gala.)

The revolving door extended all the way to O'Bagy, who was simultaneously lobbying for regime change at SETF while working at the ISW, a fact left undisclosed in her *Wall Street Journal* op-ed. Furthermore, according to *Time* magazine, she had acted as "McCain's Sherpa for his surprise trip into Syria" while serving as "the face of the moderate Syrian opposition, batting down dovish anxieties that the rebels were riddled with al Qaeda and arming them would ultimately harm US interests."

Days after being unmasked as a paid Syrian opposition lobbyist, O'Bagy was exposed for faking her PhD in Arabic studies. As soon as the humiliated Kagan fired O'Bagy, the academic fraudster took another pass through the revolving door, striding into the halls of Congress as McCain's newest foreign policy aide.

The Syrian opposition had banked everything on American intervention, but to their dismay, diplomacy wound up winning the day. Russian foreign minister Sergey Lavrov rescued Obama from the interventionists, arranging a last-minute deal that required the Syrian government to dispose of its entire stock of chemical weapons under the supervision of the OPCW. The agreement was a rare example of de-escalation in an era of permanent war. For its successful destruction of the Syrian chemical stocks, the OPCW was awarded a Nobel Peace Prize.

Nevertheless, the West and its Gulf allies continued to fuel the civil war, pumping more resources into their proxies, both in Syria and in Washington.

Moderate Members of Al Qaeda

"There's a playbook in Washington that presidents are supposed to follow," President Obama complained to the *Atlantic* magazine's Jeffrey Goldberg, referring directly to the debate to authorize war on Syria. "It's a playbook that comes out of the foreign-policy establishment. And the playbook prescribes responses to different events, and these responses tend to be militarized responses."

At the heart of the Washington playbook was the ambition for regime change, either through massive CIA-led operations or through direct military intervention. Even after the failure to achieve this goal in 2013, Syria remained atop the interventionist target list. Within the conglomeration of think tanks that stretched from downtown Washington to the city's embassy row, support for Syria's rebels had only deepened. This was in large part due to the influence of the Gulf states, pro-Israel donors and the defense industry. Hoping to leverage American power for their own narrow interests, these regressive forces exerted decisive financial control over think tanks from the Atlantic Council to the Brookings Institute to the Middle East Institute (MEI), while paying for sponsored content at the *Daily Beast* and bankrolling *Foreign Policy* magazine's annual "Peace Games" in Dubai. Within these institutions, calls for air strikes and tanks consistently overrode efforts to think.

The Obama White House eventually became so frustrated with Gulf pressure on Washington's foreign policy establishment that some aides resorted to nasty characterizations: "I've heard one [Obama] administration official refer to Massachusetts Avenue, the home of many of these think tanks, as 'Arab-occupied territory,'" Goldberg reported.

The MEI, a think tank that claimed to provide "non-partisan, expert information and analysis on the Middle

East," emerged after the failure of the red line strategy as one of the Beltway's most aggressive advocates for regime change in Syria. The institution was backed by no less than $20 million from the United Arab Emirates. Steven Simon, former National Security Council advisor, was hired as a senior fellow by the MEI after he left the Obama administration. But as soon as he began challenging the regime change narrative on Syria, publishing a series of op-eds questioning the strategic logic of intervening on behalf of a jihadist-dominated opposition, he was unceremoniously fired.

Simon reflected, "Americans don't support think tanks for this kind of thing. The foreign funding for think tanks which produce policy advocacy as though it were American when it reads like it was written in advance by Saudi embassy—that's really pretty awful. The whole thing is a scandal."

After Simon's forced departure, MEI became home to one of the most consequential self-styled experts on the Syrian civil war. Posing as an objective analyst on the ideology and goals of the various armed groups, having placed their leaders under the microscope through a series of interviews he conducted at conferences in Riyadh, Charles Lister was also one of the rebels' most influential advocates.

A former intern for the British Conservative Party, Lister rose to prominence at the Brookings Institute's Doha Center, a wing of the think tank established at the behest of the Qatari royal family. He kept especially close contact with the Turkish-backed Salafist militia, Ahrar al-Sham, frequently conveying statements by its official spokesman, Labib al-Nahhas, especially when other members of the group made extremist proclamations. Delivering sound-bites in British pronunciation, the fresh-faced, bespectacled Englishman quickly emerged as one of the most sought-after Syria commentators in Washington. That the non-Arabic speaker had conducted a substantial portion of his fieldwork on the opposition from the air conditioned lobby of a luxury hotel in Riyadh, and had only made a brief jaunt into Syria, was of little consequence to the journalists who turned to him for quotes and analysis. The line Lister took—not necessarily his insights—had earned him the foreign policy elite's stamp of approval.

In 2015, Lister produced a comprehensive list of the rebel groups that deserved designation as "moderate," and who therefore qualified for advanced weaponry from the West. He larded his report with Kurdish groups that had no connection to the anti-Assad opposition, claiming that the number of moderate rebels stood at a whopping 70,000. His research informed an internal report by the British Joint Intelligence Committee, and prompted Prime Minister Cameron, a major patron of the opposition, to publicly claim that there were "about 70,000 Syrian opposition fighters on the ground who do not belong to extremist groups."

Lister said of his own analysis, "Many of the groups who fall within both these categories are armed factions the Islamist-averse United States' CIA has already 'vetted' and assessed as 'moderate' enough to receive lethal assistance." Indeed, the CIA had begun equipping the groups listed in his report with advanced TOW missiles and sophisticated communications equipment, part of a $500 million authorization request Obama had sent to Congress in June 2014. The only problem was that many, if not most, of the rebel factions he flagged as moderates were actually hard-line Islamists that would ultimately align with either al-Nusra or Ahrar al-Sham.

Among the groups at the top of the list was Nour al-Din al-Zenki, a Salafist fighting unit that had been rewarded with American-made BGM-71 TOW missiles after it helped seize control of eastern Aleppo. The weapons had arrived through the CIA's Turkey-based operations room, a clearinghouse for arms provided by the United States, Saudi Arabia, Qatar and Turkey. "Most of the support from governments who back the rebels is now channeled through the [CIA's] Military Operations Command," the *New York Times* reported. At its peak, the CIA was spending $1 out of every $15 in its entire budget on covert operations in Syria.

The al-Zenki militia was founded by Sheikh Tawfiq Shahabuddin, a Salafi cleric with no formal religious education and a background as a butcher of camel meat. Shahabuddin had served jail time in Syria for murdering his sister, the breadwinner of his family, in a grisly 1999 honor killing. In 2014, a year before Lister publicly blessed the sheikh's Zinki faction with the stamp of moderation and the same year the group was rewarded with CIA assistance, Zinki carried out a wave of kidnappings and the torture of activists and journalists in rebel-held eastern Aleppo. Just a year later, the neoconservative Institute for the Study of War listed al-Zinki as a "power broker" and a moderate group "independent" of Al Qaeda in its "Syrian Opposition Guide."

The group's atrocities were becoming increasingly difficult for even its most zealous promoters to whitewash, however. In July 2016, commanders of al-Zenki captured Abdullah Issa, a nineteen-year-old fighter from Liwa al-Quds, a Palestinian militia that fought on the side of the Syrian government. From the bed of a pickup truck, the fighters filmed themselves taunting the teen, then sawed off his head with a knife and dangled it before a cell phone camera.

By the time of the beheading, al-Zenki had lost its overt support from the CIA. But inside the Beltway, it still managed to maintain influential cheerleaders. At the Century Foundation, a New York- and Washington-based think tank that described itself as "progressive, non-partisan," and dedicated to "reduc[ing] inequality," senior fellow Sam Heller dedicated a lengthy editorial in August 2016 to arguing that the United States "will have to back Zenki and other groups like it." While acknowledging that an al-Zenki commander had "sawed off his prisoner's head in the back of a pickup truck," and even conceding that the group often "fought side-by-side" with al-Nusra, Heller pronounced al-Zenki to be "a natural, if unpalatable, partner" that deserved Washington's backing. "But if Washington insists on keeping its hands perfectly clean," Heller insisted, "there's probably no Syrian faction—in the opposition, or on any side of the war—that merits support."

At a January 2017 panel discussion at the Atlantic Council—a major Washington think tank funded by NATO, the governments of Turkey, Saudi Arabia, Qatar and major defense contractors—Lister joined several interventionist pundits announcing a major report on "Combating Al Qaeda in Syria." While the fresh-faced young British pundit conceded that Al Qaeda was being "mainstreamed" within rebel-held territories, he and his fellow talking heads on the panel placed the blame squarely on the Syrian government and its Iranian backers for the bloodshed and demanded more arms for the rebels.

When I asked Lister why, three years earlier, he had so confidently designated al-Zenki as a moderate organization, he claimed, "Not in a million years did they represent the organization they represent today, which I would completely, and I have said publicly, does not deserve any kind of relationship with the United States or any of our allies."

Just three months earlier, however, Lister had published an op-ed in the *Washington Post* arguing for a massive infusion of weapons to Syrian rebel groups just like al-Zenki. He and his co-author, John Allen, a Hillary Clinton campaign surrogate and retired four-star general who had led the international coalition against ISIS, demanded Obama do what "the Russians believe the United States will never do: Escalate the conflict."

The duo argued that if the president failed to further arm the rebels occupying eastern Aleppo, "al-Qaeda would reap the rewards of our shortcomings." It was an odd claim considering the blunt assessment that Pentagon spokesman Colonel Steve Warren offered in April 2016: "It's primarily al-Nusra [Al Qaeda] who holds Aleppo."

Seated in the front row at the Atlantic Council's event on combating Al Qaeda and listening attentively to the speakers was David Petraeus. The former CIA director and four-star general had been forced from public life when he was exposed for carrying on a romantic affair with his biographer, Paula Broadwell. Since 2015, following his fall from grace, Petraeus began lobbying national security officials for direct American support to Al Qaeda, or as the *Daily Beast* put it, "using so-called moderate members of al Qaeda's Nusra Front to fight ISIS in Syria."

By February 2017, al-Zenki—the Salafist militia once branded as "moderate" by Lister and armed through the US joint Military Operations Command in Turkey—had entered into a formal coalition with al-Nusra. Called Hay'at Tahrir al-Sham, the rebel umbrella group also included a militia named the Bin Laden Front. The merger of a former American proxy with affiliates of Al Qaeda that openly celebrated the author of the 9/11 attacks posed an uncomfortable quandary for Washington. In May the State Department quietly removed Hay'at Tahrir al-Sham from a press release classifying the jihadist coalition as a terrorist group, replacing it with al-Nusra. The motivation was clear: if the United States placed a former CIA proxy like al-Zenki on its terror list, it risked opening itself up to lawsuits from the group's many victims.

No matter how far the Syrian armed opposition lurched toward jihadism, there always seemed to be foreign policy pundits in Washington eager to promote them. In September 2015, an op-ed entitled "The Right Salafis Can Make All The Difference" appeared on the Atlantic Council's website courtesy of a nonresident fellow named Mona Alami. The author singled out Zahran Alloush, the leader of Jaysh al-Islam (the Army of Islam), as a moderate who has "reversed previous policies hostile to Western values," and argued that he deserved support.

Eli Lake, a neoconservative columnist at Bloomberg News who was one of Ahmed Chalabi's chief boosters during the run-up to invading Iraq, echoed Alami's charitable assessment of Jaysh al-Islam, trumpeting the group's supposed willingness to accommodate Israel. In a subsequent editorial, Lake complained that the militia's leader was being "smeared in [Arab media] as a terrorist in league with al Qaeda."

Alloush was the son of a Salafi cleric from Saudi Arabia. Released from Syria's Saydnyah prison in 2011 after the Assad government heeded the opposition's demand for a general amnesty for jailed militant leaders, he was immediately recruited by the Saudi prince, Bandar bin Sultan, to lead a new coalition of Islamist rebels east of Damascus. Alloush made clear in a video message that any ideological difference between himself and Al Qaeda was skin deep, repeatedly insisting on his commitment to an Islamic State. Addressing his supporters, Alloush pledged to ethnically cleanse Syria of Shi'ites and Alawites. "Oh, you enemies of Islam ... we will step on your heads," he rumbled into the camera. An Obama administration official brushed off any concerns about Alloush's gang at the time, remarking, "We don't have a problem with the Islamic Front."

With Saudi funding and training from Pakistani special forces, Jaysh al-Islam proceeded to loot US State Department supplies warehoused in the town of Atmeh, then kidnapped Razan Zeitouneh, one of the last prominent secular opposition activists still active in Syria. True to Alloush's pledge to brutalize Syria's Alawites, in November 2015 his men placed captive Alawite hostages in cages on the backs of trucks and paraded them through East Ghouta as human shields to deter Syrian government and Russian bombing.

It was not only Jaysh al-Islam that was designated "moderate" by the Washington foreign policy elites. The other major Islamist rebel group in Syria, Ahrar al-Sham, also found favor inside the Beltway. Al-Sham had been founded by Abu Khalid al-Suri, a veteran jihadist who fought alongside bin Laden in Afghanistan and was named by a Spanish court as a key figure in orchestrating Al Qaeda's Madrid train bombings in 2004. Nonetheless, the organization earned a friendly spread in *Foreign Affairs*, with a bipartisan trio of national security professionals marketing it as "an Al Qaeda linked group worth befriending."

Israel's ISIS Connection

While Washington's Gulf-funded think tank experts spun out public relations for the allies of Al Qaeda, ISIS found defenders in Israel. At the Likud Party-linked Begin-Sadat Center for Strategic Studies, its director Efraim Inbar promoted the Islamic State in Syria as a boon to Israel's strategic deterrence. In an op-ed entitled "The Destruction of Islamic State Is a Strategic Mistake," Inbar argued, "The West should seek the further weakening of Islamic State, but not its destruction." Instead, he insisted, it should exploit ISIS as a "useful tool" in the fight against Israel's true enemy, Iran and its proxy, Hezbollah, which operates on Israeli frontiers from southern Lebanon. "A weak IS is, counterintuitively, preferable to a destroyed IS," Inbar concluded. Inbar went on to argue for prolonging the conflict in Syria for as long as possible on the grounds that extended sectarian bloodshed would produce "positive change."

As bracing as it might have been, Inbar's argument provided a perfect distillation of the Israeli government's position on the Syrian civil war. "In Syria, if the choice is between Iran and the Islamic State, I choose the Islamic State," Israel's former defense minister, Moshe Ya'alon, bluntly stated in 2016. Eager to see an Iranian ally weakened from within and without, the Israeli army occasionally bombed in support of the rebels operating around the southern city of Quneitra and attacked Damascus several times.

The end goal of the Israelis was to establish a buffer zone between itself and Hezbollah, with Sunni Islamists, including Al Qaeda affiliates, acting as its proxies. A rebel commander revealed to the US news outlet *Al-Monitor*, "The battle to capture Quneitra on Sept. 27 [2014] was preceded by coordination and communications between Abu Dardaa, a leader of Jabhat al-Nusra [Al Qaeda], and the Israeli army to pave the way for the attack."

The Israeli military-intelligence apparatus even funded its own unit of the Free Syrian Army, the Golan Knights. "Israel stood by our side in a heroic way," Moatasem al-Golani, a spokesman for the Golan Knights, told the *Wall Street Journal*. "We wouldn't have survived without Israel's assistance.

In 2016, Israel established a liaison unit to support the efforts of the rebels in southern Syria, according to journalist Nour Samaha, "facilitating cross-border travel for residents into Israel, regular deliveries of food, clothing, construction equipment and educational materials, airstrikes on pro-government positions and the establishment of an Israeli-backed opposition faction in rebel-held southern Syria."

When journalist Bryan Bender visited top Israeli military officials in the occupied Golan Heights, he heard unapologetic arguments for supporting Al Qaeda and ISIS against the Syrian government, Iran and Hezbollah. "If I can be frank, the radical axis headed by Iran is more risky than the global jihad one," said Army Brigadier General Ram Yavne, the head of the IDF's Strategic Division. "It is much more knowledgeable, stronger, with a bigger arsenal." When Bender asked another Israeli official if the United States should allow ISIS to maintain its caliphate in eastern Syria, he replied, "Why not?"

While Israeli military honchos took satisfaction from the bloodshed of Syria's civil war, ISIS commanders tiptoed around the Israeli military. During a public forum in Israel, the ever-candid former minister of defense, Ya'alon, revealed that an ISIS cell operating alongside the rebels in southern Syria had accidentally launched a mortar into Israeli-controlled territory. "On most occasions, firing comes from regions under the control of the regime," Ya'alon commented. "But once the firing came from ISIS positions—and it immediately apologized."

Pushed by Israeli media to clarify his statement about ISIS formally apologizing to Israel—an open admission of an Israeli backchannel to the jihadists—Ya'alon refused further comment.

In Washington, meanwhile, top officials in the Obama administration, including Hillary Clinton, kept their complaints about the channels of state support to ISIS and other jihadist rebel factions confined to private discussions. There was a lot to lose in venting their frustrations in public, including the massive donations their own political operations received from the very same sources.

When Hillary Clinton left the State Department in late 2013, she immediately joined the board of the Clinton Foundation. The New York-based nonprofit touted its charitable good works around the world, from making AIDS medication more affordable to "working toward a world where more girls and women can achieve full participation in all aspects of life." At the same time, the Clinton Foundation raked in between $10 and $25 million from the government of Saudi Arabia, and as much as $5 million from a front group called "Friends of Saudi Arabia." Tens of millions more flowed into the Clinton foundation coffers from Qatar, Kuwait and the United Arab Emirates.

All along, Clinton knew that the major donors to her family's vehicle for charity and influence peddling—a key platform for her forthcoming presidential campaign—were propping up ISIS and Al Qaeda in Syria. In a 2014 email to her longtime political confidant John Podesta, Clinton singled out Qatar and Saudi Arabia as the principal benefactors of the Islamic State. "While this military/para-military operation is moving forward," she wrote, citing Western and US intelligence sources, "we need to use our diplomatic and more traditional intelligence assets to bring pressure on the governments of Qatar and Saudi Arabia, which are providing clandestine financial and logistic support to ISIL and other radical Sunni groups in the region."

Vice President Joseph Biden was even more explicit. Discussing the challenges facing America in Syria, he stated, "Our biggest problem is our allies." Singling out Turkey and Saudi Arabia, Biden complained at Harvard's Kennedy School of Government in October 2014, "They were so determined to take down Assad and essentially have a proxy Sunni–Shia war; what did they do? They poured hundreds of millions of dollars and thousands of tons of weapons into anyone who would fight against Assad. Except that the people who were being supplied were Al-Nusra and Al Qaeda and the extremist elements of jihadis coming from other parts of the world."

Biden's candid comments were immediately labeled as a "gaffe" by the *Washington Post*'s Adam Taylor, who grumbled about the "worrying habit of lumping al-Qaeda's al-Nusra Front in with Islamic State." For daring to give credence to what was already widely known, Biden was forced to embark on the equivalent of an international apology tour the same month, issuing "a formal clarification" to Turkey's Erdoğan and thanking Saudi Arabia's foreign minister for his country's supposed cooperation in the fight against ISIS. After Biden's pathetic retreat, scarcely anyone in Washington, whether in government, the world of think tank experts, or in the press corps, dared to openly confront America's core Middle Eastern allies for their backing of Al Qaeda and ISIS.

Besides Saudi Arabia and Qatar, there was ample evidence that Turkey was taking a lead role in fueling Islamist militancy in Syria's north. A leaked 2015 report from the Turkish Gendarmerie General Command found that lorries filled with heavy weapons had been sent by the Turkish intelligence services to resupply al-Nusra. "The trucks were carrying weapons and supplies to the al-Qaeda terror organization," the report read. The government of Turkish president Erdoğan promptly banned all media coverage of the scandal and placed the soldiers who carried out the searches on trial for espionage.

A twenty-nine-year-old Lebanese American named Serena Shim had been reporting on these developments on the Turkish border for Press TV, the Iranian government's English language channel. She was among the first correspondents to cover the transfer of arms from the Incirlik US air base in Turkey to insurgents in Syria. Her sister, Fatmeh, told local media in her hometown of Detroit, Michigan, that Shim "caught [Turkish intelligence] bringing ISIS high-ranked members into Syria from Turkey into camps, which are supposed to be Syrian refugee camps." Shim began to fear for her life, complaining that Turkish intelligence considered her a spy. "I'm hoping that nothing is going to happen, that it's going to blow over," she told Press TV, the Iranian network, on October 18.

One day later, Shim died in a car accident. The story of her death was buried, with no acknowledgement from Reporters Without Borders or the Committee to Protect Journalists. American media scarcely covered it at all. Press TV said the car that she died in and its driver had disappeared. Her family never accepted the official version of events and has pressed in vain for an investigation.

The Eagle versus the Anvil

While Washington deepened its support for the rebels, the Syrian government and its allies faced down jihadist forces on several fronts. ISIS had easily demolished a collection of rebels around the far eastern city of Deir Ezzor, and was determined to move in and impose its theocratic rule on the city's 150,000 residents. With Deir Ezzor besieged on all sides and dependent on Russian airdrops for basic supplies, the overstretched Syrian army was left as its last line of defense.

On September 13, 2016, the Syrian and Russian militaries agreed to a ceasefire with the rebels. The deal called for the establishment of a US-Russian "joint integration center" (JIC) to coordinate strikes against ISIS. The secretary of defense, Ashton Carter, expressed serious reservations about coordinating with the Russians, but his objections were vetoed by Obama. The Pentagon then embarked on a public relations push against the JIC, leaking negative assessments to friendly reporters while Carter berated Kerry in private. Four days later, the United States inexplicably attacked a Syrian army unit holding a strategic mountaintop in Deir Ezzor, killing over 100. In the moments after the attack, ISIS seized key points around Deir Ezzor's airport and threatened to overrun the city entirely. The United States claimed the air strike was a mistake, but the explanation never washed with the Syrian and Russian governments.

"The Deir Ezzor strike appears to have been timed to provoke a breakdown of the cease-fire before the JIC could be formed, which was originally to be after seven days of effective truce—meaning Sept. 19," journalist Gareth Porter wrote. By that date, the ceasefire had been called off and the JIC was never to be—a development that satisfied Carter and the Pentagon. The Syrian army, meanwhile, managed to hold off the ISIS onslaught that the United States had assisted.

From Idlib to Palmyra, home of some of the world's most treasured antiquities, areas across Syria were being overrun by jihadist forces, all thanks to a flood of weapons from the United States, the UK and their Gulf allies. And back in Washington, the most well known liberal interventionist pundit in the country, Thomas Friedman, was clamoring in the *New York Times* for the United States to "simply back off fighting territorial ISIS in Syria and make it entirely a problem for Iran, Russia, Hezbollah and Assad."

It was not without good cause that 82 percent of Syrians polled by the British opinion monitoring firm ORB International agreed that ISIS was a "US and foreign made group."

In audio leaked from a closed meeting with Syrian opposition activists, Secretary of State Kerry offered a stunning admission that the United States had used ISIS as a tool for applying negotiating pressure on the Syrian government. Kerry also acknowledged that the growth of ISIS and Washington's refusal to stanch it was the key factor in triggering direct Russian intervention in October 2015. The cynical American strategy he revealed recalled Brzezinski's "bear trap," which aimed to provoke the Soviets into invading Afghanistan by providing Islamist insurgents with advanced weaponry.

"I mean, the reason Russia came in is because ISIL was getting stronger," Kerry explained to the activists, who were grumbling audibly. "Daesh [ISIS] was threatening the possibility of going into Damascus and so forth. And that's why Russia came in. Because they didn't want a Daesh government. And [the Russians] supported Assad. And we know that this was growing. We were watching. We saw that Daesh was growing in strength and we thought Assad was threatened. We thought, however, we could probably manage, you know, that Assad might negotiate and instead of negotiating, you got Assad, ah, you got Putin supporting him."

Nir Rosen, a former journalist who has overseen conflict negotiations on the ground in Syria, arranging numerous ceasefires and reconciliation deals, recalled to me, "the US and Europe consistently opposed and undermined attempts to negotiate local ceasefires in Syria and discouraged the UN special envoy from involving himself in them. They only gave it their support once it became clear that regime change was not going to happen and the Russian intervention had changed the game. But before then, the US and EU viewed de-escalating the conflict and local ceasefires as a tool to 'help the regime win' and preferred to see the war go on than see the war end on terms they disliked."

With the help of the Russian military, the Syrian army began rolling back jihadist insurgents from eastern Aleppo to Palmyra to Hama. The defeat of the militants triggered a paroxysm of outrage in Washington that helped set the stage for a return to Cold War-era paranoia, with Putin cast as a modern-day Bond villain hell-bent on world domination and Assad portrayed as his bloodthirsty mini-me. The testimonies of average Syrians who supported their government's campaigns against the Western and Gulf-backed insurgency, or who expressed gratitude about the expulsion of rebels from their neighborhoods, were scarcely, if ever, conveyed back to the Western public.

By late March 2016, thanks to Russian air support, the Syrian army was beginning to retake Palmyra and salvage what was left of its Roman-era antiquities, which ISIS regarded as blasphemous idols and had begun to destroy. A widely overlooked study issued a year later by *IHS Jane's*, one of the world's premier military affairs journals, found that between April 2016 and March 2017, the majority of ISIS's engagements had been with the Syrian military: "The Syrian government is essentially the anvil to the US-led Coalition's hammer. While US-backed forces surround Raqqa, the Islamic State is engaged in intense fighting with the Syrian government around Palmyra and in other parts of Homs and Deir al-Zour provinces."

The reality that the Syrian military was doing the bulk of fighting against ISIS was apparently too inconvenient for Washington to accept. At a March 24, 2016, press briefing, a reporter asked US State Department spokesman Mark Toner, "Do you want to see the [Syrian] regime retake Palmyra, or would you prefer that it stays in Daesh's [ISIS] hands?"

Unwilling to provide a direct answer to what seemed like an easy question, Toner strung together empty platitudes for a full minute.

"You're not answering my question," the reporter protested.

Toner emitted a nervous laugh and conceded, "I know I'm not."

8

Regions of Savagery

While a narrative prevailed in Washington that held regime change as the best strategy to combat ISIS, Syrians living inside the country told a different story. Some 7 million of them had fled from rebel-held areas—"liberated territory," according to opposition activists—and taken shelter in government-controlled cities like Damascus.

The Salafist rebel groups that held sway across parts of Syria generally shared ISIS's theocratic vision and were implementing it to various degrees in the territories they had seized from the government.

Like so many areas conquered by proxy forces backed by the United States and its allies over the past four decades, Idlib underwent a swift process of "Talibanization." The town square became the site of executions, including that of a young woman shot in the head in January 2015 for supposedly committing adultery. Lindsey Snell was one of the last Western journalists to enter Idlib after it fell under al-Nusra control, and has made seven trips to rebel-held areas. She entered in 2014, passing checkpoints that contained billboards informing women to fully cover their faces with niqab and ordering men not to smoke tobacco. Before she left, she was arrested by al-Nusra and transferred to a prison in Turkey, where she was later rescued by US special forces.

In Idlib, Snell documented how al-Nusra and its jihadist allies cannibalized one US-backed "moderate" faction after another until they no longer existed. First, it destroyed Harakat Hazm, a favorite of the CIA and think tank pundits in Washington, targeting its commanders in improvised explosive attacks and seizing its antitank TOW missiles.

Next, in March 2016, al-Nusra overran the headquarters of the US-backed Division 13, seizing two storage facilities of heavy weapons, including a tank and armored vehicles. Finally, al-Nusra arrested the most skilled TOW operator of Division 13, Suhail Hammad, known by rebels as "Abu Tow." Hammad's crime was posting a photo of himself smoking a cigarette next to an al-Nusra billboard that read, "smoking shisha is haram [forbidden under Islamic law]."

Among the most vividly disturbing records of life in rebel-held Syria was the documentary *Undercover in Idlib*, produced by journalist Jenan Moussa for the UAE-based news outlet Akhbar. Relying on footage secretly filmed by three residents of Idlib, all opponents of the Syrian government, the documentary revealed the full extent of al-Nusra's control over the area. The abandoned homes of Christians were spray painted with numbers and handed over to Salafi loyalists, not only by al-Nusra, but by the Turkish-backed Ahrar al-Sham militia. The elderly Christians who were not able to flee were forced to convert, while the statue of the Virgin Mary outside their local church was decapitated, its head replaced with the black flag of Al Qaeda. The nearby town of Jisr al-Shughour, an early base of armed revolt, had been destroyed and turned to a ghost town. Its only inhabitants were a collection of Turkistani and Chinese Uighur jihadists, with the Uighurs seizing Syrian real estate to establish their own colonies. Many thousands of Uighurs and Turkmen had settled in Idlib, according to Moussa's report.

Turkey not only provided weapons and logistical support to

the rebels controlling Idlib, it controlled the external borders, supplying passes for select residents to enter and exit. More disturbingly, the Akhbar documentary team found that Turkey had supplied religious texts to local clerics explaining how to implement Sharia law on matters including the treatment of female slaves. The streets of Idlib were plastered with pro–Al Qaeda graffiti, including quotes by Ayman al-Zawahiri. "Democracy is Polytheism," read a highway banner credited to Ahrar al-Sham. Over time, al-Nusra replaced the stark road signs with colorful, family-friendly graphics emphasizing the importance of Sharia.

At Radio Fresh, the USAID-funded media outlet in Idlib, host Raed Fares—one of the US State Department's favorite activists in rebel-held Syria—was reduced to broadcasting the sound of bleating goats and bird chirps to circumvent the music ban. Ordered to fire all his female employees, Fares instead relied on a computer program that auto-tuned their voices to make them sound male. "They now sound more like robots," he commented.

With the help of the United States and the so-called "Friends of Syria," Idlib and eastern Aleppo embodied stark visions of theocratic dystopia that could have been lifted from the crudest of Islamophobic imaginations. The United States and its allies were providing tens of millions in civil infrastructure to help construct a de facto Islamic State, funding radio stations, schools and the hospitals provided by the Syrian American Medical Society (SAMS), which had received at least $5.2 million from USAID to operate exclusively within rebel-controlled areas. But no group operating within the armed opposition received as much funding from the American government, or adulation from the Western public, as the civil defense and media organization known as the White Helmets.

The Hidden Soldiers

At the 2017 Oscars ceremony in Hollywood, the Syrian civil war took center stage with the Motion Picture Academy's presentation of Best Documentary Short to filmmakers Orlando von Einsiedel and Joanna Natasegara for their Netflix film on the Syrian rescue workers known as the White Helmets. As Natasegara fought back tears, Einsiedel read a prepared statement from Raed al-Saleh, the director of the White Helmets: "Our organization is guided by a verse in the Quran: 'To save one life is to save all of humanity.' We have saved more than 82,000 civilian lives."

The Oscar was just the latest in a raft of glowing accolades presented to the White Helmets. In 2016, the group narrowly missed out on a Nobel Peace Prize nomination after receiving the "alternative Nobel" award known as the Right Livelihood Award. Endorsements for the group poured in from celebrities, including George Clooney and Justin Timberlake, as well as from Hillary Clinton and a host of politicians—from the British Foreign Ministry's Boris Johnson to Secretary of State Kerry to Senator Bernie Sanders. Articles in major news outlets touting the group's heroism, invariably describing how the courageous rescue workers "run to the bombs," appeared in a flood as the Nobel Prize voting approached. In the French parliament, where measures declaring emergency law across the country had just been enacted after a series of murderous attacks by Al Qaeda sympathizers, lawmakers greeted Saleh and his colleagues with a thunderous standing ovation.

For journalists and human rights groups covering Syria from afar, the White Helmets became a go-to resource, providing a steady stream of vivid and bracing footage from the front lines of rebel-held areas that represent a no-go zone for most Western reporters. Media reports on casualty numbers in rebel-held areas routinely referred to sourcing from "civil defense workers," citing the White Helmets as the authority on the ground without independently verifying their claims. Reporters covering the Syrian conflict for top Western publications developed such close relationships with the White Helmets that some, like Australian Broadcasting Corporation correspondent Sophie McNeil, even took to social media to fundraise for the group.

Though the White Helmets' leadership and promoters insisted on a commitment to saving lives regardless of their political affiliation, the group represented the leading edge of the Syrian opposition's campaign to spur regime change. During the fall of 2016, as the Syrian military made steady gains against the Salafi-jihadi rebels that controlled eastern Aleppo, the White Helmets' slick website directed visitors to a request to sign a petition for a no-fly zone to "stop the bombs" in Syria. The website was created and operated by the Syria Campaign, a UK-based public relations organization funded by a British Syrian billionaire, Ayman Asfari, who was committed to the overthrow of the government of President Assad. And the no-fly zone was an interventionist device for spurring a war of regime change that Hillary Clinton herself acknowledged would "kill a lot of Syrians," and which US general Joseph Dunford worried would require a hot war with Russia and Syria.

In May 2015, the White Helmets' Saleh met privately with UN and EU officials to push for a no-fly zone. A month later, his colleague Farouq Habib testified before the US House Committee on Foreign Affairs in support of a no-fly zone, claiming to possess firsthand knowledge of chemical weapons attacks by the Syrian government. With the Obama administration having drawn its "red line" at the deployment of chemical weapons, allegations like these were potential trigger points for full-scale US military intervention. In November 2016, Saleh was back in Washington to lobby alongside Mouaz Moustafa of the SETF and Representative Elliot Engel, one of the most avid supporters of Israel on Capitol Hill, for expanded sanctions on Syria targeting the country's central banking system and blocking replacement parts for its civilian airliners.

Marketed to the public as a mere band of "rescuers" rushing toward the bombs to pluck helpless babies from the rubble, the White Helmets had revealed themselves as an international influence operation that lobbied on behalf of the Western governments and military-intelligence officials that conceived it to drive the regime change agenda. Indeed, the group was not born in the rubble of a Syrian conflict zone, but in public relations offices and the boardrooms of private defense contractors.

~

Back in July 2012, a year after the Syrian conflict began, USAID, operating under the auspices of the State Department, began to lay the groundwork for its Syria Regional Option. With American analysts excitedly proclaiming the imminent downfall of Assad and his government, USAID rushed to "provide support to emerging civil authorities to build the foundation for a peaceful and democratic Syria," according to a USAlD executive report from that year.

The grants were authorized by USAID's Office of Transitional Initiatives (OTI), a division of the State Department notorious for spearheading failed attempts at regime change in countries that resisted diktats from Washington. Following a series of pilot programs carried out by a for-profit, Washington DC-based contractor called Development Alternatives International (DAI), at a cost of $290,756 to US taxpayers, the OTI began setting up local councils in rebel-held Syrian territory. The idea was to establish a parallel governing structure in insurgent-held areas that could one day supplant the current government in Damascus. USAID's 2012 executive summary on the Syria Regional Option acknowledged that "foreign extremist entities" already held sway across the country.

In March 2013, a former British infantry officer named James Le Mesurier turned up on the Turkish border of Syria. Le Mesurier was a veteran of NATO interventions in Bosnia and Kosovo who moved into the lucrative private mercenary industry after his army days ended. But running security for the UAE's oil and gas fields left him feeling unfulfilled with his career as a hired gun. He wanted to be a part of something more meaningful. So he became a leading participant in USAID's Syria Regional Option.

Le Mesurier's job was to train men in areas controlled by Syria's armed opposition to rescue civilians in bombed out structures, and to film themselves doing it. In 2014, he established Mayday Rescue, a non-profit based in Turkey that grew out of the Dubai-based "research, conflict transformation, and consultancy" firm known as Analysis, Research and Knowledge, or ARK. That company, which employed Le Mesurier while overseeing the White Helmets' training, has been sustained through grants from Western governments and the British Ministry of Defense. Though they were known as Syrian Civil Defense, graduates of Le Mesurier's course became popularly identified by the signature headgear they wore in the field: white helmets.

Since being founded under the watch of Mayday Rescue, the White Helmets have received grants totaling at least $100 million from the UK Foreign and Commonwealth Office, Japan and USAID, as well as an untold sum from Qatar. USAID says the $32 million it has contributed to the White Helmets "supports impartial emergency responders." The sum represents an unusually large contribution to a supposed civil defense project operating in a war zone. It is unclear how much of this generous funding supported rescue efforts inside Syria, and how much contributed to the White Helmets' sophisticated public relations apparatus, which included a state-of-the-art communications center in Gaziantep, Turkey.

Mark Ward, director of the Syria Transition Assistance and Response Team at the State Department, highlighted the political dimension of the White Helmets' funding in an interview with *Men's Journal*: "[Funding the White Helmets is] one of the most important things we can do to increase the effectiveness and legitimacy of civil authorities in liberated areas of Syria."

In the Oscar-winning Netflix documentary *The White Helmets*, Mayday Rescue is never identified as the administrator of the group, nor does Le Mesurier ever appear on screen. USAID and Chemonics, the for-profit, DC-based contractor that supplies the group, are also omitted from the film.

For many languishing in rebel-held territory in Syria, however, USAID and contractors like Chemonics were little more than financial feeding tubes for the ultra-Islamist fiefdoms set up by Gulf-backed insurgent groups. As Brett Eng and Jose Ciro Martinez wrote in *Foreign Policy*—not exactly a hub of anti-imperialist opinion—USAID's involvement in Syria "has created another unhealthy form of dependence in opposition-controlled areas like Daraa. Instead of the Assad regime, it is the United

States, Jordan, and the for-profit development organization Chemonics that civilians in Daraa are beholden to."

Eng and Martinez also warned that USAID might be inadvertently propping up some of the more unsavory rebel factions, writing, "without a well-defined, inclusive opposition group, it is unclear to whom civilian loyalties are being redirected."

Frankie Sturm, a public information officer at the State Department, told me that Chemonics "has put in place third-party monitors to verify that assistance reaches intended beneficiaries and for intended purposes."

When I asked Chemonics for the names of these monitors, it directed my questions back to USAID, which refused to provide an answer on security grounds. Then USAID spokesperson Sam Ostrander told me his agency "works with another firm, completely separate from Chemonics" to monitor the assistance to the White Helmets, but didn't name the company or disclose how much public funding it received.

In 2014, USAID produced the first and only evaluation report to date on its Syria-related "transition initiatives." It was not exactly a portrait of success. "The extent to which OTI's efforts were successfully building inclusive and accountable governance structures was still unclear," the report concluded, also noting that "the ongoing conflict resulted in challenges that have led to delays in development and implementation of these activities."

Just as USAID expanded its operations inside rebel-held territory, a top public relations firm received a contract to market the rescue workers it was funding to the Western public as the true heroes of the Syrian conflict.

Were it not for the Syria Campaign, the White Helmets would likely be looked on with the same amount of interest by Western media consumers as rescue workers in conflict zones like Palestine and Yemen—with almost no concern at all. But thanks to the public relations outfit's multimillion-dollar campaign, the Syrian opposition has generated its most effective vehicle for promoting regime change and papering over the real face of the armed Salafist groups driving its agenda on the ground.

Presented as an authentic "voice of the Syrian people," the Syria Campaign was essentially a front for a slick public relations operation backed by wealthy foundations and donors with a clear interest in regime change. It drew on the model established by John Train's Afghanistan Relief Committee, a CIA front that aimed to produce documentaries portraying the mujahedin as anticommunist freedom fighters. The success of some of the post–Cold War era's most successful humanitarian intervention ploys also seemed to be a source of inspiration, from the stage-managed congressional testimony of "Nayirah," whose lies about babies murdered in their incubators by Saddam's army helped propel the United States into the first Gulf War, to ZunZuneo, the USAID-created social media network that mixed fake news with flash mobs in a failed attempt to trigger a "Cuban spring" that would topple Fidel Castro.

Back in 2014, after the "red line" policy failed to trigger Western intervention, a Syrian British oil and gas billionaire named Ayman Asfari decided to direct his fortune into a significant upgrade of the opposition's propaganda machine. Asfari turned to an activist-oriented public relations firm with offices in New York City and London. Called Purpose, the firm was best known for its work on liberal social issues with well-funded progressive clients like the ACLU and police reform group Campaign Zero. It promised to deliver its clients creatively executed campaigns that produced either a "behavior change," "perception change," "policy change" or "infrastructure change."

With $180,000 in seed money from Asfari, $120,000 more from the Rockefeller Brothers Fund—one of the CIA's favorite pass-throughs during the Cold War—and half a million more from anonymous donors, Purpose was venturing to effect a regime change.

To fulfill the goal of its new contract, Purpose blasted out a job listing for a "Syrian Voices project," boasting, "Purpose grew out of some of the most impactful new models for social change," including "the now 30 million strong action network avaaz.org." In fact, the Syria Campaign's founder, Purpose co-founder Jeremy Heimans, was also one of the original founders of Avaaz. As he told Forbes, "I co-founded Avaaz and [the Australian activist group] Get Up, which inspired the creation of Purpose."

What was Avaaz? Back in 2011, the global "clicktivist" organization introduced a public campaign for a no-fly zone in Libya and delivered a petition with 1.2 million signatures to the UN supporting Western intervention. A year later, after NATO shattered Libya's government and the country was overrun by a collection of Islamist armed militias, Avaaz sent hundreds of thousands of dollars of communications equipment to rebel activists in Syria, along with trainers to assist them in the use of satphones. It even smuggled at least thirty-four foreign correspondents into rebel-held areas, including the French photographer Rémi Ochlik, who was killed alongside *Sunday Times* correspondent Marie Colvin in Homs. As the armed insurgency intensified, Avaaz smuggled $2 million worth of supplies to the rebels' medical teams, according to the *Guardian*.

The cozy relationship that Avaaz enjoyed with the journalist corps that parachuted into Syria transferred over to the Syria Campaign, which drew heavily from the directors of Avaaz and Purpose. As foreign correspondents became increasingly unable to enter the country, either because the Syrian government refused to grant them visas or because the insurgents had developed a nasty habit of kidnapping and sometimes executing journalists, they turned increasingly to the public relations outfit for a steady stream of quotes, photos and even storylines from opposition activists.

James Sadri, former director of the Syria Campaign, acknowledged to me that his operation had been involved in shopping editorials to major publications. "There have been op-eds in the past that we've helped get published, written by people on the ground. There's a lot of op-eds going out from people inside Syria," he told me.

In July 2016, staffers of the PR company appeared in the studios of Channel 4 in London at a gathering of wealthy donors known as the Funding Network. The goal was to raise funds for a documentary about the White Helmets that would air on Netflix. "The Syria Campaign made a fantastic pitch for funding for their outreach work surrounding *The White Helmets*," the Funding Network reported. The group noted, however, that "for reasons of confidentiality, we are unable to post the Syria Campaign's pitch for the time being."

Soon after the documentary aired on Netflix in October 2016, it was nominated for an Oscar.

Thanks to the almost seamless nexus between opposition-funded public relations firms and the Western media, the viewing public was sold on a parade of colorful characters designed to distract them from the ugly reality of the armed insurgency. The most captivating of these figures was Bilal Abdul Kareem, an African American former stand-up comedian from Harlem, New York City, who converted to Islam and somehow popped up in rebel-held Syrian territory with a sophisticated media operation. Abdul Kareem's videography skills earned him a freelance gig with CNN, during which he led the network's top foreign correspondent, Clarissa Ward, into insurgent-held eastern Aleppo for an award-winning, unmistakably pro-opposition special broadcast. He also produced reports for Channel 4, the BBC, and was even named Al Jazeera English's "personality of the week." During the final days of the battle of Aleppo, CNN International's Hala Gorani introduced Abdul Kareem as an "independent journalist."

Abdul Kareem's relationship with major Western outlets was almost as cozy as the one he enjoyed with some of the most ferocious Al Qaeda–linked figures in Syria. Abdullah al-Muhaysini, the Saudi cleric who emerged as the most prominent voice of Al Qaeda's forces in Syria, celebrated Abdul Kareem in a friendly sit-down: "Greetings to our media man, the great innovator, Bilal Abdul Kareem!" Though Abdul Kareem denied being a member of Al Qaeda, Abdullah Abu Azzam, an activist affiliated with the rebel group Kataib Thawar al-Sham, told me that the American exile had produced videos for an array of jihadist clerics under the pseudonym "Abu Omar." Meanwhile, Akif

Razaq, an employee of Abdul Kareem's online media group, On the Ground News, was stripped of British citizenship on the grounds that he was "aligned with an al-Qaeda-aligned group" and "presents a risk to the national security of the United Kingdom."

Inarguably the most successful propaganda mascot of the Syrian opposition was a seven-year-old girl named Bana al-Abed. Bana became an instant international celebrity and won droves of Western fans who followed her every move thanks to the video messages and pleas for intervention published each day at her Twitter account—"it's better to start 3rd world war," read one of them. Though she faked it as best as she could, Bana had no ability to understand English; her mother and a collection of helpers appeared to be writing her tweets and scripting her video soliloquies with help from editors at CNN and Turkish state media. During the battle for rebel-held eastern Aleppo, where al-Abed and her family were embedded, CNN host Jake Tapper introduced the little girl as "the face of innocent civilian suffering in Syria" and read a tweet from the girl's Twitter account beseeching Trump to "do something for the children of Syria." Matthew Rycroft, British ambassador to the UN, also quoted al-Abed as he made his case for intervention at the Security Council.

After Aleppo was taken from the insurgents, Bana and her family joined jihadist forces on a bus convoy to Al Qaeda–held Idlib. From there, they were shepherded into Turkey, where Bana became a centerpiece of state propaganda and was made a citizen following a bizarre photo-op with its Islamist president, Erdoğan. She was also granted an audience at Erdoğan's palace with American actress Lindsay Lohan, who spoke in a bizarrely put-on Arabic accent. Though Bana could not read, write or speak English, Simon & Schuster granted the girl a major book contract following dealings with the literary agency of J.K. Rowling, who had helped promote Bana's Twitter account and cultivated the child as a global celebrity. At the 2018 Academy Awards ceremony in Hollywood, Bana made a cameo appearance on stage during a performance of the liberal feel-good anthem, "Stand Up For Something," by rapper Common and singer Andra Day. By this point, the revelations that Bana's father, Ghassan al-Abed, had been an armed member of one of the Islamist militias that formerly occupied eastern Aleppo had tumbled down the Orwellian memory hole.

However, even as the White Helmets drove the Western media's narrative about the conflict, the Syria Campaign struggled to suppress the myriad reports appearing in alternative and social media of group members' involvement with jihadist groups, and even their direct involvement in atrocities.

During the victory party in Idlib's central square in March 2015, when al-Nusra and its Salafi-jihadist allies captured the city of Idlib from the government, several White Helmet members appeared alongside gunmen from al-Nusra at the city's main clock tower to celebrate. Across Idlib, they were filmed carrying rifles for the conquering rebels and standing triumphantly with al-Nusra fighters atop a Syrian government flag.

Among the celebrating White Helmets was Muawiya Hassan Agha. The same month that al-Nusra took Idlib, Agha provided an extensive eyewitness account to an opposition human rights group known as the Violations Documentation Center on the alleged deployment of chemical weapons by Syrian government warplanes. The report described him as a "media activist," when in fact, Agha's own Facebook page offered copious evidence that he had also fought as a member of al-Nusra. A year later, Agha appeared in a video depicting his rebel cohorts torturing two captured Syrian conscripts they later executed. The White Helmets forced him to resign only after his violence was exposed by pro-government social media activists.

The rebel conquest of northern Syria was captured on camera in vivid detail by Hadi al-Abdallah, a media activist from the USAID-funded media outlet Radio Fresh, whom the Syria Campaign frequently promoted. A fearless presence in Syria's deadly combat zones, al-Abdallah was also an unabashed cheerleader for the Al Qaeda–led coalition known as Jaish al-Fatah. When these jihadist rebels took al-Mastuma camp in Idlib, al-Abdullah was there to promote those he called "the heroes of Jaish al-Fatah." Among those he interviewed in the camp was Abu Qaswarah, a triumphant commander of the jihadist group Jund al-Aqsa, which was formed as an offshoot of ISIS.

"Syria will remain Sunni! Syria is Sunni, not Shi'ite!" Qaswarah exclaimed before al-Abdallah exchanged congratulatory hugs with his troops.

In one particularly ghoulish on-camera appearance, al-Abdallah toyed with a group of Syrian soldiers trapped in a collapsed building as they begged for their lives—"Oh, now you know God?" he asked tauntingly, guffawing as the soldiers pleaded for mercy.

Like the White Helmets, al-Abdallah had benefited from heavy promotion by the Syria Campaign. With the group's help, he was awarded the prestigious Press Freedom Award by the French NGO, Reporters Without Borders, honoring him for "enabl[ing] civil society's actors to speak to the outside world." On Twitter, the US embassy in Syria—an entity that only existed online—congratulated al-Abdallah for his award, while the *New York Times* produced a ten-minute documentary puff piece about the rebel media activist called *Dying to Be Heard*.

Consolidating his status as a star of the Western-backed Syrian opposition, al-Abdallah appeared in the HBO documentary, *Cries From Syria*, a two-hour-long commercial for Syria's opposition. Following a screening of the film inside the US Capitol, where it was introduced by Republican representative Adam Kinzinger and Democratic representative Brendan Boyle—a perfect portrait of the bipartisan foreign policy establishment in action—its Russian Israeli director Evgeny Afineevsky melted down when journalist Dan Cohen confronted him with videos of al-Abdallah celebrating with jihadist rebels and taunting trapped soldiers. After denying the authenticity of the videos, Afineevsky stutteringly accusing Cohen of participating in Russian propaganda.

Afineevsky was no less irked when Cohen whipped out his cell phone to show him an execution filmed in 2015 in the rebel-held town of Haritan. It featured two members of the White

Helmets waiting just off camera while a member of al-Nusra shot a man dressed in street clothes in the head after reading out a death sentence. Seconds later, the White Helmets team tossed the freshly executed man on a stretcher and scrambled away.

The video of the two White Helmets members immediately packing up the man's body prompted a carefully worded statement by the organization condemning the killing and claiming its members were simply fulfilling their task to perform "the emergency burial of the dead."

This was not the only footage of White Helmets participating in public executions. In May 2017, Syrian opposition activists uploaded a cell phone video of a public execution in the rebel-held city of Jasim, in Syria's southern Daraa province. The video showed three men from the White Helmets rushing into the center of a crowd, mere seconds after the alleged criminal sentenced to death was shot in the head, and taking away the body on a stretcher. A member of the White Helmets can be seen celebrating along with the crowd of onlookers.

Members of the White Helmets had even been filmed operating alongside ISIS, as British journalist and ISIS hostage John Cantlie inadvertently acknowledged when he referred to a White Helmets' team working behind him as "the Islamic State's fire brigade." Cantlie had been forced to appear in the propaganda video, posing as a journalist and promoting the Islamic State's narrative in exchange for his own survival.

In March 2017, in a video message honoring the sixth anniversary of the Syrian uprising, Abu Jaber, a leader of the new Al Qaeda–led rebel coalition in Syria, Hay'at Tahrir al-Sham, hailed the White Helmets as the "hidden soldiers of the revolution."

The intimate bond between the White Helmets and extremist insurgents is the most striking evidence that the United States and other Western governments have provided civil infrastructure for the very jihadists they had sworn to destroy during the so-called "war on terror." Yet the group's seamy side has never been reported in mainstream Western media—mere mention of the group's ties to Al Qaeda and its allies is strictly taboo. In fact, one of the only mainstream mentions of the White Helmets' involvement with jihadist rebels was in Snopes, the supposedly methodical fact-checking site, which dismissed the preponderance of evidence of jihadist ties as "false"—and with negligible explanation.

Meanwhile, the Syria Campaign produced a lengthy paper, "Killing The Truth," on how "Russia is fueling a disinformation campaign to cover up war crimes in Syria," and blaming the Russian-backed network, RT, for criticism of the White Helmets' relationship with extremist militias. At no point, however, did the Syria Campaign or any of the mainstream pundits who similarly blamed Russia for tarring the White Helmets' heroic image debunk a single piece of "disinformation." Instead, they resorted to condescending dismissal, branding their opponents as "conspiracists," "Assadists," and "useful idiots."

The cover-up of the White Helmets' real activities suggested that an elaborate scam had been deployed to deflect from the scandalous operation to flood Syria with weapons and empower those that Hillary Clinton once described as "the hard men with guns." But for ordinary Syrians who bore the brunt of the chaos, and for Europeans beset with an unprecedented refugee crisis, no amount of propaganda could obscure the ghastly consequences of the West's dirty war on another formerly stable Arab state.

9

Collateral Damage, Indirect Benefits

The Syrian civil war produced perhaps the worst refugee crisis since World War II. A staggering 5 million refugees were forced outside Syria's borders, with many settling in camps that amounted to human warehouses, while a million others fled to Europe. By the end of 2016, the crisis had a seismic impact on the West, with the refugee question swinging elections across Europe and driving politics to the farthest shores of the right. Members of the Western political establishment behind the policies that had fueled the conflict placed the full weight of responsibility on President Assad, Russia and Iran—anyone but themselves. But the reality behind the conflict was more complex and far too inconvenient for them to acknowledge.

The refugees I met in 2013 in the Zaatari refugee camp slept in tents in the windswept desert along the Jordanian-Syrian border. It was the third largest city in Jordan at the time, but it was not really a city at all. Many residents were forced to dig holes for toilets, subsisted on donated food and water, and a few told me they spent nights fending off packs of wild dogs. The majority of the camp's residents were under the age of eighteen and only slightly more than half of them had any access to education.

Why were they there? These refugees hailed from the early bases of rebellions against Assad like Daraa, a bastion of conservative Sunni opposition to the government's rule. They had paid a terrible price for rising up and were now warehoused indefinitely, surrounded by Jordanian and French intelligence stations and separated from the nearest city by kilometers of desert. Among the few able to leave were two young men I witnessed walking past a Jordanian intelligence station toward the Syrian border. When my guide asked them where they were going, one responded simply, "To make jihad."

But not all refugees fled for the same reason. Max Abrahms, the political scientist from Northeastern University, oversaw a specialized seven-person research team deployed across the western Balkan migration route to Europe in 2015 and 2016. Abrahms' team conducted 130 in-depth interviews with Syrian refugees in camps, transit centers and across the migration route. What he and his colleagues found shattered the conventional interventionist narrative about the refugee crisis. According to the data they collected, only 16 percent of refugees held Assad entirely responsible for their flight. The vast majority—77 percent—blamed both the Syrian government and the foreign-backed armed groups committed to its overthrow.

"The conventional wisdom was that all the refugees were fleeing from Assad. Part of the Western narrative was that the Syrian conflict was a one-sided genocide," Abrahms explained to me. "But the refugees we interviewed were much less likely to blame their leaving on Assad than they were to blame multiple belligerents—to blame Assad and the armed [insurgent] groups. At least according to the population, they left because they found the overall situation really dangerous and didn't align with any of the warring parties."

Another pivotal factor driving the refugee crisis was the crushing sanctions imposed on Syria by the United States and its allies.

The Syrian Center for Policy and Research found that following the collapse of domestic production of pharmaceuticals two years into the conflict, sanctions had "affected the importation of lifesaving medicines used in the treatment of hepatitis, cancer, and [a] variety of inoculations not produced in Syria." Sanctions also caused Syria's manufacturing sector to contract by a staggering 70 percent, while its mining and tourism industry was shattered. Air travel, meanwhile, had grown increasingly perilous thanks to American restrictions on the import of civilian airliner parts. In short, the United States and EU had waged all-out economic warfare on Syria and its civilians, and all because its government refused to stand down in the face of an armed insurgency.

In September 2015, a three-year-old Syrian Kurdish boy named Alan Kurdi was found dead on a beach at Bodrum, Turkey. He was one among thousands of casualties of the smuggling route to Europe. Along with his mother, Rehanna, his father, Abdullah, and his five-year-old brother, Ghalib, Alan's family had fled Damascus when the armed revolt broke out in 2011, then were forced to escape from the Kurdish town of Kobane after it became the site of heavy fighting between ISIS and US-backed Kurdish fighters. The Kurdi family found sanctuary in Turkey, but their application for asylum to Canada was repeatedly rejected despite the best efforts of Abdullah's sister, Tima, who was already living in British Columbia.

In desperation, the family paid a smuggler $4,400—far more than the cost of a flight to Canada—to ferry them to the Greek island of Kos. But almost as soon as the rickety boat was in the water, it was struck by powerful waves, the captain fled, and Abdullah struggled in vain to save his family as they were swallowed by the Mediterranean. The heartrending image of three-year-old Alan lying face down in a red shirt, blue shorts and Velcro shoes became an instant international symbol of the refugee crisis. The photograph was carried on newspaper covers across Western capitals, generated reams of editorials demanding emergency assistance for refugees and put Canada's right-wing government on the defensive. "It was something about that picture," Tima Kurdi reflected. "God put the light on that picture to wake up the world.

Tima arrived on the Capitol Hill lawn on an unusually balmy day in February 2017. She was a petite woman with an outsized presence and voluminous mane of dyed blonde hair. She had been invited to Washington by Representative Tulsi Gabbard to help press the case for her bill, the Stop Arming Terrorists Act. The proposal called for the United States to end all overt and covert assistance to the Syrian rebels.

Hailing from a liberal district in Honolulu, Hawaii, Gabbard was a telegenic thirty-six-year-old veteran of the Iraq War who had been considered one of the Democratic Party's rising progressive stars. She had been a top surrogate of Senator Bernie Sanders in his quixotic run for the presidency and a guest on national political gabfests like HBO's *Real Time with Bill Maher*. By disrupting the near-total consensus over the arming of the rebels, and by attempting to make their jihadist composition the subject of public debate, Gabbard had touched the third rail of Washington political culture.

Gabbard's Stop Arming Terrorists Act was a by-product of her trip in January 2017 to Syria, where she met with Syrians in government-held territory, including internally displaced people who had fled from the rebels and ISIS. During the visit, Gabbard accepted an impromptu invitation to meet with Assad. "In order for any peace agreement, in order for any possibility of a viable peace agreement to occur, there has to be a conversation with him," Gabbard said of Assad, flagrantly rejecting the Washington consensus on regime change. "I think we should be ready to meet with anyone if there's a chance it can help bring about an end to this war, which is causing the Syrian people so much suffering."

On her return, Gabbard was pilloried for challenging the interventionist line. Among those who lashed into her was Josh Rogin, the *Washington Post* neoconservative columnist, who branded the congresswoman as "Assad's mouthpiece in Washington." Representative Adam Kinzinger, a recipient of substantial funding from arms industry giants, and one of the most reliable allies of the multimillion dollar Saudi lobby, piled on, calling Gabbard's meeting with Assad "a disgrace." Against these powerful bipartisan interests, Gabbard stood virtually alone.

For all the attention and enmity she had received for her trip to Syria, Gabbard's press conference on the Capitol lawn was virtually ignored by the Beltway press corps. While scores of activists from the women's reproductive rights group Planned Parenthood held an exuberant rally a hundred yards away, Gabbard found herself introducing Tima Kurdi before a crowd of four reporters and three onlookers. The nephew of Tima Kurdi, little Alan Kurdi, might have been an icon of the Syrian refugee crisis, but most Capitol Hill reporters had kept away from the presser.

After the event, I spoke to Kurdi about her path to political activism. She told me it began during a trip to Brussels, where she met Syrian refugees across the city and heard their stories. "One group of refugees would tell me a heartbreaking story about how they lost their kids to Assad," she said. "Then I'd meet another group who'd tell me they lost theirs to the rebels. But when I would watch the news, it was always, 'Assad is evil,' but they never talked about all the people who were suffering from the rebels."

Kurdi said she began doing research and discovered that the rebel groups "were funded to keep fighting and divide Syria, and it's all become about money and power with civilians caught in the middle. And this was not fair to me," she decided. "The reality is, they don't want to end the war in Syria, they want to keep funding the rebels."

After Alan Kurdi became an international symbol of the plight of Syrian refugees, Tima Kurdi said she was approached by the Syria Campaign, the opposition-funded public relations firm. "They came to me and asked me to support the overthrow of Bashar but I said, no, Bashar did not chase my family away, ISIS did."

Kurdi pointed to Iraq as a lesson in the dangers of regime change. She and her family loathed Saddam Hussein for his treatment of the Kurds, especially his massacre of the villagers at Halabja with chemical weapons. "I will never forget how he buried that town alive," she said. "Look at Libya. It's the same thing. I'm not for Bashar and I wasn't for Saddam but we need to change the policy of regime change."

Kurdi saw the instability that wars of regime change had caused as inextricably linked to the rise of Islamophobia. She told me that for her prominence as a relative of perhaps the most memorable and tragic symbol of refugee plight, she was deluged with attacks from right-wing supporters of President Donald Trump. "It took me three days to recover from being called so many names," she said.

Prime-time Soldiers

All across the European continent, the refugee crisis was propelling the rise of far-right parties that had been confined to the margins only years before. With austerity-induced rioting spreading and thousands of refugees washing up on the continent's southern shores each day, working and middle class Europeans increasingly fell under the sway of rightist demagogues determined to channel their anti-elitist resentment toward an easy scapegoat.

I witnessed the power of migrant baiting at a massive far-right rally in Helsinki, Finland, where the country's second-largest party joined forces with bands of neo-Nazis. Because much of Finland was fixated on the nationally televised Independence Day festivities on December 6, 2015, downtown Helsinki was eerily empty. A thousand or so far-right activists had taken over the streets, rallying first on a frosty square. The demonstration was planned in coordination with the True Finns, the anti-migrant populist party that held the second largest number of seats in the country's parliament at the time.

One after another, speakers invoked the popular conspiracy theory that had helped send the True Finns to power. According to these activists, the refugee crisis was not the blowback from wars and instability fueled by the West and its regional allies, but a calculated plot to destroy traditional European culture.

Terhi Kiemunki, a member of the board of the True Finns party, pointed to ISIS as the source of the plot: "A couple of years ago, the ISIS leader Abu Bakr al-Baghdadi set the goal that Western countries that cannot be militarily taken should be invaded from within." Kiemunki then asked her audience, "Have you thought about why the wave of refugees started from Iraq and Afghanistan started only now, even though there has been a war there for more than a decade?"

"In 2030," another activist from a far-right group called Close The Borders warned, "we'll have, like, half a million immigrants. I don't know about you, but this sounds like genocide!"

At the height of the rally, a large screen was unfurled on stage for a showing of a viral online piece of agitprop that had become one of the global far-right's top recruiting vehicles. It was a documentary called *With Open Gates: The Forced Collective Suicide of European Nations*, and it depicted a continent under assault from a wave of Arab and black conflict zombies yearning to sexually vandalize as many fair white maidens as possible and live high on the welfare hog. Promoted by Breitbart as "a dispatch from the future," the nineteen-minute film garnered 1.5 million hits on YouTube in the first five days after its initial release.

The real villains in *Open Gates* were not the migrants themselves, but the liberal dupes who celebrated their mass influx, particularly German chancellor Angela Merkel, who had staked her legacy on her commitment to taking in more than 1 million refugees. At the same time, the film introduced terrified viewers to a rising hero from across the Atlantic: Donald Trump.

"Look, I've been watching this migration, and I see the people," Trump intoned to an interviewer as montages of menacing crowds of migrants flash on screen. "They're men, and they're strong men! These are young men and they're physically strong men. They look like prime-time soldiers." Having just launched his campaign for president of the United States, Trump was channeling the sensibility of Europe's far right and its rising obsession with demographic threats.

At the rally in Helsinki, activists appeared obsessed with the sexual danger posed by refugees. From the stage, True Finns youth leader and former Big Brother Finland reality show star Sebastian Tynkkynen wondered aloud, "When so-called tolerant people open their hearts to those who take advantage of our society and cannot integrate, our women and daughters have to open their legs. Who is the next victim? Is it my own sister?"

The True Finns were led by Jussi Halla-aho, a member of the European parliament. Halla-aho's anti-Muslim diatribes resulted in his conviction in the Finnish Supreme Court for racial defamation and disturbing the sanctity of religion. The high-profile trial enabled him to portray himself before his party's nativist base as a champion of free speech under siege by the politically correct establishment. Having risen to fame through his blog, *Scripta: Diaries From The Declining West*, Halla-aho warned, "We are repeating every mistake Sweden, for instance, has made before us. Most Finnish cities will be surrounded by a ring of burning ghettoes."

The Independence Day march represented a convergence between the more mainstream rightist organizations like True Finns and the militant Nordic Resistance Movement. The Resistance Movement, which received resources from its more numerous neo-Nazi cousins next door in Sweden, appeared at the march in black bomber jackets and jeans, bearing torches that illuminated the darkened streets of Helsinki. As the march passed a group of leftist counter-demonstrators held back by militarized police firing fusillades of FN 303 "less lethal" plastic bullets, the far-right forces chanted, "Thank you, police!" (Less than a year later, Resistance Movement members beat a protester to death at their rally in central Helsinki.)

"There hasn't been a lot of cooperation before between the different actors but we saw ... that these marches are an important way to gather actors from different parts of the nationalist scene," Li Andersson, a twenty-nine-year-old member of parliament and leader of Finland's Left Alliance, explained to me. "It's a problem because it normalizes them more but I would say it makes them stronger when they're able to cooperate in this way."

Andersson was the co-author of the first critical book-length survey of the Finnish far right. As payback for her work, she became the target of a sustained deluge of rape threats, including from activists at the Independence Day march, who joked from the stage about sexually assaulting her with a cactus. "The whole irony here is it's coming from the same guys who say they're now worried about the rights of women in Finland because of these rape issues [from asylum seekers]," Andersson said.

As the Independence Day marchers proceeded away from downtown Helsinki, Finnish police dragged scattered leftist counter-demonstrators into paddy wagons, clearing a path to the rally's final destination. There, in a vast graveyard, as a hard rain poured from the darkened sky, the marchers gathered before a memorial to the Finnish veterans who had fought alongside the Nazi SS in World War II. The tombs of these fallen soldiers contained much more than the skeletons of a collaborationist army that fended off the Soviets. In the minds of the nationalist marchers, they housed the spirit of a once-pure culture sullied by a foreign invasion and the globalist elites that orchestrated it. And so they laid candles and roses at the base of the tomb and bowed their heads in silent tribute.

Sex Crime Panic

All over Europe, extremist outfits were moving from the farthest shores of the right to the mainstream, propelled by a simple promise to voters: we will bring stable work back to your country and keep the Muslims out of your neighborhood. The message resonated with a war-weary population that had seen its standard of living decline under a combination of center-right and center-left rule, and they could hardly differentiate between the two sides any longer.

A model of ultra-nationalist leadership lay in Hungary, where Prime Minister Victor Orban had won widespread support and made himself the bane of Brussels with his "zero refugee strategy." The walls Orban had built on Hungary's southern border, designed to prevent the influx of refugees, had become a model for the kind Trump promised to erect on the US-Mexico border. In France, meanwhile, Marine Le Pen's anti-immigrant National Front, founded by her Holocaust revisionist father, Jean-Marie, had moved out of its southern base and made her a national contender. After the wholesale collapse of France's center-left Socialist Party, Le Pen was narrowly defeated for prime minister by Emmanuel Macron, a multimillionaire businessman with no political experience who represented an aggressively neoliberal brand of French Republicanism. Macron immediately set out to co-opt his challenger's immigrant restrictionism, prompting the National Front to tout its "political victory."

In Norway, just two years after the killing spree by Anders Breivik, a self-styled "counter-jihadist" inspired by the key voices of America's Islamophobia industry, his former party, the Progress Party, had become a junior partner in the country's government. Among its first items of business was the rejection of Syrian refugees on the grounds that they were mentally unfit. When I visited Oslo in 2015, the city was buzzing with reports that an ISIS flag had been unfurled in the town center, an isolated event that right-wing forces exploited to reinforce the sense of Western civilization under siege from within.

Next door, in the Scandinavian country that stood as a model of democratic socialism, a previously marginal party established by openly white supremacists, the Swedish Democrats, was suddenly polling right behind the ruling Social Democrats, hammering the government's decision to take in 160,000 refugees in 2015. In downtown Stockholm in early 2016, a gang of forty men dressed in all black, with black armbands, was filmed hunting down and beating refugees, or anyone who didn't look like a native Swede. They left behind manifestos that read, "We refuse to accept the repeated assaults and harassment against Swedish women."

The antirefugee moral panic reached terrifying heights on the final night of 2015, when a group of over sixty asylum seekers engaged in what appeared to be coordinated sexual assaults on women out to enjoy New Year's Eve celebrations in the German city of Cologne. The attackers hailed mostly from Morocco and were not among the newly arrived batch of asylum seekers Merkel had accepted. None of them appeared to be from Syria.

During one documented incident, in fact, a group of Syrian refugees valiantly protected a victim of assault and guided her to her boyfriend. Covered for days in German media, reports of the sex attacks in cities across the country began to pour in to local police departments, prompting a social media campaign that fueled the fire of grassroots groups like Pegida. Recognizing how the far-right pressure had stimulated the outrage of the general public, Germany's mainstream media and political class exploited the indignation for maximum effect.

The tabloid empire of right-wing media baron Axel Springer was a predictable source of antirefugee red meat in the days after the attacks, but liberal publications chimed in as well. *Süddeutsche Zeitung*, a mainstream outlet, featured a black hand penetrating into the pelvic region of a white female silhouette in its cover story on the Cologne attacks. As the town of Bornheim, just outside Cologne, banned all male refugees from its public swimming pools, citing a string of harassment complaints, the liberal daily *Tagesspiegel* featured an op-ed blaming the whole religion of Islam for the scandal. According to the author, "an Islamic socialization creates an image of woman which ends in such crimes." Nine months later, in German regional elections, the anti immigrant Alternative for Germany Party (AFD) won the largest share of the vote of any far-right party since World War II.

The unsettling results highlighted a trend that was put on display in the United States after 9/11 and which had been masked momentarily by the election of Barack Obama. It was what the sociologist Christopher Bail called the "fringe effect," where anti-Muslim and extremist organizations successfully hijack the mainstream media by mobilizing public outrage, amplifying their influence and overwhelming their liberal opponents with a narrative rooted in fear and anger. But there was another ingredient in the far-right parties' mainstream appeal, the product of a long-term strategy focused on submerging their history of anti-Semitism in the politics of ultra-Zionism. For its own opportunistic reasons, Israel's transatlantic lobbying apparatus was eager to play along.

Their Fight Is Our Fight

In Germany, the country that prided itself more than any other European nation on having reconciled with the ghosts of its fascist past, Chancellor Angela Merkel's decision to admit over 1 million newly arrived refugees generated a terrible backlash. The membership of the grassroots anti-Muslim Pegida movement swelled across the country, providing a seemingly legitimate popular cover for hardcore activists from the Young National Democrats and other neo-Nazi groupings. In 2015, the year that Pegida took to the streets, German police recorded more than 1,000 attacks on refugee homes.

The AFD, meanwhile, was making major inroads in local elections by branding Merkel as a *Volksverraeter*, or a traitor to the German people. The brazen insult represented the resurgence of a Nazi-era phrase that had been taboo since 1945. Formed out of the right wing of Germany's Christian Democratic Union (CDU), the AFD drew on the political tradition of figures like Alfred Dregger, a Nazi war veteran who campaigned heartily for the release of German war criminals. Alexander Gauland, a founder of the AFD, emerged out of Dregger's political network in Brandenburg, while Dregger's successor in the German Bundestag, Martin Hohmann, helped form the AFD after being expelled from the CDU for blaming a Jewish plot for the Bolshevik revolution.

Next door, the Austrian Freedom Party drew on a similar tradition. Founded in 1950 by a former officer of the Waffen SS, the Freedom Party enjoyed its first swell of popularity in the 1990s under the leadership of the late Jorg Haider, who described the SS as "men of character" and routinely soft-pedaled the Holocaust. Under the leadership of Heinz Christian Strache, who seized the reins of the party from Haider in 2005, the Freedom Party made strides to mainstream respectability by transmuting its traditional anti-Semitism into the increasingly popular politics of Islamophobia. The alliance that Strache formed with Israel's Likud Party and his flamboyant displays of Zionism were key to his strategy.

A conference on the "new anti-Semitism" sponsored by the Freedom Party put the far right's play for mainstream appeal on bold display. Held in an opulent downtown Vienna hotel in November 2016, the conference starred the hard-line Israeli former army chief of staff Rafael Eitan, who advocated the ethnic cleansing of Palestinians he described as "cockroaches," and Michael Kleiner, a top Likud Party apparatchik. The event's theme revolved around a concept rolled out by the pro-Israel lobby, which held that a "new" anti-Semitism of Muslims had joined forces with leftist opponents to Zionism to supplant the old bigotry against Jews that once emanated from the Christian West. Earlier that year, Strache had traveled to Israel at the invitation of the Likud Party, which hosted him for a visit to the Yad Vashem Holocaust memorial.

The Freedom Party's conference on anti-Semitism was timed to advance the hopes of Norbert Hofer, its candidate for the presidency. At the time, he was running neck and neck with the Green Party-affiliated Alexander Van der Bellen. "Islam is not a part of Austria," Hofer proclaimed. "By the year 2050, 50 percent of the children [in Austria] under 12 will be Muslims ... The kind of politics that is permitting a changing face of Austria and Europe has to be opposed." Hofer failed in his bid for the presidency; however, by the end of 2017, the Freedom Party had won enough seats in parliament to gain a role in the governing coalition. Strache thus became vice chancellor while his party took control of three major ministries.

The Freedom Party's ultra-Zionism was part of a wider trend that saw far-right parties across western Europe exploiting Israel and Zionism to paper over their unsavory anti-Semitic roots. Marine Le Pen—the leader of France's National Front, which was founded by her father, Jean Marie, a notorious Holocaust minimizer—played on Jewish fears of Muslim immigrants, insisting to them "that the Front National is not your enemy, but that it is without a doubt the best shield to protect you against the one true enemy, Islamic fundamentalism." In the Netherlands, the far-right Party of Freedom leader Geert Wilders had risen from the backbench of parliament to presidential contender with his pledge to ban the Quran and forcibly drive out Moroccan immigrants from Dutch cities. Unlike Le Pen, whom the Israeli government treated with suspicion (while forging ties in private), Wilders was welcomed with open arms in Israel.

More than anyone, he represented the power of the new right-wing axis that stretched from Washington through Europe and reached its ideological source in Netanyahu's Israel, the garrison state that marketed itself as a Fort Apache on the front lines of the clash of civilizations.

Wilders claimed to have formed his views about Muslims during the time he worked on an Israeli cooperative farm in the 1980s. "If Jerusalem falls into the hands of the Muslims, Athens and Rome will be next," Wilders warned in 2010. "Thus, Jerusalem is the main front protecting the West. It is not a conflict over territory but rather an ideological battle, between the mentality of the liberated West and the ideology of Islamic barbarism."

Disgust with Europe's political establishment was not limited to the lower middle class voters who typically swung right in times of crisis. It was deeply felt among the metropolitan and unionized base of the UK Labour Party as well. In September 2015, Labour voters followed the trend of left populism embodied by parties from Spain's Podemos to Greece's Syriza and elected Jeremy Corbyn as the party's leader in September 2015.

A backbencher who had been largely unknown outside activist circles, Corbyn resisted a tidal wave of smears from the British tabloids by mobilizing tens of thousands of new Labour members in support of his leadership bid. He had gained popularity not only by railing against the US–EU Transatlantic Trade and Investment Partnership, a corporate trade deal, and the pro-austerity consensus, but by laying down a hard line against military intervention. An acolyte of the Labour Party's leftist icon Tony Benn, Corbyn maintained close ties to Stop the War UK, the grassroots movement Benn helped found to oppose the invasion of Iraq. With an army of committed volunteers behind him, Corbyn was able to put down one challenge after another to his leadership from Labour's centrist-liberal establishment, each one more nasty than the last.

Unlike his opponents among the Blairite center and the reactionary right, Corbyn's response to the refugee crisis that confronted Europe was informed by a keen understanding of its origins. "What comes around goes around. What goes around comes around," he remarked to journalist Amy Goodman. "And I think we've got to think very carefully about the policies we've had over the past fourteen years, ever since 9/11. 9/11 was a disaster—dreadful, awful, appalling. We bombed Afghanistan. Fourteen years later, Britain, mainly, has left Afghanistan; the US is still there. Is it a country at peace? No, there are many people now fleeing from Afghanistan because of the continued instability there. Surely, the future of this world has to be looking into the fundamental causes of these conflicts, not just dealing with the symptoms."

Corbyn's anti-interventionism extended to Syria, where he opposed the imposition of another NATO no-fly zone that would have provided a pretext for a war of regime change. His position provoked harsh condemnation from more established Labour members and galvanized their crusade to replace him with a figure closer to the neoliberal center. Leading the charge against Corbyn's stance on Syria was Jo Cox, a former policy director for the international aid industry's bastion, Oxfam, an ardent campaigner for the R2P doctrine and one of Labour's most forceful voices of military humanism.

Determined to force through a vote supporting a military assault targeting the Syrian government in October 2015, Cox joined forces with Andrew Mitchell, a member of parliament from the ruling Conservative Party. "Some may think that a military component has no place in an ethical response to Syria. We completely disagree," Cox and Mitchell wrote in an op-ed.

The two proceeded to form an intra-parliamentary "Friends of Syria" group to promote military intervention in Syria under the guise of "civilian protection."

Cox ultimately abstained on the vote to authorize air strikes against ISIS because they did not target the Syrian government as well—"by refusing to tackle Assad's brutality we may actively alienate more of the Sunni population, driving them towards ISIS," she argued in the parliamentary debate. She advanced this argument as ISIS was planning a new offensive to retake Palmyra from the Syrian government.

Within British politics, there were few politicians who were more ardent in their support for the Syrian opposition than Cox. In media appearances and op-eds, the self-proclaimed feminist promoted "the moderate [rebel] forces on the ground—the much discussed 70,000," citing the discredited number cooked up by the Gulf-funded Beltway think tank pundit Charles Lister. "We must not let America sell out the Syrian rebels to Putin and Assad," Cox demanded.

While passionately advocating for her government to accept more unaccompanied children fleeing from Syria, she had simultaneously lobbied for extending the country's civil war by funneling more arms to the rebels, implicitly rejecting any resolution to the crisis short of regime change. In maintaining such a seemingly contradictory position, Cox was firmly in line with western Europe's center-left, from Germany's Green Party to France's ruling Socialists.

On June 16, 2016, Cox was shot and stabbed to death on her way to a constituent meeting in West Yorkshire. Her attacker was Thomas Mair, a fanatical white supremacist and mentally disturbed recluse with a twenty-year history of support for the neo-Nazi National Alliance and Britain First. Mair blamed "white liberals and traitors" for contaminating Europe's traditionally white culture with their immigrant-friendly policies. He was immediately celebrated on white nationalist online forums like Stormfront for eliminating a race traitor.

"Britain first, keep Britain independent, Britain will always come first!" Mair shouted as he plunged a knife into Cox's chest again and again. "This is for Britain!"

Cox' s murder occurred in the final weeks before the June 2017 Brexit referendum, when the nation voted to leave the economic and political European Union. In fact, the phrase Mair had bellowed out as he murdered Cox was a slogan of the right-wing populist UK Independent Party (UKIP), which was one of the leading forces for Brexit. Cox had been a stalwart supporter of the Remain campaign, and had even attacked Corbyn for failing to support the EU with sufficient fervor.

UKIP's founder, Nigel Farage, mobilized support for the Leave campaign by stirring up a Kulturkampf against the EU for threatening Britain's white Christian identity. His appeals spoke to extremists like Mair, convincing them that they had a mainstream voice. Just hours before Mair killed Cox, Farage unfurled a new billboard ad for Brexit that showed a mass of Syrian refugees marching across the Balkans, heading ominously toward Western Europe. The apparently darkened image was accompanied by words that hinted at white demographic destruction: "Breaking Point."

Cox's death spurred a national outpouring of grief and made her a martyr of the Remain campaign. However, a far-right online hub run by neo-Nazi activist and former apartheid South African intelligence asset Arthur Kemp claimed that the killing of Cox galvanized antiestablishment fury against the EU and helped propel the popularity of Brexit.

Less than a third of exit polls predicted a Leave victory, filling opponents with confidence as voting on the referendum began on June 23, 2016. But in the end, London, a virtual bubble of affluence and cosmopolitanism, was the only region in England where voters overwhelmingly backed remaining in the EU. The vote to leave the EU had triumphed by a million votes, a stunning victory for Euroskeptic forces and the populist right across the West. Arriving at Trump Turnberry in Scotland for the reopening of his renovated open-venue golf resort, Donald Trump pronounced Brexit a "great thing." He had forged a close bond with Farage during the campaign and saw his triumph—and the xenophobic politics that propelled it—as a model for his own campaign.

In a wide ranging and unfailingly friendly interview with Michael Gove, the Conservative member of parliament who became a face of the center-right's pro-Leave forces, Trump pointed to the Syrian refugee crisis as the most powerful factor driving support for Brexit. "People, countries want their own identity and the UK wanted its own identity but, I do believe this, if they hadn't been forced to take in all of the refugees, so many, with all the problems that it, you know, entails, I think that you wouldn't have a Brexit," Trump said. "It probably could have worked out but, this was the final straw, this was the final straw that broke the camel's back."

Then Trump went further, blaming the West's interventions in the Middle East for creating the crisis. "Look, this whole thing should have never happened," he said in response to Gove's question on Merkel's refugee-friendly policies. "Iraq should not have been attacked in the first place, all right? It was one of the worst decisions, possibly the worst decision ever made in the history of our country. We've unleashed—it's like throwing rocks into a beehive."

That the refugee crisis was driving Europe to the hard right was undeniable. Trump's critique of Brexit was backed up by polling data that showed nearly 73 percent of prospective "leave" voters citing immigration as the most important issue in the referendum, just as the government had agreed to accept 20,000 Syrian refugees.

A comparative media study commissioned by the United Nations High Commissioner for Refugees confirmed that the "fringe effect" had also played a part in Brexit's success, finding that British media coverage of refugees was the "most hostile" of any European country. If there was any other factor that drove Leave voters, it was the sheer disgust they felt with the country's establishment and the sense that it would never change unless it was sent a powerful message of rejection.

In the wake of its rebuke from British voters, the Labour

Party's centrist wing seemed unusually eager to confirm the public's jaundiced perception of its agenda. The delusional politics of this faction were perfectly embodied in a report entitled "The Cost of Doing Nothing: The Price of Inaction in the Face of Mass Atrocities" that had been initiated by Jo Cox, and which was published in her memory by a collection of her interventionist party mates.

The paper had been initially timed as a response to the British government's Chilcot inquiry that found the government of Tony Blair guilty for deliberately misleading the British public about the threat of Saddam Hussein, choosing war over more viable diplomatic options, and ignoring manifold warnings about the imminence of sectarian bloodletting in Iraq. Delayed by Cox's murder, the publication was announced in January 2017 by Gordon Brown, the former Labour minister of defense who supported invading Iraq as "the right decision for the right reasons."

The paper amounted to a thirty-two-page defense of the Responsibility to Protect doctrine, arguing for more unilateral military campaigns in the name of "civil protection" and slamming antiwar elements—or what its authors branded as "knee jerk isolationism, unthinking pacifism and anti-interventionism in Britain." The paper lamented the UK's failure to enact a war of regime change in Syria, where pro-government forces were restoring control over large swaths of territory previously controlled by Al Qaeda–allied rebels and ISIS. How the toppling of another Middle Eastern government would not deepen the refugee crisis driving right-wing reactionary politics across Europe was left unexplained.

Just prior to the paper's release, Jo Cox's husband, Brendan, issued a fundraising appeal in his murdered wife's name for Hope Not Hate, a UK government-funded antiracist organization, and the Syrian White Helmets, the US- and British-backed first responder group that operated alongside Al Qaeda's local affiliate and even ISIS. Though Corbyn made a passionate appeal on behalf of the fundraising drive, Brendan Cox slammed the Labour leader's spokesman,

Seamus Milne, for urging protests outside the American embassy in London alongside those Cox had helped organize at the Russian embassy, calling his sentiments "absolutely disgraceful."

10

Attacking Our Team

With the lessons of Afghanistan, Iraq, Libya and Syria staring it in the face, and with the far right marching across Europe as a result of the blowback from these calamitous campaigns, the British Labour establishment remained defiantly wedded to the ideology of military interventionism. This tragic dynamic replicated itself across the Atlantic, on a much more dramatic scale, within the presidential campaign of Hillary Clinton. More than any other active politician, Clinton bore the legacy of the wars that had destabilized the Middle East and emboldened the populist right throughout the West. She entered the contest against Trump supremely confident, but as it dragged on, the ghosts of her interventionist past came back to haunt her.

If Donald Trump entered the 2016 presidential contest with low expectations, it was due in large part to the myopia of a Beltway press corps that shared all the prejudices of Washington's established political class. Over the course of a succession of corporate trade deals and post-9/11 interventions, the country's political culture had changed beneath them, but Beltway elites were too detached to notice.

The emails released by WikiLeaks from the hacked email account of Clinton campaign chief John Podesta provided an especially intimate portrait of a political establishment hovering above the lived experiences of average Americans and shuttling blithely between redoubts of coastal elitism. Throughout the email exchanges, Podesta can be found at "Hamptons and Vineyard money events," in Silicon Valley talking "philanthropy and social action" with Mark Zuckerberg, in Davos and back at the affluent island resort of Martha's Vineyard sipping "specially selected wines" with a rich investor at a "shoes optional" beachside party.

Along with his brother, Tony, John Podesta was the co-founder of the Podesta Group, a Washington lobbying firm that raked in millions each year from a stable of foreign government clients, including some of the world's most despotic, corrupt leaders. With a "fixture in Republican politics" at its helm, Jeb Bush deputy campaign manager Kimberley Fritts, the Podesta Group reaped over $1.7 million in a contract with Saudi Arabia's state-owned oil company and nearly $100,000 more from the Center for Studies and Media Affairs at the Saudi Royal Court.

The relationship with the Gulf states extended to the Center for American Progress, with a donation of $500,000 to $999,000 from the UAE embassy. Overseen by John Podesta, the think tank was farming out its staff to Hillary Clinton's presidential campaign, along with the foreign policy orthodoxy—the "Washington playbook"—they adhered to with almost religious dedication.

Trump's handlers had made a calculated decision to not only campaign against Clinton, but to treat the entire establishment—the mainstream media, Hollywood, and Washington's permanent bipartisan political class—as an opposition party. Trump's opening salvo came in the form of *Clinton Cash*, a 186-page read of foreign donations to the Clinton Foundation with special attention to its relationship with the royal families of Saudi Arabia and Qatar.

Authored by Peter Schweizer, the book was the brainchild of Steven Bannon, then editor-in-chief of Breitbart. Its research was funded by billionaire Robert Mercer through the Government Accountability Institute (GAI) that Bannon oversaw. Thanks to prepublication deals Bannon arranged with the *New York Times* and *Washington Post*, the book's most damaging revelations appeared first in mainstream media, shaping a narrative that steadily eroded Clinton's claim to be a "champion for everyday Americans." Though the illegality of her actions could not be established, an aroma of corruption trailed Clinton for the remainder of the campaign.

An all-out assault on Jeb Bush, a charter member of PNAC and the Great White Hope of the Republican Party's corporate backers, was the logical next step for the Trump campaign. Following the release of another book produced through GAI research, *Bush Bucks*, Trump roasted Bush and his family's neoconservative legacy of military failures.

The fireworks began at a November 2015 debate, when Bush began detailing a convoluted plan for a no-fly zone in Syria that would protect those he described as "moderate Islamists." Trump saw an opening and pounced: "Assad is a bad guy but we have no idea about the rebels. I read about the rebels, the moderate rebels, nobody even knows who they are," he proclaimed. Summarizing a conversation with an anonymous military official on the Syrian rebels, Trump said, "We're giving hundreds of millions of dollars in equipment to these people—we have no idea who they are! ... They may be far worse than Assad. Look at Libya, look at Iraq, look at the mess we have after spending trillions of dollars, thousands of lives, wounded warriors all over the place, who I love, all over, we have nothing!"

Trump's diatribe was among the most incendiary attacks on military interventionism ever witnessed by a nationally televised audience. And it was perhaps the first time the Bush family had been so publicly and personally skewered for the damage their wars had done to the country's social fabric. Defying the polling data that showed a bare majority of Republicans still voicing support for the invasion of Iraq, GOP primary voters lapped it up, sending Trump surging ahead of Bush by twenty points.

At a February 2016 Republican primary debate, Trump intensified his attack on Bush. The exchange began with Jeb Bush complaining that Trump was siding with Russia while it was "attacking our team" in Syria—a reference to the Salafist rebels allied with Al Qaeda.

"Jeb is so wrong!" Trump erupted. "We've spent five trillion dollars all over the Middle East, we have to rebuild our country, rebuild our infrastructure—you listen to [Bush] and you're gonna be there for another fifteen years."

As Bush reiterated his call for regime change in Syria, Trump cut in on him. "We're supporting troops and we don't even know who they are!" Trump barked, referring to the Syrian rebels. "We have no idea who they are!"

Bush attempted to punch back but only fell further into Trump's trap. "While Donald Trump was building a reality show," Bush said, referring to Trump's prime time reality TV vehicle *The Apprentice*, "my brother was building a security apparatus to keep us safe, and I'm proud of what he did."

"The World Trade Center came down under your brother's reign. Remember that?" Trump roared. "That's not keeping us safe!"

Trump had crossed a line, or at least the crowd of lobbyists, white-gloved party activists and campaign aides that filled the hall that night in South Carolina thought so, responding with a chorus of angry boos. The rebel billionaire had especially offended Marco Rubio, a dreary Cuban American senator from Florida and neoconservative pet project who was taking advice from a DC think tank called the Foreign Policy Institute, which had been spun out of PNAC.

"George W. Bush enforced what the international community refused to do," Rubio insisted, pounding his lectern in defense of invading Iraq. "And again, he kept us safe and I'm forever grateful for what he did for this country."

"How did he keep us safe when the World Trade Center came down?" Trump interjected. "I lost hundreds of friends—the World Trade Center came down during the reign of George Bush!"

Trump's rhetoric stunned Beltway political professionals. "Everything we know about political strategy suggests that

Trump's decision to attack George W. Bush will backfire," Curt Anderson, a mainline Republican strategist told *Politico*. "If it doesn't backfire, then it will be official; nothing can stop him."

Trump lamented the consequences of regime change in Iraq, proclaiming that Saddam Hussein "killed terrorists ... Today, Iraq is Harvard for terrorism." CNN spun his fundamentally accurate assessment as "express[ing] his preference for keeping dictators in power in the Middle East."

The political class had underestimated the depth of antiwar sentiment across middle America, and the depth of visceral hatred average Americans held for the political establishment. After a series of mind-bogglingly pointless interventions that had made legless, armless and otherwise combat-singed veterans a common sight across the country, even the Republican base that had once rallied around Bush's wars was demonstrating its willingness to take a chance on Trump.

The same phenomenon was witnessed within the Democratic Party's base, where Senator Bernie Sanders was being rewarded not only for his constant diatribes against the "millionaire and billionaire class," but also for hammering Clinton on her 2002 vote to authorize force against Iraq.

When Clinton and her surrogates criticized Sanders' plan for tuition-free college as reckless and unserious, for example, the self-described socialist reminded voters of her support for occupying Iraq: "When we went to war in Iraq, the trillions we spent there—not a problem." Clinton had no response to his quip.

Throughout the campaign, Clinton clutched to liberal interventionist orthodoxy with an almost faith-based dedication. In debates with both Sanders and Trump, she aggressively championed a no-fly zone over Syria, an effective call for regime change that would have placed the US military in direct conflict with Russia's. And, as a result, in May 2016, months before the general election began in earnest, Trump began chipping away at Clinton's foreign policy record: "Crooked Hillary Clinton's foreign interventions unleashed ISIS in Syria, Iraq and Libya. She is reckless and dangerous!" candidate Trump tweeted, earning over 7,000 retweets.

By this point, Trump was sending neoconservatives into a state of petulant frenzy. They turned to Clinton in droves, regarding her astutely as a lighter shade of neocon who would faithfully uphold the doctrine of American exceptionalism. She did nothing to discourage the perception. David Frum, a Canadian neoconservative and former Bush speechwriter who conceived the term "axis of evil" to help sway public opinion in support of invading Iraq, wound up issuing "The Conservative Case For Voting for Clinton" in the pages of the *Atlantic*, the putatively liberal magazine where he served as senior editor. Max Boot, the hyper-militaristic columnist who once wrote that "US imperialism has been the greatest force for good in the world," hailed Clinton for "supporting the Afghan surge [and] the intervention in Libya," and even vouched for her national security credentials in an online ad released by her campaign.

Michael Morell, a former CIA director who openly called for covert operations to "'make the Iranians pay a price in Syria ... make the Russians pay a price in Syria," joined Clinton's campaign foreign policy team. The consulting firm that employed Morell, Beacon Global Strategies, was a perfect symbol of the permanent state, representing almost a dozen clients from the arms industry, while providing foreign policy advice to the campaigns of Republican hawks Ted Cruz, Marco Rubio, Lindsey Graham, Carly Fiorina and Jeb Bush—almost the entire GOP field. The Washington-based firm had been founded by top foreign policy advisors to the Clinton campaign, Philippe Reines and Andrew Shapiro.

Perhaps the most consequential neoconservative supporter of Clinton's presidential bid was Robert Kagan, a co-founder of PNAC who had outlined a plan for America's "benevolent empire." In July 2016, Kagan hosted a "foreign policy professionals for Hillary" fundraiser at a Washington townhouse in July 2016. "I would say all Republican foreign policy professionals are anti-Trump," Kagan remarked at the bipartisan confab, where $25,000 was raised for Clinton. "I would say that a majority of people in my circle will vote for Hillary."

Fifth Columns and Fake News

In her bid to court the Republican establishment, Clinton carefully bifurcated the GOP into the bigots rallying behind Trump and "honorable Republicans" like John McCain, the neoconservatives' most reliable voice in the Senate. Clinton's strategy was on display during a speech in Reno, Nevada, in August 2016, where she painted Trump as the "temperamentally unfit" leader of "an emerging racist ideology known as the 'Alt-Right.'"

"A fringe element has effectively taken over the Republican Party," Clinton declared, outlining the antiblack, anti-Semitic politics of the alt-right and pronouncing Putin their global "godfather." It was as though the racist elements at the Republican base had emerged out of a clear blue sky, and not from the Southern strategy conceived in Nixon's campaign office back in 1972. Clinton then praised George W. Bush for condemning anti-Muslim bigotry after 9/11, omitting everything that came afterward, from the Patriot Act to the invasion of Iraq to the crackdowns on Muslim civil society leaders.

"Every day, more Americans are standing up and saying 'enough is enough'—including a lot of Republicans," she said. "I'm honored to have their support."

Clinton's strategy followed the logic that American voters would ratify the bipartisan establishment that her campaign symbolized rather than take a chance on an intemperate billionaire who spoke his mind with reckless abandon. With a wink and a nod, she had also signaled her eagerness to accommodate neoconservatives who reviled Trump's "America First" message.

From inside the Ritz Carlton, where the Clinton family presided over an "inspiring women"-themed insurance industry fundraiser during the Democratic National Convention, while protesters rallied in the downtown Philadelphia streets outside, the country seemed to be doing fine. "Despite what you hear, we don't need to make America great again. America has never stopped being great," Clinton insisted, repudiating Trump's campaign slogan, "Make America Great Again," and his constant refrain that "our country is going to hell."

early 1980s, the Islamophobes and flimflam artists of the far right fringe rapidly positioned themselves as the counter to the ossified conservative counter-establishment. Like the neocons, they saw their role as supplying their chosen candidate with a sharpened language and ideological ballast that set him apart from the field, not to turn out masses of voters. Trump was eager to play along, even catering to the icons of the 9/11 Truth movement and making several appearances on the nationally popular program of right-wing online media jock Alex Jones. "Your reputation is amazing. I will not let you down," Trump pledged to Jones. And Jones returned the favor with a blood oath. "I'm ready to die for Trump!" the gravel-voiced conspiracy monger proclaimed.

The massacre of forty-nine people at an Orlando nightclub on June 12, 2016, by Omar Mateen, a self-proclaimed "Islamic soldier" of ISIS during the height of the campaign, helped ground Trump's darkest visions in a plausible version of reality. This only fueled the sense Trump sought to encourage: that the clash of civilizations had finally come home. Just as 9/11 had helped propel Bush to re-election, the Orlando massacre was the catastrophic and catalyzing event Trump needed to electrify his campaign.

Following the bloodbath Mateen committed inside the gay-oriented Orlando, Florida nightclub known as Pulse, where he gunned down close to 50 people, police revealed to the public that the shooter had sworn allegiance to ISIS during the massacre, and that his name was decidedly non-Anglo and seemingly Middle Eastern. He was not someone who would have been banned under Trump's proposed Muslim travel ban, but a US citizen from Port Lucie, Florida. These facts were just enough to jolt the country during the height of a presidential election.

A flurry of rumors circulated after the massacre that Mateen had been a repressed homosexual who targeted a gay nightclub because it represented all he loathed within himself. His father, Seddique, told local media that Omar once flew into a rage at the sight of two men kissing on a sidewalk, but the FBI found no record of a double life, either on online dating forums or through interviews with patrons of Pulse.

The tapes of Mateen's calls with the police negotiator, Andy, revealed a determined killer explicitly tracing the source of his rage to the civil war in Syria and the American campaign against ISIS. Though he had never been to the Syrian battlefield or trained with any jihadist group, Mateen had clearly immersed himself in the group's propaganda, as well as in mainstream American news coverage that was invariably critical of the Syrian government and its Russian ally's campaign to roll back the rebels.

Though the killer singled out Russian air strikes for condemnation, he framed his paroxysm of murderous rage as an act of revenge for American assassinations of ISIS leadership in Iraq and Syria. As he said during his final moments, "Even though it's not air strikes, it's strikes fucking here ... Now you feel how it is."

Mateen's path to ISIS began where it ended: in a quintessentially American atmosphere suffused with violence and racial hatred. Having been ruthlessly bullied by classmates at a junior high school for severely emotionally disturbed students, Mateen came of age fantasizing about a career in law enforcement, applying to various police departments and seething at the rejections he invited with his outbursts of rage. He settled on a career as a private security guard, working for the global firm G4S and yearning for the gallantry of uniforms, shiny badges and powerful service weapons.

While doling out abuse to the weak, he endured it at the hands of his superiors. While working as a G4S guard at the Port Lucie courthouse, Mateen endured sustained harassment from racist co-workers. In a formal complaint he filed with G4S on September 27, 2013, Mateen alleged in painstaking detail a lengthy series of incidents of harassment by fellow security guards and cops who appeared to have been stirred into an anti-Muslim lather by the leading voices of the Islamophobia industry.

In the document, Mateen alleged that a sheriff's deputy named John Roleau taunted him, asking, "Don't you Arabs sleep with goats?" Mateen was of Afghan descent, not an Arab, and he was born in the United States.

He also claimed that Robert McNamara, a deputy and Gulf War veteran said to have a reputation for right-wing views, hailed the vehemently anti-Muslim former Republican representative Alan West as a hero, then declared, "we need to kill all the fucking Muslims."

Mateen also reported that someone had taunted him by slapping Representative Alan West campaign stickers on his car and deflating his front two tires while he was parked at the courthouse. (West was the far-right lawmaker who had boasted of brutally beating information out of an Iraqi civilian while serving in the army.)

According to notes by the deputy general counsel for G4S, Michael Hogsten, Mateen admitted that he had made outrageous claims of loyalty to Islamic extremist groups to get the racist cops off his back: "After Boston bombing occurred—everyone got really nasty—I said—know what I'm related to, Boston bomber is my first cousin and matter of [fact]—related to fort hood [sic] shooter—I know Kenya mall shooters—said so they would leave me alone," Mateen told him.

Under the mounting duress, Mateen confided to a local friend named Mohammed Malik that he had been shaken by the racial harassment he had endured at work. He told Malik that he had begun watching YouTube clips of speeches by Anwar al-Awlaki and that they moved him deeply. Al-Awlaki was a charismatic Yemeni American imam who had gravitated from the mainstream of America's Muslim community to the battlefield of southern Yemen, where he joined the country's Al Qaeda affiliate. Killed in a CIA drone assassination alongside his son, a sixteen-year-old American citizen named Abdulrahman, al-Awlaki lived on through his sermons.

Delivered in fluent English and with magnetic charisma, al-Awlaki's online diatribes racked up hundreds of thousands of views on YouTube. They became so popular, in fact, that Google monetized them by placing banner ads for iTunes and Hollywood blockbuster films alongside them. (It was not until late 2017 that Google wiped al-Awlaki's videos from its YouTube service.) His videos played an acknowledged role in influencing everyone from the Fort Hood shooter Nidal Hasan to the San Bernardino shooter Syed Rizwan Farook to so-called "underwear bomber" Umar Farouk Abdulmutallab. They also helped clarify the stark worldview that an acquaintance of Mateen's, Moner Mohammad Abusalha, adopted as he came to a decision in 2014 to make jihad in Syria.

Abusalha, referred to in Mateen's phone exchanges with a police negotiator as "my homie," was the twenty-two-year-old son of a Palestinian American and an American convert to Islam from Fort Pierce, Florida. In 2014, after intensive viewing of al-Awlaki's online sermons, Abusalha traveled to Syria to help establish an Islamic State. He found his way to Aleppo, joining up with the Al Qaeda–led rebels that had seized the city's eastern districts and had held them alongside an array of rebel factions.

In May 2014, after pledging loyalty to al-Nusra, Abusalha became the first American to carry out a suicide attack in Syria, driving a truck bomb into a restaurant filled with Syrian government soldiers. "This life sucked …" he complained in a final video message. "All you do is work forty, fifty, sixty hours a week, and then you go waste it on garbage, and then you do the same thing."

Abusalha and Mateen had not, in fact, been homies. At best, they were loose acquaintances who had attended the same mosque in Fort Pierce. Mateen's friend, Malik, had known Abusalha much better and was shocked when he learned that the young man had fallen into jihadist adventurism. Even more troubling to Malik was Mateen's confession that he had been consuming al-Awlaki videos as well. Malik called the FBI and informed them about his friend. The bureau had already been made aware of Mateen's outburst against his coworkers at the courthouse.

After interviewing Mateen, the FBI dispatched an informant to provoke him into a controlled terror plot that was supposed to result in his prosecution. As Sheriff Ken Mascara of Florida's

St. Lucie County told the Vero Beach *Press Journal*, the FBI dispatched an informant to "lure Omar into some kind of act and Omar did not bite."

Pawns in the Game

Completely overlooked in mainstream media coverage of the Orlando massacre, the revelation of FBI meddling raised questions about the bureau's role in Mateen's path to murder. Since 9/11, the FBI had relied heavily on informants to entrap scores of young, often mentally troubled Muslim men and send them to prison for as long as twenty-five years. These prosecutions hyped the threat of ISIS and Al Qaeda in the American mind, producing scores of high-profile convictions each year for terror plots that never would have taken place if the FBI had not hatched them.

In early 2016, the FBI encouraged an obviously inept convicted felon and recent convert to Islam named James Medina to bomb a South Florida synagogue and pledge allegiance to ISIS. He had never expressed any interest in the militant group before the FBI approached him, nor did he appear to have had any contact with it. On trial for planning to commit an act of terror with a weapon of mass destruction, Medina was portrayed in Jewish-oriented media outlets as a hardcore ISIS member spreading anti-Semitic terror. Medina's lawyer, however, insisted that his client was mentally ill and that he been a victim of entrapment.

Trevor Aaronson, the author of *Terror Factory: Inside the FBI's Manufactured War on Terror*, reported that nearly half of all terror prosecutions between September 11, 2001 and 2010 involved informants, including some with criminal backgrounds raking in as much as $100,000 from the FBI. Following the blueprint established by FBI informant Emad Salem in the 1995 "Day of Terror" trial, the FBI's assets often preyed on mentally ill men with little capacity to resist their provocations.

Though these dubious prosecutions were intensely covered by

mainstream media, from cable news networks to local papers, the role of FBI agents in ginning up terror plots and inflating the threat of groups like ISIS were rarely mentioned in reporting of the trials of hapless young Muslim men. Having fueled the rise of Al Qaeda and ISIS across the Middle East, the US government was now exaggerating the presence of their members inside America by ginning up terror plots.

The zealous prosecutions that resulted from manufactured terror plots were a rarely acknowledged but particularly corrosive aspect of Obama's legacy. As Aaronson noted, "the US government didn't prosecute anyone from a terrorism sting" during George W. Bush's last year in office. When Obama assumed power, however, sting operations resumed with staggering frequency, a tactic designed to cast his administration as just as tough on terror as any Republican. Under Obama, federal prosecutors announced an arrest resulting from a terrorism sting every sixty days, "suggesting that there are a lot of ineffective terrorists in the United States, or that the FBI has become effective at creating the very enemy it is hunting."

As a result, the public was left with the impression that sleeper cells were gestating in cities across the country, and was pressured to support the most reactionary policies proposed in the wake of real ISIS-inspired attacks like those witnessed in Orlando, San Bernardino and Boston. Following the 2013 Boston marathon bombings, while SWAT teams hunted down Dzhokhar Tsarnaev, who was unarmed at the time, Bostonians obeyed a voluntary "lockdown order" without a second thought, turning the city into a virtual ghost town and demonstrating how a state of emergency could be imposed with only the mildest coercion.

"This is a request that the public stay inside and they are adhering to it," Massachusetts state trooper Todd Nolan told *Time*. "There has been no law mentioned or any idea that if you went outside you'd be arrested."

While the FBI was unable to explain how many of the suspects arrested in sting operations might have ever otherwise engaged in terrorism, there is evidence to suggest the bureau's informant program played a role in provoking real violence.

According to Coleen Rowley, a former FBI agent and division counsel whose May 2002 memo to the FBI's director shed new light on the FBI's pre-9/11 failures, "In the case of Mateen, since he already worked for a security contractor [G4S], he was either too savvy to bite on the pitch [to carry out a terror attack] or he may have even become indignant that he was targeted in that fashion. These pitches and use of people can backfire."

In the case of Elton Simpson, the FBI played an undeniable role in pushing him toward violence. Back in 2007, after Simpson converted, he fell under the influence of Wahhabist extremism. Following a tip-off, the Phoenix FBI hired a local Muslim named Dabla Deng to befriend Simpson and record hundreds of hours of phone calls. The bureau enticed Deng, an economically vulnerable refugee from Somalia, with a whopping $132,000 for the job. When Simpson lied to the FBI about his plans to go overseas to wage jihad, he was given three years' probation. The sting operation drove Simpson to new depths of rage. As Usama Shami, the imam of the mosque where Simpson converted, told *60 Minutes*: "When he found out that this guy was spying on him, and taping him and then finding out that the government was doing that, I think something clicked in him. And the mosque, we couldn't do anything. Because we don't know what he did."

Simpson was out of prison in 2015 when he became enraged by a "Draw Muhammad" contest hosted by anti-Muslim activist Pamela Geller in May 2015 at a community center in Garland, Texas. He had learned of the attack from a Twitter user named Australi Witness, who tweeted the address of the event and a Breitbart article promoting it. According to Rita Katz, the self-styled terror expert and founder of the SITE Intelligence Group, Australi Witness was "part of the hard core of a group of individuals who constantly look for targets for other people to attack."

This mysterious Twitter user later retweeted a jihadi account urging "brothers in Texas" to "go there with your weapons, bombs or with knives." The incitement of Australi Witness was retweeted by Simpson, a clear mark of approval.

Inside the Draw Muhammad contest, the racist propensity of

contestants was incentivized with a $10,000 prize. They were also treated to a guest appearance by Geert Wilders, the far-right Dutch politician who had proposed banning the Quran. Throughout the event, Wilders and Geller were surrounded by a phalanx of militarized Bureau of Alcohol, Tobacco, Firearms and Explosives (ATF) officers at a cost of over $10,000 to taxpayers.

Though ISIS had issued a call for Western loyalists who could not make their way to Syria to carry out attacks in their own lands, the FBI chimed in to ensure Simpson might carry through on the violent plan: "Tear up Texas," an FBI informant texted Simpson before Geller's event took place.

"U know what happened in Paris," Simpson responded, referring to the *Charlie Hebdo* massacre in February that year. "So that goes without saying ... No need to be direct."

Before Simpson descended on Garland, armed to the teeth and accompanied by his roommate, Nadir Soofi, he changed his Twitter avatar to a photo of Anwar al-Awlaki. The two bungling fanatics did not even manage to enter the community center before they were cut down by a private security guard and a police offer.

The video of the shooting was recorded on a cell phone by an FBI agent who happened to be in the car right behind Simpson and Soofi– who followed the two to the event, fully aware that they were about to attempt a massacre. Beyond recording the attack, the FBI agent did nothing to stop it. Whether the agent acted to encourage the violence is still unknown.

"I can't tell you whether the FBI knew the attack was gonna occur," Dan Maynard, the lawyer for a friend of Simpson and Soofi who was later prosecuted by the FBI, told *60 Minutes*. "I don't like to think that they let it occur. But it is shocking to me that an undercover agent sees fellas jumping out of a car and he drives on. I find that shocking."

Australi Witness, the Twitter user who helped inspire Simpson and Soofi to target the cartoon contest, was arrested a year later by the FBI. It turned out he was not the "hardcore" Islamist terror leader that Rita Katz thought he was, but a twenty-one-year-old Jewish American from the suburbs of Jacksonville,

Florida, named Joshua Ryne Goldberg. Goldberg had invented an array of online personalities, from a radical Zionist to an ultra-feminist to a fanatical jihadist, in order to generate a raft of high-profile online hoaxes, often inciting terrorist violence against soft targets.

The deranged young man's criminal hearings were conducted partly in private, and his trial never took place, with both the defense and government prosecution teams insisting that the young man was mentally unfit to stand trial. In the end, Goldberg pleaded guilty to attempted malicious damage and destruction by an explosive of a building. His conviction occurred with negligible media fanfare—a stark contrast to the government's high-profile Muslim terror busts.

Hours after the Garland attack, Geller and Wilders posed for a triumphant photo with the federal agents hired to protect them. The following day, Geller exploited her platform on CNN to paint herself as a First Amendment crusader. "I will not abridge my freedoms so as not to offend savages," Geller proclaimed. "Freedom of speech is under violent assault here."

ISIS, meanwhile, claimed credit for the attack, although the FBI and a Jewish Internet troll from Florida played the most important operational roles in it. The bizarre incident was the latest clarifying example of the symbiotic relationship the anti-Muslim far-right enjoyed with jihadists, this time with the FBI playing a crucial role in helping both elements achieve their propaganda goals—the Islamophobes as free-speech crusaders and ISIS as fearless warriors with international reach.

In the case of Mateen, there appeared to be an intertwined mess of motives behind his killing spree that were as personal as they were political. Was he merely a twenty-first century incarnation of Travis Bickle, the romantically inept, pill-popping antihero of Martin Scorsese's dystopic post-Vietnam drama *Taxi Driver*, another angry beta male who shattered his depressing existence through a spasm of moralistic violence? Or was he the hardcore "Islamic soldier" he claimed to be? Perhaps he was just a toxic, quintessentially American concoction of both.

The complex reality of Mateen and the context from which he emerged mattered little to those who were setting the agenda for him. In the end, he was just a pawn in their game.

11

Extinction of the Grayzone

Mateen was, above all, a pawn in ISIS's game, which was designed to draw the United States into costly conflicts at home and abroad. A February 2015 article in *Dabiq*, the official magazine of ISIS, offered a clear window into the organization's emerging strategy. Published in the immediate aftermath of the *Charlie Hebdo* massacre, where self-proclaimed French jihadists murdered nine staff members of the anti-Muslim satirical magazine, the manifesto was titled, "The Extinction of the Grayzone."

"The presence of the Khilafa [Islamic Caliphate] magnifies the political, social, economic, and emotional impact of any operation carried out by the mujahadin against the enraged crusaders," *Dabiq* stated. "This magnified impact compels the crusaders to actively destroy the grayzone themselves, the zone in which many of the hypocrites and deviant innovators living in the West are hiding."

ISIS thus revealed its intention to unravel the democratic fabric of Western civil society—what it called the "grayzone"—by provoking its elected leaders into disproportionate military reprisals and draconian security crackdowns. Once repression and Islamophobia in Western societies reached sufficiently unbearable levels for Muslims, the author wrote, "The Muslims in the West will quickly find themselves between one of two choices, they either apostatize and adopt the *kufri* [infidel] religion propagated by Bush, Obama, Blair, Cameron, Sarkozy, and Hollande in the name of Islam so as to live amongst the *kuffar* [infidels] without hardship, or they perform *hijrah* [emigrate] to the Islamic State and thereby escape persecution from the crusader governments and citizens."

With its strategy, ISIS ideologues exuded a keen understanding of the rightward shift in Western politics and the way in which their activities had accelerated the process. Denizens of the far right also saw political benefits in the establishment of an Islamic State and its claims to have inspired killing sprees from Paris to San Bernardino to Orlando. In his manifesto, the far-right Norwegian "counter-jihadist" mass shooter Anders Breivik stated in no uncertain terms his wish for an Islamic State. Like any jihadist fanboy, Breivik saw Al Qaeda as the purest embodiment of Islam. And like jihadists, the Islamophobic ideologues who inspired him aimed to encourage *hijrah,* or Muslim migration to the Middle East through mass deportation and even civil war.

Trump's candidacy provided a perfect opportunity for ISIS and the "counter-jihadists" of the far right to collaborate on a shared plan to extinguish the "grayzone." A recruitment video released by Somali Al Qaeda franchise al-Shabaab provided perhaps the best example of the symbiotic relationship the two seemingly conflicting elements enjoyed. The video began with an appearance by Anwar al-Awlaki. "Yesterday, America was a land of slavery, segregation, lynching and the Ku Klux Klan," al-Awlaki intoned in English, with a black Al Qaeda flag draped behind him. "And tomorrow it will be a land of religious discrimination and concentration camps."

Next, Trump appeared on screen announcing his discriminatory Muslim travel ban: "Donald J. Trump is calling for a total and complete shutdown of Muslims to the United States until its representatives can figure out what the hell is going on," Trump declared to a chorus of cheers on December 7, 2015.

The juxtaposition was intended to use Trump's words—and his policy proposals—to reinforce al-Awlaki's condemnations. It was a devastatingly effective recruitment tool.

In the hours after Mateen was identified as the shooter, Michael Oren, a former Israeli ambassador to the United States and veteran neoconservative with close ties to the Republican Party, urged Trump to continue chipping away at the "grayzone." "If I was Donald Trump, I would have come out the minute that the FBI started to indicate this morning that we are talking about a guy who was operating from Islamic motivations," Oren said on an Israeli news program. "Just his name alone ... a Muslim name, the son of Afghan immigrants who apparently maintained connections of some sort to extremist Islamic organizations, that in itself will greatly influence the presidential race."

Now, Mateen was a pawn in Trump's game as well. "Because our leaders are weak, I said this was going to happen—and it is only going to get worse," Trump said in a prepared statement on Orlando, warning that immigrants from Muslim-majority countries were seeking to impose Sharia law on America. "I am trying to save lives and prevent the next terrorist attack. We can't afford to be politically correct anymore."

Mateen's assault on a gay nightclub created the occasion for a novel political appeal by Trump. At the Republican National Convention, where the party's Christian right forces had enshrined the usual antigay language into the convention plank, Trump invoked the Orlando massacre and promised, "I will do everything in my power to protect our LGBTQ citizens from the violence and oppression of the hateful, foreign ideology—believe me."

It was the first time in Republican Party history that a presidential nominee had dared use the acronym "LGBTQ" or appealed so directly to a group that many members of the party base believed were possessed by Satanic demons. By laundering progay politicking behind the narrative of Islamophobia, Trump was able to neutralize any evangelical backlash while targeting a demographic that had turned solidly against the GOP.

Hillary Clinton had won the fulsome endorsement of every major American gay rights organization; however, Trump exploited the Orlando shooting to hammer her as a threat to the safety of gays. "Clinton wants to allow radical Islamic terrorists to pour into our country—they enslave women, and murder gays," Trump thundered. "I don't want them in our country."

With his seemingly contradictory fusion of Islamophobia and social tolerance, Trump borrowed from the liberalized rhetoric of European right-wing populists, who presented Muslim immigration as an existential threat to the rights of women and homosexuals, and channeled the "pinkwashing" public relations tactic of Israel's right wing, which deployed Israel's comparatively gay-friendly policies to deflect from its record of human rights abuses against Palestinians.

The Trump campaign appeared to be coordinating its messaging strategy with Milo Yiannopoulos, the comically pretentious, almost self-satirically gay face and British-accented voice of the alt-right. Just days after the Orlando massacre, Yiannopoulos appeared outside the Pulse nightclub for a provocative press conference that was livestreamed by Breitbart, where he served as an editor. Dressed in a dark, neatly tailored suit, flanked by a burly, sunburned bodyguard on one side and Gavin McInnes, the racist, openly anti-Jewish hipster ad man and co-founder of the Vice media empire, on the other, Yiannopoulos unleashed a rambling tirade against Muslims, collectively blaming them for Mateen's massacre. "We will shoot back," the preening former tech entrepreneur vowed, dabbing the sweat pouring from his brow with a handkerchief.

Though he posed as a rogue operator, Yiannopoulos was clearly acting in tandem with the Trump campaign. "Trump is probably the most gay-friendly candidate for president in either party in decades," Yiannopoulos proclaimed. "He could be the most gay-friendly president in history."

Yiannopoulos was not willing to take his schtick as far as Richard Spencer (no relation to the "counter-jihadist" Robert Spencer) had. Having coined the term "alt-right," Spencer had become the subject of a stream of profiles glamorizing him as the trend-setting "dapper face of white nationalism" who "aims to make white nationalism cool again," as the liberal magazine *Mother Jones* put it.

Spencer belittled Yiannopoulos's politics as "alt-light," a diluted "entry point, gateway drug pushing towards us." But, unlike Spencer, Yiannopoulos had proven adept at inspiring harsh repercussions against the targets of his toxic trolling. During his press conference in Orlando, he seemed to lament that the police presence around the mosque that Mateen had attended in nearby Fort Pierce had prevented enraged citizens from taking righteous revenge, which he downplayed as "being rude to Muslims."

Months later, on the fifteenth anniversary of the 9/11 attacks, a Trump supporter named Joseph Michael Schreiber did just that, setting fire to the mosque that Mateen had occasionally visited and which Yiannopoulos had singled out. Schreiber's Facebook page was a portrait of yet another right-wing beta male shut-in, one who openly admired both Trump and Netanyahu. "ALL ISLAM IS RADICAL, and should be considered TERRORIST AND CRIMANALS [sic]," Schreiber ranted a month after the Orlando massacre.

In the year leading up to the election, a wave of violence targeting Muslims swept across the country, from shootings to mosque arsons. The highest number of recorded attacks on mosques in the country occurred in 2016, according to the Council on American Islamic Relations. Relentless incitement since 9/11 and a succession of failed military interventions in the Middle East had driven disapproval of Muslims to record levels, a September 2016 University of Minnesota study found. In railing against America's most disliked religious demographic, the Trump campaign was merely doing the math.

The Republican nominee also found ISIS to be an unusually useful tool for deflecting damaging revelations. When he was grilled by moderator Anderson Cooper in an October 6 presidential debate about leaked audiotapes revealing him boasting about sexually assaulting random women by "grabbing 'em by the pussy," Trump immediately and shamelessly pivoted to ISIS:

"I am embarrassed by it and I hate it," Trump said of his own comments on the tapes, "but it's locker-room talk and one of those things. I will knock the hell out of ISIS. We are going to defeat ISIS. It happened a number of years ago in a vacuum that was left. Because of bad judgment. I will tell you, I will take care of ISIS."

In August, when Clinton descended on the Orlando area, a base of Democratic support in perhaps the most important swing state, her appearance backfired in spectacularly bizarre fashion. Addressing a crowd of thousands, Clinton poured out heartfelt condolences to the victims of the Orlando massacre. Lurking behind her throughout the stump speech was a mustachioed man waving a homemade sign that praised Clinton as "good for national security."

The man was the father of Omar Mateen, Seddique, an eccentric local figure who hosted an Afghan public affairs show on a US-based satellite channel where he sometimes appeared in full military regalia and railed against Pakistan and its Inter-Services Intelligence—"the killer ISI," he called them—for the damage they had done to Afghanistan.

"Clinton is good for United States versus Donald Trump," Seddique told a local news affiliate after the rally, deepening the embarrassment to Clinton. His spontaneous appearance was one of the weirdest moments of an especially weird presidential campaign. Trump immediately seized on Seddique Mateen's presence at the Clinton rally to call for his deportation, even though he was a naturalized US citizen: "I'd throw him out," Trump vowed. "Whether it's racial profiling or politically correct, we better get smart," Trump continued, pointing to race as a criteria for immigration. "We are letting tens of thousands of people into our country. We don't know what the hell we're doing."

But the US government knew a lot more than it was letting on about its relationship with both Omar Mateen and his father, Seddique. In the fallout after the bloodbath in Orlando, the Department of Justice attempted to prosecute Nour Salman, the abused widow of Omar Mateen, alleging that she was an accomplice to his shooting. The case fell apart when the FBI was forced to admit that it not only attempted to groom Omar as an informant; it had successfully recruited Seddique and worked with him for a decade—all the way up to the date of the Pulse massacre.

What's more, the government had known that Omar was searching for tickets to Istanbul in the days before his shooting. This city was often the first destination for foreign jihadis on their way across the Turkish border to Syria. The government also found that Seddique had transferred money to an unknown source in Turkey right under its watch. As the embarrassing revelations piled on, the government quietly dropped its case, and its troubling relationship with the Mateens conveniently tumbled down the mainstream media's memory hole.

As the panic over ISIS subsided inside the United States, states across the Middle East were still struggling to eject the jihadist group from areas destabilized by Western intervention.

Unintended Consequences

By the summer of 2016, the hometown of Muammar Gaddafi had been transformed into a vision of hell thanks to NATO's intervention. The beaches of Sirte were a tableau for one of ISIS's most shocking execution videos, a high-definition snuff film showing black-masked terminators decapitating a dozen Egyptian Christian Coptic migrant workers and saturating the incoming waves with their blood.

Tripoli, meanwhile, was largely under the control of Abdelhakim Belhadj, the former Libyan Islamic Fighting Group warlord hailed by Senator McCain as a "hero." Belhadj, a former ally of Al Qaeda who fought alongside the Taliban, had emerged as an influential business tycoon, with interests in the airline Libyan Wings and the Al Jazeera–style channel, Al Nabaa. With funding from Qatar, he had helped lead the now-defunct Islamist "Libyan Dawn" government into power in Tripoli through a violent coup that had displaced hundreds of thousands. Among his key allies was Sheikh Sadiq Al-Ghariani, the fundamentalist Grand Mufti who said of Ansar al-Sharia—the group that killed the former US ambassador to Libya, Christopher Stevens—"they kill and they have their reasons."

In a February 2015 report on Libya, the International Crisis Group had warned, "On the current trajectory, the most likely medium-term prospect is not one side's triumph, but that rival local warlords and radical groups will proliferate, what remains of state institutions will collapse, financial reserves ... will be depleted, and hardship for ordinary Libyans will increase exponentially."

Over a year later, even top US military officials openly conceded that Libya was a failed state, its public coffers and oil reserves looted by the foreign powers that oversaw the 2011 war of regime change. Its shores had become a main disembarkation point for migrants, where women fleeing conflict and poverty in sub-Saharan Africa were beaten, raped and starved in "living hellholes," according to UNICEF. After the United Nations International Organization for Migration recorded testimony of open-air slave markets in Libya, where migrants from West Africa were bought and sold, CNN produced footage of the auctions—a shocking visual document of the return of slavery to the African continent thanks in no small part to US military intervention.t

As in Iraq, where even former opponents of Saddam Hussein had become nostalgic for the relative stability he guaranteed, many Libyans had begun to pine for the days of Gaddafi. "I hate to say it but our life was better under the previous regime," Fayza al-Naas, a pharmacist in Tripoli, told Agence France-Presse. While Gaddafi's Green Movement was attempting a comeback, Libya's Western-imposed rulers continued to lay waste to the country.

On the campaign trail, Hillary Clinton refused to admit any fault for her role in the Libyan catastrophe. Not only did she defend the intervention, she touted it as a successful exercise in freedom spreading: "I think President Obama made the right decision at the time," she said. "And the Libyan people had a free election [for] the first time since 1951. And you know what, they voted for moderates, they voted with the hope of democracy."

Senator Bernie Sanders countered Clinton's flowery prognosis of Libya's burgeoning democracy by cautioning, "Regime change often has unintended consequences—in Iraq, in Libya, where ISIS has a dangerous foothold."

But Sanders' criticism of Clinton's Libyan misadventures was muted. Like most members of Congress from both parties, he had voted in support of the intervention. An eleventh-hour resolution by the libertarian Republican senator Rand Paul that declared the attack unconstitutional had failed to pick up a single Democratic vote, and garnered support from only ten Republicans. Paul's resolution had rankled many Democratic senators by asking them to endorse a statement Obama had made one year before he entered the White House: "the president does not have power under the Constitution to unilaterally authorize a military attack in a situation that does not involve stopping an actual or imminent threat to the nation."

The House Select Committee on Benghazi spent little time investigating the real scandals of the Libyan intervention, from Clinton's decision to push for a military campaign on false premises to her bloodcurdling comments—"We came, we saw, he died"—upon hearing that Gaddafi had been sodomized to death with a bayonet. The committee also ignored McCain's promotion of Belhadj, a former Al Qaeda ally, as well as the role of CIA and America's Gulf allies in arming jihadist and Salafist militias, which ultimately transformed a formerly stable, functional state into a safe haven for ISIS.

Serious interrogation of a failed intervention launched on the most specious grounds would have thrown a ratchet into the interventionist agenda and cast inconvenient light onto the ongoing proxy war in Syria. By diverting discussion of Libya from the systematic dismantling of a functional state to crude partisan politics, the Benghazi committee fulfilled its role in protecting the Washington playbook. As Representative Richard Hanna, a Republican member of the committee, freely admitted, "This may not be politically correct, but I think that there was a big part of this investigation that was designed to go after people and an individual, Hillary Clinton."

Over the course of seventeen months, the Benghazi committee burned through $8 million to carry out a political show trial that ultimately focused more on Clinton's emails with her coterie of advisors than on anything related to the catastrophic war of regime change that reduced a formerly prosperous Libya to a failed state. The committee amounted to a taxpayer-funded opposition research firm that rolled out its findings through right-wing operatives like K.T. McFarland, a Fox News national security contributor who had complained during her failed 2006 Senate campaign against Clinton: "Hillary Clinton is really worried about me, and is so worried, in fact, that she had helicopters flying over my house in Southampton today taking pictures."

In February 2015, as the committee gathered steam, subpoenaing witnesses and generating reams of negative media, Clinton's public disapproval rating exceeded her approval rating for the first time since she was appointed secretary of state in 2009. The ratings steadily worsened, with disapproval reaching a staggering 55 percent by Election Day. An NBC-*Wall Street Journal* poll in late June 2016 revealed that 69 percent of respondents found Clinton untrustworthy, and though the same percentage of respondents saw Trump in the same light, a majority stated their opinion that he said what he truly believed—that he spoke from conviction, even when delivering half-truths.

"Everybody thought Hillary Clinton was unbeatable, right? But we put together a Benghazi special committee, a select committee," said Republican representative Kevin McCarthy in a moment of remarkable candor. "What are her numbers today? Her numbers are dropping. Why? Because she's untrustable. But no one would have known any of that had happened, had we not fought."

The first day of the Republican National Convention in July 2016 was staged as a greatest hits compilation of the Benghazi committee. The extravaganza opened with a tale of betrayal by two of the burly guards who battled Ansar Al-Sharia at the US consulate, Mark Geist and John Teigen, and who had just sold their story to the cinematic schlockmeister Michael Bay. Then came Patricia Smith, the bereaved mother of Sean Smith, a US informational management officer who was killed at Benghazi. Alternating between sorrow and unsheathed rage, Smith exclaimed, "I blame Hillary Clinton personally for the death of my son," leading the Republican crowd in a chant that had become the unofficial slogan of the Trump campaign: "Lock her up! Lock her up!"

The spectacle at the Republican National Convention was a tragic portrait of misplaced anger. Though their lives had been upended by a war waged without formal congressional authorization, and their loved ones had been killed by Islamist rebels covertly armed by the United States and its allies, the stars of the Republicans' Benghazi passion play had earned their place on stage through their willingness to participate in a hyper-partisan political theater without examining the real factors that had suffused their lives with heartrending loss.

The same was true for Clinton, who used her opening statement before the Benghazi committee as occasion to reassert the militaristic mind-set that had guided the United States into the Libyan disaster in the first place. "We have learned the hard way when America is absent," she said, "especially from unstable places, there are consequences. Extremism takes root, aggressors seek to fill the vacuum and security everywhere is threatened, including here at home."

But it was America's very presence in Libya that had opened the floodgates of chaos, not only inside the country, but across several geographic regions. The intervention had not only shattered one of Africa's most prosperous states, it destabilized large parts of Nigeria, inflamed the conflict in Somalia and helped flood Syria with heavy weapons.

The intervention also resulted in unintended consequences inside the West, and not only by playing a contributing role in Clinton's loss to one of the most erratic, seemingly toxic candidates in modern American political history—an indirect result, at least, of the catastrophe in Benghazi and the national scandal that ensued. Across the Atlantic, the most emphatic case of blowback from the Libyan intervention took place in Manchester, the city that had been home to a community of exiles that the British intelligence services had used as pawns on the imperial chessboard, but whom it was proving increasingly powerless to control.

Blowback in Britain

Sometime in late April 2017, twenty-two-year-old Salman Abedi returned from Libya to the Whalley Range neighborhood where he was born and raised in Manchester, England. Upon Abedi's arrival, the FBI sent an alarming dispatch to its counterparts in the British MI5 intelligence service warning that Abedi was planning a high-level political assassination on behalf of ISIS or another jihadist cell. The warning was ignored. Three weeks later, on May 22, Abedi entered a concert by Ariana Grande, a pop singer whose audience consisted largely of preteen and teenage girls. In the middle of a crowd, Abedi detonated a powerful bomb packed with nails and ball bearings, killing himself and twenty-two others. It was the deadliest terror attack ever carried out on British soil.

"It seems likely—possible—that he wasn't doing this on his own," Britain's home secretary, Amber Rudd, speculated to the BBC. She described the bomb as "more sophisticated than some of the attacks we've seen before."

Rudd's statement was proven true, but in an ironic way that she and her colleagues would have loathed to acknowledge. Indeed, Abedi was a product of the ratline that the British intelligence service operated from Manchester, where the MI6 oversaw a large community of Libyan exiles, to the anti-Gaddafi insurgency in Libya, to the extremist wastelands established by Gulf-backed jihadist "rebels" in Syria.

Soon after the bloodbath in Manchester, Theresa May's government set about burying the facts that threatened to expose the devil's game it had played for so many decades in the Middle East. Reverting to warmed-over Islamophobia, May obscured the political context behind the attack by connecting it to another terror attack three months earlier on London's Westminster Bridge, claiming the two were "bound together by the single evil ideology of Islamist extremism."

Behind the prime minister's bluster lay a series of uncomfortable questions that would have threatened the survival of her government if they had been answered in the full light of day: Why had the MI5 ignored warnings about Abedi delivered by the FBI in the days ahead of the attack? And why had the British authorities failed to act on an earlier report to a counter-terror hotline by neighbors of the Abedi family who had heard Salman proclaiming his support for suicide bombings?

When these warnings arrived, May had been serving as home secretary and was in charge of monitoring the MI5 and its international arm, the MI6. This raised further questions: Did British intelligence ignore the red alerts because it was attempting to groom Abedi as an informant, as it had tried and failed to do with Mohammed Emwazi, the wayward London youth who somehow wound up in ISIS-controlled territory in Syria as the fearsome decapitator known as "Jihadi John"?

There were even more troubling issues for the MI6 that related to the bomber's father, Ramadan Abedi.

Back in 2011, when the Libyan insurgency erupted against Gaddafi amid the tumult of the Arab Spring, the MI6 turned back on its old proxies in Manchester, hustling them to the front lines. Even locals under government control orders for alleged involvement with extremist groups were handed back their passports. "I was allowed to go [to Libya], no questions asked," a British Libyan who had been under house arrest at the time for extremist ties told *Middle East Eye*. "We were in the same group over there—we called ourselves the Manchester fighters—we even had our own logo," a mechanic named Akram Ramadan told the *Guardian*. "Three-quarters of the fighters at the beginning of the revolution were from Manchester—

the rest came from London, Sheffield, China and Japan. From everywhere."

Among those who took the MI5's ratline from Manchester to Libya was Ramadan Abedi. He arrived on the battlefield just as arms began pouring in from France and Qatar, funneled to the LIFG through the National Transitional Council. Ramadan Abedi returned home to Manchester only briefly to sort out some paperwork while his son, Salman, was in college.

Unfamiliar with their homeland and alienated by their adopted country's chaotically cosmopolitan culture, Salman and his brother, Hashem, gravitated toward the nihilistic worldview propagated through online jihadist channels. Before long, they followed their father into Libya, arriving as part of a larger group of second-generation Libyan youth who were doing the same. The youngsters all wound up joining the local ISIS affiliate, according to *The Times* of London. Abedi was then able to travel to Syria and shuttled to ISIS territory, where he deepened his propensity for violence and his skill in carrying it out.

It was a straight line from there to the bloodbath in Manchester. As a former schoolmate of Salman Abedi's put it: "He was an outgoing, fun guy, but since he went to Libya in 2011 he came back a different guy."

In July 2018, a review of the Manchester bombing found that the British national security apparatus had been more intimately involved in the activities of the Abedis than previously believed. Four years earlier, during the height of the Libyan civil war, in which both Ramadan and Salman Abedi acted as foreign fighters, the Royal Navy's *HMS Enterprise* docked in Tripoli and welcomed both men aboard along with some 100 others. They were escorted to Malta and then flown back to the UK. A month before he was ferried home to the UK, Salman Abedi had been removed from a security services watch list.

What were the two men doing in Libya at the time, and why were they sent home without a second thought? These questions were scarcely engaged with by the British press, which reporting the Royal Navy's suspect sealift in passing and with little to no follow-up, branding it as a "rescue" operation.

The West's wars in the Middle East were drawing to an ignominious close by this point. From Washington to London, the so-called war on terror no longer generated the same level of public hysteria—or paychecks—it once had. But as the dust cleared from two decades of regime change campaigns, a new cast of evildoers was coming into focus.

Afterword

Active Measures

The election of Donald Trump triggered a moral panic about foreign meddling and supplied America's security state with a convenient and familiar national enemy to replace the evildoers of the so-called "war on terror." Trump's anti-interventionist posturing on the campaign trail, his lambasting of Bush's wars in Afghanistan and Iraq, his stated refusal to arm Syrian "moderate rebels," his suspicion of NATO, his apparent interest in détente with Russia, and the promise of a buffoonish reality show star as the captain of America's empire—all of this, no matter how disingenuous Trump's anti-interventionist appeals might have been—had engendered a wild hysteria among foreign policy elites. Joining with the dead-enders of Hillary Clinton's campaign, who were desperate to deflect from their crushing loss, the mandarins of the national security state worked their media contacts to generate the narrative of Trump-Russia collusion.

Out of the postelection despair of liberals and national security elites, the furor of Russiagate was born.

This national outrage substituted Russia for ISIS as the country's new folk devil and painted Trump as Russian president Vladimir Putin's Manchurian candidate. Rather than assailing Trump as the imperious, bigoted oligarch he was, the established opposition dusted off the phantasmagoria of the McCarthy era to brand the president as a Russian sleeper agent—and "the Russians" as a singular source of evil. "And just the historical practices of the Russians, who typically are almost genetically driven to co-opt, penetrate, gain favor, whatever, which is a typical Russian technique," declared James Clapper, then director of national intelligence (DNI), in May 2017 comments channeling the xenophobia suddenly coursing through the Democratic Party's political veins.

By uniting against a foreign evil that supposedly controlled the White House, liberals had unwittingly become infected with the same tendency exhibited by right-wing Tea Party activists, who had sought to cast Obama as a crypto-Muslim with no American birth certificate. Almost overnight, hundreds of thousands of liberals were showing up at postelection rallies with placards depicting Trump in Russian garb and surrounded by Soviet hammer-and-sickle symbols. Typical of the phantasmagoria of the liberal "resistance" was a giant projection above the Apple Store near the Manhattan gay mecca of Chelsea that portrayed a shirtless Putin lovingly embracing a pregnant, effeminate Trump. Complimented with the hashtag #LoveThroughHate, the image conveyed the sense that Putin and Trump were gay together, and that Trump was the bottom in the relationship. For the first time in history, a majority of registered Democrats told pollsters that they believed Americans should fight and die to defend NATO members like Latvia from a hypothetical Russian invasion. With the strange and sudden transformation of the Democrats into a paranoid war party, a quiet neoconservative campaign set into motion over a decade before was being realized.

~

This book began in Afghanistan, where the CIA weaponized political Islam to stop the spread of socialism in Central Asia and bleed the Soviet Union from its soft underbelly. The defeat the Soviets suffered at the hands of the US-backed mujahedin left a deep psychological scar that weakened their national resolve at an elemental level. When the Soviet Union collapsed under the weight of economic pressure from without and within, Washington poured salt on the fresh wounds of the newly formed Russian Federation. Not only did the administration of President George H.W. Bush declare victory in the Cold War, effectively taunting a fallen foe, it began expanding NATO's military tentacles eastward in clear abrogation of verbal agreements with the deposed Soviet president Mikhail Gorbachev. The goal was clear: to encircle the largest and most militarily powerful nation in Eurasia and gradually transform it into a toothless, economically dependent vassal of the United States.

During the 1990s, Russia witnessed the wholesale looting of its state assets by "the Harvard boys," a collection of neoliberal American economists dispatched by President Bill Clinton's administration to impose "shock therapy" privatization under the watch of then treasury secretary Lawrence Summers. A new class of oligarchs blossomed while millions of Russians lost their pensions and public benefits, resulting in 3 million "excess deaths"—twice as many citizens as Russia lost during World War I. Diseases like diphtheria and tuberculosis, which had been wiped out under Soviet rule, experienced a resurgence, while HIV/AIDS spread like wildfire, driven by heroin imported from Afghanistan, where the Soviet-backed government had been replaced by a collection of warlords armed by the CIA. Life expectancy among Russian men immediately declined by five years, while grandmotherly babushkas saw their life savings disappear.

"Many hung around for a while, wandering around town," wrote journalist Paul Klebnikov, who was later murdered for his work exposing Russian crime syndicates. "The men became drunks sprawled at the icy gutter; the women became bone-thin ladies begging at the entrance of churches; then they died.

The younger generation had turned its back on its elders and allowed them to perish."

By the end of the tenure of Boris Yeltsin, the vodka-sodden, American-installed president, Russia's poverty rate had risen from 2 percent to a staggering 40 percent, an economic collapse worse than that of America during the Great Depression. The carefully managed harvest of death and economic devastation should have stood alongside some of the most titanic crimes of the twentieth century. In Washington, however, the looting was celebrated in reams of op-eds as "free-market reform" and "liberalization," while its catastrophic consequences were only quietly acknowledged in scarcely read official reports. "By pursuing a policy of 'reform' that required the political victory of *their* reformers by whatever means necessary, the administration undermined the democratic process itself," a 2000 US congressional report on the Clinton administration's Russia policies concluded, foreshadowing the era of Yeltsin's handpicked successor, Vladimir Putin. (The report also found that "millions of US taxpayer dollars provided directly to" Clinton's handpicked shock therapists from agencies like USAID "would be unaccounted for.")

Though Putin was cut from the same privatizing cloth as Yeltsin, he embodied the experience of a KGB man who had witnessed the nation's tragic collapse from the inside. He valued stability above all else and entered the Kremlin determined to impose it on his country by any means. The project of national revival entailed a crackdown on the oligarchs who defied his model of state-centered capitalism, as well as an array of internal political threats through sometimes less than savory methods. By 2007, the Russian economy was on its way to recovering from the crisis imposed on it during the 1990s. The country's national security apparatus had clearly recovered its confidence as well. That year, Putin delivered a touchstone address at the Munich Security Conference that skewered American interventionism as a driver of "global destabilization." With a glowering Senator John McCain seated just feet away in the front row, Putin slammed "illegitimate actions" like the Iraq invasion for "new human tragedies and creat[ing] new centers of tension."

In Washington, the pressure for a confrontation with Putin's Russia was steadily building. In 2004, three years after the Bush administration's unilateral withdrawal from an antiballistic missile treaty with Russia, a conglomeration of Iraq war neocons and liberal interventionists composed an open letter to EU and NATO leaders that slammed Putin for turning his back on the supposed achievements of the Yeltsin era. Published under the letterhead of the US-funded National Endowment for Democracy's *Journal of Democracy*, the letter was authored by neocon movement figureheads Robert Kagan and William Kristol, along with then senator Joseph Biden, Madeleine Albright and Tom Malinowski, a lobbyist for Human Rights Watch. Its authors expressed anger that "the instruments of state power appear to be being rebuilt," a clear reference to Putin's restoration of the Kremlin's control over national affairs at the expense of Western-friendly oligarchs like Boris Berezovsky, who later faced prosecution for their widespread theft of state resources. While Americans were transfixed by Bush's "war on terror" drama, a bipartisan coalition was quietly coalescing to confront the resurgent Russian menace.

So-called color revolutions were spreading across eastern Europe, meanwhile, leveraging funds from US-backed soft-power NGOs like the National Endowment for Democracy, George Soros's Open Society Institute and exiled oligarchs such as Berezovsky to topple governments in former Soviet satellite states. Mikheil Saakashvili, the president of Georgia, was one of Washington's favorite pet projects; one of his top advisors was Bruce P. Jackson, an American former military intelligence officer who helped found the neoconservative Committee for the Liberation of Iraq.

In 2008, with backchannel approval from then vice president Dick Cheney, Saakashvili sent Georgian troops into the semi-sovereign Russian territory of South Ossetia, claiming it as his own. His men were resoundingly clobbered in a punishing Russian counterattack. A humiliated Saakashvili was seen chewing his tie in agony on national television as news arrived of his defeat. Congress erupted in bipartisan denunciation of Putin for having the chutzpah to repel an ally's aggression. Across Russia, meanwhile, Putin's public approval rating soared.

When President Obama attempted a diplomatic "reset" in 2009 with Putin's replacement, Dmitry Medvedev, he was met by an angry open letter from the Foreign Policy Initiative, a rebranded version of Robert Kagan's PNAC that helped conceive the US invasion of Iraq. For his part, Medvedev appeared so determined to repair the damaged relationship with the United States that when NATO was on the verge of intervening in Libya in 2011, Russia abstained on a UN Security Council vote authorizing the Western military alliance to establish a no-fly zone.

Putin was livid over the move, slamming it as a capitulation. "In Bill Clinton's times," Putin declared in comments aimed straight at Medvedev, "Yugoslavia and Belgrade were bombed. Bush sent armed forces into Afghanistan. A far-fetched and totally false pretext was used to invade Iraq, and the entire Iraqi leadership was eliminated, even children in Saddam Hussein's family died. And now, it's Libya's turn—under the pretext of protecting civilians. But it's the civilian population who dies during those airstrikes against (Libyan) territory. Where is the logic and the conscience? There is neither."

Putin's fury at his country's failure to obstruct yet another disastrous regime change operation helped propel his run for the presidency a year later. The chaos that had washed over Libya vindicated his warnings and sealed Medvedev's fate as a failed placeholder. That same year, Obama mocked his Republican opponent, Mitt Romney, for referring to Russia as America's top enemy. "The 1980s are now calling and they want their foreign policy back because the Cold War's been over for twenty years," Obama said in a widely applauded debate zinger. The Washington press corps shrugged off Romney's comments as a gaffe, unaware that his neoconservative foreign policy team was driving a campaign to turn his words into reality. Four months before the presidential debate, and mostly below the radar of the national media, the Senate had effectively destroyed Obama's "reset" initiative with Moscow by passing the Magnitsky Act. The bill ushered in the first round of sanctions on Putin's inner circle and opened up the American attack on Russia's resurgent economy. Putin responded by banning American adoptions of Russian orphans. Unlike in the United States, where Congress passed the Magnitsky Act unanimously and without debate, Putin's retaliation was met with consternation by some members of Russia's Duma.

The sanctions had been generated thanks to the fortune of Bill Browder, a vulture capitalist hedge fund manager who cashed in on Russia's vast sell-off of public assets during the 1990s. Browder, who gave up his American citizenship to avoid paying taxes, turned to the Ashcroft Group, a high-flying lobbying firm run by right-wing former attorney general John Ashcroft, to turn lawmakers like Democratic senator Ben Cardin into de facto clients and ply members of the State Department. Years before, Browder had left his accountant, Sergei Magnitsky, to face the consequences after he bolted from the country to avoid paying $19 million in a civil tax judgment. While being held in prison, Magnitsky died from what Russian authorities said was cardiac arrest; Browder claimed his former bookkeeper had been beaten to death, incorrectly painting him as a whistle-blowing lawyer who had exposed a $230 million theft by the Russian government.

A documentary film by Andrei Nekrasov, a Russian dissident and noted critic of Putin, raised serious questions about whether Browder had concocted large parts of his story. While he posed as a courageous truth teller in testimony before Congress and on cable news networks, recasting what appeared to be a financial dispute into an international human rights drama, Browder fought with general success to ban screenings of Nekrasov's *The Magnitksy Act: Behind the Scenes*. He even toiled to avoid telling his story under oath, once fleeing on foot when served with a subpoena in a case brought by one of the companies impacted by the Magnitsky sanctions. It was clear that one of the key architects of the new Cold War had much to hide.

By 2014, US-Russian relations had reached a boiling point over Ukraine. The country's elected president, Viktor Yanukovych, had rejected an EU economic association agreement that would have imposed harsh austerity on his country in favor of a more generous deal with neighboring Russia. Carl Gershman, a veteran neoconservative activist who served as chairman of the US government-funded National Endowment for Democracy (NED) that had financed color revolutions across Europe, had argued a year before that "Ukraine's choice to join Europe will accelerate the demise of the ideology of Russian imperialism that Putin represents." With Yanukovych siding with Russia, he threatened to prevent Washington from achieving what Gershman called "the biggest prize": regime change in Moscow.

Within months, another color revolution swept through Kiev, with millions in money from the NED and allied NGOs pouring in to establish new opposition media outlets and mobilize activists. Obama's assistant secretary for European and Eurasian affairs in the State Department, Victoria Nuland, personally presided over the operation, marshaling a coalition of neoliberal technocrats and ultra-nationalist street muscle to drive out Yanukovych. "We've invested over five billions dollars," Nuland said, "to help Ukraine achieve its European aspirations." Nuland happened to be the wife of Robert Kagan, the PNAC co-founder and former Romney advisor. She was so committed to the project of regime change in Ukraine that she appeared alongside then US ambassador Geoffrey Pyatt to hand out cookies to protesters in Kiev's Maidan Square. "I think, to help glue this thing and to have the UN help glue it and, you know, fuck the EU," Nuland declared in a phone call to Pyatt.

Following the ouster of Yanukovych, Putin annexed the Ukrainian region of Crimea, where the mostly Russian-speaking population had voted in a referendum to join the Russian Federation. Fighting between pro-Russian separatists and the Ukrainian military—including the neo-Nazi Azov battalion, incorporated into the country's national guard—began in the eastern Donbass region, which remained contested and where both Russia and the Pentagon quietly supplied assistance.

Nuland's machinations had plunged Ukraine into instability, and the EU association deal that the new pro-Western government in Kiev was compelled to sign wound up deepening the economic ruin. However, she had served the neoconservative agenda successfully, elevating the conflict they sought with Russia to new heights.

The uproar over Russia's annexation of Crimea consolidated anti-Russian hostility across partisan lines in Congress and mobilized Cold War fever within national security circles. Still William Kristol lamented at the time that the US public had grown "war weary" and was not yet invested in a new confrontation. "All that's needed is the rallying," he maintained. "And the turnaround can be fast."

That moment would arrive amid the 2016 general election, when allegations of Russian hacking dominated headlines and triggered Democratic Party outrage.

Before a packed hearing room in the Capitol's Longworth Building on March 20, 2017, just two months after Trump's inauguration, Democratic representative Adam Schiff distilled what had become the conventional wisdom in Washington into his opening remarks. With FBI director James Comey seated before him as a witness, Schiff addressed the House Select Committee on Intelligence:

"Last summer, at the height of a highly contested and bitterly adversarial presidential campaign, a foreign power intervened in an effort to weaken our democracy and to influence the outcome for one candidate and against the other," Schiff alleged in a stiff but authoritative monotone he had perfected during his years as a prosecutor. "That foreign adversary was, of course, Russia, and it acted through its intelligence agencies and on the instruction of its autocratic ruler, Vladimir Putin, in order to help Donald J. Trump become president of the United States."

Invoking the term du jour of Russia-obsessed Democrats—"active measures"—Schiff claimed that Russia's Federal Security Service (FSB) had stolen emails from the server of the Democratic National Committee (DNC) and hacked the email account of John

Podesta, Hillary Clinton's campaign manager. Then, according to Schiff, the FSB orchestrated a "daily drip" of damaging material through third-party hosting sites like WikiLeaks. "It does not matter" whether the leaks proved decisive, or even relevant, in swinging the election to Trump, Schiff insisted. "What does matter is this," he said, building to a dramatic climax: "The Russians successfully meddled in our democracy and our intelligence agencies have concluded they will do so again."

The ranking member of the Intelligence Committee proceeded to raise questions about whether US citizens had colluded actively with the Russian government to influence the election in Trump's favor, or if bribery or blackmail had been a factor in Trump's decision-making toward Russia. With public sources, Schiff was able to demonstrate that several Trump advisors had met with Russian diplomats and done business with fellow oligarchs, but the evidence to support his most consequential claim, that Russia had hacked the DNC server in direct coordination with the Trump campaign, was just that—a claim with no evidence to back it up.

By this point, the Democrats were relying on a single source to demonstrate that Russian intelligence agents had hacked the DNC's emails during the 2016 election. It was a private cybersecurity firm called CrowdStrike. The president of this firm, Shawn Henry, was a former FBI executive assistant director and a paid cybersecurity consultant to NBC. CrowdStrike's director, Dmitri Alperovitch, was a Russian exile working as a senior fellow at the Washington DC-based Atlantic Council.

With heavy funding from NATO, weapons manufacturers like Raytheon and Gulf monarchies from Saudi Arabia to Bahrain and Kuwait, the Atlantic Council had become a key proponent of military interventionism and anti-Russian fervor. Besides pumping up regime change in Syria and promoting Salafist insurgents as "moderate rebels," the think tank hired a cadre of anti-Kremlin operatives like Alperovitch with financial support from Ukrainian oligarch Victor Pinchuk. Pinchuk also happened to be a close associate of Bill Clinton and a top contributor to the Clinton Foundation.

CrowdStrike laid out its findings on Russian hacking in a June 2016 report called "Bears in the Midst." The paper's title referred to a hacking outfit called Fancy Bear, fingering it as a Kremlin asset that the Russian government had used to hack the DNC's servers. CrowdStrike relied on entirely speculative claims authored in highly technical, authoritative language to support its dramatic conclusions. Its report was also filled with contradictory claims, asserting, for instance, that Fancy Bear's "tradecraft is superb," though the supposed hacking group had been so sloppy it left behind Cyrillic comments on the documents it disseminated online.

Before the DNC had hired CrowdStrike, Comey had sent "multiple requests at different levels" of the DNC for access to the hacked email servers. "The FBI repeatedly stressed to DNC officials the necessity of obtaining direct access to servers and data, only to be rebuffed until well after the initial compromise had been mitigated," an FBI official confirmed. With the FBI denied access to the DNC's servers, the only source on the Russian government connection to the hack was CrowdStrike.

Though they were never given the DNC servers to directly examine, the Department of Homeland Security and FBI reinforced CrowdStrike's attribution in reports declaring "high confidence" in it. During his widely televised address before the House Intelligence Committee, Representative Schiff also turned to a dossier composed by a former MI6 agent named Christopher Steele to reinforce the narrative of Trump–Russia collusion.

Marketed as a rock-solid piece of spycraft, this dossier was in fact the product of collaboration between the Clinton campaign and a private research firm, Fusion GPS, that employed Steele. The Clinton campaign had effectively paid for a collection of mostly unverified and salacious claims concerning Trump's relationship with the Russian government and about the evil intent of Russians in general. Before the dossier became a Clinton campaign weapon, it was presented to Secretary of State John Kerry and other US officials in the form of a two-page summary by Jonathan Winer. A former State Department official, Winer had lobbied on behalf of Bill Browder and later helped the fugitive oligarch craft the Magnitsky Act. He also forged a relationship with the British spy Steele. "While I was at the State Department," Winer recounted, "[Steele] provided me some 120 documents about Russia and Ukraine ... about what Russia was doing in the national security area that was relevant to the United States." The dossier included the allegation that Trump had been secretly filmed by Russian intelligence services while gleefully watching sex workers urinate on the bed where President Barack Obama had slept. It alleged that Putin was holding the video as *kompromat*, or blackmail material, to keep the president in line. Delivered in the kind of clinical spook-speak that John Le Carré fans lapped up, and packed with enough salacious morsels for the tabloid press to feast on, the document read like a classic piece of gray propaganda.

Once Clinton cut Steele loose during the campaign, Comey attempted to hire him to continue collecting dirt on Trump and Russia. The arrangement fell through when Steele violated FBI policy by feeding confidential information to the media. However, Comey had also inserted a confidential operative, veteran US foreign policy analyst and CIA asset Stefan Halper, inside the Trump campaign to "investigate" the candidate's Russian ties. Meanwhile, the Steele dossier was used as the lone piece of evidence by a Foreign Intelligence Surveillance Act judge to justify authorizing the FBI to place a Trump campaign advisor, Carter Page, under FBI surveillance. Though Comey was forced to terminate Steele's contract a day before Trump's election in November 2016, Steele continued to communicate with the FBI through an agent named Bruce Ohr, whose wife happened to work for Fusion GPS—the same research firm that had hired Steele.

The week of Trump's inauguration, James Clapper arranged for the existence of the Steele dossier, including its most explosive contents—the so-called "pee pee tape"—to be leaked to CNN through some of the FBI's most trusted stenographers in the Beltway press corps. The story sent shockwaves through Washington and brought Trump's tense relationship with the intelligence directors to a boiling point. While liberals reveled in the president's embarrassment, Trump's right-wing base began to see him as a victim of the opaque, unelected "deep state." (Clapper was hired as an analyst by CNN soon after the imbroglio.)

Eager to excuse the historically inept candidacy they had overseen, the dead-enders of the Clinton campaign did all they could to reinforce the narrative of Trump-Russia collusion and the general atmosphere of anti-Russian hostility. An insider account of the Clinton campaign published after her loss, *Shattered*, confirmed that "in the days after the election, Hillary declined to take responsibility for her own loss." Her top advisers were summoned the following day, according to the book, "to engineer the case that the election wasn't entirely on the up-and-up ... Already, Russian hacking was the centerpiece of the argument." Two months later, Jennifer Palmieri, the communications director of Hillary Clinton's campaign, urged Democrats to push the narrative of Trump-Russia collusion "relentlessly and above all else." Party leadership accepted the marching orders in total lockstep.

Trump might have been the most immediate target of Russiagate, but the manufactured scandal had far-reaching consequences for America's political culture, and particularly for media outlets that diverged from the consensus narrative. A DNI report issued days after Trump entered office declared that a broad campaign of Russian interference had influenced the 2016 elections, yet asserted "high confidence" in place of providing concrete evidence. In fact, one third of the report was dedicated to content analysis of the Russian-backed English-language news network RT, homing in on two shows that were no longer on air and accusing their hosts of spreading "radical discontent." Soon after, the House and Senate intelligence committees initiated a series of stormy hearings on Russian interference, prompting the Department of Justice to force RT to register as a foreign agent. No other foreign state broadcaster was required to do the same under threat of arrest and prosecution.

The front pages of trusted newspapers filled with stories sourced to unnamed "US officials" alleging unproven acts of

Russian sabotage against American voting systems, electricity grids and even the minds of average Americans via Kremlin-directed "active measures." The alleged Russian hacking of the DNC servers during the 2016 campaign was freely compared to Pearl Harbor and 9/11 by everyone from Hillary Clinton to Senator Ben Cardin. Russia hysteria dominated the coverage of the two major anti-Trump cable networks, MSNBC and CNN, with the top-rated MSNBC host, Rachel Maddow, dedicating more coverage to Russia than any other issue. Former intelligence agency higher-ups, from ex-CIA directors John Brennan and Michael Hayden to former DNI James Clapper, were hired as network contributors, and by the end of 2017, books by these operatives and by James Comey on the Trump-Russia furor dominated bestseller lists.

Under the influence of a cultural coup orchestrated by the national security state, American liberals united to defend some of the country's most conservative institutions against Trump's barrage of insults. The FBI, the "intelligence community" and the corporate mainstream media emerged as their victim-heroes, while NATO—the US-dominated military alliance that had transformed Libya into a failed state, helped destabilize Afghanistan and turned up tensions with Russia by expanding across Eastern Europe—each earned special protected status among those taken in by the Trump-Russia collusion narrative. In its obsession with Moscow's supposed meddling, the Democratic Party elite eagerly rehabilitated the Bush-era neoconservatives, welcoming PNAC founder William Kristol and "axis of evil" author David Frum into the ranks of the so-called "resistance." The Center for American Progress, the semiofficial think tank of the Democratic Party, consolidated the liberal-neocon alliance by forging a formal working partnership with the American Enterprise Institute, the nest of the Iraq war neocons, to "stand up to Russia."

The narrative of Russiagate provided the national security state with all the political latitude it needed to carry out a longstanding goal that had previously been unworkable. Now, a top-down campaign to tame the online wilds where establishment media faced a stiff challenge from alternative and independent news sources could be marketed to the general public as a crusade against "fake news."

In her first public appearance after losing to Trump, Hillary Clinton demanded that measures be taken against "the epidemic of malicious fake news and false propaganda that flooded social media over the past year," one of the many external factors she blamed for her defeat. The concept was assumed to encompass everything from phony clickbait sites to online conspiracism to virtually anything that offended elite sensibilities. Because mainstream media had failed to decide on a concrete definition of fake news, Trump was easily able to co-opt the term and turn it back on his enemies among the Beltway press corps. Elements in the national security state also seized the opportunity to clamp down on dissent.

Soon after Trump's inauguration, a shadowy website called PropOrNot mysteriously emerged with a blacklist of alternative media outlets, including many hubs of progressive left-wing opinion. PropOrNot accused them of "echoing Kremlin propaganda" and serving as platforms for Russian "active measures." The *Washington Post* immediately picked up on the site's blacklist and promoted it in a front-page feature. Hamilton 68, a similarly themed but more polished initiative backed by the German Marshall Fund, followed up months later with a seemingly sophisticated "dashboard" that claimed to track the amplification of media sources and political issues by Russian bots. Though the dashboard's developers refused to name a single bot account they tracked, and eventually admitted that many "bots" were real people who were not even Russian, this initiative was treated as the gold standard in Russian "active measure" monitoring by Congress and mainstream media. Meanwhile, the Atlantic Council in Washington, funded by NATO, the arms industry, and Gulf allies, created its own special Digital Forensic Research Lab (DFRLab) unit to hunt down the Kremlin's most devious online influencers. Despite its researchers misidentifying a British pensioner and a Ukrainian American concert pianist as Russian bots, the DFRLab was hired in June 2018 by Facebook to purge its platform of digital evildoers. This meant that one of the most militaristic think tanks in DC, whose very existence was predicated on its ability to advance corporate and Western imperial interests around the globe, had been granted the ability to censor content on the private website that had come to represent America's digital commons.

Throughout 2017, Silicon Valley executives were hauled before the Senate Intelligence Committee and pressured to cleanse their social media sites of Russian bots, trolls and alternative media scofflaws. The first casualty of the centrist censorship campaign was the easiest target: Alex Jones. In the pages of this book, Jones was seen channeling skepticism about the official story of the 9/11 attacks into a far-right cult of personality centered around himself. He eventually emerged as one of Trump's most potent grassroots allies and stalwart defenders. Amid the online purge, Jones and his archive were disappeared from almost every major social media platform, from YouTube to Pinterest to Facebook—his archives were simply erased under government pressure. Democratic senator Chris Murphy suggested that Jones would not be the last voice silenced by the establishment: "These companies must do more than take down one website," Murphy declared. "The survival of our democracy depends on it." Soon enough, leftist outlets—including teleSUR, the Latin American, socialist-oriented broadcaster—were forced to fight to reinstate their Facebook pages following arbitrary takedowns.

Russiagate had provided the national security state with a convenient lever for reasserting its authority over the national discourse. But its underlying narrative of America-under-siege reflected mounting frustration with the reality of America's waning influence on the world stage. The fraying of the hegemonic American project was most pronounced in Syria, where Washington's multibillion dollar covert arm-and-equip operation had collapsed in the face of a combined intervention by Russia and Iran. After Iraq and Libya, Syria was supposed to have been next to fall under Western military pressure. But by calling on its allies and effectively mobilizing its own resources, the government in Damascus had managed to hold on. The reaction in Washington's national security circles was predictably overwrought.

By 2017, ISIS was well on its way to defeat. The "regions of savagery" it had carved out in northeastern Syria, from Raqqa to Deir Ezzor, were rapidly caving under pressure from the Syrian military, Russian air support, and US-backed Kurdish forces. Meanwhile, Syria and its allies were pulverizing the Islamist insurgents suffering from dwindling foreign support. President Assad was winning the diplomatic war as well, having extracted an official reversal on March 30 of Washington's policy from US ambassador to the UN Nikki Haley and then secretary of state Rex Tillerson, who each declared that the United States would no longer seek regime change in Syria. A scheduled April 5 gathering of Western diplomats in Brussels to plan reconstruction efforts represented another significant diplomatic victory for Damascus.

Still, insurgents held an important card in the form of the "red line" policy enacted by the Obama administration back in 2013. According to the "red line," if the Syrian government could be plausibly accused of deploying chemical weapons in any form, the Trump administration would have to provide military intervention. At the same time, as the Syrian army closed in on rebel strongholds, US intervention was the insurgents' only hope to stave off total defeat.

Like clockwork—just forty-eight hours before diplomats convened in Brussels—images and allegations began to pour in through the Syrian opposition's social media channels depicting a calamitous attack on rebel-held territory. According to the Syrian Observatory for Human Rights, a one-man operation based in England and funded by the British Foreign Office, on April 3, 2017, some sixty civilians were killed in an apparent chemical weapons attack on Khan Shaykhun, a town within the Idlib governorate. Since 2015, Idlib has been under control of Al Qaeda's affiliate in Syria, known as Hay'at Tahrir al-Sham.

Immediately, photos emerged in the media of members of the US- and UK-funded White Helmets splashing water on writhing children piled on the back of a pickup truck, an unusual procedure for the treatment of sarin victims. Other outlets showed the White Helmets treating victims without gloves, a procedure that would have exposed rescuers to sarin had it indeed been deployed. No munitions were ever produced; the only visual evidence of a chemical-based air strike was a photograph of a single crater in the road in Khan Shaykhun.

The impact of these gut-wrenching viral images of dead children was immediate, sparking outrage across the globe and renewing demands for regime change from Western capitals. At an April 5 press conference in the White House's Rose Garden, one reporter after another pushed Trump to bomb. "Do you feel like you bear responsibility for responding to the chemical attacks and does the chemical attack cross a red line for you?" Julie Pace of the Associated Press asked Trump.

"Will you go after them? What message will you give them today? Will you work with the Russians to ground the Syrian air force and to establish safe zones?" another reporter asked.

Trump seemed lost, babbling incoherently about ISIS while slamming the Iran nuclear deal. The same reporter kept up the pressure: "But sir, I'm talking about the Iranian militias in Syria supporting the Syrian regime, separate of the nuclear deal. What message do you have for them today?"

"You will see," Trump declared. "They will have a message. You will see what the message will be."

Behind the scenes, Trump's foreign policy was increasingly under the management of a cast of former four-star generals who comprised much of his national security inner circle. Meanwhile, his daughter, Ivanka Trump, approached him with the photos of dead children in Khan Shaykhun to ratchet up the pressure for military intervention. The first daughter was "heartbroken and outraged" by the images, according to her brother. "Ivanka is a mother of three kids and she has influence. I'm sure she said, 'listen, this is horrible stuff.' My father will act in times like that," said presidential son Eric Trump.

"It crossed a lot of lines for me," President Trump said of the images. "When you kill innocent children, innocent babies ...

with a chemical gas that is so lethal that people were shocked to hear what gas it was, that crosses many, many lines. Beyond a red line. Many, many times."

On the evening of April 5, at his resort in Mar-a-Lago, Trump authorized the launch of fifty-nine cruise missiles from two naval destroyers parked in the Mediterranean. Their target was Shayrat airbase, a central node of the Syrian military's operations, where air strikes against ISIS-held territory in Palmyra and even far-off Deir Ezzor had been launched. Whether the base had any role in the chemical attack on Khan Shaykhun was still unknown.

Trump's bombing run won high praise from the military humanists who had been behind some of the Obama administration's most catastrophic regime change operations. "Donald Trump has done the right thing on Syria. Finally!! After years of useless handwringing in the face of hideous atrocities," Anne Marie Slaughtert declared.

Nicholas Kristof, the *New York Times* columnist who boosted NATO's intervention in Libya and advocated for another war of regime change in Syria, proclaimed, "Trump is right to make Syria pay a price for war crimes, and taking out airfields is the best approach." His only concern, he said, was in Trump's "execution." (During Israel's 2014 assault on the Gaza Strip, the reliably pro-intervention Kristof complained that "too many [Palestinians] define nonviolence to include rock-throwing. No, that doesn't cut it.")

Having clashed openly with a media he had referred to as "an enemy of the people," Trump suddenly found cheerleaders in newsrooms across the country. Out of forty-seven major newspaper editorial boards, only one—the *Houston Chronicle*—opposed Trump's strikes on Syria. While the *Washington Post*'s David Ignatius, a reliable barometer of national security state opinion, lauded Trump for "mov[ing] slightly towards pillars of traditional foreign policy," CNN described Trump as "lean[ing] towards [a] moderate voice." The network's leading foreign policy analyst, Fareed Zakaria, exulted in the bombing, exclaiming that "Donald Trump became president of the United States last night. I think this was a big moment." (Zakaria echoed his colleague at CNN, liberal commentator Van Jones, who said two months earlier that Trump "became president" when he honored the widow of a Navy SEAL killed in a botched special forces raid that left as many as twenty-five civilians dead in Yemen.)

Jake Tapper, the CNN anchor who had positioned himself as the Trump's arch-antagonist, joined the war party. On Twitter, Tapper quoted a "Syrian activist" who had texted him to exclaim, "Finally thank God!!!" The following day, CNN revealed the identity of that "activist": He was Mouaz Moustafa, the State Department-funded opposition lobbyist who helped drive the failed campaign for US military intervention in Syria back in 2013, and who took Senator John McCain on his illegal trip into Syria, where the senator posed for an embarrassing photo-op with two insurgents accused of kidnapping Shia pilgrims.

Trump's bombing earned praise from even more unlikely quarters. On their private Telegram channels, ISIS, Al Qaeda and the Syrian Salafi insurgent group Ahrar al-Shạm cheered on the president and demanded more airstrikes. In Al Qaeda–controlled Idlib, a local falafel salesman renamed his shop after Trump, while Syrian opposition supporters took to social media to hail the president—the arch-Islamophobe author of the discriminatory travel ban targeting Muslims—by nicknaming him "Abu Ivanka al-Amriki."

Among the isolated voices of criticism was one of the world's most experienced weapons inspectors, Hans Blix. As the former head of the International Atomic Energy Agency, Blix's attempts to investigate the existence of weapons of mass destruction in Iraq had been sabotaged by Bush's invasion. In Syria he saw history repeating itself. "I don't know whether in Washington they presented any evidence but I did not see that in the Security Council," Blix complained to the German outlet *Deutsche Welle*. "Merely pictures of victims that were held up, that the whole world can see with horror, such pictures are not necessarily evidence of who did it."

Blaming an emotionally charged atmosphere for Trump's

impulsive decision, Blix asked, "If you had a murder and you strongly suspect one fellow, do you go to judgment and execution straight away? Three days after the murder?" (Not one major American or British news outlet covered Blix's critical comments.)

The rare swell of positive reinforcement from elements which seemed dedicated to Trump's undoing fulfilled the president's almost animalistic yearning for approval. He seemed so overcome with self-satisfaction that he was able to remember what he was eating at the time of the missile strike better than the name of the country he had just bombed.

"I was sitting at the table, we had finished dinner," he recalled in a bizarre interview with Maria Bartiromo of Fox Business. "We're now having dessert—and we had the most beautiful piece of chocolate cake that you've ever seen—and [Chinese] President Xi was enjoying it." Trump continued, his face ruddy with delight: "So what happens is I said, 'We've just launched fifty-nine missiles heading to Iraq, and I wanted you to know this. And [Xi] was eating his cake. And he was silent."

"Towards Syria?" Bartiromo interjected, correcting the president.

"Yes, heading toward Syria," Trump sheepishly conceded, quickly returning to a detailed play-by-play of how Xi finished his dessert.

Though Trump might have been ignorant of the international implications of the missile strikes or even where the missiles landed, he seemed acutely aware of the domestic political benefits of bombing a Russian ally. Under constant fire from Russia-baiting Democrats in Congress and the Beltway press corps, Trump found an opportunity to co-opt their narrative. "If Russia didn't go in and back this animal, you wouldn't have the problem you have now," he told Fox Business, referring to Assad in the most derogatory terms he could muster.

Eric Trump echoed his father's attempt to pushback at the narrative of Russiagate, insisting, "If there was anything that [attacking] Syria did, it was to validate the fact that there is no Russia tie."

The day after the missile strikes, cable news producers were like putty in the hands of the national security state. The Pentagon piped footage of the Tomahawk launches from the Pentagon to the American public through CNN while prime-time panels filled up with former generals and ex-intelligence agents. Brian Williams, the MSNBC anchor who had been suspended from his job for fabricating a dramatic war story about surviving a fusillade of RPG fire from insurgents during a helicopter flight over Iraq, was overcome with an almost erotic exuberance as he commented on a Pentagon-supplied video of the missile launch.

"I am guided by the beauty of our weapons," Williams gushed, quoting a Leonard Cohen lyric from a piece the singer-songwriter once described as a "terrorist song."

Once the national media finally completed its love bombing of Trump, the Syrian military resumed sorties from the Shayrat airbase, still intact despite salvos of cruise missile strikes. Hoping to seize the moment, the national security state's most radical elements dusted off a well-worn blueprint and channeled it *sotto voce* through the pundit who represented one of their most trusted ciphers.

"Back off fighting territorial ISIS" and instead harness the jihadist group as a proxy to "bleed" Russia, Iran and the Syrian government, Thomas Friedman urged in the *New York Times*. Advising Washington *against* defeating ISIS, Friedman demanded massive arms shipments to the "moderate rebels" in Idlib and a no-fly zone to protect them, either unaware or unconcerned that the area was under the iron grip of the local franchise of Al Qaeda.

Friedman pointed to the covert war initiated by the CIA in 1979 in Afghanistan as his blueprint: "In Syria, Trump should let ISIS be Assad's, Iran's, Hezbollah's, and Russia's headache—the same way we encouraged the mujahedeen fighters to bleed Russia in Afghanistan."

As deranged as Friedman's prescription might have seemed, it was hardly different than the policy Washington had put in place when it began arming the insurgency in 2012. Washington's meddling had produced the birth of the ISIS caliphate across wide swaths of Iraq and Syria, along with the rise of the largest

Al Qaeda franchise since 9/11. For average people across the Middle East, this proxy war compounded the agony of the invasion of Iraq to an unbearable degree. For the managers of savagery in Washington, however, the destabilizing impact of the semi-covert policy had been a boon, enabling the fragmentation of a previously stable and secular state that had obstructed American and Israeli designs in the region.

Seven years later, though Syria had finally begun to reconstitute itself, the country bore all the scars of a world war played out on a miniature scale. Military personnel from Russia and Iran lay scattered across regions of government control, while Turkey had taken de facto possession of Idlib and was on its way toward invading and occupying Afrin, a mostly Kurdish area in northern Syria. Israel continued to harass the country, using the Iranian presence as a pretext to launch attacks deep inside Syrian territory. Meanwhile, the United States held on to a tenuous presence in the northeast, embedding thousands of troops among Kurdish fighters and entrenching itself in the oil-rich region despite having completed its mission against ISIS. A July 2018 report by the UN Security Council Sanctions Monitoring Team implicitly accused the United States of giving ISIS "breathing space" in order to justify prolonging the American military's presence.

The Russians and Iranians had been invited guests of the Syrian government, and Turkey was a regional neighbor, though not necessarily a friendly one. However, President Assad stated in no uncertain terms that the Americans were unwelcome "invaders." And as the three major players—Russia, Iran and Turkey—negotiated over Syria's future at the Sochi peace talks, the United States stood on the sidelines, rumbling idle threats alongside its monarchic Gulf partners. Washington was clearly the odd man out. While Trump appeared to recognize this reality, he would have to overcome the iron opposition of a firmly entrenched national security state to do anything about it.

During an April 3, 2018, White House meeting—exactly a year after the Khan Shaykhun incident—Trump clashed with his defense secretary, Jim "Mad Dog" Mattis; General Joseph Dunford, the chief of the Pentagon's central command; and an assorted group of Pentagon officials over Syria. When the president proposed an immediate withdrawal of US troops from the country, Mattis and the generals pushed back, citing unspecified "residual pockets of Islamic State fighters." "How long do you need to do that?" a frustrated Trump complained. The generals refused to provide a clear time line. It appeared as though they favored a near-permanent US presence, possibly to keep the oil wells in Syria's northeast in American custody.

The stormy meeting resembled a confrontation that occurred months earlier between Trump and his national security team over Afghanistan, where the president erupted in a stream of profanities against the generals' plan for a massive surge of US troops. With only the ultra-nationalist aide Steve Bannon on his side, Trump found himself cornered. In a matter of days, the generals had secured their plans for a major escalation in Afghanistan and Bannon had been unceremoniously drummed out, completing the purge of Trump's inner circle of loyalists.

Among the president's right-wing constituent base, events like these fueled the perception that a "deep state" of unelected national security operatives had systematically sabotaged the president's non-interventionist "America first" agenda and supplanted it with the "globalist" consensus favored by cosmopolitan elites and the mainstream media. Given the rapidly shifting tenor of the president's rhetoric and the composition of his foreign policy team, the perception was understandable. Trump's inner circle had been overtaken by hard-line militarists like John Bolton, the national security advisor who favored military campaigns from Iran to North Korea, and former South Carolina governor Nikki Haley, a marionette in the hands of neoconservatives who treated the UN as a grand stage to inveigh against Iran and Russia. Under the watch of Secretary of State Mike Pompeo, an evangelical zealot and anti-Iran hard-liner, neoconservative retreads were filling up mid-level posts. In just over a year, the Trump administration was beginning to resemble the second coming of George W. Bush's first term.

Back in Syria, the final pockets of Salafi-jihadi insurgency were being steamrolled by the Syrian army with Russian and Iranian military assistance. The strongest insurgent holdout lay in East Ghouta, an area in the suburbs of Damascus that had been used as a staging point for constant mortar attacks on the Syrian capital and even attempts to down civilian airliners taking off from the nearby airport. Jaysh al-Islam (the Army of Islam) had established a hard-line Islamist fiefdom in this area, relying on arms and untold millions in funding from Saudi Arabia. But as the Syrian army closed in, Jaysh al-Islam's foreign backing collapsed, forcing its leadership to hash out a series of deals that enabled its evacuation. Now, the only remaining pocket of resistance lay in the adjacent suburb of Duma, where a hard-line faction refused to accept any bargain with Damascus. Its defeat was imminent.

On April 7—just four days after Trump's confrontation with the generals over pulling US troops from Syria—a new wave of videos and photos came tumbling in from the familiar opposition media channels alleging that a chemical attack had taken place. As before, concrete evidence was nonexistent; Western media consumers were simply asked to accept on faith that photographs of lifeless women and children in a basement and videos of children being hosed off by White Helmet personnel constituted a chemical attack. They were also expected to shut off their critical faculties and avoid asking why Syria's armed opposition alleged a chemical attack seemingly whenever it was on the brink of a major defeat. In the hyper-charged atmosphere of Russiagate, where any prominent opinion maker who questioned the wisdom of a revamped Cold War or challenged Washington's hostility toward Moscow could be branded a traitor, skeptics of the official narrative on Duma were swiftly dismissed as "conspiracists" or, worse, as Kremlin agents.

Hours after the chemical allegations emerged, Trump mustered the most cartoonishly menacing threat he could conceive, vowing that "Animal Assad" would pay a "big price" for the attack. His tirade was followed by a volley of 126 cruise missiles from the deck of a US warship stationed in the Mediterranean. They struck at targets like the Barzeh science research laboratory, which international inspectors from the OPCW had inspected a year prior and determined to be a civilian science research facility with no chemical weapons on site. Hours later, Mattis emerged before the Washington press corps to announce the immediate end of operations.

The attack was a largely symbolic strike carried out from a distance and aimed as much at American public opinion as it was at a "rogue nation." In that respect, it was positively Clintonian, recalling the US cruise missile on the al-Shifa medical factory in 1998 that wiped out much of Sudan's supply of pharmaceutical drugs in the name of retaliating against bin Laden. Interventionist pundits spent days shrieking about Trump's failure to dent the "Assad regime," but with Russia and Iran's militaries fully invested in guaranteeing Syria's survival, there was little the United States could do toward that end without risking a devastating regional conflagration. Once again, America's national security state had been checkmated on the world stage.

Khan Shaykhun, the town in Al Qaeda–dominated Idlib where a chemical attack was alleged to have taken place, had remained off limits to international inspectors and journalists; however, the liberation of Duma and East Ghouta from insurgent control provided an unprecedented opportunity for outside investigation. When the veteran Middle East correspondent for the UK *Independent*, Robert Fisk, visited Duma, he met a local doctor who insisted that no chemical attack had occurred, but that the Islamist gunmen who occupied the area exploited the destruction of conventional bombings to create the appearance of one. A reporter from the conservative American network OAN named Pearson Sharp visited the local hospital and heard the same story from local doctors: "the rebels were desperate, and they needed a ploy to get the Syrian army off their backs so they could escape."

The most illuminating testimony came from Hassan Diab, a local boy who appeared in widely disseminated footage being frantically hosed down by insurgent-affiliated medical staff. "We were outside, and they told all of us to go into the hospital. I was immediately taken upstairs, and they started pouring water on me," Diab recalled to a reporter from RT Arabic. "The doctors started filming us here [in the hospital], they were pouring water and taking videos." Diab's father complained that his son had been stripped and sprayed with cold water despite suffering no injuries from any chemical weapons—that he had been used as a stage prop to convince Westerners that the red line had been crossed.

Though other eyewitnesses, including doctors from the Duma hospital, confirmed Diab's testimony in a press conference at The Hague, Western pundits dismissed their words entirely on the grounds that the Russian foreign ministry had organized the press meeting. But a preliminary report by the OPCW on the Duma attacks provided further credence to skeptics of the official line. Unlike the OPCW's report on the incident in Khan Shaykhun, which found that a nerve agent had been used, but which relied on partisan third parties linked to the insurgents to deliver the biomedical samples, the investigation into Duma was conducted with a full chain of custody.

This report found that no nerve agents had been present and found no chlorine in the biomedical samples it took from supposed victims on site. The only thing inspectors discovered was "various chlorinated organic chemicals"— the kind of substances that could originate from ordinary household cleansers and swimming pools. Tellingly, findings that suggested the West had waged another military operation on the basis of a deception were scarcely reported by the same media outlets that had blared news of a chemical attack with near-total certainty. (The *New York Times* had even sought to reinforce the official narrative by hiring a cartoonist to dramatize a chemical attack in Duma; the paper marketed its article as "augmented reality.")

No organization had been more instrumental than the White Helmets in supplying the mood music for Western military intervention. Treated as neutral lifesavers imbued with the spirit of Gandhi in Western mainstream media, nominated for a Nobel Prize, and awarded an Oscar for a Netflix documentary propagandizing on their behalf, the White Helmets were, in fact, an influence operation funded to the tune of at least $90 million by the US State Department and the British Foreign Office. They were also a party to the conflict, having been embedded among virtually every faction of the armed opposition—including ISIS—and filmed participating in grisly public executions.

Since their creation in southern Turkey in 2014 by a former British military officer and information warfare specialist named James Le Mesurier, the White Helmets had served as the go-to source for Western correspondents seeking dramatic footage of civil servants extracting children from rubble. While parading in public as lifesavers, White Helmet leaders lobbied Congress for sanctions on Syria and pleaded for Western military intervention. But as one insurgent pocket after another collapsed across Syria, this internationally famous and assiduously whitewashed organization rapidly shed its usefulness.

In July 2018, following the defeat of Islamist insurgents in southern Syria, including ISIS factions, 422 self-identified White Helmet members were evacuated by the Israeli military through the occupied Golan Heights to Jordan, a US client state that had served as a base for covert operations against Syria's government. The war may not have been entirely over, but this event signaled more than any other that the campaign to shatter Syria as an independent nation-state was close to its end. Not only had the White Helmets been treated to a special evacuation not afforded to any other Syrians in distress, it had arrived courtesy of Israel, a malicious adversary whose very existence was opposed across the Arab world. Nothing could have better reinforced the critique of this group as a collection of cynical mercenaries—and of the Syrian armed opposition as a whole—than this scene of retreat.

Consumed in bitterness over its failure in Syria, America's national security state lashed out with vengeful fury. Biting sanctions were crafted to target Russia for its role in preventing regime change in Syria. Meanwhile, the Trump administration reoriented its national security doctrine toward what Defense Secretary Mattis called "great power conflict" with Russia and China. The new doctrine did not even mention ISIS or any "war on terror."

A budget-busting defense authorization bill appropriately named for Senator John McCain ratified the drive toward confrontation with Russia and China, removing congressional oversight from the production of new nuclear weapons and demanding a "whole of government" strategy against China. The bill also widened the military's latitude for action against Iran, which the Trump administration had just placed back on the regime change target board after unilaterally reneging on the nuclear deal the United States had signed with Tehran. Under heavy influence from pro-Israel oligarchs like Sheldon Adelson and the think tanks he's funded, the Trump administration established a special "Iran Action Group" to spearhead the State Department's campaign of pressure and sabotage. The new anti-Iran unit distinctly resembled the George W. Bush Pentagon's Office of Special Plans, the propaganda operation set up by neoconservative operative Douglas Feith to cook up intelligence linking Saddam Hussein to Al Qaeda. Below the radar of the Washington press corps, Feith's son, David, had been hired to work directly under the Iran Action Group's director, Brian Hook.

Through covert operations and overt invasions, America's national security state had destabilized entire regions, from the Levant to North Africa, unleashed a migration crisis of unprecedented proportions onto Europe and spurred an inevitable right-wing backlash that was unraveling the neoliberal consensus they sought to protect. This process had crashed against the hard rocks of reality in Syria, and with it, the unipolar bliss that America had briefly enjoyed after the Cold War began to evaporate. As a new order emerged, Russiagate had become the ultimate expression of the national security state's anxieties.

Just one day before Trump's scheduled summit in Helsinki, special counsel Robert Mueller released the most dramatic document in his eighteen-month-long federal investigation into Trump's relationship with Russia. It was a detailed indictment of twelve Russian officers of the military intelligence unit GRU, accusing them of hacking into the DNC's computers to disrupt the 2016 presidential campaign. The timing of the indictment ensured that Trump would be met with the furor of the Washington press corps tailing him to Helsinki, with one question another about "collusion" with Putin and *kompromat*—and zero questions about substantive issues like antiballistic missile negotiations or de-escalation in Syria. Because the accused intelligence officers were likely to never appear in court, Mueller's charges couldn't be proven. (When another group of Russians accused by Mueller of interfering in the 2016 election through the Internet Research Agency online troll farm did appear in court, he rejected their request for discovery and frustratingly passed the case off to other attorneys.) However, the contents of the special counsel's indictment were enough to convict Trump in the eyes of the national security state. "He is wholly in the pocket of Putin," former CIA director Brennan declared following the Helsinki summit with Putin. Brennan added that Trump's performance was "nothing short of treasonous."

By painting Trump as Putin's puppet and branding anyone who favored détente with Russia as traitorous, the national security establishment rallied the public behind diplomatic degradation, all-out hostility and budget-busting defense expenditures. And by reviving the anticommunist paranoia of the Cold War, Russiagate enabled smear campaigns against socialist challengers like UK Labour Party leader Jeremy Corbyn, an antiwar stalwart, and even Bernie Sanders, who presented only a faint challenge to the foreign policy consensus.

In the face of their own failure, America's national security elites had successfully engineered a new Cold War, wagering that the reignited conflict would preserve their management of savagery abroad and postpone the terrible reckoning they deserved at home.

Notes

p. 2 McCain Defense Authorization Bill: HR 5515: John S. McCain National Defense Authorization Act for Fiscal Year 2019, govtrack.us, August 13, 2018.

p. 2 "biggest Resistance gathering yet": Susan B. Glasser, "John McCain's Funeral Was the Biggest Resistance Gathering Yet," *New Yorker*, September 1, 2018.

p. 2 "America was always great": Ellen Cranley, "'America Was Always Great': Meghan McCain Delivered a Fiery Rebuke of Trump in an Emotional Eulogy at her Father's Funeral," *Business Insider*, September 1, 2018.

p. 2 editorial excoriating Trump: Anonymous, "I Am Part of the Resistance Inside the Trump Administration," *New York Times*, September 5, 2018.

p. 7 Morton Kondracke observed: Edward Said, *Covering Islam*, Vintage, 1981, lxiii.

p. 7 Benjamin Netanyahu organized a conference: Remi Brulin, "Israel's Decades-Long Effort to Turn the Word 'Terrorism' Into an Ideological Weapon," *Mondoweiss*, August 26, 2014. Also see Brulin interview with Glenn Greenwald, Salon Radio, salon.com, March 14, 2010.

p. 8 "part of a much larger struggle": "Rolling Back the Barbarians,"

New York Times, May 18, 1986.

p. 9 **Utaybi soaked in the jeremiads (p. 9):** Yaroslav Trofimov, *The Siege of Mecca*, Anchor Books, 2007, 27–28.

p. 9 **Bin Baz issued decrees:** Ibid.

p. 10 **the royals were forced to turn to their sworn foe:** Ibid., 87, 151.

p. 10 **forbade them from shaking hands with men:** "The Ruling on Shaking Hands Between Men and Women," abdurrahman.org.

p. 10 **he endorsed the use of Viagra:** Adel Darwish, "Obituary: Sheikh Abdul Aziz Ibn Baz," *Independent*, May 13, 1999. Also see Mai Yamani, "War of the Fatwas," *Guardian*, October 29, 2007.

p. 10 **make exodus from non-Muslim countries:** "The Ruling on Muslims Residing in a Non-Muslim Country," salafi-dawah.com.

p. 10 **"illegalize movie theaters:** Alan Cowell and David D. Kirkpatrick, "Saudi Arabia to Allow Movie Theaters after 35-Year Ban," *New York Times*, December 11, 2017.

p. 11 **"to induce a Soviet military intervention":** Zbigniew Bzezinski interviewed by *Le Nouvel Observateur*, 1998, translated from French by William Blum and David N. Gibbs. This translation was published in Gibbs, "Afghanistan: The Soviet Invasion in Retrospect," *International Politics* 37, no. 2, 2000, 241–42.

p. 11 **1977 interagency memo:** Steven Aftergood, "Intelligence Reform in the Jimmy Carter Era," *FAS*, June 2, 2016.

p. 11 **most consequential covert intelligence operation:** Robert Pear, "Arming Afghan Guerrillas: A Huge Effort Led by US," *New York Times*, April 18, 1988.

p. 11 **Pakistan's nuclear weapons program advanced:** Interview with Jack Blum, Washington, DC, February 3, 2017.

p. 12 **"Pakistan is like Israel":** P.R. Kumaraswamy "The Strangely Parallel Careers of Israel and Pakistan," *Middle East Quarterly*, June 1997, 31–39.

p. 12 **Zia's ISI gave preference:** Ahmed Rashid, *Jihad: The Rise of Militant Islam in Central Asia*, Yale University Press, 2002, 210.

p. 12 **Mahmood Mamdani wrote:** Mahmood Mamdani, *Good Muslim, Bad Muslim*, Pantheon Books, 2004, 130.

p. 12 **"concert with Islamic countries":** Mark Curtis, *Secret Affairs: Britain's Collusion with Radical Islam*, Word Power Books, excerpted at MarkCurtis.info on September 30, 2016.

p. 12 **Saudi backing was crucial:** Pear, "Arming Afghan Guerrillas: A Huge Effort Led by US," *New York Times*, April 18, 1988.

p. 13 **issued a new fatwa:** "His Eminence Shaykh 'Abdul-'Aziz ibn 'Abdullah ibn Baz in an Interview With 'Al-Mujahid,' Kingdom of Saudi Arabia Portal of the General Presidency of Scholarly Research and Ifta," no. 5, 151, alifta.net.

p. 13 **Azzam instructed a young Osama:** Lawrence Wright, *The Looming Tower*, Vintage Books, 2006, 109–10.

p. 13 **its construction blueprints were used:** Yaroslav Trofimov, *The Siege of Mecca*, Random House, 2007, 124.

p. 13 **left him captivated by Utaybi's vision:** Ibid., 247.

p. 13 **including Muhammad Amir Sulayman Saqr:** Ibid., 248.

p. 14 **"at the forefront" of jihad:** Sam Roe, Laurie Cohen and Stephen Franklin, "How Saudi Wealth Fueled Holy War," *Chicago Tribune*, February 22, 2004.

p. 15 **"I was expecting to have to debate it":** "The True Story of Charlie Wilson's War," History Channel documentary, 2007, youtube.com.

p. 15 **$40 million in .22-millimeter canons:** Robert Pear, "Arming Afghan Guerrillas: A Huge Effort Led by US," *New York Times*, April 18, 1988. See also Gary J. Schmitt, "My War With Charlie Wilson," *American Enterprise Institute*, December 28, 2007.

p. 15 **Wilson also owned some $250,000 worth of stocks:** Melissa Roddy, "Charlie Wilson: I Come Not to Praise Him, but to Bury Him," Huffington Post, April 13, 2010.

p. 16 **experienced contractor named Osama bin Laden:** Jonathan Steele, "Bin Laden May Flee in Tunnels," *Guardian*, September 18, 2001.

p. 16 **$51 million grant:** Joe Stephens and David B. Ottaway, "From US, the ABCs of Jihad," *Washington Post*, March 23, 2002.

p. 16 **volunteer who directed the center, Thomas Gouttierre:** Joel Whitney, *Finks*, OR Books, 2017, 263.

p. 16 **"This type of reform":** Michael J. Berens, "University Helped US Reach out to Taliban," *Chicago Tribune*, October 22, 2001.

p. 17 **"a relatively young leader":** Ken Silverstein, "Blasts from the Past," Salon.com, September 22, 2001.

p. 17 **academic group called "the professors":** Olivier Roy, *Islam and Resistance in Afghanistan*, Cambridge Middle East Library, 1985, 71.

p. 17 **the Asia Foundation:** General CIA Records, publication date: March 22, 1967, declassified on February 5, 1999, cia.gov/library/readingroom/document/cia-rdp75-00149r000100550007-7.

pp. 17–18 **Hezb-i-Islami was playing a long game:** Henry Kamm,

"Afghan Rebel Opposes Talks; Vows Battle for Islamic State," *New York Times*, March 19, 1988.

p. 18 **suspected to be involved in the murder**: Ibid.

p. 18 **"a pure Islamic state"**: Ibid.

p. 18 **Thatcher traveled to a refugee camp**: "Margaret Thatcher on State Visit to Pakistan," YouTube clip of October 1981 report by David Rose, youtube.com.

p. 18 **"We had better leave"**: "Thatcher Surprises Afghan Guards with a Handshake," *Montreal Gazette*, October 9, 1981.

pp. 18–19 **his affection for the mujahedin**: Russian diplomat "How Many Russians Did Sikorski Kill?," Radio Poland, August 8, 2011, thenews.pl.

p. 19 **"succeeded only in hitting the outer wall"**: Andrew Osborn and Matthew Day, "Russian Takes a Potshot at Past of Polish Minister," *Daily Telegraph*, August 10, 2011.

p. 19 **In Train's spy-ops fantasy**: Whitney, *Finks*, 259–68.

p. 20 **"I hate the gooks"**: C.W. Nevius, Marc Sandalow and John Wildermuth, "McCain Criticized for Slur / He Says He'll Keep Using Term for Ex-captors in Vietnam," *San Francisco Chronicle*, February 18, 2000.

p. 20 **McCain shot down by Soviet officer**: Miriam Elder, "Russian Who Shot Down John McCain Should be Given a Medal, Say Communists," *The Telegraph*, November 22, 2008.

p. 20 **McCain provided the Vietnamese with valuable intelligence**: Douglas Valentine, "McNasty," Counterpunch, June 13, 2008.

p. 20 **So committed was McCain**: Chip Berlet, "McCain Advised Ultra-Right Group Tied to Death Squads," Huffington Post, May 25, 2011.

p. 20 **Stetsko, the Ukrainian Nazi collaborator**: John-Paul Himka, "The Lviv Pogrom of 1941," *Kyiv Post*, September 23, 2010.

p. 21 **Boucher casually dismissed**: Joan Mower, "State Department Plays Down Afghan Rebel Massacre," Associated Press, July 19, 1989.

p. 21 **he was rebuked. McWilliams explained**: Andrew Cockburn, "A Special Relationship," *Harper's*, January 2016.

p. 22 **"victims of political instrumentalization"**: Rudiger Schoch, *Afghan Refugees in Pakistan During the 1980s: Cold War Politics and Registration Practice*, UNHCR, June 2008, unhcr.org.

p. 22 **first right-wing terror attack**: Sindre Bangstad, *Anders Breivik and the Rise of Islamophobia*, Zed Books, 2014, 120.

p. 22 "resistance movement": Ibid.

p. 23 concentration camp in Oakdale, Louisiana: Lisa Belkin, "For Many Arab-Americans, FBI Scrutiny Renews Fears," *New York Times*, January 12, 1991.

p. 23 "a place of pivotal importance": Alfred McCoy, "Washington's Great Game and Why Its Failing," TomDispatch, June 7, 2015.

p. 23 Rubin … told journalist Robert Friedman: Robert I. Friedman, "The CIA's Jihad," *New Yorker*, March 17, 1995.

p. 24 the CIA paid Abdel-Rahman's way: Ibid.

p. 24 "he would create a new reality": Wright, *The Looming Tower*, 246.

p. 25 as journalist Peter Lance argued: Peter Lance, *Triple Cross*, WilliamMR, 2006, 20; Lance published the first book-length profile of Mohamed. Though Lance relied at points on problematic figures like Steven Emerson, a self-styled investigative reporter now widely regarded as a discredited anti-Muslim ideologue, Lance's central claim—that the CIA and FBI protected Mohamed as he penetrated America's national security infrastructure—is well documented and has not been disproven.

p. 25 "Everyone in the community knew": Ibid., 28–29.

p. 26 "Now, what outside agency?": Ibid., 34.

p. 26 Mohamed was sent home: Ibid., 42.

p. 26 De Atkine … foreword to *The Arab Mind*: Raphael Patai, *The Arab Mind*, Recovery Resources Press, revised 2007 edition. See also Seymour M. Hersh, "The Gray Zone," *New Yorker*, May 24, 2004. Hersh explains how Patai's book influenced "the notion that Arabs are particularly vulnerable to sexual humiliation," ultimately leading to the sadistic tactics put on display in the US-run Abu Ghraib prison.

p. 27 "we do not have moderates": Triple Cross, "Bin Laden's Spy in America," Nat Geo, 2006, youtube.com.

p. 27 "I don't think he was anti-American": Benjamin Weiser, "US Ex-Sergeant Linked to bin Laden Conspiracy," *New York Times*, October 30, 1998. In four articles between 1999 and 2000, the *New York Times* mentioned Mohamed's links to US intelligence services only once, noting that he had begun a relationship with the FBI in 1993, providing them with information on members of "sleeper" cells.

p. 27 one of the most important hubs of the Afghan proxy war: John

Cooley, *Unholy Wars*, Pluto Press, 2002, 71.

p. 28 "I believe that there was an [FBI] agent": Lance, *Triple Cross*, 44.

p. 28 Mohamed's army evaluation report: Julia A. Coyner to Lt. McGraw, US Army Reserve Personnel Center Public Affairs Office, October 5, 1995.

p. 28 "top secret for training": The manuals taken by Mohamed from Ft. Bragg were discovered by the FBI at the apartment of El-Sayyid Nosair and were viewed by this author. They contain an assortment of documents, from "Location of selected units" of US special forces in December 1988, to a manual entitled "Prepare An M72A2 Light Antitank Weapon for Firing."

p. 28 "Without the revolution, what would I be?": "Specter of Islam Troubles Kabul," *Detroit Free Press* via Knight Ridder, April 27, 1988.

p. 29 beseeching them for American cooperation: "Gorbachev to Cut Troops: Meets Reagan, Bush After Telling UN of 500,000 Reduction: Friendly Farewells by 2 World Leaders," *LA Times* Wire Services, December 7, 1988.

p. 30 Weinberger helped arrange: Jonathan Marshall, "Saudi Arabia and the Reagan Doctrine," *Middle East Research and Information*, November/December 1988.

p. 30 "An extremist seizure of Kabul": Steve Coll, *Ghost Wars*, Penguin, 2004, 232.

p. 30 amounts of cash and weapons to Hekmatyar: Ibid., 238.

p. 31 "these same techniques reappear": Cooley, *Unholy Wars*, 71.

p. 31 According to Cooley, Abu Sayyaf: Ibid., 50.

p. 31 "CIA monster": Edmundo Santuario III, "Abu Sayyaf The CIA's Monster Gone Berserk," *Bulatlat*.

p. 31 "begin treating the Bosnians as we did the Contras and mujahedin": *Daily Journal* via Associated Press, June 19, 1995.

p. 31 "wealthy Saudi Arabian emigre [sic] Osama Binladen": John Pomfret, "Bosnia's Muslims Dodged Embargo," *Washington Post*, September 22, 1996.

p. 32 Benevolence International was among: Sam Roe, Laurie Cohen and Stephen Franklin, "How Saudi Wealth Fueled Holy War," *Chicago Tribune*, February 22, 2004.

p. 32 "the United States did not push the matter": Ibid.

p. 32 When Blum testified before the Senate: Transcript of the hearing of the Senate Select Intelligence Committee on alleged CIA drug trafficking to fund Nicaraguan Contras in the 1980s, October 23, 1996, angelfire.com.

p. 33 "Thank you for bringing the Americans to help us": Wright, *The Looming Tower*, 172.

p. 34 "forbidden blood would be spilled": Thomas Hegghammer, "Abdallah Azzam and Palestine," Norwegian Defense Establishment (FFI), 2013, hegghammer.com.

p. 34 Wright … speculated that Zawahiri: Wright, *The Looming Tower*, 164.

p. 34 (the Blind Sheikh), entered the United States on a visa: Douglas Jehl, "CIA Officers Played Role in Sheik Visas," *New York Times*, July 22, 1993.

p. 35 "This will not be considered as mercenary recruiting": 1989 internal FBI communique FOIA'ed by Thomas Hegghammer and published on Twitter.com on March 2, 2018.

p. 35 a 1995 report in the *Boston Globe*: Paul Quinn-Judge and Charles M. Sennott, "Figure Cited in Terrorism Case Said to Enter US with CIA Help," *Boston Globe*, February 3, 1995.

p. 35 the newspaper's editor retracted the story: Lance, *Triple Cross*, 127.

p. 36 "those stupid bastards at the CIA": Andrew Cockburn, "A Special Relationship," *Harper's*, January 2016.

p. 36 But Shalabi wanted to spent the funds: Lance, *Triple Cross*, 66.

p. 36 the murder investigation was hastily closed: Ibid., 67.

p. 37 he grew depressed, popping Prozac: John Kifner, "Police Say Kahane Suspect Took Anti-Depression Drugs," *New York Times*, November 9, 1990.

Prozac … acts of violence: Maia Szalavitz, "Top Ten Legal Drugs Linked to Violence," *Time*, January 7, 2011.

p. 37 left him with lingering injuries: Kifner, "Police Say Kahane Suspect Took Anti-Depression Drugs."

p. 37 Undercover FBI agents tailed them: Lance, *Triple Cross*, 207.

p. 37 tools in the FBI's campaign: Jonathan Schoenwald, "Reforming the FBI After September 11: Lessons From the 1960s," *FindLaw*, March 14, 2002.

p. 38 Kahane … group he called ZEERO: Rabbi Meir Kahane's HY"D last speech "JEW, LEAVE THE EXILE" at ZEERO Conference, youtube.com.

p. 38 Israel's chief rabbi: Abraham Rabinovich, "Kahane Buried in Jerusalem: Violence Mars Funeral of Rabbi Slain in US," *Sun-Sentinel*, November 8, 1990.

p. 38 Kahane's ... into the Israeli mainstream: Tony Greenstein, "Kahane Was Right! Labour Leader Barak Supports Kahane's Loyalty Oaths," October 18, 2010, azvsas.blogspot.com. See also Chaim Levinson, "Kahane's Vision for Loyalty Oath Was Not So Different than Barak's," *Haaretz*, October 15, 2010.

p. 39 "to be done by means of destroying": Robert I. Friedman, "The CIA's Jihad," *New Yorker*, March 27, 1995.

p. 39 store in Jersey City called Sphinx Trading: Lance, *Triple Cross*, 373.

p. 41 Bin Laden had brought battle plans: Wright, *The Looming Tower*, 178–9.

p. 42 *The Gulf War Did Not Take Place*: Jean Baudrillard, *The Gulf War Did Not Take Place*, Indiana University Press, 1991.

pp. 42–3 "Nayirah" ... incubators of Kuwaiti babies: John Stauber and Sheldon Rampton, "Lies, Damn Lies, and the Public Relations Industry," Common Courage Press, chapter 10, prwatch.org/books/tsigfy10.html.

p. 43 his caucus was renting discounted office space: John R. Macarthur, "Deception on Capitol Hill," *New York Times*, January 15, 1992.

p. 43 "none had more impact on American public opinion": John R. Macarthur, *Second Front: Censorship and Propaganda in the Gulf War*, University of California Press, 1992.

p. 44 A study that year by Martin Lee and Norman Solomon: Martin A. Lee and Norman Solomon, *Unreliable Sources: A Guide to Detecting Bias in News Media*, Lyle Stuart, 1991, xvii.

p. 44 to gather information on Arab American business: Ronald J. Ostrow and Dan Shannon, "FBI Agents Interview Arab-American Business Leaders : Terrorism: US Hopes to Head Off Acts of the Type Threatened by Hussein," *LA Times*, January 8, 1991.

p. 45 "the end point of mankind's ideological evolution": Francis Fukuyama, "The End of History?," *National Interest*, Summer 1989.

p. 45 "we've got five, maybe ten, years to clean up": Wesley Clark, *A Time to Lead*, Palgrave MacMillan, 2007, 150.

p. 46 "Anti-Soviet Warrior Puts His Army": Robert Fisk, "Anti-Soviet Warrior Puts His Army on the Road to Peace: The Saudi Businessman Who Recruited Mujahedin Now Uses Them for Large-Scale

Building Projects in Sudan," *Independent*, December 6, 1993.

p. 46 bin Laden had already taken credit: Michael Scheuer, *Through Our Enemies' Eyes: Osama bin Laden, Radical Islam, and the Future of America*, revised edition, Potomac Books, 2006, 147.

p. 46 "The CIA had trained whoever had conducted them": Scott Stewart, "A Look Back at the 1993 World Trade Center Bombing," Stratfor Worldview, February 26, 2015.

p. 46 "It would be almost a year before I heard the term 'al Qaeda'": Ibid.

p. 47 Yousef ... to establish Abu Sayyaf: Zachary Abuza, "Balik-Terrorism: The Return of The Abu Sayyaf Group," Strategic Studies Institute at the Army War College, September 2005, 3.

p. 47 "We promise you that next time will be very precise": Lance, *Triple Cross*, 116.

p. 47 Pakistani intelligence ... Mercy International: Anwar Iqbal, "Pakistan unearthing Yousef's roots," UPI, April 11, 1995.

p. 48 "with the assistance of .... the CIA": Richard Labévière, *Dollars for Terror*, Algora Publishing, 2000, 364.

p. 48 train his cadres at the Khost camp: Lance, *Triple Cross*, 103–4.

p. 48 He was accompanied by Essam Hafez Marzouk: Ibid., 123–5.

p. 49 Mohamed ... his training of Al Qaeda recruits: Wright, *The Looming Tower*, 205–6. See also Lance, *Triple Cross*, 129.

p. 49 Mohamed led his mentor, Zawahiri: Lance, *Triple Cross*, 197–9.

p. 49 Al-Kifah ... Bosnia: William J. Kole, "Intelligence Report: Islamic Extremists Have Been Crossing Balkans for Years," Associated Press, April 17, 2006.

p. 50 to never have to wear a wire: Lance, *Triple Cross*, 81.

p. 50 Salem ... A serial liar: James C. McKinley Jr., "Key Witness in Bomb-Plot Trial Admits Lying about His Exploits," *New York Times*, March 8, 1995.

p. 50 Salem's ... whopping $1 million: Lance, *Triple Cross*, 118.

p. 50 Victor Alvarez, a twenty-nine-year-old idler: Joseph P. Fried, "Defendant in Bomb Case Is Described as Retarded," *New York Times*, August 29, 1995.

p. 52 Mohamed was busy training a terror cell: Ibid., 45.

p. 52 "Bravo, Attorney General McCarthy": Andrew C. McCarthy, "Bravo Attorney General Mukasey," *National Review*, July 15, 2008.

p. 53 "McCarthy advised Ali Mohamed to ignore": Lance, *Triple Cross*, 175.

p. 53 the government blocked [De Atkine]: Interview with Roger

Stavis, June 1, 2017.

p. 54 **"the result of an action initiated by Langley"**: Paul Quinn-Judge and Charles M. Sennott, "Figure Cited in Terrorism Case Said to Enter US with CIA Help Defense Says Defendants Trained by Him," *Boston Globe*, February 3, 1995.

p. 54 **largest and most complex terror conspiracy**: Richard Bernstein, "Trial for 12 Opens in Plot for Bombing New York Buildings," *New York Times*, January 10, 1995.

p. 54 **"would have resulted in the murder of hundreds if not thousands"**: Joseph P. Fried, "Sheikh Sentenced to Life in Prison in Bombing Plot," *New York Times*, January 18, 1996.

p. 50 **"They bought their conviction with a million dollars"**: Brian Jenkins, "Defense: Juror Bias in Terror Verdicts," CNN, October 1, 1995.

p. 50 **"This country has experienced militant fascism"**: Joseph P. Fried, "Sheikh Sentenced to Life in Prison in Bombing Plot," *New York Times*, January 18, 1996.

p. 50 **"God will make (America) disappear from the surface of the Earth"**: Mike Dorning, "World Trade Terrorist Gets Life, No Parole," *Chicago Tribune*, January 18, 1996.

p. 55 **"We're preparing for the worst"**: Times Wire Services, "Tight Security Aims to Forestall Terror Attacks," *Chattanooga Times*, October 3, 1995.

p. 56 **Robert Fox ... in a nationally televised 1993 broadcast**: Cooley, *Unholy Wars*, 199.

p. 56 **Laurie Mylroie, a disgruntled**: Peter Bergen, "Did One Woman's Obsession Take America to War?," *Guardian*, July 5, 2004.

p. 57 **Rabbani, one of the mujahedin's founding fathers**: Melody Emachild Chavis, *Meena, Heroine of Afghanistan*, MacMillan, 2003.

p. 57 **he had just beheaded five political opponents**: Andrew Cockburn, "A Special Relationship," *Harper's*, January 2016.

p. 59 **"Nobody had ever imagined that the situation could get this bad"**: Ahmed Rashid, *Taliban*, Yale University Press, 2000, 204.

p. 59 **Pakistan then helped to set up a wireless network**: Ibid., 45.

p. 59 **the Saudis directly armed the movement**: Ibid.

p. 59 **"There was not a word of US criticism"**: Ibid., 177.

p. 60 **Chris Taggart publicly volunteered his opinion**: Ibid., 166.

p. 60 **Human Rights Watch documented a white-painted C-130 Hercules**: Human Rights Watch, "Pakistan's Support of the Taliban," hrw.org, 2001.

p. 60 **Saudi Arabia kicked in millions:** Ibid.

p. 60 **women forbidden from attending school:** Revolutionary Association of Women in Afghanistan (RAWA), "Some of the Restrictions Imposed by Taliban on Women in Afghanistan," rawa.org.

p. 60 **Music was banned:** Nicholas Wroe, "A Culture Muted," *Guardian*, October 13, 2001.

p. 60 **walls bulldozed atop accused homosexuals:** Associated Press, "Execution by Taliban: Crushed under Wall," *New York Times*, January 16, 1999.

p. 60 **with recycled USAID-designed textbooks as their guide:** Rob Crilly, "'Infidels Are Our Enemy': Afghan Fighters Cherish Old American Schoolbooks," Al Jazeera America, December 7, 2014, america.aljazeera.com/articles/2014/12/7/afghan-fighters-americantextbooks.html.

p. 60 **Gouttierre, was paid:** Michael J. Berens, "University Helped US Reach Out to Taliban," *Chicago Tribune*, October 22, 2001.

pp. 60–1 **Taliban commanders and a few Al Qaeda operatives:** Ibid.

p. 61 **the United States found "nothing objectionable":** Rashid, *Taliban*, 166.

p. 61 **"The Taliban will probably develop like Saudi Arabia":** Ibid., 179.

p. 61 **Samira Goetschel asked Brzezinski:** Samira Goetschel, "Our Own Private Bin Laden," 2006, youtube.com.

p. 62 **"I call on Muslims to support this nation":** Public Broadcasting System (PBS), "Jihad: The Men and Ideas Behind Al Qaeda," 2007, youtube.com.

p. 62 **"A very hard war between Muslims and Westerners":** Ibid.

p. 62 **The Egyptian government had struck a deal in July 1997:** Wright, *The Looming Tower*, 290–91.

p. 63 **butchered fifty-eight tourists and six Egyptian locals:** Ibid., 292–3.

p. 63 **attended by President Mubarak and Sean Connery:** Cooley, *Unholy Wars*, 155.

p. 63 **"had been so rare as to be unknown until then in Egypt":** Ibid.

p. 63 **he and bin Laden festered in a squalid encampment:** PBS, "Jihad: The Men and Ideas behind Al Qaeda."

p. 63 **"we did not see Osama bin Laden":** Shahir Shahidsaless, "The Khobar Towers Bombing: Its Perpetrators and Political Fallout," Middle East Eye, September 3, 2015.

p. 63 **Libya became the first country:** Simon Denyer, "Gaddafi's Libya

Reminds US It Issued the First bin Laden Arrest Warrant," *Washington Post*, May 4, 2011.

p. 63 **according to French journalist Guillaume Dasquié:** Max Blumenthal, "The Manchester Bombing Is Blowback from the West's Disastrous Interventions and Covert Proxy Wars," AlterNet, May 25, 2017.

p. 64 **It was Mohamed who scouted:** "Former GI Pleads Guilty in Embassy Bombings/Egyptian-born Ex-sergeant Says He Helped bin Laden," *San Francisco Gate*, October 21, 2000.

p. 64 **"I took pictures, drew diagrams":** Ibid.

p. 64 **they knew of the existence of the East African cell:** Lance, *Triple Cross*, 273.

p. 64 **"This is the most dangerous man I have ever met":** Ibid., 278–80.

p. 65 **eLance was faced with a libel lawsuit:** Boris Kachka, "Prosecutor as Book Publicist," *New York Magazine,* June 5, 2009.

p. 65 **Mohamed ... accepted a subpoena to testify:** Lance, *Triple Cross*, 302–4.

p. 65 **he tore pages from his notebooks:** Ibid.

p. 66 **"The Bureau couldn't risk that kind of embarrassment":** Ibid., 372.

p. 66 **"I've read what you read and I can't comment":** Jonathan Towers, "Triple Cross: Bin Laden's Spy in America," *National Geographic Channel*, 2006, youtube.com. See also Benjamin Weiser, "US Ex-Sergeant Linked to bin Laden Conspiracy," *New York Times*, October 30, 1998.

pp. 66–7 **strikes, launched on the basis of bunk intelligence:** Wright, *The Looming Tower,* 320.

p. 67 **50 percent of the medicine to one of the poorest countries:** Patrick Wintour, *Observer*, December 20, 1998, cited in Nafeez Masaddeq Ahmed, "United States Terrorism in Sudan," October 22, 2001, mediamonitors.net.

p. 67 **sold them on the black market for $10 million each:** Wright, *The Looming Tower,* 323.

p. 67 **"It was like a script [bin Laden] has written for the Americans":** PBS, "Jihad: The Men and Ideas behind Al Qaeda," 2007.

p. 67 **"Bin Laden's interest was not in killing a few Americans":** Ibid.

p. 68 **"a propagandist for the Israelis":** Leon T. Hadar, "Binyamin Netanyahu: The Joe Isuzu of the Middle East Media Wars," *Washington Report on Middle East Affairs*, July 1991, 32.

p. 68 the *Washington Times* recommended: Ibid.

p. 68 Perle was overheard on an FBI wiretap: Janine R. Wedel, *Shadow Elite*, Basic Books, 2009, 148.

p. 68 Feith was fired from a job: Ibid., 148–9.

p. 69 the prime minister tapped Feith and his allies: Jason Vest, "Turkey, Israel and the US," *Nation*, August 23, 2002.

p. 69 "A Clean Break: A New Strategy for Securing the Realm": *A Clean Break: A New Strategy for Securing the Realm*, Institute for Advanced Strategy and Political Studies, 1996; authors of the paper included Richard Perle, James Colbert, Charles Fairbanks Jr., Douglas Feith, Robert Loewenberg, David Wurmser, and Meyrav Wurmser; see informationclearinghouse.info.

p. 69 high colonial-era "Iron Wall" manifesto: Vladimir Jabotinsky, "The Iron Wall," first published in Russian, *Rssvyet*, November 4, 1923, and in English in the *South African Jewish Herald* on November 26, 1937; transcribed and revised by Lenni Brenner for Die Roten and published online at marxists.de.

p. 70 "Toward a Neo-Reaganite Foreign Policy": William Kristol and Robert Kagan, "Toward a Neo-Reaganite Foreign Policy," *Foreign Affairs*, July/August 1996.

p. 71 "dual containment" … by Martin Indyk: F. Gregory Gause III, "The Illogic of Dual Containment," *Foreign Affairs*, March/April 1994. Gause's criticism of the Clinton administration's dual containment strategy proved to be remarkably prophetic. Warning of the consequences of Iraqi regime change, he wrote, "The policy could end up encouraging the very results, regional conflict and increased Iranian power that the United States seeks to prevent."

p. 71 576,000 children under the age of five had died: Barbara Crossette, "Iraq Sanctions Kill Children, UN Reports," *New York Times*, December 1, 1995. The UNICEF study was challenged in a 2017 paper by London School of Economics researchers, alleging, "Saddam Hussein's government successfully manipulated the 1999 survey in order to convey a very false impression." See Tim Dyson and Valeria Cetorelli, "Changing Views on Child Mortality and Economic Sanctions in Iraq: A history of Lies, Damned Lies and Statistics," *BJM Global Team*, July 24, 2017. Nevertheless, Albright justified the sanctions policy even as she accepted the 576,000 infant death toll as fact. What's more, Dyson and Cetorelli do little to explain how the insertion of Iraqi Ministry of Health researchers among the UNICEF team contaminated its study or resulted in fabrication.

p. 72 **Albright ... containment policy was "worth it"**: Rahul Mahajan, "We Think the Price Is Worth It," *Fairness and Accuracy in Reporting*, November 2001, fair.org.

p. 72 **when he signed the Iraq Liberation Act**: Johanna Mcgeary, "Taking Out Saddam," CNN, November 30, 1998.

p. 72 **Zinni ... dismissed the scheme as "harebrained"**: Ibid.

p. 73 **"No one has done what Saddam Hussein has done"**: "US Policy on Iraq Draws Fire in Ohio," CNN, February 18, 1998.

p. 75 **a February 2001 wedding ceremony**: PBS, "Jihad: The Men and Ideas behind Al Qaeda," 2007. See also: Wright, *The Looming Tower*, 376–7.

p. 75 **Ahmed Zaidan ... was ferried to the wedding**: Ibid.

p. 75 **"She sails into the waves flanked by arrogance"**: Ibid.

p. 76 **"The destroyer represented the West"**: Lawrence Wright, "The Agent," *New Yorker*, July 10, 2006.

p. 76 **"what will happen in the coming five years"**: PBS, "Jihad: The Men and Ideas Behind Al Qaeda," 2007.

p. 76 **deployed into the faceless suburbs**: Jamie Reno, "Terrorist Cell Was Embedded Deeply in San Diego," *North County Times*, September 10, 2011.

p. 76 **followed the jihadi trail through Bosnia**: The 9/11 Commission, "Final Report of the National Commission on Terrorist Attacks on the United States," 2004, 155.

p. 76 **Mihdhar later trained in Afghanistan**: "The Men Who Brought the World to the Brink of War," *Guardian*, September 22, 2001.

pp. 76–7 **The two landed at Los Angeles International Airport**: Jamie Reno, "Terrorist Cell Was Embedded Deeply in San Diego," *North County Times*, September 10, 2011.

p. 77 **CIA operatives broke into Mihdhar's hotel room**: Wright, "The Agent."

p. 77 **Curiously, the CIA refused to supply the information to the FBI**: Ibid.

p. 77 **"Mihdhar and Hazmi could have seemed"**: Ibid.

p. 77 **they were met at the airport by Omar Bayoumi**: Reno, "Terrorist Cell Was Embedded Deeply in San Diego."

p. 77 **the two worshipped at the King Fahad Mosque**: Possible link between hijackers, Culver City mosque questioned in newly released twenty-eight pages from 9/11 report," CBS LA/AP, July 15, 2016.

p. 77 they were "immediately assigned an individual": Dan Christensen, "Secrets of 9/11: FBI Probe in 2012 Focused on Alleged Supporters of Hijackers," *Miami Herald*, December 20, 2016. See also Patrick J. McDonnell, "Saudi Envoy in LA Is Deported," *LA Times*, May 10, 2003. This article was one of the first public mentions of Fahad al-Thumairy and his alleged connections to extremists. It failed to connect him to the 9/11 plot, however.

p. 78 they co-signed an apartment lease: The 9/11 Commission, "Final Report of the National Commission on Terrorist Attacks on the United States," 2004, 517.

p. 78 his salary shot up from $500 a month to $3,500: David Johnston and Douglas Jehl, "Bush Refuses to Declassify Saudi Section of Report," *New York Times*, July 29, 2003.

p. 78 "One of the FBI's best sources in San Diego": James Risen, "Threats and Responses: The Intelligence; Informant for FBI Had Contacts with Two 9/11 Hijackers," *New York Times*, July 25, 2003.

p. 78 Bayoumi and Thumairy's phones registered twenty-one calls: Philip Shenon, "Declassified Documents Detail 9/11 Commission's Inquiry Into Saudi Arabia," *Guardian*, May 13, 2016.

p. 78 Bayoumi logged nearly 100 calls to Saudi officials: HG Reza, "What Was Omar al-Bayoumi Doing in San Diego?," *San Diego Reader*, September 11, 2016.

p. 78 Bayoumi ... traveled frequently to Saudi consular offices: see chapter 5 from Office of the FBI Inspector General, "A Review of the FBI's Handling of Intelligence Information Prior to the September 11 Attacks," November 2004, oig.justice.gov.

p. 78 welcoming party Bayoumi organized: Amy Goldstein and William Booth, "Hijackers Found Welcome Mat on West Coast," *Washington Post*, December 29, 2001.

p. 78 worshipping at his Al-Ribat Al-Islami mosque: Reno, "Terrorist Cell Was Embedded Deeply in San Diego."

p. 78 "There was always a series of cars": John Cloud, "The Plot Comes into Focus," *Time*, September 23, 2001.

p. 79 Action Required: None: The House Permanent Select Committee on Intelligence and the Senate Select Committee on Intelligence "Report of the Joint Inquiry Into the Terrorist Attacks of September 11, 2001," December 2002.

p. 79 a different kind of Republican: "Bush Visits NAACP—A Different

Kind of Republican," The Hotline, July 11, 2000.

p. 79 **Jim Yardley praised Bush's "bipartisan, above-the-fray image":** The Hotline, April 17, 2000.

p. 79 **"healing a divided nation":** *CNN Late Edition with Wolf Blitzer*, CNN, December 17, 2000.

p. 79 **"Cheney is the ultimate man of moderation":** "Will Dick Cheney Be a Good Running Mate for George W. Bush?," CNN Crossfire, July 24, 2000.

p. 79 **"should be what is described as a 911 global police force":** *CNN Late Edition with Wolf Blitzer*, December 17, 2000.

p. 79 **"Cheney is the ultimate man of moderation":** "Will Dick Cheney Be a Good Running Mate for George W. Bush?," *CNN Crossfire*, July 24, 2000.

p. 80 **"Cheney is the ultimate man of moderation":** "Will Dick Cheney be a good running mate for George W. Bush?," *CNN Crossfire*, July 24, 2000.

p. 80 **Mylroie ... as a terror consultant in the Pentagon:** Peter Bergen, "Did One Woman's Obsession Take America to War?," *Guardian*, July 5, 2004.

p. 80 **"an astonishing number of unheeded warnings":** James Mann, *Rise of the Vulcans*, Penguin Books, 2004, 291.

p. 80 **"Bin Laden Threats Are Real":** The 9/11 Commission, "Final Report of the National Commission on Terrorist Attacks on the United States," 2004, 259.

p. 81 **"the summer of the shark":** Amy Dempsey, "'Summer of the Shark' Was a Story Media Could Sink Their Teeth Into," TheStar.com, August 28, 2016.

p. 81 **The number of shark attacks was actually down:** Ibid.

p. 81 **he fielded thirty to fifty calls from reporters every day:** Ibid.

p. 81 **"the system was blinking red":** Rupert Cornwell, "The System Was Blinking Red," *Independent*, July 22, 2004.

p. 81 **"Bin Laden Determined to Strike Inside the US":** The 9/11 Commission, "Final Report of the National Commission on Terrorist Attacks on the United States," 2004, pp. 260–2.

p. 81 **"a Bin Laden cell in New York was recruiting Muslim-American youth":** Ibid.

pp. 81–82 **Al Qaeda operatives ... maintained:** Jonathan Miller, "A Plea Deal, Then Freedom, in Terror Case Where Prosecutors Kept Evidence a Secret," *New York Times*, March 8, 2003.

p. 82 Waleed Al-Noor ... had been named as an unindicted co-conspirator: Peter Lance, "Al Qaeda and the Mob: How the FBI Blew it on 9/11," Huffington Post, November 17, 2006.

p. 82 Passaic County detectives accused Christie: Lance, *Triple Cross*, 382.

p. 82 He exuded an "expansive mood": Dana Milbank and Mike Allen, "Bush Gave No Sign of Worry in August 2001," *Washington Post*, April 11, 2004.

p. 82 "we are going to be struck soon": Cofer Black, Briefing to Department of Defense Annual Convention on Counterterrorism, August 15, 2001, fas.org.

pp. 82–3 Howard Stern ... "Pam Anderson's Jet": Howard Stern's 9/11 Broadcast with Paired Footage, youtube.com.

p. 84 earning him praise for channeling the outrage: Douglas Barclay, "On 9/11, Howard Stern Refused to Stop His Radio Show and Helped New Yorkers Process the Madness Around Them," *Rare*, September 11, 2015.

pp. 84–5 won the *Late Show with David Letterman*, the real Dan Rather: *Late Show with David Letterman*, September 17, 2001, youtube.com.

p. 85 "We're going to attack Iraq," the general grumbled: Joe Conason, "Seven Countries in Five Years," Salon.com, October 12, 2007.

p. 86 President George W. Bush appeared at the Islamic Center: "'Islam is Peace' Says President," The White House, September 2001, georgewbush-whitehouse.archives.gov.

p. 86 a "pro-American" vigil ... transformed into a racist mob: Don Terry and Noreen S. Ahmed-Ullah, "Protesters Turn Anger on Muslim Americans," *Chicago Tribune*, September 14, 2001.

p. 86 Sikhs were targeted: "History of Hate: Crimes against Sikhs Since 9/11," Huffington Post, August 7, 2012.

pp. 86–7 Christopher Smith ... credited a 1994 documentary: "One Man's War on Terror," *Brown Alumni Magazine*, November/December 2002.

p. 87 "creating mass hysteria against American Arabs": John F. Sugg, "Steven Emerson's Crusade," FAIR, January 1999, fair.org.

pp. 87–8 "We are Israeli. We are not your problem": "Were Israelis Detained on Sept. 11 Spies?" ABC News, June 21, 2002.

p. 88 "Please! Call Congress": Alexander Zaitchik, "Meet Alex Jones," *Rolling Stone*, March 2, 2011.

p. 88 Branded by *Talkers* magazine as "an early trailblazer": Ibid.

p. 88 "The twenty-first century is gonna be a new century": Richard Linklater, "Waking Life," *Thousand Words*, October 2001.

p. 89 accusing it of orchestrating "controlled demolitions": Alexander Zaitchik, "Meet Alex Jones," *Rolling Stone*, March 2, 2011.

p. 89 "wherever [Bush] wants me to line up, just tell me where": Peter Hard, "Rather's Real Bias," FAIR, April 2005, fair.org.

p. 89 like MSNBC's Phil Donahue: Amy Goodman and Juan Gonzalez, "Phil Donahue on His 2003 Firing from MSBC, when Liberal Network Couldn't Tolerate Anti-war Voices," *Democracy Now!*, March 21, 2013.

p. 89 public trust in the federal government had plummeted: "Beyond Distrust: How Americans View Their Government," *Pew Research Center*, November 23, 2015.

p. 89 more online listeners than America's top conservative radio jock: Zaitchik, "Meet Alex Jones."

p. 90 increase risk of heart attacks and sperm damage: Alexander Nazaryan, "Is Alex Jones Peddling Lead-tainted, Sperm-killing Products? Toxic Heavy Metal Found in Two Infowars Supplements," *Newsweek*, October 17, 2017.

p. 90 Dylan Avery, a twentysomething waiter at Red Lobster: Nancy Jo Sales, "Click Here for Conspiracy," *Vanity Fair*, August 2006.

p. 90 making himself its executive producer: Paul Joseph Watson, "Alex Jones Announces Loose Change Role," Prison Planet, May 18, 2007.

p. 90 finding interest from filmmaking legend David Lynch: "David Lynch Questions 9/11," Wereldgastern VPRO, December 3, 2006, youtube.com.

p. 90 actor Charlie Sheen and the oligarch Mark Cubane: Paul Joseph Watson and Alex Jones, "The Truth About Charlie Sheen and Loose Change," *Prison Planet*, May 28, 2007.

p. 90 in 2006, 42 percent of Americans told pollsters: Mike Berger, "Zogby Poll Finds Over 70 Million Voting Age Americans Support New 9/11 Investigation," 911Truth.org, May 21, 2006.

p. 91 Twenty-eight pages ... had been redacted: Mark Mazzetti, "In 9/11 Document, View of a Saudi Effort to Thwart US Action on Al Qaeda," *New York Times*, July 15, 2016.

p. 91 showing contacts between one of the hijackers: "Indirect 9/11 Link to Saudi Royal Revealed in 28 Unclassified Pages Revealed to

Be Prince Bandar bin Sultan," *Daily Mail*, August 5, 2016.

p. 91 forked over millions to powerhouse DC firms like Qorvis: Brian P. McGlinchey, "Document Exposes Inconsistent Disclosure of Saudi Hand in Campaign Against JASTA," 28Pages.org, September 26, 2017.

p. 91 Bush and Obama administrations were staunchly against: Seung Min Kim, "Obama Vetoes Saudi 9/11 Bill," *Politico*, September 23, 2016.

p. 91 "an Afghan national resistance movement": The 9/11 Commission, The 9/11 Commisision Report: Final Report of the National Commission on Terrorist Attacks upon the United States, W.W. Norton & Co., 2004, 55.

p. 91 "compared to the Soviet Union, and to its collapse": Samira Goetschel, "Our Own Private Bin Laden," 2006, youtube.com.

p. 92 Jones opened … the Minutemen: Glenn Spencer, "Border Fence Plans Were All about Amnesty," The Alex Jones Channel, January 17, 2011, youtube.com.

p. 92 "could possibly cause flooding akin to Noah's ark": Fiona Miller, "Expert: Chemtrails Could Wipe Out Humanity," Infowars.com, November 15, 2016.

p. 92 engineered the 1995 … bombing: TheAlexJonesChannel, "Proof the OKC Bombing Was an Inside Job," InfoWars.com, December 17, 2011.

p. 93 on the *Late Show with David Letterman* that Arab "sleeper cells": *Late Show with David Letterman*, September 17, 2001, youtube.com.

p. 94 In fact, al-Arian had known both men: Phone interview with Sami al-Arian, May 2, 2017.

p. 95 "I delivered," he said. "Now it's your turn": Ibid.

p. 95 rising wave of attacks from right-wing radio jocks: Eric Boehlert, "The Prime-time Smearing of Sami al-Arian," Salon.com, January 23, 2002.

p. 95 "one of the world's most lethal terrorist factions": John F. Sugg, "Steve Emerson's Crusade," FAIR, January 1999, fair.org.

p. 96 Attorney General John Ashcroft touted the case: Khadijah Qamar and Hamdan Azhar, "How the US Falsely Accused a Palestinian Teacher of Aiding Terror," Electronic Intifada, October 1, 2014..

p. 96 Gordon Kromberg, an outspoken supporter of Israel: Melva Underbakke, "The Ordeal of Dr. Sami Al-Arian," *Washington Report on Middle East Affairs*, April 2007.

p. 96 **two full-time court translators had been paid:** Interview with Sami al-Arian, February 5, 2017; interview with Linda Moreno, former lead attorney on al-Arian's defense team, June 8, 2017.

p. 96 **the former think tank of ... AIPAC:** Right Web, *Washington Institute for Near East Policy*, June 30, 2015, rightweb.irc-online.org.

pp. 96–7 **An investigation and prosecution ... cost taxpayers upwards of $50 million:** Ken Silverstein, "The Trials of Sami al-Arian," *Harper's*, March 7, 2008.

p. 97 **thanks to the personal intervention of President Recep Tayyip Erdoğan:** Interview with Sami al-Arian, February 5, 2017.

p. 97 **Emerson's ... as an NBC commentator:** Zachary Block, "One Man's War on Terror," *Brown Alumni Magazine*, November/December 2002.

p. 97 **millions to a private for-profit company:** Bob Smietana, "Anti-Muslim Crusaders Make Millions Spreading Fear," *Tennessean*, October 24, 2010.

p. 98 **Kohlman "admitted he had never interviewed any members of the group":** Petra Bartosiewicz, "Experts in Terror," *Nation*, January 17, 2008.

p. 98 **her field work largely consisted of:** Aaron Leibel, "Undercover in the War on Terror," Jewish Telegraphic Agency, July 28, 2003.

p. 98 **She appeared on *60 Minutes* to promote the book:** Marc Perelman, "Muslim Charities Sue CBS Investigator," *Forward*, June 13, 2003.

p. 98 **Katz went on to form her own company:** Benjamin Wallace-Wells, "Private Jihad," *New Yorker*, May 29, 2006.

p. 98 **"They translate the statements into English on our behalf":** Ibid.

p. 99 **Philip Pearlman, had been the guitarist:** Raffi Khatchadourian, "Azzam the American," *New Yorker*, January 22, 2007.

p. 99 **writing about his obsession with death metal:** Ibid.

pp. 99–100 **Gadahn's "State of the Ummah" series:** "State of the Ummah Part 1," *As-Sahab Media*, 2001, republished by Internet Media Archive, archive.org/details/stateoftheummah1.

p. 100 **"Civilized people throughout the world are speaking out in horror":** Laura Bush, "Laura Bush on Taliban Oppression of Women," *Washington Post*, November 17, 2001.

p. 100 **"There will be 300-page [haircare] manuals and instructional videos":** David Halbfinger, "After the Veil, a Makeover Rush," *New*

York Times, September 1, 2002.

p. 101 **Hekmatyar returned to his former power base:** Robert Dreyfuss, "Your Tax Dollars at War," *Mother Jones*, May/June 2009.

p. 101 **"Courtesy of the Red, White and Blue" … at top:** Rob Walker, "Toby Keith's Two Fisted 9/11 Song," Slate.com, August 12, 2002.

p. 101 **the United States "lit up" a wedding celebration:** "Afghan: US Bomb Hits Wedding Party," CNN, July 1, 2002.

p. 101 **Karzai was one of the so-called "Gucci Guerrillas":** Derek Brown, "Hamid Karzai: Rebel with a Cause," *Guardian*, December 7, 2001.

p. 102 **working closely with his fellow Pashtun tribesman, Zalmay Khalilzad:** "Friendly Ally Who Has Yet to Be Tested," *Irish Times*, June 22, 2002.

p. 102 **Karzai helped organize the movement into a potent force:** Sarah Chayes, "Hamid Karzai's Cozy History with the Taliban," *LA Times*, February 9, 2014.

p. 102 **Ahmed Wali Karzai, an accused heroin trafficker:** James Risen, "Reports Link Karzai's Brother to Afghanistan Heroin Trade," *New York Times*, October 4, 2008.

p. 102 **Ahmed Wali Karzai was put on the CIA payroll:** Dexter Filkins, Mark Mazzetti and James Risen, "Brother of Afghan Leader Said to Be Paid by CIA," *New York Times*, October 27, 2009.

p. 102 **Tora Bora cave complex with only fifty-seven captured:** George Friedman, *America's Secret War*, Doubleday, 2004, 199.

pp. 102–3 **"He knew every ridge and mountain pass":** Mary Anne Weaver, "Lost at Tora Bora," *New York Times Magazine*, September 11, 2005.

p. 103 **"kaleidoscope of brigands, fanatics, and opportunists":** Ibid., 198.

p. 103 **Bush … did not publicly admit to its failure at Tora Bora:** Barton Gellman and Thomas E. Ricks, "US Concludes Bin Laden Escaped at Tora Bora," *Washington Post*, April 17, 2002.

p. 103 **"take action to deter and prevent acts of international terrorism":** Congress.gov, SJ Res. 23—Authorization for Use of Military Force, 107th Congress, 2001–02, congress.gov.

p. 105 **Office of Special Plans, a pet project:** Julian Borger, "The Spies Who Pushed for War," *Guardian*, July 17, 2003.

p. 105 **Office of Special Plans … "an unofficial 'Iraqi intelligence cell'":** Julian Coman, "Fury Over Pentagon Cell That Briefed White House on Iraq's 'Imaginary' al-Qaeda links," *Daily Telegraph*, July 11, 2004.

p. 106 **$97 million to Chalabi's Iraqi National Congress:** *SourceWatch*, Center for Media and Democracy, "Iraq Liberation Act of 1998," sourcewatch.org.

p. 106 **Bush's State Department attempted to appropriate $8 million:** Eli J. Lake, "US Plans for Post-Saddam Iraqi Government," UPI, June 5, 2002.

p. 106 **a pledge that Feith found "quite moving":** Evan Thomas, "The Rise and Fall of Chalabi: Bush's Mr. Wrong," *Newsweek*, May 30, 2004.

p. 106 **Chalabi delivered Adnan al-Hadeiri:** James Bamford, "The Man Who Sold the War," *Rolling Stone*, November 18, 2005.

p. 106 **Chalabi, for his part, allegedly received $1 million:** Abdel Bari Atwan, *The Secret History of Al Qaeda*, University of California Press, 2006, 213.

p. 106 **al-Hadeiri had failed a polygraph test:** Bamford, "The Man Who Sold the War."

p. 106 **Among those that cashed in on the contract was the Rendon Group:** Ibid.

p. 107 **"It was the first in a long line of hyped and fraudulent stories":** Ibid.

p. 107 **Pentagon inspector general and senator, Jay Rockefeller, later called "inappropriate":** Jonathan S. Landay, "Pentagon Office Produced 'Alternative' Intelligence on Iraq," McClatchy, February 8, 2007.

p. 107 **"Saddam is seeking, is working, is advancing towards the development of nuclear weapons":** C-Span, "Israeli Perspective on Conflict with Iraq," September 12, 2002.

p. 107 **"America must not ignore the threat gathering against us":** "Bush: Don't Wait for Mushroom Cloud," CNN, October 8, 2002.

p. 107 **"The line was the brainchild of two speechwriters":** Bryan Burrough, Eugenia Peretz, David Rose and David Wise, "The Path to War," *Vanity Fair*, May 2004.

p. 108 **"We needed to go over there [to Iraq], basically, and take out a very big stick":** Dan Murphy and Thomas Friedman, "Iraq War Booster," *Christian Science Monitor*, March 18, 2013.

p. 108 **"United States needs to pick up some small crappy little country":** Jonah Goldberg, "Baghdad Delenda Est, Part Two," *National Review*, April 23, 2002.

p. 108 **"Saddam Hussein has ... chemical and biological weapons stock"**: Hillary Clinton Senate floor speech on SJ Res 45, "A Resolution to Authorize the Use of United States Armed Forces Against Iraq," October 10, 2002, democraticunderground.com.

p. 108 **"Yet this Chamber is, for the most part, silent"**: Robert C. Byrd, "The Arrogance of Power," Senate floor speech, March 19, 2003, americanrhetoric.com.

p. 109 **Phil Donahue, was summarily yanked from the airwaves**: Amy Goodman, "Phil Donahue on His 2003 Firing When Liberal Network Couldn't Tolerate Anti-war Voices," *Democracy Now!* March 21, 2013.

p. 109 **Clear Channel ... memorandum**: "158 Songs Banned by Clear Channel after 9/11, Plus all by Rage against the Machine," RT.com, September 11, 2016.

p. 109 **"Freedom's untidy"**: Pamela Hess, "Rumsfeld: Looting Is Transition to Freedom," UPI, April 11, 2003.

p. 109 **some 250,000 tons of ammo and explosives disappeared**: "377 Tons Small Part of Absent Iraq Explosives," Associated Press, October 31, 2004, nbcnews.com.

p. 110 **"Wahhabism is going to spread in the Arab nation"**: John Nixon, *Debriefing the President*, Penguin Books, 2016, 4.

p. 110 **the war in Iraq as "A Christian's Duty"**: Max Blumenthal, "Onward Christian Soldiers," Salon.com, April 15, 2003.

p. 110 **Hizb ut-Tahrir ... "Destroy the Fourth Crusader War"**: Ibid.

p. 111 **"Baghdad's little America"**: Rajiv Chandrasekaran, *Imperial Life in the Emerald City: Inside Iraq's Green Zone*, Vintage Books, 2007.

p. 111 **"privatization that sort of occurs naturally"**: Ibid., 120.

p. 111 **"establish the basic legal framework"**: Ibid., 68.

p. 111 **Bremer issued dozens more orders**: Antonia Juhasz, "The Handover That Wasn't," *Foreign Policy in Focus*, July 20, 2004.

p. 112 **Feith ... proposal for a "De-Baathification of Iraqi Society"**: James P. Pfiffner, "US Blunders in Iraq: De-Baathification and Disbanding the Army," *Intelligence and National Security* 25, no. 1, February 2010, 76–85.

p. 112 **"What happened to everyone there?"**: Sidney Blumenthal, "Emerald City Exposed," Salon.com, September 14, 2006.

p. 112 **January 2003 National Intelligence Council paper**: Michael R. Gordon, "Poor Intelligence Misled Troops About Risk of Drawn-out

War," *New York Times*, October 20, 2004.

p. 113 **Zarqawi took the namesake ... in the autonomous Kurdish region:** Nir Rosen, *Aftermath*, Nation Books, 2010, 139–43.

p. 114 **Powell falsely described Zarqawi as the link:** Transcript of Powell's UN presentation, CNN, February 6, 2003.

p. 114 **Zarqawi ... sought an open war with the Shia:** Rosen, *Aftermath*, 144.

p. 114 **"many Sunni areas will stand with the mujahedin":** William McCants, *The ISIS Apocalypse*, Picador, 2015, 13.

p. 115 **Bin Laden and Zawahiri expressed severe reservations:** Ibid., 14. Also see Rosen, *Aftermath*, 144.

p. 115 **"the al Qaeda network's propaganda, recruitment":** Alan Cowell, "Britain Assails Critical Report on Role in Iraq," *New York Times*, July 19, 2005.

p. 115 **"welcome a US military intervention in Syria":** Atwan, *The Secret History of Al Qaeda*, 218.

p. 116 **Iraqi civilian casualties stood at 665,000:** David Brown, "Study Claims Iraq's "Excess" Death Toll Has Reached 655,000," *Washington Post*, October 11, 2006.

p. 116 **Al Qaeda's franchise in Iraq:** McCants, *The ISIS Apocalypse*, 15.

p. 116 **Abu Ghraib ... first exposed by Seymour Hersh:** Seymour Hersh, "Torture at Abu Ghraib," *New Yorker*, May 10, 2004.

p. 116 **grisly torture, brutality and even rape:** Julian Borger, "US Military in Torture Scandal," *Guardian*, April 30, 2004.

p. 117 **"We're already being compared to ... Sharon":** Julian Borger, "Israel Trains US Assassination Squads in Iraq," *Guardian*, December 8, 2003.

p. 117 **the "Salvador Option" ... James Steele:** Mona Mahmood, Maggie O'Kane, Chavala Madlena, Teresa Smith, Ben Ferguson, Patrick Farrelly, Guy Grandjean, Josh Strauss, Roisin Glynn, Irene Baqué, Marcus Morgan, Jake Zervudachi and Joshua Boswell, "From El Salvador to Iraq: Washington's Man Behind Brutal Police Squads," *Guardian*, March 6, 2013.

p. 118 **"Iraq is a prison, and now I live in my own little prison":** Steve Niva, "Walling off Iraq: Israel's imprint on US Counterinsurgency Doctrine," *Middle East Policy Council* 15, Fall 2008, No. 3.

p. 118 **"Israelis changed the way" ... JINSA-sponsored trip:** Max Blumenthal, "The Israelification of Domestic Security," *Al Akhbar*, December 2, 2011.

p. 119 **Dichter ... "fighting crimiterrorists"**: Ibid.

p. 119 **1033 Program ... 84,258 assault rifles**: Eyder Peralta, "White House Ban on Militarized Gear for Policy May Mean Little," NPR, May 21, 2015.

p. 119 **$699 million in military vehicles to local police**: Celisa Calacal, "Does the Militarization of Police Lead to More People Killed? Research Says Yes," AlterNet, July 7, 2017.

p. 119 **$111 million COPS Hiring Program**: "$111 Million in COPS Grants Support Military Veterans," Department of Justice Archives, June 26, 2012.

p. 120 **"They move unnoticed"**: "Attorney General Prepared Remarks on the National Entry-Exit Registration System," Department of Justice, June 6, 2002.

p. 120 **NYPD ... "Demographics Unit"**: Adam Goldman and Matt Apuzzo, "NYPD: Muslim Spying Led to no Leads, Terror Cases," Associated Press, August 21, 2012.

p. 120 **NYPD commissioner Ray Kelly ... Tel Aviv**: "NYPD commissioner: Israel Improved Our Ability to Combat Terror," YNet, March 2, 2010.

p. 121 **Pew Research poll ... comprehensive withdrawal**: Andrew Kohl, "Foreign Policy: The Public Sends a Muddled Message," Pew Research Center, March 8, 2007.

p. 121 **4,222 Americans had been killed in Iraq**: "Names of the Dead," *New York Times*, January 22, 2009.

p. 121 **white phosphorous ... heats human flesh to 5,000 degrees**: "M15 White Phosphorous Grenade" FAS Military Analysis Network, fas.org.

p. 121 **"Justified kill. They're all listed as insurgents"**: Max Blumenthal, "Max Blumenthal Interviews Marine Mom Tina Richards," youtube.com, July 7, 2007.

p. 122 **as many as twenty veterans killed themselves each day**: Leo Shane III and Patricia Kime, "New VA Study Finds 20 Veterans Commit Suicide Each Day," *Military Times*, July 7, 2016.

p. 122 **"NO BETTER FRIEND, NO WORST ENEMY"**: Steve Fishman, "Hell's Kitchen," nymag.com, n.d.

p. 122 **Allen West ... discharged from the military**: "US Officer Fined for Harsh Interrogation Tactics," CNN, December 13, 2003.

p. 123 **Islam a "theo-political belief system and construct"**: Brian Tashman, "Meet Allen West, Fanatical Opponent of Muslims,

Immigrants, Progressives, and Obama," *Right Wing Watch*, November 9, 2010.

p. 123 **Chris Kyle ... inflated the number of service medals:** "Navy Revises 'American Sniper' Chris Kyle's Medal Count," Fox News, July 10, 2016.

p. 123 **stall tales ... Superdome:** Jarvis DeBerry, "The 'American Sniper's' Preposterous New Orleans Story," *Times-Picayune*, January 20, 2015.

p. 123 **unverified story ... Jesse Ventura:** Nicholas Shmidle, "In the Crosshairs," *New Yorker*, June 3, 2013.

p. 123 **Marcus Luttrell ... Mohammad Gulab:** R.M. Schneiderman, "Marcus Luttrell's Savior, Mohammad Gulab, Claims 'Lone Survivor' Got It Wrong," *Newsweek*, May 11, 2016.

p. 124 **Luttrell ... ad for the National Rifle Association:** Luttrell NRA Commercial, youtube.com.

p. 126 **"Destroying the Great Satan: The Rise of Islamic Facism [sic] in America":** Matea Gold, "Bannon Film Outline Warned US Could Turn Into Islamic States of America," *Washington Post*, February 3, 2017.

p. 126 **Walid Phares ... Lebanese Fifth Bureau:** Sarah Lazare, "Trump's New Foreign Policy Advisor Is a Hardcore Neocon Tied to Notorious Lebanese Militia That Massacred Civilians," Alternet's Grayzone Project, March 21, 2016, alternet.org..

p. 127 **Spencer ... partnership with Pamela Geller:** Max Blumenthal, "The Great Fear," *Tom Dispatch*, December 19, 2010.

p. 127 **divorce settlement ... Oshry, wound up dying:** Ibid.

p. 127 **Geller ... Yerushalmi:** Ibid.

p. 128 **David Horowitz Freedom Center ... Chernick:** Ibid.

p. 128 **Another top supporter ... Nina Rosenwald:** Max Blumenthal, "The Sugarmama of Anti-Muslim Hate," *Nation*, June 14, 2012.

p. 128 **Horowitz ... Islamofascism Awareness Week:** Max Blumenthal, "The Demons of David Horowitz," *Huffington Post*, November 6, 2007.

p. 129 **"Instead of opening eyes, we are fastening blindfolds":** Andrew Kacynski and Chris Massie, "In College, Trump Aide Stephen Miller Led Controversial 'Terrorism Awareness Project' Warning of 'Islamophobia,'" CNN, February 15, 2017.

p. 129 **Miller ... Rabbi Ben Packer:** Ben Packer, "Our Friend Stephen Miller," Arutz Sheva, December 15, 2016. Also see Michael F. Brown,

"'Fire Up the Bulldozers,' Says Trump's Biggest Fan in Jerusalem," *Electronic Intifada*, January 19, 2017.

p. 129 **He was Raphael Shore:** Ibid.

p. 129 **At Aish, Shore oversaw ... the Clarion Project:** Ali Ghraib and Eli Clifton, "Meet the Donors Behind the Clarion Fund's Islamophobic Documentary 'The Third Jihad'," *Think Progress*, January 24, 2012.

p. 130 **During the 2008 election ... a film called *Obsession*:** Max Blumenthal, "The Great Fear," *Tom Dispatch*, December 19, 2010.

p. 130 **Obama was ... of Malcolm X:** Alex Parent, "Bombshell: Obama Malcolm X's Love Child?," *Gawker*, October 30, 2008.

p. 130 **Gaffney tendered donations:** Eli Clifton, "Far-right Birther's Secret Funders: Look Who's Backing Islamophobe Frank Gaffney," Salon.com, October 1, 2014.

p. 131 **Shoebat ... "A secular dogma":** Ed Pilkington, "US Counter-Terrorism Training 'Presents Islam as Inherently Violent'," *Guardian*, March 9, 2011.

p. 131 **He received his PhD ... circumstances:** Daniel Nexon, "Sebastian Gorka May Be a Far-right Nativist, but for Sure He's a Terrible Scholar," *Foreign Policy*, March 17, 2017.

p. 131 **"the rise of the transcendentalist terror":** Andrew Reynolds, "Stop Calling Him 'Dr': The Academic Fraud of Sebastian Gorka, Trump's Terrorism 'Expert,'" *Haaretz*, April 27, 2017.

p. 132 **Berntsen ran a long-shot Tea Party campaign:** David M. Halbfinger, "Ex-spy Is a Long Shot to Oust Schumer," *New York Times*, July 1, 2010.

p. 132 ***How Obama Embraces Islam's Sharia Agenda*:** Andrew C. McCarthy, *How Obama Embraces Islam's Sharia Agenda*, *Encounter Broadside*, 2010.

p. 132 **"a center to the victims ... of jihadi wars":** "Protesters Descend on Ground Zero for Anti-mosque Demonstration," CNN, June 7, 2010.

p. 132 **Gingrich reinforced the righteous narrative:** Andy Barr, "Newt Compares Mosque to Nazis," *Politico*, August 16, 2010.

p. 133 **Mercer, who paid for a $1 million ad blitz:** Mobashra Tazamal, "Robert Mercer's Financing of Islamophobia," *The Bridge Initiative*, March 20, 2018.

p. 133 **Under Breitbart's direction:** Thomas Hedges, "The Bizarre Far-right Billionaire Behind Trump's Presidency," *Real News*, January 13, 2017.

p. 133 **Breitbart ... junketed to Israel:** Larry Solov, "Breitbart News Network: Born in USA, Conceived in Israel," Breitbart, November 17, 2015.

p. 133 **"the Leni Riefenstahl of the Tea Party movement":** Alex Kotch, "Trump Campaign Leaders Made Movies Comparable to Nazi Propaganda," Alternet, October 6, 2016.

p. 133 ***The Roots of Political Correctness*:** "William S. Lind on the Origins of Political Correctness," youtube.com.

p. 135 **"a platform for the alt-right":** Jim Naureckas, "How Breitbart Provides a 'Platform for the Alt-right,'" FAIR, January 2017.

p. 135 ***Generation Zero*:** *Generation Zero*, youtube.com.

p. 135 **hires at Breitbart was Julia Hahn:** Peter Maas, "Birth of a Radical," *Intercept*, May 7, 2017.

p. 135 **Titled *Camp of the Saints*:** "Racist Book, *Camp of the Saints*, Gains in Popularity," Southern Poverty Law Center, March 21, 2001.

p. 136 **Bannon clearly sought to transplant:** Paul Blumenthal and J.M. Rieger, "This Stunningly Racist French Novel Is How Steve Bannon Explains the World," *Huffington Post*, March 6, 2017.

p. 136 **"Against radical Islam, we're in a 100-year war":** Paul Blumenthal and J.M. Rieger, "Steve Bannon Believes the Apocalypse Is Coming and War Is Inevitable," *Huffington Post*, February 18, 2017.

p. 136 **battling ... Hekmatyar and Jalaluddin Haqqani:** "Pakistan, Taliban, Haqqani Network and Gulbuddin Hekmatyar Working Together in Afghanistan: Report," *Nation*, December 30, 2010.

p. 137 **Obama ... "the killing or capture of bin Laden":** Macon Phillips, "Osama Bin Laden Dead," Obama White House Archives, May 2, 2011, obamawhitehouse.archives.gov.

p. 137 **Hersh ... reported in 2015 that bin Laden:** Seymour M. Hersh, "The Killing of Osama bin Laden," *London Review of Books*, May 21, 2015.

p. 138 **Carlotta Gall ... also the journalism of R.J. Hillhouse:** Gabrielle Bluestone, "*New York Times* and NBC Reporters Back Portions of Osama bin Laden Story," *Gawker*, May 12, 2015.

p. 138 **Obama's late-night announcement:** "USA celebrates Osama bin Laden's Death," youtube.com. See also youtube.com/watch?v=rFCU_hRJ1OE; youtube.com/watch?v=kXvjz7KkkEM; and youtube.com/watch?v=WfkCEffFENo.

p. 139 **"The death of bin Laden was a focusing event":** Jeff Grabmeier, "Survey: Killing of bin Laden Worsened America's Views of

US Muslims," Ohio State University, July 20, 2011, news.osu.edu.

p. 140 **"gays, beer drinkers and pot smokers"**: Marc Fisher, "Meet the Architect of the New Libya," *Washington Post*, December 9, 2011.

p. 140 **Monitor Group, to "introduce to Libya important international figures"**: Paresh Dave, "Gaddafi Paid Millions to Spin His Image in American Media," Annenberg Media Center, March 3, 2011, neontommy.com.

p. 140 **policymakers like Anne-Marie Slaughter were junketed**: Aaron Klein, "Hillary's Close Adviser Caught in Libya Scandal," *WordNetDaily*, March 20, 2011. *WorldNetDaily* is a far-right website that occasionally traffics in conspiratorial thinking. Its lead writer, Aaron Klein, obtained documents from the Monitor Group on Slaughter's trip to Libya and is therefore cited here.

pp. 140–1 ***Slouching Towards Sirte***: Maximillian Forte, *Slouching Toward Sirte: NATO's War on Libya and Africa*, Baraka Books, 2012.

p. 141 **the president had "signed ... support to the Libyan rebels"**: Mark Mazzetti and Eric Schmitt, "CIA Agents in Libya Aid Airstrikes and Meet Rebels," *New York Times*, March 30, 2011.

p. 141 **Gaddafi reached out to Tony Blair**: Forte, *Slouching Toward Sirte*, 119–20.

p. 141 **former Guantanamo detainee ... Qumu**: Abu Sufian Ibrahim Ahmed Hamuda bin Qumu, "The Guantanamo Docket," *New York Times*, n.d.

p. 142 **Qumu was now leading the forces**: Charles Levinson, "Ex-Mujahedeen Help Lead Libya Rebels," *Wall Street Journal*, April 2, 2011.

p. 142 **"Muammar Gaddafi has lost legitimacy to lead"**: "Obama Demands Gaddafi Step Down," *Sydney Morning Herald*, March 4, 2011.

p. 142 **"There are millions of blacks who could come to the Mediterranean"**: "Western States Need Libyan Partnership: Gaddafi," Reuters, March 7, 2011.

p. 142 **"Libya may become the Somalia of North Africa, of the Mediterranean"**: Corky Siemaszko, "Khadafy Offers to Flee Libya in Exchange for Safe Passage, but Libyan Rebels Turn Him Down: Report," *New York Daily News*, March 7, 2011.

p. 142 **"Libya has been a strong partner in the war against terrorism"**:

"US Embassy Cables: Profile of 'Intellectually Curious' but 'Notoriously Mercurial' Gaddafi," *Guardian*, December 7, 2010.

p. 144 **NATO bombed Serb forces:** Evan Osnos, "In the Land of the Possible," *New Yorker*, December 22, 2014.

p. 144 ***A Problem from Hell*, Power lashed:** Max Blumenthal, "Samantha Power, Obama's Atrocity Enabler," *AlterNet*, October 27, 2014.

p. 144 **"The Smartest Woman in America":** Howie Kahn, "The Smartest Woman in America," *Marie Claire*, February 7, 2008.

p. 144 **Susan Rice ... product of elite academic institutions:** Mike Unger, "10,000 Hours: DC Native, Foreign Policy Expert," *American University*, April 2018.

p. 144 **Power "really put on the agenda the use of military power":** Evan Osnos, "In the Land of the Possible," *New Yorker*, December 22, 2014.

p. 145 **"there will be a million reasons NOT to act":** Anne Marie Slaughter, Hillary Clinton Email Archive, *WikiLeaks*, February 21, 2011, forum.wikileaks.org.

p. 145 **At a March 14, 2011 meeting:** Steven Erlanger, "By His Own Reckoning, One Man Made Libya a French Cause," *New York Times*, April 1, 2011.

p. 145 **"protect civilians from a possible genocide like ... Rwanda":** Jeffrey Scott Shapiro and Kelly Riddell, "Exclusive: Secret Tapes Undermine Hillary Clinton on Libyan War," *Washington Times*, January 28, 2015.

p. 145 **"They gave us what we wanted to hear":** Jo Becker and Scott Shane, "Hillary Clinton, 'Smart Power,' and a Dictator's Fall," *New York Times*, February 27, 2016.

p. 145 **Obama ... Nobel Peace Prize lecture:** Barack H. Obama, Nobel Peace Prize 2009, Nobelprize.org, December 10, 2009.

p. 146 **he derided as "backbenchers":** Becker and Shane, "Hillary Clinton, 'Smart Power,' and a Dictator's Fall."

p. 146 **"that keeps Saif on our side without any bloodshed in Benghazi":** Charles R. Kubic, "Hillary's Huge Libya Disaster," *National Interest*, June 15, 2016.

p. 146 **"stupid, stupid facts":** Jeffrey Scott Shapiro and Kelly Riddell, "Exclusive: Secret Tapes Undermine Hillary Clinton on Libyan War," *Washington Times*, January 28, 2015.

p. 146 **"gangsters and terrorists":** Ibid.

p. 146 **"Qaddafi did not perpetrate a 'bloodbath'":** Alan Kuperman,

"Lessons from Libya: How Not to Intervene," *Harvard Kennedy School Quarterly Journal*, September 2013.

p. 147 "a real bloodbath, a massacre like we saw in Rwanda": Mohammed Abbas, "Gaddafi Forces Push towards Benghazi, no UN Move Yet," Reuters, March 14, 2011.

p. 147 "Qaddafi threatens a bloodbath that could destabilize an entire region": "President Obama says the Mission in Libya Is Succeeding," White House Office of the Press Secretary, March 26, 2011.

p. 147 "There's some information with Viagra. So, it's like a machete": "ICC to Investigate Reports of Viagra-Fueled Gang-Rapes in Libya," CNN, May 17, 2011.

p. 147 Libya inquiry by the British House of Commons': "Libya: Examination of Intervention and Collapse and the UK's Future Policy Options Inquiry," UK parliament, September 9, 2016, publications.parliament.uk.

p. 148 "scores of civilian casualties": CJ Chivers and Eric Schmitt, "In Strikes on Libya by NATO, an Unspoken Civilian Toll," *New York Times*, December 17, 2011.

p. 148 Mahari Hotel, all Gaddafi loyalists: "Libya: New Proof of Mass Killings at Gaddafi Death Site," *Human Rights Watch*, October 17, 2012.

p. 148 In towns like Tawergha: Tarik Kafala, "'Cleansed' Libyan Town Spills Its Terrible Secrets," *BBC News*, December 12, 2011.

p. 148 an American drone controlled by a joystick jockey: Thomas Hardin, "Col Gaddafi Killed: Convoy Bombed by Drone Flown by Pilot in Las Vegas," *Daily Telegraph*, October 20, 2011.

p. 148 then proceeded to sodomize him: Tracey Shelton, "'Gaddafi Sodomized': Video Shows Abuse Frame by Frame," *Global Post*, October 24, 2011.

p. 148 Gaddafi's body was laid out to rot: Rania El Gamal, "Gaddafi Still on Show, Rotting as Wrangling Goes on," Reuters India, October 24, 2011.

p. 148 "We came, we saw, he died!" Corbett Daly, "Clinton on Qaddafi: 'We Came, We Saw, He Died'," CBS News, October 20, 2011.

p. 149 "use military tools to advance humanitarian causes": Nicholas Kristof, "Thank you, America!" *New York Times*, August 31, 2011.

p. 149 "intelligence on the extent ... was inadequate": "Libya: Examination of Intervention and Collapse and the UK's Future Policy Options Inquiry," UK parliament, September 9, 2016.

p. 150 **"the imperative for solidarity with the Libyan rebels"**: Ahmad Shokr and Anjali Kamat, "Libya's Reformist Revolutionaries," *Economic and Political Weekly,* March 19, 2011.

p. 150 **Clinton ... "skin in the game"**: Becker and Shane, "Hillary Clinton, 'Smart Power' and a Dictator's Fall.

p. 150 **"Good! This is the only language that Qaddafi is understanding"**: Ibid.

p. 150 **"ask our Arab friends"**: Ibid.

p. 150 **British intelligence tapped its contacts in the LIFG**: Martin Bright, "MI6 'Halted Bid to Arrest bin Laden,'" *Guardian*, November 9, 2002.

p. 151 **Belhaj was ... "no longer a danger to society"**: Ian Black, "The Libyan Islamic Fighting Group—From Al Qaida to the Arab Spring," *Guardian*, September 5, 2011.

p. 151 **Belhaj found an eager promoter in John McCain**: John McCain, "Statement by Senator McCain in Benghazi," McCain.Senate.Gov, April 22, 2011.

p. 151 **Belhaj partnered closely with Ali Sallabi**: Labib Nasir and Alastair Macdonald, "Libyan Islamist Commander Swaps Combat Rig for Suit," Reuters, November 11, 2011.

p. 151 **Sallabi became Qatar's main conduit**: Marc Fisher, "Meet the Architect of the New Libya," *Washington Post*, December 9, 2011.

p. 151 **Belhaj moved into mainstream politics**: Sudarsan Raghavan, "These Libyans Were Once Linked to al-Qaeda. Now They Are Politicians and Businessmen," *Washington Post*, September 28, 2017.

p. 151 **"Islamic law is the source of legislation in Libya"**: Ken Hanly, "Libya Makes Sharia Law Basis for Law and State Institutions, *Digital Journal*, December 7, 2013.

p. 151 **homosexuality "affect[s] religion"**: Stephen Gray, "Libya: UN Delegate Says Gays 'Affect Continuation of Humanity,'" *Pink News*, February 14, 2012.

p. 152 **the Nawasi Brigade ... kidnapped and threatened**: George Grant, "Gay Men in Libya Tell of Beatings by the Local Militia," *Times of London*, December 1, 2012.

p. 152 ***The Innocence of Muslims***: Max Blumenthal, "Inside the Strange Hollywood Scam That Spread Chaos across the Middle East," *Guardian*, September 13, 2012.

p. 153 ***The Innocence of Muslims*** **to Egypt**: Nancy A. Youssef and

Amina Ismail, "Exportation of *The Innocence of Muslims* to Egypt," McClatchy Newspapers, September 15, 2012. Also see Angry Marmot, "From Film to Protests: The Publication of Innocence of Muslims' in Egypt," *Daily Kos Community*, September 24, 2012.

p. 154 "how violent the religion and people are": Blumenthal, "Inside the Strange Hollywood Scam That Spread Chaos across the Middle East."

p. 154 the boldface headine: MUSLIM RAGE: Ayaan Hirsi Ali, "Ayaan Hirsi Ali on the Islamists' Final Stand," *Newsweek*, September 17, 2012.

pp. 154–5 Egyptian satellite television networks popular in Benghazi": David D. Kirkpatrick, "A Deadly Mix in Benghazi," *New York Times*, December 28, 2013.

p. 155 *Innocence of Muslims* had played a part: Alexander Abad-Santos, "What Susan Rice Said versus What the CIA Gave Her," *Atlantic*, November 16, 2012.

p. 155 Clinton's approval rating sank: Jonathan Easley, "Poll: Hillary Clinton's favorability rating dives amid Benghazi probe," *Hill*, May 31, 2013.

p. 155 "'Benghazi' is a joke about GOP obsession": David Mizner, "Worse than Benghazi," *Jacobin*, July 17, 2015.

p. 156 UNICEF called "living hellholes": Karen McVeigh, "Refugee Women and Children 'Beaten, Raped and Starved in Libya Hellholes'," *Guardian*, February 28, 2017

p. 156 at least 25,000 unaccompanied children: Ibid.

p. 156 "the proliferation of weapons from Libya has continued": "Libyan Weaponry Fueling Regional Conflicts," *North Africa Post*, April 12, 2013.

p. 156 Heavy weapons also flowed to ... Syria: Sheera Frenkel, "Syrian Rebels Squabble over Weapons as Biggest Shipload Arrives from Libya," *Times* of London, September 14, 2012.

p. 156 Belhaj ... met with Syrian rebel: Ruth Sherlock, "Leading Libyan Islamist Met Free Syrian Army Opposition Group," *Daily Telegraph*, November 27, 2011.

p. 157 "for all their brilliance and hubris and sense of themselves": Victor S. Navasky, "How We Got into the Messiest War in Our History," *New York Times Book Review*, November 12, 1972.

p. 157 one top Clinton aide called it the "bank shot": Scott Shane and Jo Becker, "A New Libya, with 'Very Little Time Left'," *New York*

Times, February 27, 2016.

p. 159 **"The youth's civil resistance is unfettered by ideology"**: Haytham Manna, "Syria Must Change or Be Changed," *Guardian*, March 31, 2011.

p. 159 **the head of the dissent movement in the city**: "'House-to-House Raids' in Syrian Cities," Al Jazeera English, May 9, 2011.

p. 160 **"We demand, first, banning [gender] mixed schools!"**: Kevork Almasian, "Syria: NOT a Revolution," *Syrian Analysis*, March 18, 2017; Almasian, a Syrian-Armenian refugee in Germany, has produced a series of English-language videos that provide a corrective to Western media characterizations of the Syrian conflict. While he makes no secret of his support for the Syrian government, he has relied on primary sources like video of Ayrout's sermons in Baniyas, which were faithfully translated. Almasian's characterization of the initial motives for protests was corroborated from an alternately opposed angle by a documentary by the US State Department-funded Syria Untold and produced by Dellair Youssef, *Baniyas: Beginnings*, youtube.com.

p. 160 **"They were upset about the ban of the niqab, or full veil"**: Nir Rosen, "A Tale of Two Syrian Villages: Part Two," Aljazeera.com, October 26, 2011.

p. 160 **"We are all jihadists! We will exterminate Alawites!"**: Monitor 360, "Country Report: Syria," Open Source Center, June 2012, p. 31; The Open Source center is a CIA intelligence center focusing on analysis of open-source and "gray" material. Video of the Homs chants are also featured in Almasian, "Syria: NOT a Revolution."

p. 160 **Yougov poll funded by the Qatar Foundation**: Jonathan Steele, "Most Syrians Back President Assad, but You'd Never Know from Western Media," *Guardian*, January 17, 2012.

p. 161 **death of a local fruit vendor, Nidal Janoud**: "Nidal Jannoud Killers," youtube.com.

p. 161 **Two days later, on April 12**: Joshua Landis, "Western Press Misled—Who Shot the Nine Soldiers in Banyas? Not Syrian Security Forces," April 13, 2011, joshualandis.com.

p. 161 **"Syrian army, security agencies and the vague paramilitary"**: Q&A: Nir Rosen on Syria's armed opposition, Al Jazeera English, February 13, 2012.

p. 161 **On June 6, 2011, in Jisr al-Shugour**: "Syria Troops 'Killed in Clashes' in Jisr al-Shughour," *BBC News*, June 6, 2011.

p. 161 **Once again, the opposition claimed**: "Syria Crisis: Investigating

Jisr al-Shughour," *BBC News*, June 22, 2011.

p. 161 **burned government employees alive:** Philip Caulfield, "Video Reportedly Shows Syrian Rebels Throwing Bodies off Post Office Roof in Al-Bab, Outside of Aleppo," *New York Daily News,* August 13, 2012.

p. 162 **governments of Turkey and Qatar successfully pushing:** Christopher Philips, "Eyes Bigger than Stomachs: Turkey, Saudi Arabia and Qatar in Syria," *Middle East Policy Council*, 24, mepc.org.

p. 162 **"The government is running against the terrorist armed groups":** Anderson Cooper with Syrian Ambassador to the UN, Bashar Jaafari, FLV, youtube.com.

p. 164 **"grind the flesh" of Alawite government loyalists:** "The Charm of Telesalafism," *Economist*, October 20, 2012.

p. 164 **Edward Dark ... "seeing black Qaeda flags at a checkpoint":** Rania Khalek, "Ignored by Western Media, Syrians Describe the Nightmare the Armed Opposition Brought Them," Alternet's Grayzone Project, May 15, 2017, alternet.org.

p. 165 **"United States to promote reform across the region":** Barack Obama, "Remarks by the President on the Middle East and North Africa," White House, May 19, 2011.

p. 165 **"the time has come for President Assad to step aside":** President Obama: "The Future of Syria Must be Determined by Its People, but President Bashar al-Assad Is Standing in Their Way," Obama White House Archives, August 18, 2011.

p. 165 **White House was "certain Assad is on his way out":** "US Certain Assad Is 'on His Way out': Official," Reuters.com, August 18, 2011.

p. 166 **viewer poll: "Do you think Alawites brought genocide":** Faisal al-Qasim, "Do the Alawites Deserve Genocide?" Al Jazeera Arabic, May 8, 2015, youtube.com.

pp. 166–7 **Prince Bandar bin Sultan, who had directed weapons:** Mark Mazetti and Matt Apuzzo, "US Relies Heavily on Saudi Money to Support Syrian Rebels," *New York Times*, January 23, 2016.

p. 167 **"Thank God for the Saudis":** "McCain: Christie Can Move Past Scandal," *CNN Press Room*, January 12, 2014.

p. 167 **"Syria: Scenarios of Dramatic Political Change":** Brad Hoff, "New Declassified CIA Memo Presents Blueprint for Syrian Regime Collapse," *Libertarian Institute*, February 26, 2017, reprinted at *Zero Hedge*, zerohedge.com; original document here: cia.gov/library/readingroom/docs/CIA-RDP86T01017R000100770001-5.pdf.

p. 168 al-Qurayshi … frequently quoted Mao: McCants, *The ISIS Apocalypse*, 81.

pp. 168–9 Zawahiri … "form a group and send it to" Syria: Ibid., 85.

p. 169 "Bucca was a factory. It made us all. It built our ideology": Martin Chulov, "ISIS: The Inside Story," *Guardian*, December 11, 2014.

p. 169 Born Ibrahim al-Awwad: William McCants, *The ISIS Apocalypse*, 72.

p. 169 Hardan … Baghdadi was also held: William McCants, "The Believer," Brookings, September 1, 2015.

p. 170 *The Management of Savagery*: Abu Bakr Naji, *The Management of Savagery: The Most Critical Stage Through Which the Umma Will Pass*, translated by William McCants, May 23, 2006, azelin.files.wordpress.com.

p. 171 On December 23, 2011, a series of bombings: Kareem Fahim, "Syria Blames Al Qaeda after Bombs Kill Dozens in Damascus," *New York Times*, December 23, 2011.

p. 171 "Salafist principality in eastern Syria": Brad Hoff, "2012 Defense Intelligence Agency Document: West Will Facilitate Rise of Islamic State 'in Order to Isolate the Syrian Regime'," *Levant Report*, May 19, 2015.

p. 172 "sweeping generalizations": State Department Daily Press Briefing, June 4, 2015, https://2009-2017.state.gov/r/pa/prs/dpb/2015.

p. 172 "the major forces driving the insurgency in Syria": Retired US general: Drones Cause More Damage than Good," Al Jazeera English, July 16, 2015.

pp. 172–3 "the hard men with the guns": Jeffrey Goldberg, "Hillary Clinton: 'Failure' to Help Syrian Rebels Led to the Rise of ISIS," *Atlantic*, August 10, 2014.

p. 173 "transition on Yemen as the model": Harvey Morris, "West Floats Clemency Offer if Assad Goes Quietly," *New York Times*, June 21, 2012.

p. 173 "automatic rifles, rocket-propelled grenades": Eric Schmitt, "CIA Said to Aid in Steering Arms to Syrian Opposition," *New York Times*, June 21, 2012.

p. 173 "There were no moderates": Brad Hoff, "The CIA's Top Spy in Syria Knew Nothing about Syria," *Canary*, August 1, 2016. Also see Douglas Laux, *Left of Boom: How a Young CIA Case Officer*

Penetrated the Taliban and Al-Qaeda, St. Martin's Press, 2017.

p. 174 **"Most of the arms shipped ... are going to hard-line Islamic jihadists"**: David E. Sanger, "Rebel Arms Flow Is Said to Benefit Jihadists in Syria," *New York Times*, October 14, 2012.

p. 174 **"most of the injured and dead FSA are Jabhat al-Nusra"**: David Ignatius, "Al-Qaeda Affiliate Playing Larger Role in Syria Rebellion," *Washington Post*, November 30, 2012.

p. 174 **"moderate rebels have often been very immoderate and ineffective"**: Ben Hubbard, Eric Schmitt and Mark Mazzetti, "US Pins Hope on Syrian Rebels With Loyalties All over the Map," *New York Times*, September 11, 2014.

p. 174 **"You are not going to find this neat, clean, secular rebel group"**: Ibid.

p. 175 **Baghdadi demanded that Jolani exploit**: Aaron Lund, "As Rifts Open Up in Syria's al-Qaeda Franchise, Secrets Spill Out," Carnegie Middle East Center, August 10, 2015.

p. 176 **killed in the fighting was one of the emirs**: "Advancing Army Kills Jihadist Emir in Syria's Latakia: Activists," *Agence France Presse*, August 18, 2013.

p. 176 **"create a balance of terror"**: "Syrian Rebel Sheikh Calls for War on Assad's Alawite Heartland," Reuters, July 10, 2013.

p. 177 **"even though they were unarmed and trying to flee"**: "Executions, Indiscriminate Shootings, and Hostage Taking by Opposition Forces in Latakia Countryside," Human Rights Watch, October 10, 2013.

p. 177 **"I saw a baby's head hanging from a tree"**: Jonathan Steele, "Syria: Massacre Reports Emerge From Assad's Alawite Heartland," *Guardian*, October 2, 2013.

p. 177 **al-Okaidi ... a "main recipient"**: Ruth Sherlock, "Syria Rebel Quits after Battlefield Defeat," *Daily Telegraph*, November 4, 2013.

p. 177 **Benjamin Hall ... the base "only fell"**: Brad Hoff, "ISIS Leader Omar al-Shishani Fought Under US Umbrella as Late as 2013," *Levant Report*, September 18, 2015.

p. 178 **"a mix of jihadist and Free Syrian Army leaders, who stood together"**: Anne Barnard and Eric Schmitt, "As Foreign Fighters Flood Syria, Fears of a New Extremist Haven," *New York Times*, August 8, 2013.

p. 178 **"oh Alawites, we came to slaughter you!"**: Brad Hoff, "ISIS as US Creation: The Clearest Authenticated Video Evidence to Date," *Levant Report*, September 13, 2014.

p. 178 "My relationship with the brothers in ISIS is good": "US Key Man in Syria Worked Closely with ISIL and Jabhat al Nusra," youtube.com.

p. 178 "We truly did not see from them anything except good morals": Ibid.

p. 178 Ford was "running around the country": John Dolan, "Meet Robert Ford, the US Diplomat Who Helped Send Syria to Hell in the Name of Democracy," Alternet's Grayzone Project, June 1, 2017, alternet.org.

p. 179 Raqqa … "icon of the revolution": "How Did Raqqa Fall to the Islamic State of Iraq and Syria?," *Syria Untold*, January 13, 2014.

p. 179 "We accompanied the jihad in Iraq as military escorts": Aymenn Jawad al-Tamimi, "The Islamic State of Iraq and Al-Sham,": ME Forum, December 11, 2013.

p. 180 "those who were with the people joined Jabhat al-Nusra": Alison Tahmizian, "Raqqa's FSA Brigades Join Jabhat al-Nusra," *News Deeply*, September 20, 2013.

p. 181 "we're about to become Al Qaeda's air force now?": Julian Pecquet, "Kucinich: Syria Strike Would Turn US Into 'al Qaeda's Air Force'," *Hill*, August 23, 2013.

p. 183 Israeli's intelligence services … determined: Max Blumenthal, "Dubious Intelligence and Iran Blackmail: How Israel Is Driving the US to War in Syria," *Mondoweiss*, September 1, 2013.

p. 183 Obama inaugurated the policy: "Remarks by the President to the White House Press Corps," White House archives, August 20, 2012.

p. 183 complained to journalist Charles Glass: Charles Glass, "Tell Me How This Ends," *Harper's Magazine*, February 2019.

p. 183 complain of hundreds of chlorine attacks: Syrian American Medical Society, "A New Normal: Ongoing Chemical Weapons Attacks in Syria," sams-usa.net. SAMS is a US-funded Syrian exile organization dedicated to regime change. It operates hospitals in rebel-held areas while lobbying in Washington for military intervention and support for the opposition's civil society apparatus. In its 2015 report, SAMS alleged without scientific evidence that "161 documented chemical attacks have led to at least 1,491 deaths and 14,581 injuries from chemical exposure." For more on SAMS, see Max Blumenthal, "How the Syrian American Medical Society Is Selling Regime Change and Driving the US to War," *Truthdig*, April 12, 2018.

p. 184 **Libyan intervention was a "shit show"**: Jeffrey Goldberg, "The Obama Doctrine," *Atlantic*, April 2016.

p. 184 **rebels were a ragtag band of "farmers and doctors and carpenters"**: Ibid.

p. 185 **"chemical weapons personnel were on the ground"**: "Kerry: 'High Confidence' that Syria Government Responsible for Chemical Attack That Killed at Least 1,426 People," *Huffington Post*, August 30, 2013.

p. 185 **Clapper ... no "slam dunk"**: Goldberg, "The Obama Doctrine."

p. 185 **Ahmet Üzümcü, had issued a statement of deep concern**: Statement by the OPCW Director-General on Allegations of Chemical Weapons Use in Syria, OPCW, March 19, 2013, opcw.org.

p. 185 **OPCW team ... the way to Damascus**: Executive Council Briefed on UN Secretary-General's Request to Assist Investigation of Alleged Use of Chemical Weapons in Syria, OPCW, March 27, 2013, opcw.org.

p. 185 **"Some people say that it's already too late, and I can definitely understand that"**: Ian Sample, "UN Team Heads to Syria to Inspect Sites of Alleged Chemical Weapon Attacks," *Guardian*, August 1, 2013.

p. 186 **Del Ponte found ... "strong, concrete suspicions"**: "UN Has Testimony that Syrian Rebels Used Sarin Gas: Investigator," Reuters, May 5, 2013.

p. 186 **Hersh cited testimony ... al-Nusra had acquired sarin**: Seymour Hersh, "Whose Sarin?," *London Review of Books*, December 19, 2013. Also see Hersh, "The Red Line and the Rat Line," *London Review of Books*, April 17, 2014.

p. 186 **branding him a conspiratorial loon**: Eliot Higgins, "Sy Hersh's Chemical Misfire," *Foreign Policy*, December 9, 2013.

p. 186 **Cameron's ... own Conservative Party staged an unlikely revolt**: "Syria Crisis: Cameron Loses Commons Vote on Syria Action," *BBC News*, August 30, 2013.

p. 186 **McCain ... excoriated**: "John McCain Ripped on Syria at Town Hall," youtube.com.

p. 187 ***Red Lines* was ... a public relations vehicle for Moustafa**: *Red Lines*, Spark Media, 2014.

p. 188 **Kahana ... "financed the opposition group"**: Moti Kahana bio at amaliah.org/team.

p. 188 **"This could be like his Benghazi moment"**: *Red Lines*, Spark Media, 2014.

p. 188 McCain met with a small group of rebels: Lauren Williams, "McCain Crosses Paths with Rebel Kidnapper," *Lebanon Daily Star*, May 31, 2013.

p. 189 mockery from *Daily Show* host Jon Stewart: "John McCain's Syrian Photo Op," *Daily Show with Jon Stewart*, June 3, 2013.

p. 189 Moustafa angrily protested: John Hudson, "Reps. Ed Royce and Eliot Engel Dispatch Aides Near Syrian Border," *Foreign Policy*, June 6, 2013.

p. 189 "She's fluent in Arabic and spent an enormous amount of time": Max Blumenthal, "Shady PR Operatives, Pro-Israel Ties, Anti-Castro Money: Inside the Syrian Opposition's DC Spin Machine," *Mondoweiss*, September 7, 2013.

p. 189 Institute for the Study of War ... revolving door culture: Rajiv Chandrasekaran, "Civilian Analysts Gained Petraeus's Ear While He Was Commander in Afghanistan," *Washington Post,* December 18, 2012.

p. 190 "McCain's Sherpa for his surprise trip into Syria": Jay Newton-Small, "The Rise and Fall of Elizabeth O'Bagy," *Time*, September 17, 2013.

p. 190 O'Bagy was exposed for faking her PhD: Gordon Lubold and Shane Harris, "Exclusive: McCain Hires Controversial Syria Analyst Elizabeth O'Bagy," *Foreign Policy*, September 27, 2013.

p. 190 OPCW was awarded a Nobel Peace Prize: Peter Walker, "Nobel Peace Prize Won by Chemical Weapons Watchdog for Work in Syria," *Guardian*, October 11, 2013.

p. 191 "There's a playbook in Washington": Jeffrey Goldberg, "The Obama Doctrine."

p. 191 "Peace Games" in Dubai: Max Blumenthal, "'Peace Games' of @ForeignPolicy magazine, brought to you by the government of UAE currently besieging Yemen," Twitter, March 7, 2017.

p. 191 think tanks, as 'Arab-occupied territory': Jeffrey Goldberg, "The Obama Doctrine."

p. 191 UAE backing for MEI: Ryan Grim, "Gulf Government Gave Secret $20 Million Gift to DC Think Tank," *Intercept*, August 9, 2017.

p. 192 Steven Simon's firing: Rania Khalek, "Meet the Mystery Fixer Who Negotiated Syria out of Seven Years of War," Alternet's Grayzone Project, August 2, 2018, alternet.org.

p. 192 Lister rose to prominence: ICWatch, Charles Lister entry, April 20, 2015, icwatch.wikileaks.org.

p. 192 kept especially close … Ahrar al-Sham: Yalla La Barra, "Qatar Mouthpiece Charles Lister Insists Islamist Militants Be Part of the Solution in Syria," wordpress.com, November 19, 2015.

p. 192 Lister was also one of the rebels' … advocates: "'Roadmap Without Assad': Syrian Opposition Riyadh Meeting Kicks off," *New Arab/Al Araby*, August 12, 2015.

p. 192 Lister produced a comprehensive list: Charles Lister, "Yes, There Are 70,000 Moderate Opposition Fighters in Syria. Here's What We Know About Them," *Spectator*, November 27, 2015.

p. 193 part of a $500 million authorization request: Karen DeYoung, "Obama Asks for Authorization to Provide Direct Military Training to Syrian Rebels," *Washington Post*, June 26, 2014.

p. 193 "Most of the support from governments who back the rebels": Ben Hubbard, "US Goal Is to Make Syrian Rebels Viable," *New York Times*, September 18, 2014.

p. 193 $1 out of every $15 … operations in Syria: Greg Miller and Karen DeYoung, "$1 out of Every $15 in CIA's Budget to Syrian Rebels," *Washington Post*, June 12, 2015.

p. 193 Shahabuddin served jail time: "Washington's 'Moderate' Terrorists Are under the Microscope of Criminal History, Banditry and Corruption," Thawra.sy, July 26, 2016. Thawra added: "Since [Shahabuddin's] appearance on the scene, he was considered very close to Turkey and was responsible for the kidnapping of Italian activists Vanessa Marzolo and Greta Ramili in August 2014, and when Turkey demanded their release, he harshly criticized Turkey. He had a good relationship with Qatar and was one of the personalities that Al Jazeera was interested in. It contributed to his promotion and held interviews with him, to confirm him as a "moderate" man who was opposed to Damascus. He was also a prominent figure close to Washington, who met with US secretary of state John Kerry in Turkey, as part of a group of 'moderate group leaders.' Tawfiq receives American support through the Jordan Operations Room, and appeared in Istanbul in late 2014 at an armed factions conference wearing an unusually formal suit and speaking at his press conference on freedom and humanity and fighting terrorism."

p. 194 Zinki carried out a wave of kidnappings: ANSA, "Ransom of 11 mn paid for aid workers release," October 5, 2015, ansa.it. In October 2015, media across the West reported that Zinki had been paid 11 million euros by the government of Italy as ransom for two Italian aid workers, Greta Ramelli and Vanessa Marzullo, whom the group abducted in July 2014. Zinki was described by the Italian news outfit ANSA at the time as "part of the al-Nusra Front, Syria's al-Qaeda affiliate." Shockingly, just one month after this high-profile hostage release, Charles Lister listed Zinki as "moderate."

p. 194 **al-Zinki as a "power broker"**: Jennifer Cafarella, "Syrian Opposition Guide," Institute for the Study of War, October 7, 2015.

p. 194 **Abdullah Issa ... sawed off his head**: "Syria Conflict: Boy Beheaded by Rebels 'Was Fighter,'" *BBC News*, July 21, 2016.

p. 194 **Century Foundation ... as "progressive, non-partisan"**: "About The Century Foundation," tcf.org/about/.

p. 194 **United States "will have to back Zenki and other groups like it"**: Sam Heller, "In Syrian Proxy War, America Can Keep Its Hands Clean or It Can Get Things Done," Century Foundation, August 17, 2016.

p. 194 **Atlantic Council ... Lister joined a panel**: "Max Blumenthal Challenges Charles Lister on 'Moderate Opposition' in Syria," youtube.com.

p. 195 **"Escalate the conflict"**: John Allen and Charles R. Lister, "Bring Syria's Assad and His Backers to Account Now," *Washington Post*, October 21, 2016.

p. 195 **"It's primarily al-Nusra [Al Qaeda] who holds Aleppo"**: "Defense Dept: 'It's Primarily al-Nusra Who Holds Aleppo,'" April 2016," youtube.com.

p. 195 **"using so-called moderate members of al Qaeda's Nusra Front"**: Nancy A. Youssef and Shane Harris, "Petraeus: Use Al Qaeda Fighters to Beat ISIS," *Daily Beast*, August 31, 2015.

p. 196 **if the United States placed ... al-Zenki on its terror list**: Benjamin Norton, Twitter, "The version of the press release on the US embassy in Syria site has not yet been updated. It still says HTS—not JAN," posted on May 15, 2017.

p. 196 **"The Right Salafis Can Make All the Difference"**: Mona Alami, "Syria: The Right Salafis Can Make All the Difference," Atlantic Council, September 14, 2015.

p. 196 **"smeared ... as a terrorist in league with al Qaeda"**: Eli Lake, "Syria's Army of Islam Faces Backlash after Comments on Israel," *Bloomberg*, October 4, 2016.

p. 196 **Alloush ... recruited by the Saudi prince**: Ian Black, "Syria

Crisis: Saudi Arabia to Spend Millions to Train New Rebel Force," *Guardian*, November 7, 2013.

p. 197 **Alawite hostages ... as human shields**: "Syrian Rebels Using Caged Civilian Captives as 'Human Shields,'" Agence France Presse, November 2, 2015.

p. 197 **"an Al Qaeda linked group worth befriending"**: Michael Doran, William McCants, Clint Watts, "The Good and Bad of Ahrar al-Sham," *Foreign Affairs*, January 13, 2014.

p. 197 **"West should seek the further weakening of Islamic State, but not its destruction"**: Ephraim Anbar, "The Destruction of Islamic State Is a Strategic Mistake," BESA Center Perspectives, August 2, 2016.

p. 198 **"I choose the Islamic State"**: Judah Ari Gross, "Ya'alon: I Would Prefer Islamic State to Iran in Syria," *Times of Israel*, January 19, 2016.

p. 198 **Israeli army occasionally bombed**: MEE Staff, "Al-Nusra Front Captures Syrian Golan Heights Crossing," Middle East Eye, August 27, 2014.

p. 198 **Abu Dardaa, a leader of Jabhat al-Nusra**: Khaled Atallah, "Are Israel and Jabhat al-Nusra Coordinating Attacks in Syria?," *Al Monitor*, June 4, 2016. Translation: informationclearinghouse.info/article44804.htm.

p. 198 **"Israel stood by our side in a heroic way"**: Rory Jones, Noam Raydan and Suha Ma'ayeh, "Israel Gives Secret Aid to Syrian Rebels," *Wall Street Journal*, June 18, 2017.

p. 198 **"facilitating cross-border travel for residents into Israel"**: Nour Samaha, "Israel's Quiet Campaign to Gain a Foothold in Southern Syria," *News Deeply*, June 15, 2017.

p. 198 **"the radical axis headed by Iran is more risky than the global jihad one"**: Brian Bender, "Israeli Officers: You're Doing ISIS Wrong," Politico, May 22, 2017.

p. 199 **firing came from ISIS ... immediately apologized"**: Richard Silverstein, "BREAKING: Former Israeli Defense Minister Confirms Israeli Collaboration with ISIS in Syria," *Tikun Olam*, April 23, 2017.

p. 199 **"a world where more girls and women"**: "Girls and Women," Clinton Foundation, clintonfoundation.org.

p. 199 **Tens of millions more flowed**: Nick Gass, "Clinton Foundation Scandals Will Be Good Fodder for Trump," *Politico*, June 22, 2016.

p. 200 **"While this military/para-military operation is moving forward"**: "Podesta Emails, Congrats!," WikiLeaks, September 9,

2014.

p. 200 **Biden was even more explicit:** "Joe Biden—ISIS Terrorists Armed by Turkey, Qatar, Saudi Arabia, UAE," youtube.com

p. 200 **"worrying habit of lumping al-Qaeda's al-Nusra Front":** Adam Taylor, "Behind Biden's Gaffe Lie Real Concerns about Allies' Role in Rise of the Islamic State," *Washington Post*, October 6, 2014.

p. 200 **Biden ... issuing a "formal clarification":** Associated Press, "Joe Biden Forced to Apologise to UAE and Turkey over Syria Remarks," *Daily Telegraph*, October 6, 2014.

p. 201 **"trucks were carrying weapons and supplies to the al-Qaeda terror organization":** "Turkish Military Says Turkish Intelligence Shipped Weapons to Al Qaeda," *Al Monitor*, January 15, 2015.

p. 201 **Shim "caught [Turkish intelligence] bringing ISIS":** Kevin Dietz, "Defenders: A Young Reporter's Mysterious Death," *Click on Detroit,* January 12, 2015.

p. 202 **"The Deir Ezzor strike appears to have been timed":** Gareth Porter, "Inquiry Points Toward a Pentagon Plot to Subvert Obama's Syria Policy," *Truthdig*, January 6, 2017. Also see Gareth Porter, "US strikes on Syrian Troops: Report Data Contradicts 'Mistake' Claims," Middle East Eye, December 6, 2016.

p. 202 **"back off fighting territorial ISIS":** Thomas Friedman, "Why Is Trump Fighting ISIS in Syria?," *New York Times*, April 12, 2017.

pp. 202–3 **82 percent of Syrians ... foreign made:** Sudarsan Raghavan, "One in Five Syrians Say Islamic State Is a Good Thing, Poll Says," *Washington Post*, September 15, 2015.

p. 203 **"We saw that Daesh was growing":** Leith Aboufadel, "Leaked Audio Reveals John Kerry Pushed for Intervention in Syria," *Al Masdar*, April 1, 2017.

p. 204 **"The Syrian government is essentially the anvil":** Susannah George, "Report: Weakening Syria's Government Could Help ISIS Group," Associated Press, April 18, 2017.

p. 204 **Unwilling to provide a direct answer:** "State Dept Option Palmyra: Assad or Daesh?," youtube.com.

p. 205 **a young woman shot in the head:** Adam Withnall, "Al-Qaeda Video Shows Public Execution of Woman Accused of Adultery," *Independent*, January 15, 2015.

p. 206 **In Idlib, Snell documented how al-Nusra:** Lindsey Snell, "I Visited Al Qaeda's Syrian Stronghold and Saw How US Backing of 'Moderate' Rebels Is Bolstering Jihadists," *Alternet's Grayzone*

Project, May 2, 2017, alternet.org.

p. 206 al-Nusra overran ... Division 13: "Al Qaeda Overruns US-backed Syria Rebels, Seize Weapons and Bases," Associated Press, March 14, 2016.

p. 206 *Undercover in Idlib*: Jenan Moussa, *Undercover in Idlib*, Akhbar News, youtube.com.

p. 207 "They now sound more like robots": Weedah Hamzah, "Syrian Station Uses Chirping Birds, Bleating Goats to Skirt Music Ban," DPA International, February 10, 2017.

pp. 207–8 2017 Oscars ceremony ... the White Helmets: Steve Dove, "The White Helmets is the 2017 Oscar Winner for Documentary (Short Subject)," The Oscars, February 27, 2017, oscar.go.com.

p. 208 Endorsements for the group poured in: Liam Stack, "After Years of War, Celebrities Find a Syrian Group to Back," *New York Times*, September 14, 2016.

p. 208 Right Livelihood Award: "Syria's White Helmets Win 'Alternative Nobel Prize'," BBC, September 22, 2016.

p. 208 In the French parliament ... lawmakers greeted Saleh: "French Parliament Honours Syria's 'White Helmets,'" Global News, October 18, 2016.

p. 208 Sophie McNeil ... fundraise for the group: Sophie McNeil, Twitter, August 19, 2016. McNeil stated: "I recommend donating to @sams_usa who treated Omran & @SyriaCivilDef who rescued him. Plus @MSF & @UNHCR #Syria."

p. 209 petition for a no-fly zone: "Support the White Helmets: To the UN Security Council Petition," whitehelmets.org/en ("the UN Security Council must follow through on its demand to stop the barrel bombs, by introducing a 'no-fly zone' if necessary."—Raed Saleh, head of the White Helmets, the Syrian Civil Defense.)

p. 209 "kill a lot of Syrians": Zaid Jilani, "In Secret Goldman Sachs Speech, Hillary Clinton Admitted No-Fly Zone Would 'Kill a Lot of Syrians,' *Intercept*, October 10, 2016.

p. 209 Dunford worried: "Dunford Tells Wicker Controlling Airspace in Syria Means War with Russia. McCain Throws Tantrum. Dunford Refines Answer, User Created Clip," C-Span, September 22, 2016.

p. 209 Saleh met privately with UN and EU officials: Samuel Oakford, "Syria's First Responders Say They Need a No-Fly Zone, but No One Listens," Vice News, May 18, 2015.

p. 209 Habib testified before the US: "Assad's Abhorrent Chemical

Weapons Attacks," House Foreign Affairs Committee, June 17, 2015, foreignaffairs.house.gov.

p. 209 **Saleh was back ... for expanded sanctions**: Ehsani, Twitter, "#Syrian opposition team who worked on recent caeser bill. Raed of white helmets seem plus syria task force members," November 16, 2016.

p. 210 **USAID rushed to ... "peaceful and democratic Syria"**: Max Blumenthal, "How the White Helmets Became International Heroes While Pushing US Military Intervention and Regime Change in Syria," *Alternet*, October 2, 2016.

p. 210 **USAID's 2012 executive summary**: Syria Regional Option (SRO) Final Report, *USAID/OTI Washington*, April 2013, pdf. usaid.gov/pdf_docs/paook16n.pdf.

p. 210 **Le Mesurier's job**: Bryan Schatz, "The Most Dangerous Job in the World: Syria's Elite Rescue Force," *Men's Journal*, October 12, 2014.

p. 210 **he established Mayday Rescue**: Jonathan Gornall, "Newsmaker: The White Helmets," *National*, September 29, 2016.

pp. 210–11 **That company ... grants from**: ARK, Clients, arkgroupdmcc.com/about/clients/.

p. 211 **At least $100 million from the UK**: "UK funding to White Helmets Boris Johnson Praising the White Helmets and Providing £65 Million!," youtube.com.

p. 211 **USAID says it has donated $32 million to the White Helmets**: "What We Do," USAID Transition Initiatives, February 28, 2018.

p. 211 **"increase the effectiveness and legitimacy of civil authorities"**: Bryan Schatz, "The Most Dangerous Job in the World."

p. 211 **"another unhealthy form of dependence"**: Brent Eng, Jose Ciro Martinez, "How Feeding Syrians Feeds the War," *Foreign Policy*, February 11, 2016.

p. 212 **USAID produced the first and only evaluation report**: "Audit of USAID's Office of Transition Initiatives' Syria-related Activities (Executive SummarySY)," Office of Inspector General, July 30, 2014, usaid.gov.

p. 213 **Asfari decided to direct his fortune**: Max Blumenthal, "Inside the Shadowy PR Firm That's Lobbying for Regime Change in Syria," *Alternet's Grayzone Project,* October 2, 2016, alternet.org. (The Syria Campaign confirmed to me the aforementioned funding figures.)

p. 214 **"I co-founded Avaaz and [the Australian activist group] Get Up"**: Rahim Kahani, "Jeremy Heimans of Purpose.com on Mobilizing

Millions for Change," *Forbes*, December 3, 2011.

p. 214 public campaign for a no-fly zone: "UNSC: Libya No-Fly Zone," *Avaaz*, March 17, 2011.

p. 214 Avaaz smuggled $2 million worth of supplies: Ed Pilkington, "Avaaz Faces Questions over Role at Centre of Syrian Protest Movement," *Guardian*, March 2, 2012.

p. 215 "The Syria Campaign made a fantastic pitch": "The Syria Campaign Announces Netflix Documentary," *The Funding Network*, August 16, 2016.

p. 215 Bilal Abdul Kareem … in rebel-held Syrian territory: Ben Norton and Bilal Abdul Kareem, "Prominent US 'Journalist' in Syria, Serves as Mouthpiece for Violent Extremists," *Alternet's Grayzone Project*, December 29, 2016.

p. 215 Abdul Kareem as an "independent journalist": Ben Norton and Max Blumenthal, "CNN Hired Top al-Qaeda Propagandist for Award-Winning Syria Documentary and Wants to Cover Its Tracks," *Alternet's Grayzone Project*, July 6, 2017, alternet.org.

p. 215 Abdul Kareem's relationship … Al Qaeda–linked figures: Ibid.

p. 216 Bana al-Abed … "start 3rd world war": Ben Norton, "This Call for World War III was tweeted from 7-year old Bana Alabed's Twitter account, then later deleted. Now she has a major book deal," Twitter, April 12, 2017.

p. 216 Though she faked it as best she could: @Walid970721, "Did they think ppl will believe that Bana wrote letter to Trump b/c its in her handwriting? She can't put together one proper Engl. sentence," Twitter, January 27, 2017.

p. 216 "the face of innocent civilian suffering in Syria": Max Blumenthal, "Thirsting for War, CNN's Jake Tapper Turned to Strange and Shady Syria Sources," *Alternet's Grayzone Project*, September 7, 2017 alternet.org.

p. 216 Rycroft … also quoted al-Abed: Kareem Shaheen and Julian Borger, "Where Is Bana? Fears for Syrian Girl Who Tweeted from Aleppo," *Guardian*, December 5, 2016.

p. 216 Bana and her family joined jihadist … Idlib: Nadia Khomami, "Where Is Bana? Girl Who Tweeted from Aleppo Is Safely Evacuated," *Guardian*, December 19, 2016.

p. 216 bizarre photo-op with … Erdoğan: Cumhurbaşkanı Erdoğan, "Halepli Bana Alabed ve Ailesini Kabul Etti," youtube.com.

p. 216 audience with … Lindsey Lohan: "Bana Alabed Meets Lindsay

Lohan in Turkey," youtube.com.

p. 216 dealings with the literary agency of J.K. Rowling: Max Blumenthal, "So @jk_rowling's literary agent gets a cut of the @simonschuster deal with a Turkish child exploitation PR scam," Twitter, April 20, 2017.

p. 216 At the 2018 Academy Awards ceremony: Evelyn Lau, "8-year-old Syrian Bana Al Abed Makes Appearance at the Oscars," *National*, March 5, 2018.

p. 217 Ghassan al-Abed, had been an armed member: @Walid970721, "Is @AtlanticCouncil's report denying that Bana's father Ghassan al-Abed is a radical Islamic militant? Do they think people are stupid? #Syria," twitter.com. (Photos extracted from Ghassan al-Abed's Facebook profile clearly show him holding weapons and posing with members of the Ahrar al-Sham militia and other militants active in eastern Aleppo, the rebel-held area where he and his family lived.)

p. 217 al-Nusra took Idlib, Agha provided an extensive eyewitness: Ben Norton and Max Blumenthal, "Yet Another Video Shows US-Funded White Helmets Assisting Public Executions in Rebel-Held Syria," *Alternet's Grayzone Project*, May 23, 2017, alternet.org.

p. 217 Violations Documentation Center: "Flash Report: Chemical Attacks in Idlib," Violations Documentation Center in Syria, March 2015.

p. 218 "the heroes of Jaish al-Fatah": Hadi Abdallah, "US Embassy Congratulated 'Reporter' Caught on Camera Embracing al-Nusra Front Terrorists," *Live Leak*, posted by user californiastars in 2017, liveleak.com.

p. 218 al-Abdallah toyed with a group: @GJoene, "Where were all the #WhiteHelmets to save these trapped pro-gov soldiers? @SyriaCivilDef says they are neutral. Oh, wait, they are not!," Twitter, extracted from al-Abdallah video broadcast, twitter.com.

p. 218 US embassy ... congratulated al-Abdallah: @USEmbassySyria, "Congratulations to Syrian reporter @HadiAlabdallah on winning 2016 @RSF_inter—TV5 Monde Prize," Twitter, November 7, 2016, twitter.com.

p. 218 execution filmed ... town of Haritan: Ben Norton and Max Blumenthal, "Yet Another Video Shows US-Funded White Helmets Assisting Public Executions in Rebel-Held Syria," *Alternet's Grayzone Project*, May 23, 2017, alternet.org.

p. 219 "the Islamic State's fire brigade": @MaxBlumenthal, "Not a scandal @RefugeesIntl, DC & Wall St elites are honoring the group

ISIS hostage John Cantlie called 'the Islamic State's fire brigade'?," Twitter, extracted from "Inside Halab," April 25, 2017.

p. 219 "hidden soldiers of the revolution": Brandon Turbeville, "VIDEO: Al-Qaeda Leader Praises White Helmets as 'Hidden Soldiers of the Revolution,'" *Mint Press News*, May 9, 2017.

p. 219 White Helmets' involvement with jihadist rebels: "Are the Syrian 'White Helmets' Rescue Organization Terrorists?," *Snopes*, snopes.com/fact-check/syrian-rescue-organization-the-white-helmets-are-terrorists/.

p. 220 "Russia is fuelling a disinformation campaign": "Killing the Truth," The Syria Campaign, December 20, 2017, diary.thesyria campaign.org.

p. 220 Abrahms' team conducted 130 in-depth: Max Abrahms, Denis Sullivan and Charles Simpson, "Five Myths about Syrian Refugees," *Foreign Affairs*, March 22, 2017.

p. 222 crushing sanctions imposed on Syria by the US and its allies: "The Syrian Catastrophe: Socioeconomic Monitoring Report, First Quarterly Report (January–March 2013)," *SCPR*, June 30, 2013.

p. 224 "It was something about that picture": Mukul Devichand, "Alan Kurdi's Aunt: 'My Dead Nephew's Picture Saved Thousands of Lives,'" BBC, January 2, 2016.

p. 224 "In order for any peace agreement": Julia Manchester, "Gabbard Says She Met with Assad on Syria Trip," CNN, January 25, 2017.

p. 224 "Assad's mouthpiece in Washington": Josh Rogin, "How Tulsi Gabbard Became Assad's Mouthpiece in Washington," *Washington Post*, January 29, 2017; Rogin's attack on Gabbard was marred by three major errors and was eventually amended with an extensive editor's note.

p. 226 migrant baiting at a massive far-right rally: Max Blumenthal and James Kleinfeld, "Independence Day: Neo-Fascists Take Finland," Real News, March 27, 2016.

p. 227 "a dispatch from the future": Oliver J.J. Lane, "WATCH: The Anti-Migrant Video Going Viral Across Europe," Breitbart, November 11, 2015.

p. 228 "Most Finnish cities ... ring of burning ghettoes": Blumenthal and Kleinfeld, "Independence Day."

p. 229 The walls Orban had built: "Hungary's Viktor Orban finds ally with 'black sheep' Donald Trump," *Deutsche Welle*, November 25, 2011.

p. 230 National Front ... "political victory": Elaine Ganley, "France's Emmanuel Macron Gets Tough on Migrants," Associated Press, December 26, 2017.

p. 230 Progress Party ... rejection of Syrian refugees: Sindre Bangstad, "The Rise of the Populist Right in Norway," *Boston Review*, June 3, 2015.

p. 230 men dressed in all black ... beating refugees: Sven Nordenstam, "Masked Mob Threatening Migrants Go on the Rampage in Stockholm," Reuters.com, January 30, 2016.

p. 230 sexual assaults on women: Melissa Eddy, "Reports of Attacks on Women in Germany Heighten Tension over Migrants," *New York Times*, January 5, 2016.

p. 231 Syrian refugees valiantly protected a victim: Lizzie Dearden, "Cologne Attacks: American Woman Tells How Syrian Refugees Rescued Her from New Year's Eve Sexual Assault," *Independent*, January 16, 2016.

p. 231 German media, reports of the sex attacks: Emran Feroz, "Racist Violence and Incitement against Refugees Explodes across Germany," Alternet's Grayzone Project, February 1, 2016, alternet.org.

p. 231 the "fringe effect": Sindre Bangstad, "The Rise of the Populist Right in Norway," *Boston Review*, June 3, 2015.

p. 232 more than 1,000 attacks: "Report: Five Times More Attacks on Refugee Homes in Germany in 2015," *Deutsche Welle*, January 29, 2016.

p. 232 *Volksverraeter*: "Volksverraeter, or 'Traitor to the People,' Named Germany's Worst Word of 2016," *SBS News*, January 11, 2017.

p. 232 political tradition of figures like Alfred Dregger: Nafeez Ahmed, "The Conservative Party Aided and Abetted German Fascists with Nazi Roots," medium.com, June 20, 2016.

p. 232 SS as "men of character": Kate Connolly, "Haider Rhetoric 'Trivialises' Nazism," *Guardian*, April 25, 2001.

p. 233 conference on the "new anti-Semitism": Anthony Faiola, "How the Far Right Is Trying to Woo an Unlikely Ally—Jews," *Washington Post*, November 29, 2016.

p. 233 Strache ... visit to the Yad Vashem Holocaust memorial: Luke Baker, "Far-right Austrian Leader Visits Israel's Holocaust Memorial," Reuters.com, April 12, 2016.

p. 233 "Islam is not a part of Austria": Tessa Szyszkowitz, "Austria Flirts with the Far Right," Carnegie Europe, December 2, 2016.

p. 233 Freedom Party had won … coalition: Nicola Slawson, "Austrian President Approves Far-right Freedom Party Joining Coalition Government," *Guardian*, December 16, 2017.

pp. 233–4 "the Front National is not your enemy": Itay Lotem, "In a Bid to Detoxify the Far Right, Marine Le Pen Wants to Appeal to French Jews," Yahoo News, March 22, 2017.

p. 234 "If Jerusalem falls into the hands of the Muslims": Roee Nahmias and Geert Wilders, "Change Jordan's Name to Palestine," YNet, June 20, 2010.

p. 235 "What comes around goes around": "Jeremy Corbyn Connects Western Bombing Campaigns and Refugee Crisis: 'What Goes Around Comes Around,'" *Democracy Now!*, December 8, 2015.

p. 235 against Corbyn's stance on Syria was Jo Cox: Toby Helm and Daniel Boffey, "More than 50 Labour MPs to Defy Jeremy Corbyn in Vote on Syria," *Guardian*, October 10, 2015.

p. 235 "We completely disagree": Steven Hopkins, "Labour: Claims Dozens of MPs 'Ready to Back Military Action in Syria'," *Huffington Post UK*, December 10, 2015.

p. 236 "by refusing to tackle Assad's brutality": Jo Cox, "With Regret, I Feel I Have No Other Option but to Abstain on Syria," *Huffington Post UK*, December 2, 2015.

p. 236 "not let America sell out the Syrian rebels": Jo Cox and Omid Nouripour, "We Must Not Let America Sell Out the Syrian Rebels to Putin and Assad," *Daily Telegraph*, February 4, 2016.

p. 236 "white liberals and traitors": Ian Cobain, Nazia Parveen and Matthew Taylor, "The Slow-Burning Hatred That Led Thomas Mair to Murder Jo Cox," *Guardian*, November 23, 2016.

p. 237 billboard ad … "Breaking Point": Josh Lowe, "Brexit: UKIP Launches 'Breaking Point' Immigration Poster," *Newsweek*, June 16, 2016.

p. 237 Kemp claimed that the killing of Cox: TNO Staff, "Brexit: 'Remain' Weaker After Cox Murder," *New Observer*, June 18, 2016.

p. 237 Less than a third of exit polls predicted: Pamela Duncan, "How the Pollsters Got It Wrong on the EU Referendum," *Guardian*, June 24, 2016.

p. 237 Trump pronounced Brexit "a great thing": Graeme Demianyk, "Donald Trump Says Brexit Will Be a 'Great Thing' and Others Will Quit EU," *Huffington Post UK*, January 15, 2017.

p. 238 "countries want their own identity": Ibid.

p. 238 prospective "leave" voters citing immigration: Jon Cohen and John Lapinski, "Poll: British Voters Split on Brexit but Think EU Exit Vote Will Fail," NBC News, June 17, 2016.

p. 238 coverage of refugees was the "most hostile": Mike Berry, Inaki Garcia-Blanco and Kerry Moore, "Press Coverage of the Refugee and Migrant Crisis in the EU: A Content Analysis of Five European Countries," UNHCR, December 2015, unhcr.org.

p. 239 "The Cost of Doing Nothing": Jo Cox, Tom Tughenat, John Bew and Alison McGowan, "The Cost of Doing Nothing: The Price of Inaction in the Face of Mass Atrocities," *Policy Exchange*, January 26, 2017.

p. 239 Hope not Hate: "What Do They Know," correspondence between Stephen Green and Marina O'Neill, February 6, 2014, whatdotheyknow.com.

p. 239 White Helmets ... operated alongside Al Qaeda's local: "Syria Civil Defense Statement," Syria Civil Defense, January 26, 2017. The statement reads: "It is true that our 121 clinics operate only in areas not under the control of the Syrian regime."

p. 239 "absolutely disgraceful": Brendan Cox, "This isn't just wrong, it's absolutely disgraceful," Twitter, October 12, 2016.

p. 242 email exchanges, Podesta can be found: The Podesta Emails, *WikiLeaks*, released on October 7, 2016, wikileaks.org.

p. 242 "fixture in Republican politics": Kimberley Fritts' Podesta Group bio has been scrubbed; however, she has reappeared as CEO with the same bio at Cogent Strategies, "a bipartisan government relations and strategic communications firm," cogent-strategies.com/team.

p. 242 Podesta Group ... contract with Saudi: Catherine Ho, "Saudi Government Has Vast Network of PR, Lobby Firms in US," *Washington Post*, April 20, 2016.

p. 242 Center for American Progress ... UAE embassy: Jim Lobe, "Is CAP Shilling for the UAE?," Lobe Log, October 31, 2016.

p. 242 *Clinton Cash* ... brainchild of Steve Bannon: Joshua Green, "This Man Is the Most Dangerous Political Operative in America," Bloomberg, October 8, 2015.

p. 243 assault on Jeb Bush, a charter member of PNAC: Richard W. Behan, "Jeb Bush and His Brother's Wars," *Counterpunch*, July 10, 2015.

p. 243 *Bush Bucks*: Green, "This Man Is the Most Dangerous Political Operative in America."

p. 243 "but we have no idea about the rebels": Charlotte Alter, "Transcript: Read the Full Text of the Fourth Republican Debate in Milwaukee," *Time*, November 11, 2015.

p. 243 voters ... sending Trump surging: Nick Gass, "Trump Hits a New High in National Poll," *Politico*, December 14, 2015.

p. 244 "Jeb is so wrong!": "Transcript: Read the Full Transcript of the Ninth Republican Debate in South Carolina," *Time*, February 16, 2016.

p. 245 "If it doesn't backfire, then it will be official": Eli Stokols, "Trump crosses the 9/11 line," *Politico*, February 14, 2016.

p. 245 "express[ing] his preference for keeping dictators in power": Jeremy Diamond, "Trump Praises Saddam Hussein's Efficient Killing of 'Terrorists,' Calls Today's Iraq 'Harvard for Terrorism,'" CNN, July 6, 2016.

p. 245 "When we went to war in Iraq, the trillions we spent there": Lauren McCauley, "In Michigan, Sanders Slams Government That Has Money for War, Not for Flint," *Common Dreams*, February 16, 2016.

p. 245 "Crooked Hillary Clinton's foreign interventions": @realDonaldTrump, "Crooked Hillary Clinton's foreign interventions unleashed ISIS in Syria, Iraq and Libya. She is reckless and dangerous!" Twitter, May 21, 2016.

p. 246 "The Conservative Case For Voting for Clinton": David Frum, "The Conservative Case for Voting for Clinton," *Atlantic*, November 2, 2016.

p. 246 "US imperialism has been the greatest force for good": Max Boot, "Imperialism!," *Weekly Standard*, May 6, 2003.

p. 246 "supporting the Afghan surge": Jacob Heilbrunn, "The Next Act of the Neocons," *New York Times*, July 5, 2014.

p. 246 Max Boot ... vouched for her: Ben Norton, "Hillary Clinton Ad Features American Imperialist Max Boot, ex-CIA/NSA Director Michael Hayden," BenNorton.com, August 7, 2016.

p. 246 "Iranians pay a price in Syria": Michael Morell "We Need to Make Iran, Russia 'Pay a Price' in Syria," youtube.com.

p. 246 Clinton's campaign ... Beacon Global: Lee Fang, "Clinton, Rubio, Cruz Receive Foreign Policy Advice from Same Consulting Firm," *Intercept*, December 18, 2015.

p. 246 Kagan hosted a ... fundraiser: Rania Khalek, "Robert Kagan and Other Neocons Are Backing Hillary Clinton," *Intercept*, July

25, 2016.

p. 247 "A fringe element has effectively taken over the Republican Party": Tim Hains, "Full Replay/Transcript: Hillary Clinton Accuses Donald Trump of 'Mainstreaming' a Hate Movement," *Real Clear Politics*, August 25, 2016.

p. 247 Clinton … "inspiring women": Nicholas Confessore and Amy Chozick, "After Lying Low, Deep-pocketed Clinton Donors Return to the Fore," *New York Times*, June 28, 2016.

p. 248 "a hell of a lot worse than waterboarding": Tom McCarthy, "Donald Trump: I'd Bring Back 'a Hell of a Lot Worse Than Waterboarding,'" *Guardian*, February 7, 2016.

p. 248 Gaffney … as "senior thought leaders": Michael Crowley and Nahal Toosi, "Trump Appointees Endorsed Link between Islam and Radicalism," *Politico*, November 18, 2016.

p. 248 Gorka … $8,000 from Trump's campaign: Sarah Lazare, "Far-Right Trump Consultant to Be Honored Speaker at Illinois Police SWAT Training," *Alternet's Grayzone Project*, September 23, 2016, alternet.org.

p. 249 Gorka … Vitezi Rend: Eli Clifton, "Why Is Trump Adviser Wearing Medal of Nazi Collaborators?," Lobe Log, February 12, 2017, lobelog.com.

p. 249 "the great Trojan Horse": Joseph Tanfani, "Donald Trump Warns that Syrian Refugees Represent 'a Great Trojan Horse' to the US," *LA Times*, October 19, 2016.

p. 249 "thousands of people were cheering as that building was coming down": "Trump Says He Saw People Celebrating 9/11 in Jersey City," *Chicago Tribune*, November 22, 2015.

p. 249 *Politifact* refuted Trump's half-baked statements: Lauren Carroll, "Fact-checking Trump's Claim that Thousands in New Jersey Cheered when World Trade Center Tumbled," *Politifact*, November 22, 2015.

p. 250 "Your reputation is amazing": Eric Bradner, "Trump Praises 9/11 Truther's 'Amazing' Reputation," CNN, December 2, 2015.

p. 250 "I'm ready to die for Trump!": Alex Jones, "Alex Jones: 'I'm Ready to Die for Trump'," youtube.com.

p. 251 tapes of Mateen's calls: "Omar Mateen Calls to Police Department I," posted to soundcloud.com by Buzzfeed News.

p. 251 Mateen … harassment from racist co-workers: Max Blumenthal, "Disturbing New Documents Reveal Orlando Shooter Omar

Mateen's Allegations of Racial Harassment by Police Co-Workers," *Alternet's Grayzone Project*, August 1, 2016, alternet.org.

p. 252 **"Don't you Arabs sleep with goats?"**: Ibid.

p. 252 **Mateen admitted ... loyalty to Islamic extremist groups**: Ibid.

p. 252 **Mateen confided to ... Malik**: Mohammed Malik, "I Reported Omar Mateen to the FBI. Trump Is Wrong that Muslims Don't Do Our Part," *Washington Post*, June 20, 2016.

p. 252 **al-Awlaki's online diatribes ... Google monetized**: Arthur Martin and Lucy Osborne, "Google Cashes in on Hate Videos: Internet Giant Puts Ads alongside Thousands of Terror Rants on YouTube," *Daily Mail*, May 27, 2013.

p. 253 **Google wiped al-Awlaki's videos**: Zoey Chong, "Google Expands Terror Crackdown on YouTube," CNet, November 13, 2017.

p. 253 **his videos ... Syed Rizwan Farook**: Greg Miller, "Al-Qaeda Figure Seen as Key Inspiration for San Bernardino Attacker," *Washington Post*, December 18, 2015.

p. 253 **his videos ... Umar Farouk Abdulmutallab**: Scott Shane, "Inside Al Qaeda's Plot to Blow Up an American Airliner," *New York Times*, February 22, 2017.

p. 253 **Abusalha ... make jihad: "This life sucked"**: Adam Goldman and Greg Miller, "American Suicide Bomber's Travels in US, Middle East Went Unmonitored," *Washington Post*, October 11, 2014.

p. 253 **"my homie"**: Omar Mateen calls to Police Department I, posted to soundcloud.com by Buzzfeed News.

p. 253 **known Abusalha much better**: Mohammed A. Malik, "I Reported Omar Mateen to the FBI. Trump Is Wrong that Muslims Don't Do Our Part," *Washington Post*, June 20, 2016.

p. 254 **"lure Omar into some kind of act"**: Blumenthal and Lazare, "Disturbing New Documents Reveal Orlando Shooter Omar Mateen's Allegations of Racial Harrassment by Police Co-Workers."

p. 255 **the FBI encouraged ... James Medina**: Aviva Stahl, "FBI Is Manufacturing Terror Plots Against Jewish-Americans, Driving Divisions Between Jews and Muslims," *Alternet's Grayzone Project*, May 11, 2016, alernet.org.

p. 255 **Medina was portrayed in Jewish-oriented media**: Ibid.

p. 256 **nearly half of all terror prosecutions ... involved informants**: Trevor Aaronson, "Inside the Terror Factory," *Mother Jones*, January 11, 2013.

p. 256 **"the US government didn't prosecute anyone from a terrorism sting"**: Ibid.

pp. 256–7 Bostonians obeyed a voluntary "lockdown order": Brian Naylor, "Boston Lockdown 'Extraordinary' but Prudent, Experts Say," NPR, April 22, 2013.

p. 257 "In the case of Mateen": Blumenthal and Lazare, "Disturbing New Documents Reveal Orlando Shooter Omar Mateen's Allegations of Racial Harrassment by Police Co-Workers."

p. 257 case of Elton Simpson, the FBI played: "Anderson Cooper Investigates First ISIS-Claimed Attack in US," *60 Minutes*, March 24, 2017.

p. 257 "I think something clicked in him": Ibid.

p. 258 "part of the hard core of a group of individuals": Elise Potaka and Luke McMahon, "FBI Says 'Australian IS jihadist' Is Actually a Jewish American Troll Named Joshua Ryne Goldberg," *Sydney Morning Herald*, September 12, 2015.

p. 258 Draw Muhammad contest ... appearance by Geert Wilders: "Two Gunmen Shot Dead at 'Draw the Prophet Muhammad' Contest in Texas," *Guardian*, May 4, 2015.

p. 258 "Tear up Texas": "Anderson Cooper Investigates First ISIS-Claimed Attack in US," *60 Minutes*, March 24, 2017.

p. 258 ihe changed his Twitter avatar: "FBI Knew about 'Draw Muhammad' Gunman Elton Simpson," *Daily Beast*, May 4, 2018.

p. 258 FBI agent ... in the car right behind Simpson and Soofi: "Anderson Cooper Investigates First ISIS-Claimed Attack in US," *60 Minutes*, March 24, 2017.

p. 259 Australi Witness ... helped inspire Simpson: Nick O'Malley, "Australian Twitter User Encouraged Islamic State Fighters to Attack Prophet Mohammad Cartoon Contest in Texas: Report," *Sydney Morning Herald*, May 5, 2015.

p. 259 Australi Witness ... Goldberg: Elise Potaka and Luke McMahon, "FBI says 'Australian IS Jihadist' Is Actually a Jewish American Troll Named Joshua Ryne Goldberg," *Sydney Morning Herald*, September 12, 2015.

p. 259 "I will not abridge my freedoms so as not to offend savages": Holly Yan, "Garland Shooting: What Is the American Freedom Defense Initiative?," CNN, May 4, 2015.

p. 261 "Extinction of the Grayzone": Max Blumenthal, "How Western Militarists Are Playing into the Hands of ISIS," *AlterNet*, November 16, 2015.

p. 262 "Yesterday, America was a land of slavery": Alexandra Sims, "Donald Trump Features in al-Shabaab Terrorist Recruitment

Video," *Independent*, January 2, 2016.

p. 263 **Michael Oren ... urged Trump to continue:** Allison Kaplan Sommer, "Trump Will Be 'Greatly Strengthened' by Orlando Shooting, Says Former Israeli Ambassador to US," *Haaretz*, June 13, 2016.

p. 263 **"Because our leaders are weak":** Ryan Teague Beckwith, "Read Donald Trump's Speech on the Orlando Shooting," *Time*, June 13, 2016.

p. 264 **"I will do everything in my power to protect our LGBTQ citizens":** Dave Quinn, "Donald Trump Vows to 'Protect LGBTQ Citizens' in GOP Speech as He Evokes Orlando Massacre," *People Magazine*, July 22, 2016.

p. 264 **"Clinton wants to allow radical Islamic terrorists to pour into our country":** "Transcript: Donald Trump's National Security Speech," *Politico*, June 13, 2016.

p. 264 **"We will shoot back":** Lucas Nolan, "Milo in Orlando: Gays, like Jews, Should Say 'Never Again!,'" *Breitbart*, June 15, 2016.

p. 264 **"Trump is probably the most gay-friendly candidate":** Ibid.

p. 265 **"alt-light":** Max Blumenthal, "How Trump and His Hipster Right-Wing Allies Are Trying to Use Gay People as a Weapon Against Muslims," *Alternet's Grayzone Project*, June 18, 2016, alternet.org.

p. 265 **"ALL ISLAM IS RADICAL":** Adam Sacasa, "Port St. Lucie Man Accused of Setting Fire to Mosque 'Embarrassed' About Incident, Police Say," *Sun Sentinel*, September 15, 2016.

p. 265 **highest number of recorded attacks on mosques:** Frances Kai-Hwa Wang, "Mosque Attacks, Apparent Anti-Islam Spending Up: Report," NBC News, July 20, 2016.

p. 265 **disapproval of Muslims to record levels:** "New Study: Muslims Are More Unpopular than Atheists in the US," WETA, September 16, 2016.

p. 266 **"I will knock the hell out of ISIS":** Siobhan Fenton, "Presidential Debate: Donald Trump Says 'Sexual Assault' Critics Should Focus on 'More Important Things like Isis'," *Independent*, October 10, 2016.

p. 266 **Seddique, an eccentric local figure:** Louis Nelson, "Orlando Shooter's Father Attends Clinton Rally," *Politico*, August 9, 2016.

p. 266 **"Clinton is good for United States versus Donald Trump":** Ibid.

p. 266 **"I'd throw him out":** Aaron Blake, "Trump Suggests Racial Profiling and Says of Omar Mateen's Father, 'I'd Throw Him out,'" *Washington Post*, August 17, 2016.

p. 267 **the case fell apart when the FBI was forced:** Krista Torralva and

Gal Tziperman Lotan, "Noor Salman Trial: Pulse Gunman's Father Revealed as FBI informant, but Judge Won't Dismiss Case," *Orlando Sentinel*, March 26, 2018.

p. 267 **beaches of Sirte ... shocking execution videos**: Ian Black, "Isis Claim of Beheading Egyptian Copts in Libya Shows Group's Spread," *Guardian*, February 15, 2015.

p. 267 **Belhaj ... influential business tycoon**: Abdelhakim Belhadj, "The Militia Leader Turned International Businessman," *Africa Intelligence*, April 28, 2016.

p. 267 **"Libyan Dawn" government ... Al-Ghariani**: Josh Halliday and Chris Stephen, "Libya's Highest Spiritual Leader Banned from UK over Support of Islamists," *Guardian*, October 30, 2014.

p. 268 **"they kill and they have their reasons"**: Aya Elbrqawi and Nadia Radhwan, "Libya: Mufti Call for Violence Angers Libyans," *All Africa*, June 12, 2014.

p. 268 **"the most likely medium-term prospect"**: "Libya: Getting Geneva Right," International Crisis Group, February 26, 2015.

p. 268 **Libya was a failed state**: Richard Lardner, "US Commander in Africa Says Libya Is a Failed State," Associated Press, March 8, 2016.

p. 268 **"living hellholes"**: Karen McVeigh, "Refugee Women and Children 'Beaten, Raped and Starved in Libyan Hellholes,'" *Guardian*, February 28, 2017.

p. 268 **testimony of open-air slave markets**: "IOM Learns of 'Slave Market' Conditions Endangering Migrants in North Africa," *International Organization for Migration*, April 11, 2017, iom.int.

p. 268 **CNN produced footage of the auctions**: "People for Sale, Exposing Migrant Slave Auctions in Libya," CNN, October 2017.

p. 268 **"I hate to say it but our life was better under the previous regime"**: "War-weary Libyans Miss Life under Gaddafi," *AFR*, October 17, 2016, businessinsider.com.

p. 268 **"I think President Obama made the right decision"**: Saagar Enjeti, "Hillary Makes It through 3 Debates without Accounting for Libya," *Daily Caller*, October 20, 2016.

p. 269 **Paul's resolution had rankled**: Susan Cornwell, "Senate Blocks War Powers Vote amid Libya Action," Reuters, April 5, 2011.

pp. 269–70 **"This may not be politically correct"**: Reena Flores, "GOP Lawmaker: Benghazi Panel 'Designed to Go after' Hillary Clinton," CBS News, October 15, 2015.

p. 270 **the Benghazi committee burned through $8 million**: Mary

Troyan, "House Benghazi committee Files Final Report and Shuts Down," *USA Today*, December 12, 2016.

p. 270 **"she had helicopters flying over my house"**: Frederic U. Dicker, "Kooky KT's Spy Tale; Hill's Helicopters Watching Me: Rival," *New York Post*, March 25, 2006.

p. 270 **69 percent of respondents found Clinton untrustworthy**: Anne Gearan, "Can Hillary Clinton Overcome Her Trust Problem?," *Washington Post*, July 3, 2016.

p. 270 **"Everybody thought Hillary Clinton was unbeatable, right?"**: Jesse Byrnes, "McCarthy Links Benghazi Panel to Clinton's Falling Poll Numbers," *Hill*, September 30, 2015.

p. 271 **Geist and John Teigen, who had just sold their story to ... Bay**: Jeanette Steele, "Military Benghazi Movie: Delay Cost Lives," *San Diego Union Tribune*, January 14, 2016.

p. 271 **"I blame Hillary Clinton personally for the death of my son"**: "'I blame Hillary Clinton personally for the death of my son': Pat Smith speaks at RNC" (video), July 19, 2016, cleveland.com.

p. 271 **"We have learned the hard way when America is absent"**: "Press Release—Hillary Clinton's Statement to the House Select Committee on Benghazi," American Presidency Project, October 22, 2015, presidency.ucsb.edu.

p. 272 **"likely—possible—that he wasn't doing this on his own"**: "Manchester Bomber Known to Authorities, Likely Did Not Act Alone—Minister," Reuters, May 24, 2017.

p. 273 **May obscured the ... uncomfortable questions**: Mark Curtis and Nafeez Ahmed, "The Manchester Bombing as Blowback: The Latest Evidence," MarkCurtis.info, June 3, 2017. Also see Max Blumenthal, "The Manchester Bombing Is Blowback from the West's Disastrous Interventions and Covert Proxy Wars," *Alternet's Grayzone Project*, May 25, 2017 alternet.org.

p. 273 **"I was allowed to go [to Libya], no questions asked"**: Amandla Thomas-Johnson and Simon Hooper, "'Sorted' by MI5: How UK Government Sent British-Libyans to Fight Gaddafi," *Middle East Eye*, May 25, 2017.

p. 273 **"We were in the same group over there"**: Nazia Parveen, "Bomber's Father Fought against Gaddafi Regime with 'Terrorist' Group," *Guardian*, May 24, 2017.

p. 274 **Salman and his brother ... followed their father into Libya**: Lizzie Dearden, "Salman Abedi 'Travelled to Syria and Libya' before

Carrying out Manchester Attack," *Independent*, May 24, 2017.

p. 274 **He was an outgoing, fun guy, but since he went to Libya in 2011**: Neal Keeling, "Who Is the Suspected Suicide Bomber Salman Abedi?," *Manchester Evening News*, May 23, 2017.

Press Association, "Manchester Arena Bomber Was Rescued from Libya by Royal Navy," *Guardian*, July 30, 2018.

p. 278 **"And just the historical practices of the Russians"**: Michael Sainato, "James Clapper Tells NBC's Chuck Todd that Russians Are 'Genetically Driven' to Co-opt," *Observer*, May 30, 2017.

p. 278 **placards depicting Trump in Russian garb**: Max Blumenthal, "Liberals Rally For 'Truth' on Trump and Russia," *Real News*, June 7, 2017, youtube.com.

p. 278 **Typical of the phantasmagoria of the liberal "resistance"**: James Wilkinson, "International Relations Have Gone Too Far! Image of Pregnant Trump Being Cradled by Putin Is Projected onto New York Buildings to Promote New Dating App That Promises 'Love through Hate,'" *Daily Mail*, February 16, 2017.

p. 278 **believed Americans should fight and die to defend … Latvia**: Dina Smeltz, Ivo Daalder, Karl Friedhof and Craig Kafura, "What Americans Think about America First," Chicago Council on Global Affairs, 2017 (poll in Appendix 4 shows 52 percent of Democrats in support of sending US troops abroad "[i]f Russia invades a NATO ally like Latvia, Lithuania, or Estonia"), thechicagocouncil.org.

p. 279 **George H.W. Bush … abrogation of verbal agreements**: Svetlana Savranskaya and Tom Blanton, "NATO Expansion: What Gorbachev Heard," GWU National Security Archive, December 12, 2017, nsarchive.gwu.edu.

p. 279 **3 million "excess deaths"**: Paul Klebnikov, *Godfather of the Kremlin*, Harcourt, 2000, 105.

p. 279 **Life expectancy … declined by five years**: Judy Dempsey, "Study Looks at Mortality in Post-Soviet Era," *New York Times*, January 16, 2009.

p. 279 **"Many hung around for a while"**: Klebnikov, *Godfather of the Kremlin*, 105–6.

p. 280 **Russia's poverty rate had risen**: Joseph Stiglitz, "The Ruin of Russia," *Guardian*, April 9, 2003.

p. 280 **"By pursuing a policy of 'reform'"**: Members of the Speaker's Advisory Group on Russia, *Russia's Road to Corruption*, September 2000, fas.org.

p. 280 Putin … at the Munich Security Conference: "Speech and the Following Discussion at the Munich Conference on Security Policy," Presidency of Russia, February 10, 2007, en.kremlin.ru.

p. 281 Bush administration's unilateral withdrawal: Terence Neilan, "Bush Pulls Out of ABM Treaty; Putin Calls Move a Mistake," *New York Times*, December 13, 2001.

p. 281 letter to EU and NATO leaders that slammed Putin: "An Open Letter to the Heads of State and Government of the European Union and NATO," *Journal of Democracy*, September 28, 2004.

p. 281 color revolutions were spreading … leveraging funds: Ian Traynor, "US Campaign Behind the Turmoil in Kiev," *Guardian*, November 25, 2004. The aforementioned article is a rare acknowledgment by Western mainstream media of the role of soft power outfits in spurring regime change, and would never be seen in the pages of today's *Guardian*. Soros and NED Chairman Carl Gershman have made no attempt to conceal their heavy support for opposition civil society and media in eastern Europe, however. The documentary *Otpor!*, on the US-astroturfed "pro-democracy" movement, contains interviews with US government officials like Daniel Serwer of the US Institute for Peace taking credit for spurring protest movements against Russian-aligned leaders. See *OTPOR! Bringing Down a Dictator*, English version, 2001, posted by Vimeo user WORKSTATION1 at vimeo.com.

p. 281 Berezovsky to topple governments: Exiled Russian plutocrat Boris Berezovsky was exposed for funding Ukraine's 2004 "Orange Revolution" by a variety of sources and was seen taking credit for it in the British documentary *Russian Godfathers, Part I. The Fugitive*, posted by Youtube user "History and Economics" at youtube.com.

p. 281 Saakashvili … one of his top advisors was Bruce P. Jackson: Andrew Cockburn, "Game On," *Harper's*, January 2015.

p. 281 backchannel approval from then vice president Dick Cheney: Ibid.

p. 281 Saakashvili was seen chewing his tie: Ian Spiegelman, "Embattled Georgian Leader Eats Tie," *Gawker*, August 16, 2008.

p. 282 Putin's approval rating soared: Alberto Nardelli, Jennifer Rankin and George Arnett, "Vladimir Putin's approval rating at record levels," *Guardian*, July 23, 2015. The aforementioned article contains data demonstrating a spike in approval for Putin immediately after the Georgian campaign.

p. 282 **Obama … letter from the Foreign Policy Initiative:** Mary Katharine Ham, "Foreign Policy Initiative Letter Asks Obama to Make Human Rights Central to Talks in Russia," *Weekly Standard*, July 1, 2009.

p. 282 **Putin was livid … at Medvedev:** Jill Dougherty, "Putin and Medvedev Spar Over Libya," CNN, March 23, 2011.

p. 282 **"The 1980s are now calling and they want their foreign policy back":** Glenn Kessler, "Flashback: Obama's Debate Zinger on Romney's '1980s' Foreign Policy (video)," *Washington Post*, March 20, 2014.

p. 283 **Magnitsky Act passed unanimously:** Putin's retaliation was met with consternation: Stephen F. Cohen, "America's New Cold War with Russia," *Nation*, January 16, 2013.

p. 283 **Browder … turned to the Ashcroft Group:** Haim Isserovitz, "Architect of the Cold War," *Jerusalem Post*, September 1, 2014.

p. 283 **documentary film by Andrei Nekrasov … exposed Browder as a fabulist:** Andrei Nekrasov, *The Magnitsky Act: Behind the Scenes*, published online on August 9, 2018, vimeo.com.

p. 283 **Browder fought … to ban screenings:** Henry Johnson, "Millionaire Tries to Stop Documentary Claiming to Tell the True Story of Russia's Missing $230 Million," *Foreign Policy*, June 10, 2016.

p. 283 **Browder … to avoid telling his story under oath:** Jason Motlagh, "Fighting Putin Doesn't Make You a Saint," *New Republic*, December 31, 2015.

p. 283 **Yanukovych, had rejected … association agreement:** Ian Trainer and Oksana Grytsenko, "Ukraine Suspends Talks on EU Trade Pact as Putin Wins Tug of War," *Guardian*, November 21, 2013.

pp. 283–4 **"Ukraine's choice to join Europe":** Carl Gershman, "Former Soviet States Stand Up to Russia. Will the US?," *Washington Post*, September 26, 2013.

p. 284 **(NED) … "Ukraine's choice to join Europe":** Alec Luhn, "National Endowment for Democracy Is First 'Undesirable' NGO Banned in Russia," *Guardian*, July 28, 2015. The article confirms the involvement of Pierre Omidyar, billionaire Ebay founder and media mogul, in the funding of opposition activity in Ukraine in 2014. According to the Omidyar Network, he directly funded Hromadske, an opposition media channel founded just weeks before the Maidan coup: omidyar.com.

p. 284 **"We've invested over five billions dollars":** "Victoria Nuland:

Ukrainians Deserve for Respect from Their Government," YouTube by user US-Ukraine on December 18, 2013, youtube.com.

p. 284 **"Fuck the EU"**: Ukraine crisis: "Transcript of Leaked Nuland-Pyatt Call," BBC, February 7, 2014.

p. 284 **Crimea ... referendum to join the Russian**: "Crimea Referendum: Voters 'Back Russia Union,'" BBC, March 16, 2014. Western media, which condemned the vote as a fraud, nevertheless acknowledged a dearth of evidence proving it as such. For instance, *Forbes* claimed voter turnout totals had been cooked, but the same article noted high turnout in Sevastopol and a majority in favor of annexation across the country. See Paul Roderick Gregory, "Putin's 'Human Rights Council' Accidentally Posts Real Crimean Election Results," *Forbes*, May 5, 2014.

p. 284 **Azov ... into the country's national guard:** Gabriela Baczynska, "Ultra-Nationalist Ukrainian Battalion Gears Up for More Fighting," Reuters, March 25, 2015.

pp. 284–5 **EU association deal ... deepening the economic ruin:** Pavel Polityuk, "EU Deal Yet to Bear Fruit for Ukrainian Exporters," Reuters, April 8, 2016.

p. 285 **"All that's needed is the rallying"**: William Kristol, "War-Weariness as an Excuse," *Weekly Standard*, March 24, 2014.

p. 285 **"Last summer, at the height of a highly contested and bitterly adversarial presidential campaign"**: Adam Schiff, "Intelligence Committee Ranking Member Schiff Opening Statement During Hearing on Russian Active Measures," US House of Representatives Permanent Select Committee on Intelligence, March 20, 2017, democrats-intelligence.house.gov.

p. 286 **Alperovitch, was a Russian exile ... at the Atlantic Council.** Dmitri Alperovitch bio, Atlantic Council, atlanticcouncil.org.

p. 286 **president of this firm, Shawn Henry, was a former FBI:** Shawn Henry is the president of CrowdStrike Services and CSO; see crowdstrike.com.

p. 286 **Atlantic Council funding Honor Roll of Contributors:** Atlantic Council, atlanticcouncil.org.

pp. 286–7 **CrowdStrike laid out ... a June 2016 report:** Dmitri Alperovitch, "Bears in the Midst: Intrusion into the Democratic National Committee," Crowdstrike, June 15, 2016, crowdstrike.com.

p. 287 **FBI denied access to the DNC's servers:** Evan Perez and Daniella Diaz, "FBI: DNC Rebuffed Request to Examine Computer Servers,"

CNN, January 5, 2017.

p. 287 employed Steele. The Clinton campaign had effectively paid: Adam Entous, Devlin Barrett and Rosalind S. Helderman, "Clinton Campaign, DNC Paid for Research That Led to Russia Dossier," *Washington Post*, October 24, 2017.

p. 287 a two-page summary by Jonathan Winer: Jane Mayer, "Christopher Steele, the Man Behind the Dossier," *New Yorker*, March 12, 2018.

p. 287 Winer had lobbied on behalf of Bill Browder: "Bottom Line," *Hill*, June 16, 2008.

p. 287 helped the fugitive oligarch craft the Magnitsky Act: Haim Isserovitz, "Architect of the Cold War," *Jerusalem Post*, September 1, 2014.

p. 288 While I was at the State Department: Jonathan Winer, "Why I Turned Over the Steele Dossier," CNN, July 23, 2018, YouTube.com.

p. 288 Steele violated FBI policy: Rowan Scarborough, "Christopher Steele Broke FBI Media Rules after Being 'Admonished,' Documents Show," *Washington Times*, August 4, 2018.

p. 288 Stefan Halper, inside the Trump campaign: Rowan Scarborough, "Comey Violated FBI's Own Rulebook by Using Trump Campaign 'Spy': Expert," *Washington Times*, May 30, 2018.

p. 288 Steele continued to communicate with the FBI: Byron York, "12 Times Christopher Steele Fed Trump-Russia Allegations to FBI After the Election," *Washington Examiner*, August 3, 2018.

p. 288 Clapper arranged for the existence of the Steele dossier: Rowan Scarborough, "Obama DNI Clapper Leaked Dossier Story on Trump: House Intel Report," *Washington Times*, April 28, 2017.

p. 289 "Already, Russian hacking was the centerpiece of the argument": Aaron Maté, "Russiagate is More Fiction than Fact," *Nation*, October 6, 2017.

p. 289 Trump-Russia collusion "relentlessly and above all else": Jennifer Palmieri, "The Clinton Campaign Warned You about Russia. But Nobody Listened to Us," *Washington Post*, March 24, 2017.

p. 289 a DNI report issued ... on Russian interference: *Assessing Russian Activities and Intentions in Recent US Elections*, Office of the Director of National Intelligence, January 6, 2017, dni.gov.

p. 289 freely compared to Pearl Harbor and 9/11: Glenn Greenwald, "A Consensus Emerges: Russia Committed an 'Act of War' on Par With Pearl Harbor and 9/11. Should the US Response Be Similar?," *Intercept*, February 19, 2018.

p. 289 Department of Justice to force RT to register as a foreign agent: Aaron Mate, "RT Was Forced to Register as a Foreign Agent," *Nation*, November 16, 2017.

p. 290 Maddow, dedicating more coverage to Russia than any other issue: Aaron Maté, "MSNBC'S Rachel Maddow Sees a 'Russia Connection' Lurking around Every Corner," *Intercept*, April 12, 2017, theintercept.com/2017/04/12/msnbcs-rachel-maddow-sees-a-russia-connection-lurking-around-every-corner/.

p. 290 books by these operators … dominated bestseller lists: Alexandra Alter, "Sales Figures for Comey's 'A Higher Loyalty' Dwarf Recent Political Best Sellers," *New York Times*, April 24, 2018.

p. 290 Center for American Progress … partnership with the American Enterprise Institute: Sam Hananel, "Release: CAP and AEI Team Up to Defend Democracy and the Transatlantic Partnership," Center for American Progress, May 10, 2018.

p. 291 "the epidemic of malicious fake news and false propaganda": Mike Wending, "The (Almost) Complete History of 'Fake News,'" BBC, January 22, 2018.

p. 291 PropOrNot … *Washington Post* immediately picked up: Ben Norton and Glenn Greenwald, "Washington Post Disgracefully Promotes a McCarthyite Blacklist From a New, Hidden, and Very Shady Group," *Intercept*, November 26, 2018.

p. 291 Hamilton 68: Max Blumenthal, "McCarthyism Inc: Introducing the Counter-Terror 'Experts' Hyping Russian Threats and Undermining Our Civil Liberties," *Alternet's Grayzone Project*, November 10, 2017, alternet.org.

p. 291 DFRLab … hired in June 2018 by Facebook: @DFRLab, "Why We're Partnering with Facebook on Election Integrity," medium.com, May 17, 2018.

p. 292 Jones and his archive were disappeared … Facebook: "Enforcing Our Community Standards," *Facebook Newsroom*, August 6, 2018, newsroom.fb.com.

p. 292 "These companies must do more than take down one website": Thomas Knapp, "Murphy's Law: Big Tech Must Serve as Censorship Subcontractors," *Counterpunch*, August 17, 2018.

p. 292 teleSUR … forced to fight to reinstate their Facebook: "teleSUR English Removed from Facebook for Second Time," teleSUR, August 14, 2018, telesurtv.net.

p. 293 United States would no longer seek regime change in Syria:

Michelle Nichols, "US Priority on Syria no Longer Focused on 'Getting Assad out': Haley," Reuters, March 30, 2017.

p. 293 **Brussels to plan reconstruction efforts:** Robin Emmott and Gabriela Baczynska, "Conference on Syria Overshadowed by Chemical Attack," Reuters, April 3, 2017.

p. 293 **some sixty civilians were killed in an apparent chemical weapons attack:** "The Syrian Observatory for Human Rights continue Documenting the Casualties of the Black Tuesday's Massacre in Khan Shaykhun, Death Toll Rises to 86 about Two Third of Them Are Children and Women," SOHR, April 5, 2017, syriahr.com.

p. 293 **Syrian Observatory for Human Rights ... funded by the British Foreign Office:** "The Syrian Observatory—Funded by the Foreign Office," Media Lens, June 4, 2018, medialens.org.

p. 294 **"Do you feel like you bear responsibility for responding to the chemical attacks?":** Michael Walsh, "Trump: Syria Gas Attack Had 'a Big Impact' on Me," Yahoo News, April 5, 2017.

p. 294 **"You will see," Trump declared:** Ibid.

p. 294 **"Ivanka is a mother of three kids and she has influence":** Rebecca Savransky, "Eric Trump: Ivanka Trump Influenced Decision to Launch Syria Strikes," *Hill*, April 11, 2017.

p. 295 **"Donald Trump has done the right thing on Syria. Finally!!":** Anne-Marie Slaughter, Twitter, April 7, 2017 at 4:24 AM.

p. 295 **"Trump is right to make Syria pay a price for war crimes":** Christopher Wilson, "Trump's Media Critics Praise Syria Strikes," Yahoo News, April 7, 2017.

p. 295 **editorial boards, only one ... opposed Trump's strikes:** Adam Johnson, "Out of 47 Major Editorials on Trump's Syria Strikes, Only One Opposed," *FAIR*, April 11, 2017, fair.org.

p. 295 **Trump for "mov[ing] slightly toward pillars of traditional foreign policy":** David Ignatius, "Trump Moves Slightly Toward Pillars of Traditional Foreign Policy," *Washington Post*, April 12, 2018.

p. 295 **"Donald Trump became president of the United States last night":** Wilson, "Trump's Media Critics Praise Syria Strikes."

p. 295 **Van Jones ... civilians dead in Yemen:** Jason Kurtz, "Van Jones on Trump: 'He Became President of the United States in that Moment, Period'," CNN, March 1, 2017.

pp. 295–6 **Tapper quoted a "Syrian activist" ... Mouaz Moustafa:** Max Blumenthal, "Thirsting for War, CNN's Jake Tapper Turned to Strange and Shady Syria Sources," *Alternet's Grayzone Project*,

September 7, 2017.

p. 296 "Abu Ivanka al-Amriki": Shailaja Neelakantan, "Abu Ivanka al-Amriki—That's What Some Syrians Are Calling Trump," *Times of India*, April 8, 2017.

p. 296 "Merely pictures of victims that were held up": "EU Urges Diplomacy in Syria as Ex-weapons Inspector Says US Acted Without Proof," *Deutsche Welle*, April 7, 2017.

p. 297 "'We've just launched fifty-nine missiles' ... [Xi] was eating his cake": Jordyn Phelps, "Trump Says He Made Decision about Syrian Strike over Cake," ABC News, April 13, 2017.

p. 297 "If Russia didn't go in and back this animal": "Trump: 'If Russia Didn't Go in and Back This Animal, You Wouldn't Have the Problem You Have Now'," *Sputnik News*, April 12, 2017.

p. 297 "If there was anything that [attacking] Syria did": Eliza Relman, "Eric Trump Says Syria Strike Shows there Is no 'Tie' between President Trump and Russia," *Business Insider*, April 11, 2017.

p. 298 "I am guided by the beauty of our weapons": Lee Moran, "Brian Williams Uses Leonard Cohen Lyric to Describe 'Beautiful' Strike on Syria," *Huffington Post*, April 7, 2017.

p. 298 "Back off fighting territorial ISIS": Thomas Friedman, "Why Is Trump Fighting ISIS in Syria?" *New York Times*, April 12, 2017.

p. 299 United States of giving ISIS "breathing space": Whitney Webb, "UN Report Finds ISIS Given 'Breathing Space' in US-Occupied Areas of Syria," *Mint Press News*, August 16, 2018.

p. 299 President Assad stated ... unwelcome "invaders": Tom Perry, "Assad Calls US Forces 'Invaders,' but Still Hopeful on Trump," Reuters, March 11, 2017.

p. 299 "How long do you need to do that?": Julie Hirschfield Davis, "Trump Drops Push for Immediate Withdrawal of Troops from Syria," *New York Times*, April 4, 2018.

pp. 290–300 Trump clashed with ... group of Pentagon officials: Carol E. Lee and Courtney Kube, "Trump Says US 'Losing' Afghan War in Tense Meeting with Generals," NBC News, August 2, 2017.

p. 301 April 7 ... alleging that a chemical attack: "Syria War: What We Know about Douma 'Chemical Attack,'" BBC, July 10, 2018.

p. 301 "Animal Assad": Eli Watkins, "Trump Blames Putin, Obama for 'Animal Assad,' Tweets 'Big Price' after Reports of Syrian Chemical

Attack," CNN, April 9, 2018.

p. 301 **Barzeh ... OPCW had inspected:** "US-led Strikes on Syria: What Was Hit?," BBC, April 16, 2018.

p. 302 **Robert Fisk, visited Duma:** Robert Fisk, "The Search for Truth in the Rubble of Douma—and One Doctor's Doubts over the Chemical Attack," *Independent*, April 17, 2018.

p. 302 **"the rebels were desperate":** Tim Hains, "OAN Reporter in Syria Finds No Evidence of Chemical Weapon Attack in Douma," *Real Clear Politics*, April 18, 2018.

pp. 302–3 **the most illuminating testimony came from Hassan Diab:** "RT Visits Hospital Seen in Douma 'Chemical Attack' Video, Talks to Boy From Footage" (VIDEO), Russia Today, April 20, 2018.

p. 303 **Western pundits dismissed their words:** Robert Mackey, "Russia Brings Syrians to The Hague to Make Underwhelming Case Chemical Attack Was Fake," *Intercept*, April 26, 2018.

p. 303 **OPCW's report ... relied on partisan third parties:** Gareth Porter, "Have We Been Deceived over Syrian Sarin Attack? Scrutinizing the Evidence in an Incident Trump Used to Justify Bombing Syria," *Alternet's Grayzone Project*, September 13, 2017.

p. 303 **investigation into Duma:** "OPCW Issues Fact-Finding Mission Reports on Chemical Weapons Use Allegations in Douma, Syria in 2018 and in Al-Hamadaniya and Karm Al-Tarrab in 2016," opcw.org, July 6, 2018.

p. 303 ***New York Times* ... hiring a cartoonist to dramatize a chemical attack:** "How We Created a Virtual Crime Scene to Investigate Syria's Chemical Attack," *New York Times*, June 24, 2018.

p. 304 **White Helmet leaders lobbied Congress for sanctions:** Ehsani2, Twitter, "#Syrian opposition team who worked on recent caeser bill. Raed of white helmets seem plus syria task force members."

p. 304 **White Helmet members were evacuated by the Israeli military:** Seth Frantzman, "Israel Evacuates Hundreds of Syrian White Helmets in Humanitarian Effort," *Jerusalem Post*, July 22, 2018.

p. 304 **Mattis called "great power conflict" with Russia and China:** Ankit Panda, "With an Eye on Great Power Conflict, US Defense Department Releases 2018 National Defense Strategy," *Diplomat*, January 21, 2018.

p. 305 **established a special "Iran Action Group"**: Colum Lynch and Robbie Graemer, "Pompeo Creates New Team to Pressure Iran," *Foreign Policy*, August 16, 2018.

p. 305 **Feith's son, David, had been hired to work directly under … Brian Hook**: Alex Pfeiffer, "Third Trump Critic Gets Rewarded with State Dept Job," *Daily Caller*, September 20, 2017.

p. 305 **Mueller released the most dramatic document**: Alex Ward, "Read: Mueller Indictment Against 12 Russian Spies for DNC Hack," *Vox*, July 13, 2018.

p. 306 **Internet Research Agency online troll farm**: Kyle Cheney, "'Be Brave': Russian Firm Urges Judge to Nix Mueller Indictment," *Politico*, August 3, 2018.

p. 30 **Brennan added that Trump's performance … "treasonous"**: Dylan Scott, "Former CIA Director: Trump-Putin Press Conference 'Nothing Short of Treasonous,'" *Vox*.

Index